CW00406610

Real Options
in practice

Founded in 1807, John Wiley & Sons is the oldest independent publishing company in the United States. With offices in North America, Europe, Australia and Asia, Wiley is globally committed to developing and marketing print and electronic products and services for our customers' professional and personal knowledge and understanding.

The Wiley Finance series contains books written specifically for finance and investment professionals as well as sophisticated individual investors and their financial advisors. Book topics range from portfolio management to e-commerce, risk management, financial engineering, valuation and financial instrument analysis, as well as much more.

For a list of available titles, please visit our Web site at www.WileyFinance.com.

Real Options
in practice

MARION A. BRACH

John Wiley & Sons, Inc.

Copyright © 2003 by Marion A. Brach. All rights reserved.

Published by John Wiley & Sons, Inc., Hoboken, New Jersey
Published simultaneously in Canada

No part of this publication may be reproduced, stored in a retrieval system, or transmitted in any form or by any means, electronic, mechanical, photocopying, recording, scanning, or otherwise, except as permitted under Section 107 or 108 of the 1976 United States Copyright Act, without either the prior written permission of the Publisher, or authorization through payment of the appropriate per-copy fee to the Copyright Clearance Center, Inc., 222 Rosewood Drive, Danvers, MA 01923, 978-750-8400, fax 978-750-4470, or on the web at www.copyright.com. Requests to the Publisher for permission should be addressed to the Permissions Department, John Wiley & Sons, Inc., 111 River Street, Hoboken, NJ 07030, 201-748-6011, fax 201-748-6008, e-mail: permcoordinator@wiley.com.

Limit of Liability/Disclaimer of Warranty: While the publisher and author have used their best efforts in preparing this book, they make no representations or warranties with respect to the accuracy or completeness of the contents of this book and specifically disclaim any implied warranties of merchantability or fitness for a particular purpose. No warranty may be created or extended by sales representatives or written sales materials. The advice and strategies contained herein may not be suitable for your situation. You should consult with a professional where appropriate. Neither the publisher nor author shall be liable for any loss of profit or any other commercial damages, including but not limited to special, incidental, consequential, or other damages.

For general information on our other products and services, or technical support, please contact our Customer Care Department within the United States at 800-762-2974, outside the United States at 317-572-3993 or fax 317-572-4002.

Wiley also publishes its books in a variety of electronic formats. Some content that appears in print may not be available in electronic books.

For more information about Wiley products, visit our web site at www.wiley.com

Library of Congress Cataloging-in-Publication Data:
Brach, Marion A.
    Real options in practice / Marion A. Brach.
        p. cm. — (Wiley finance series)
    Includes bibliographical references and index.
    ISBN 0-471-26308-7 (cloth : alk. paper)
    1. Options (Finance) I. Title. II. Series.

HG6024 .B73 2002
332.64'5—dc21   2002034204

10 9 8 7 6 5 4 3 2 1

To my parents and friends for unconditional love and support

acknowledgments

Many thanks go to Dean Paxson, Professor of Finance at the Manchester Business School in the United Kingdom. Dean introduced me to the field of real options during my MBA studies in Manchester. Without his infectious enthusiasm and never-ending willingness to discover real options in all aspects of real life, I would not have obtained access to this world. It is my great pleasure to thank Dean for both professional and personal support.

This book would not have been possible without Bill Falloon at Wiley, who intiated the project and maneuvered it through all upcoming odds. Bill steered me through the procedures with great patience and tremendous support, he proved to be an invaluable editor who would not stop to encourage the work in progress and offer valuable guidelines along the way.

contents

CHAPTER 1

Real Option—
The Evolution of an Idea

REAL OPTIONS—WHAT ARE THEY
AND WHAT ARE THEY USED FOR?

An option represents freedom of choice, after the revelation of information. An option is the act of choosing, the power of choice, or the freedom of alternatives. The word comes from the medieval French and is derived from the Latin *optio*, *optare*, meaning to choose, to wish, to desire. An option is a right, but not an obligation, for example, to follow through on a business decision. In the financial markets, it is the freedom of choice after revelation of additional information that increases or decreases the value of the asset on which the option owner holds the option. A financial call option gives the owner the right, but not the obligation, to purchase the underlying stock in the future for a price fixed today. A put option gives the owner the right, but not the obligation, to sell the stock in the future for a price fixed today.

A "real" option is an option "relating to things," from the Late Latin word *realis*. Real refers to fixed, permanent, or immovable things, as opposed to illusory things. Strategic investment and budget decisions within any given firm are decisions to acquire, exercise, abandon or let expire real options. Managerial decisions create call and put options on real assets that give management the right, but not the obligation, to utilize those assets to achieve strategic goals and ultimately maximize the value of the firm.

As this book will show in practice, real options analysis is as much about valuation as it is about thorough strategic analysis. It is about defining the financial boundaries for a decision, but also about discovering new real options when laying out the option framework. The key advantage and value of real option analysis is to integrate managerial flexibility into the valuation process and thereby assist in making the best decisions. Such a concept is immediately attractive on an intuitive level to most managers. However, ambiguity and uncertainty settle in when it comes to using the concept in practice. Key questions center on defining the right input parameters and using the right methodology to value and price the option. Also, given the efforts, time, and resources likely required for making decisions based on real option analysis, the question arises whether such a level of additional sophistication will actually pay off and help make better investment decisions. Hopefully, by the end of this book, some of the ambiguity and uncertainty will be resolved and some avenues to making better investment decisions without investing heavily in the analytical side will become apparent.

Typically, within any given firm, there are multiple short- and long-term goals along the path of value maximization and, typically, managers can envision more than one way of achieving those goals. In many ways, Paul Klee's 1929 painting *Highways and Byways* is one of the most dazzling representations of just this concept (See cover).

If the goal is to reach the blue horizon at the top, then there are multiple paths to get there. These paths come in different colors and shapes. Some fork and twist, and the path to the top is rockier and perhaps a more difficult climb. Others are straighter, but still point to the same direction. More importantly, it seems the decision maker can switch between paths, much in the same way a rock climber may take many different paths to reach the summit, depending on weather conditions and his or her own physical stamina to cope with the inherent risks of each path. One could start out in the lower left and end up in the upper right, but still reach the blue horizon. Furthermore, all paths come in incremental steps. These have different appearances and may bear different degrees of difficulty and risk, but they all are clearly defined and separated from each other and are contained within certain boundaries.

Investment decisions are the firm's walk or climb to the blue horizon. They lead to strategic and financial goals, and they can follow different paths. They usually come in incremental steps. Some paths display fewer but bigger increments to navigate; others have more but smaller steps. The real option at each step in the decision-making process is the freedom of choice to embark on the next step in the climb, or to choose against doing so based on the examination of additional information.

Most managers will agree that this freedom of choice characterizes most if not all investment decisions, though admittedly within constraints. An investment decision is rarely a now-or-never decision and rarely a decision that cannot be abandoned or changed during the course of a project. In most instances, the decision can be delayed or accelerated, and often it comes in sequential steps with various decision points, including "go" and "no-go" alternatives. All of these choices are real managerial options and impact on the value of the investment opportunity. Further, managers are very conscious of preserving a certain freedom of choice to respond to future uncertainties.

Uncertainties derive from internal and external sources; they fall into several categories that include market dynamics, regulatory or political uncertainty, organizational capabilities, knowledge, and the evolution of the competitive environment. Each category is comprised of several subcategories, and those come in different flavors and have different importance for different organizations in different industries. The ability of each organization to overcome and manage internal or private uncertainties and cope with the external uncertainties is valued in the real option analysis, as it is valued in the financial market. Uncertainty, or risk, is the possibility of suffering harm or loss, according to Webster's dictionary. Corporations that are perceived as good risk managers tend to be favored by analysts and investors. Supposedly, companies that manage risk well will also succeed in making money. Banks that were caught up in the Enron crisis—and apparently had failed to manage that risk well—had to watch their stocks "go south." Bristol-Myers Squibb failed to manage the risk associated with technical uncertainty related to the lead drug of its partner company Imclone in the contractual details of the deal made between the two. The pharmaceutical giant lost 4.5% in market value within a few days after its smaller partner announced that the FDA had rejected its application for approval of the new drug, for which Bristol Myers had acquired the marketing rights.

Risk management from a corporate strategy perspective entails enterprise-wide risk management, and includes business risks such as an economic downturn, competitive entry, or an overturn of key technology. This ability drives the future asset value, a function of market penetration, market share, and cost-structure; the likelihood of getting the product to market and obtaining the market payoff; the time-frame; and the managerial ability to execute. The combination of assets and options in place and exercisable options in the pipeline drives the value of the organization. There are in essence three tools available to management to evaluate corporate risk and uncertainty, as shown in Figure 1.1.

The capital budgeting method, which looks at projects in isolation, determines the future cash flows the project may generate, and discounts those to today's value at a project-specific discount rate that reflects the perceived risk of the cash flows. Risk is measured indirectly; in fact, the discount rate represents the opportunity cost of capital, which is the rate of returns an investor expects from traded securities that carry the same risk as the project being valued.[1] Portfolio analysis looks at the investment project in relation

Method	Approach to Risk	Instrument
Capital Budgeting	Indirect	Discount Rate
Portfolio Analysis	Relative	Benchmark
Option Pricing	Direct	Probability

FIGURE 1.1 Three approaches to risk

to the assets and options already in place; risk is evaluated in the context of the existing assets and projects. Specifically, the portfolio manager is interested in identifying the relative risk contribution of the project to the overall risk profile of the portfolio, and how the new portfolio, enriched by the new project, will compare in its risk/return profile to established benchmarks. Portfolio analysis diversifies risk; it permits only those projects to be added to the existing asset portfolio that reduce risk exposure while preserving or enhancing returns. Among the three methods, only option pricing is concerned with a direct analysis of project-specific risks. Risk is quantified via probability assignment. The expected future payoff of the investment option reflects assumptions and insights on the probability of market dynamics, global economics, the competitive environment and competitive strength of the product or service to be developed, as well as the probability distribution of costs associated with the project. The risk-neutral expected payoff, discounted back to today's value at the risk-free rate, gives today's value of the investment option.

Traditional project appraisal within the context of capital budgeting assumes that the firm will embark on a rigid and inflexible path forward, ignoring and failing to respond and adjust to any changes in the market place. The method ignores, however, that the risk-pattern of the project is likely to change over time—requiring changing discount rates. It also ignores the value of managerial flexibility to react to future uncertainties. Traditional project appraisal sees and acknowledges risk, but disregards the fact that managerial actions will mitigate those risks and thereby preserve or even increase value. Very much to the contrary, real options analysis marries uncertainty and risk with flexibility in the valuation process. Real option analysis sees volatility as a potential upside factor and ascribes value to it.

Project appraisal within capital budgeting is based on expected future cash flows that are discounted back to today (DCF) at a discount rate that reflects the riskiness of those cash flows. All costs that will be incurred to create and maintain the asset are deducted and this calculation gives rise to the project's net present value (NPV). The NPV, in other words, is the difference between today's value of future cash flows that the investment project is expected to generate over its lifetime and the cost involved in implementing the project.

The basics of the NPV concept go back to 1907, when Irving Fisher, the Yale economist, first proposed in the second volume of his work on the theory of capital and investment, entitled *Rate of Interest*, to discount expected cash flow at a rate that represented best the risk associated with the project.[2] Risk, another Latin word, meant in the ancient Roman world "danger at sea." In the context of finance and investment decisions, risk refers to the volatility of potential outcomes. The fact that the future is unknown and uncertain is the foundation for the time value of money: Money today is worth more than money tomorrow. This notion is the basis for net present value analysis, which serves as the prime approach to capital budgeting. Consider the following scenario, depicted in Figure 1.2.

A firm contemplates developing a new product line. There is a chance that the product will take off in the market readily, leading to a period of substantial cash flows. Those nice cash flows are likely to attract the attention of competitors and may provoke market entry of a comparable product some time thereafter. This will cause a collapse of the cash flow and make the product unprofitable.

The rather uncompromising NPV approach assumes that cash flows are certain and ignores that, during the time needed to build the asset, new

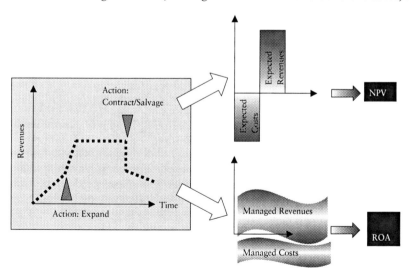

FIGURE 1.2 NPV vs. ROA

information may arrive that will change the original investment plan. It also ignores the fact that investments often come in natural, sequential steps with multiple "go" or "no-go" decision points that allow management to respond to any changes in the market or in governmental rules, or to adapt to technological advances. This approach further ignores that management may adjust to the environment by accelerating, expanding, contracting, or even abandoning the project along the way. The NPV will be based on the expected cash flows over time; management may in fact discount those future expected cash flows at a high discount rate to reflect all perceived risks, ignoring that future managerial actions may reduce those risks. It will then deduct the present value of the anticipated costs from those cash flows to arrive at the NPV.

In the real option framework, on the contrary, management acknowledges that it will have the option to expand production and distribution once the product does well, to take full advantage of the upside potential. On the contrary, if the market collapses after competitive entry, management may want to sell the asset and cash the salvage value. Both costs and revenues are flexible and adjusted to the information as it arrives. The option valuation acknowledges value creation and risk mitigation through managerial flexibility; therefore, the project appraisal not only looks better, but also more real in the real option framework.

In an NPV-based project appraisal, management adjusts for risk and uncertainty by changing the discount rate, which turns into a risk premium. For example, an investment project with an expected payoff of $100 million in three years that is perceived to have little risk may be discounted at the corporate cost of capital discount rate of 13% and then is worth today $100 million/$1.13^3$ or $69.30 million. Another project with the same future cash flow of $100 million but a much higher anticipated risk may be discounted at a risk premium of 25% and would be worth today only $51.2 million. Assume further that in order to generate this cash flow the firm has to invest $60 million today. Then the NPV for the first project is minus $60 million plus $69.3 million, equals $9.3 million, while the NPV for the second project is minus $60 million plus $51.2 million, equals minus $8.2 million, and management would accept the first project.

Option valuation also builds on expected cash flows, but the cash flows themselves are adjusted for risk and then discounted at the risk-free rate. So the less risky project may have a probability of 69% to materialize while the more risky project may have only a 51% probability to come to fruition. This translates into an expected cash flow of $69 million and $51 million, respectively. Calculation of the option value considers not only the expected value but also the assumptions on the best case scenario, which in this example is the full cash flow of $100 million assuming a 100% probability of success, as well as the worst case scenario, which equals zero cash flow in case of complete failure. These three figures are taken to calculate the risk-neutral probability, which then serves to determine the value of the option, discounted back to today's time at the risk-free rate. Following this procedure—and we will explain the underlying mathematics later—we obtain an option value of $9.3 million for the first project and an option value of zero for the second project. The investment advice is the same as for the NPV calculation: Go for project 1 and ignore project 2. Both the NPV and the option valuation arrive at the same result, provided both methods use the appropriate measure for risk, which is expressed as the discount rate for the NPV analysis and as the risk-neutral probability for the real option analysis. However, calculating the option value is only meaningful if the decision to invest in either program is subjected to some sort of managerial flexibility that could alter the course of the project and mitigate risk. If this is not the case, then there is no need or value in determining the real option value—as there is no real option.

The option approach integrates managerial flexibility in the valuation by assuming that at each stage in the future, pending on the then-prevailing market conditions, management will choose the value-maximizing and loss-minimizing path forward. Decision-making based on real option theory and practice values flexibility, while NPV ignores such flexibility. Hence, an NPV-based project appraisal is appropriate if there is uncertainty but no managerial flexibility to adjust to it. On the contrary, the real option decision-making approach is appropriate if management has the ability to react to uncertainty and a changing competitive environment, as well shape that future environment. While cash flows deliver the building blocks of investment decisions, option analysis provides the architectural framework to assemble the modular building blocks into a flexible house designed to accommodate the growing and changing needs of its inhabitants. In the absence of flexibility, the NPV and the option valuation give identical results, provided both adjust correctly for the appropriate risk, as we saw in the example above. From a practical perspective, expressing risk as a probability distribution is sometimes easier and mostly more transparent than expressing risk as a discount premium.

Imagine that you are going to build a new house and that you face several options as to how to heat the house. One decision involves whether to use a heating oil or natural gas furnace. Another may involve the decision to use an electric or natural gas range in your kitchen for cooking. You do not know how the prices for either energy source will develop in the future. You probably will do some homework and look up historic prices of both gas and oil and electricity over the past decade or so. This may give you some indication as to which energy source displays more volatility, and which one tended to be cheaper over the course of time. You then may be inclined to assume that past price movements are somewhat indicative as to what may happen to future prices. However, you will also appreciate that there is no certainty that those past price movements for these energy commodities can reliably predict future price movements. Thus, it might be of value for you to install a furnace that allows you to switch between both energy sources without any problem. That additional flexibility is likely to come at a price, a premium to be paid for a more expensive furnace that permits switching compared to a cheaper furnace that can use only one energy form. However, depending on your annual energy demand, the expected life of the furnace before it will need to be maintained or replaced, and your expectations about the future volatilities of each energy source and how they may correlate with each other, this option may well be in the money for you.

Imagine now that you were thinking about acquiring a vacation home in a new resort but were unsure how much time you would really be able to spend there. Also imagine that you were simply unsure how much you would like living there and whether the climate would really agree with you for extended living periods, rather than for a simple one-week vacation. You are faced with the following alternatives: You could buy your dream house in the new resort now and promise yourself that, if you do not like it, you would sell the house a year from now. There is a chance that within that year the house will appreciate in value to some higher price level, so that the fees associated with the purchase will be covered by, say, a third. Under those circumstances, your losses in the transaction might be reduced or even eliminated should you opt against keeping the place. Alternatively, you could enter into a lease for a year, and obtain a contractual agreement to retain the option to buy the house a year from now at favorable terms. While it may be cheaper to simply rent a house for a few weeks rather than leasing it for an entire year, with the lease you obtain an embedded growth option, namely to buy the house. You will exercise this option only if you really like the place. Inherent in the flexibility of these possible choices lies value, and this value can be determined using option analysis and option pricing.

While these examples may sound intuitive to you and invite you to use real option analysis to value your managerial options, let's investigate what others think about this concept and its implementation. Figure 1.3 summarizes some recent quotes on the subject.

These quotes from a number of sources illustrate confusion, skepticism, and misunderstanding about the concept of real options. In the same breath, however, they also convey expectations about how real option theory might be useful, and how it might or might not infiltrate daily managerial decisions. A few comments may be in order.

"To be sure, this much-vaunted alternative to the conventional method of evaluating capital-spending decisions using net present value (NPV) is catching on with more and more senior finance executives." R. Fink. *CFO.com*, September 2001.

"In ten years, real options will replace NPV as the central paradigm for investment decisions." Tom Copeland & Vladimir Antikarov. *Real Options, A Practitioner's Guide*, 2001.

"Information for evaluating real options is costly or unavailable, and asking for more money later is difficult and may be interpreted as a lack of foresight. Projects are selected by financial managers, who do not trust operational managers to exercise options properly." Fred Phillips, Professor, Oregon Graduate Institute of Science & Technology, Portland. *Business Week Online*, June 28, 1999.

"The evidence we present suggests that a significant gap exists between the promise of risk reduction offered by the real options theory and the reality of firms' apparently limited capability for managing international investments as options." Michael Leiblein, Assistant Professor of Management and Human Resources, Fisher College of Business. *Research Today*, June 2000.

"The myth of Option Pricing—Fine for the stock market and oil exploration, option pricing models don't work in valuing life sciences research." Vimal Bahuguna, Bogart Delafield Ferrier. *In vivo—The Business and Medicine Report*, May 2000.

FIGURE 1.3 Opinions on Real Options

First, real option analysis does not necessarily preclude or replace traditional DCF and NPV analysis. As pointed out before, and as will be evident throughout this book, the application of real option theory rather builds on these tools and the underlying concepts, integrates them into a new valuation paradigm, and thereby takes them to the next level of financial and strategic analysis. Second, the Black Scholes formula, which is used to price financial options, may indeed not be the right formula to price many real options. Several of the basic assumptions and constraints that come along with the Black Scholes equation simply do not hold in the real world, and we will elaborate on this later in this chapter. This, however, does not imply that the use of real options analysis is impractical or incorrect. There are other methods to price real options that can be applied. Third, inflating the value of stocks is a matter of the assumptions that go into the analysis, not a matter of the methodology used. Applied correctly, real options valuation techniques will not inflate value, but simply make visible all value that derives from managerial flexibility. In many instances, the value derived from an option analysis tends to be higher than that derived from a rigid NPV-only analysis, largely because NPV analysis ignores value created by managerial flexibility and ability to respond to future uncertainties.

The true value of real option theory can in some instances be organizational, enforcing a very thorough cross-organizational thinking process that ultimately may lead to uncovering new true real options. The case study on BestPharma[3] is a point in case. Here, the authors present a real option valuation example for a drug development program. Management of a pharmaceutical company is faced with the need to select the most promising of three early-stage research projects. Initially, the organization fails to reach an agreement as to how to prioritize these projects along established internal valuation criteria: medical need, scientific innovation, and future market size. The project that was viewed as the most innovative by the scientists was designed to address a high medical need and also had a significant market potential. The problem: it failed to compete with the other two projects in the discounted-cash flow analysis. This situation prompted the scientists to search for additional application potential of a drug to come out of the third project. The intuition of the scientists ultimately laid out several possible future indications of the third R&D program that neither of the two other alternatives would offer. The option analysis enforced organizational thinking to the degree that this future real option was identified and incorporated in the project valuation, ultimately changing the initial investment decision that was based on a simple non-strategic NPV analysis.

Some rightfully argue that identified and valued real options are worthless unless the organization that owns them also proves capable of exercising and executing them. This may be true if value is created or maximized only if management specifically decides to terminate a project, a decision many companies may find difficult to make. This thought leads us into the organizational aspects of real option valuation, a topic to be discussed later in Chapter 9.

Any real option analysis starts with framing the decision scenario, followed by the actual valuation. The interpretation of the results often instigates further discussions, re-framing and re-valuation of the option, and possibly uncovering new real options. Real option analysis should assist an organization in coping with uncertainty, which becomes contained within more certain and defined boundaries, the option space. The commitment of organizational resources to uncertainty becomes limited in extent and time and becomes visibly staged. Real option analysis helps the organization to comprehend how uncertainties impact on the value of investment decisions and to recognize what drives an option out of the money. As time proceeds and uncertainty resolves, real option analysis permits and encourages the organization to question and redefine the underlying assumption, thereby narrowing down the option space. Thinking about alternative options is part of the real option analysis process, and it will be instrumental in determining the value of managerial flexibility. Real option analysis will also assist in identifying how a given risk can be limited, and how an alternative "Plan B" should be designed to effectively hedge risk and mitigate losses.

Real option analysis supports and expands the strategic framework of an organization. It also bridges finance, strategy, and the organizational infrastructure. Real option analysis can also serve as a catalyst within an organization: it identifies trigger points that alter the course of a decision. Being capable of altering the course of a decision requires organizational discipline and an alignment of real option execution with incentive structures. Often, real option analysis will require an opening of the organization, a new level of information sharing and discussions to frame the option framework and to identify the drivers of uncertainty. Some organizations may find that it is the organizational structure, not the lack of data or the lack of financial or mathematical talent, that effectively interferes with their ability to identify the options, lay out the framework with all its drivers, and execute the real options.

To use a comparison: many viewed the information technology (IT) revolution in the corporate world, including the introduction of tools such as enterprise resource planning (ERP) software, as primarily an organizational challenge, a software "that makes a grown company cry," as the *New York Times* found out.[4] The software is designed to facilitate integration of information across the organization. However, failure or success in implementing SAP, the quintessence of some publications,[5] is driven by the ability of the organization to change in a way that allows proper use of these tools. Operating an enterprise software program such as SAP or Oracle is not simply a matter of letting the IT department install the software; it requires and promotes much more of a complete change in organizational architecture and culture.[6] The software dictates to a significant degree intra-organizational processes and procedures as well as how the organization interacts with its vendors and customers. An organization wanting to apply an ERP system needs to get ready for it, in organizational design, mindset, and culture. Similarly, implementing real options is not just another strategic management or finance tool, it is also an organizational mindset and will only work and be of value to the organization if aligned with incentive structures, performance measures, and decision-making procedures. The future may show that failure or success in identifying, analyzing, and executing real options is to a large extent driven by organizational design.

The use of real option analysis in the appraisal is not about getting bigger numbers for your projects, nor is it per se about encouraging investments early, when NPV suggests refraining from investment. Real option analysis can in fact tell you what the value is of waiting to invest. The use of real option analysis does not protect against investment decisions leading to the acquisition of options that are out of the money and, as a result, have a certain probability of expiring worthless. Like any other financial and strategic analysis tool, real option analysis is never better than the assumptions that go into the analysis. It does, however, provide a rather safe option space for any decision to be made. As time progresses and more information arrives, the boundaries of uncertainty become better defined and the option space more safe and confined. "The key issue is not avoiding failure but managing the cost of failure by limiting exposure to the downside," notes Rita McGrath, a prominent academic researcher, in her article on entrepreneurial failure.[7]

Further, the distinction between real option pricing and real option analysis is noteworthy. Real option pricing is a risk-neutral market-based method of pricing a derivative. A derivative is something resulting from derivation, such as a word formed from another word; *electricity*, for example, derives from *electric*. A financial derivative is a financial instrument whose value is derived from the value of the underlying stock. Financial derivatives include options, futures, and warrants. Futures are legally binding agreements to buy or sell an item in the future at a price fixed today, the spot price. Options, on the contrary, give the right to buy or sell in the future at a price fixed today, but imply no legal obligation to do so. Options on futures give the right, but not the obligation, to buy or sell a future contract in the future at a price specified today. Warrants entail the right to buy a stock in the future at a price specified today. All derivatives have in common that their price is dictated by the volatility of the underlying asset.

Pricing derivatives such as options and futures builds on the no-arbitrage argument. No arbitrage implies it is not possible to buy securities on one market for immediate resale on another market in order to profit from a price discrepancy. The no-arbitrage argument is intimately linked to the completeness of financial markets. If, in complete financial markets, an arbitrage opportunity exists, an agent will instantly take advantage of it by buying a security at a lower price in order to sell it in a different market at a higher price. Instantly, all agents in the market will follow the lead, and the prices of the security in the two markets will converge, killing the arbitrage opportunity—provided the markets are efficient and there is full information.

Real option analysis, on the contrary, is a strategic tool. It entails a cross-organizational exercise designed to lay out the options, discover the risks, and determine the range and reach of managerial flexibilities. It delivers the framework and structure for real option pricing, and it is the benchmark against which to measure real option execution. If real option execution fails to live up to the expectations set in the real option analysis and reflected in the real option price, the organization has to do a post-mortem to uncover where and why the three components got misaligned—to avoid similar mistakes in the future.

THE HISTORY OF REAL OPTIONS

The trade of options on real assets is older than transactions involving money. In 1728 B.C., Joseph was sold into Egypt. Genesis tells the story of Joseph, who recommended to the Pharaoh that he invest heavily in grain after learning about the Pharaoh's dreams. Joseph recognized this to be the best path into the future: exercising the option and buying all available grain now and during the coming seven productive years in order to save it for the seven years of famine. The risk Joseph and his contemporaries faced in Egypt was to die of starvation; the real option available to them was to hedge against that risk by saving grain. The exercise price to be paid was the creation of appropriate storage containers to keep the grain.

Some of the more than 20,000 ancient tablets found in the city of Mari on the Euphrates River, just north of today's border between Syria and Iraq, give rich testimony of option and future contracts negotiated in that area between 1800 and 1500 B.C. These contracts were a substitute or derivative for an underlying real asset, such as grain or metal, long before money in the form of coins was available. In Book 1 of his *Politics*, Aristotle tells the story of Thales (mid-620s B.C. to ca. 546 B.C.), the famous ancient philosopher. Thales made a fortune by acquiring call options on olive presses nine months ahead of the next harvest. Based on his readings of the stars in the firmament, he foresaw that the next harvest would be outstanding, and he decided to engage in contractual arrangements that would—for a small fee—give him the right to rent out olive presses. The risk Thales faced was the uncertainty surrounding the outcome of the next harvest. If that harvest were to be bad, there would be little need for olive presses and Thales would not rent the presses. The option acquisition cost would be sunk, the option out of the money. However, when the harvest came, it turned out to be a fruitful one. Thales rented the presses out at high prices, while paying only a small premium for the right to exercise his call option. Please note that Thales' personal goal in this transaction was not to become rich but to prove that philosophers need not be poor.

During the Tokawawa era in Japan, starting around 1600, Japanese merchants bought call options on rice. They purchased coupons from land-owning Japanese noblemen that would give them the right on rice crops exactly as specified on the coupon. If the anticipated need for rice changed, these merchants were free to trade the coupons, and hence the right to acquire the rice, at the Shogunate, a centralized market place.

Around the same time, in the 1630s, middle-class Dutchmen traded high on Real Tulip Options. These flowers, brought to Holland from Turkey, were refined and re-cultured into many variants by the early 17th century. The exotic and very expensive plants became much admired for their beauty but were affordable only to the very rich. Tulips soon became a scarce good, demand exceeded delivery by far, further enhancing their status. Unpredictable weather and climate—in the absence of greenhouses, fertilizers, or gene transfer—largely dictated the harvest. These factors also generated the level of uncertainty that finally promoted the insight that in fact a whole new market was about to emerge: the market of future tulips. People engaged in contracts that gave them the right to purchase tulips during the next season at a specified price, when the bulbs were still in the ground and nobody had seen the blossoms. If the harvest turned out to be bad, prices of tulips would go up further, giving the contract owner the right to purchase at the specified price, sell at the prevalent market price, and cash in on the difference—the value of the option. Option contracts on tulips were traded not just in the Netherlands, but also in England.[8] In the Netherlands, tulips became the hottest commodity in the early 17th century. Prices escalated to an outrageous level (a twenty-fold increase in January of 1637) and then shortly thereafter, in February 1637 finally, the tulip bubble burst. Prices were so high that people started selling them and an avalanche of tulip bulb sales set in, leading to one of the first market crashes in history.

In 1688, shortly after the Amsterdam Bourse opened, "time bargains," a contemporary term for both options and futures, started trading.[9] In the United States, a more formalized trade with futures and options did not start until the mid 19th century. The Chicago Board of Trade (CBOT), the first formal futures and option exchange, opened in 1848 and began trading futures and options contracts in the 1870s. On April 26, 1973, listed stock options began trading on the Chicago Board Options Exchange. Trading of the first equity options in 1973 coincided with the publication of the Black-Scholes seminal paper.[10] In the paper, Black and Scholes derived a mathematical formula that allowed pricing of call options on shares of stock. The arrival of this formula facilitated the growth of option markets, and became the basis for valuation and pricing. This formula, and its variations, later had even broader application in financial markets. In 1975, other exchanges began offering call options and, since 1977, put options have also been traded. Today, exchanges in a multitude of countries that cover more than 95% of the world equity market offer stock index options.

At the same time that financial options began trading, academic researchers also started viewing corporate securities as either call or put options on the assets of the firm.[11] In fact, it was Stewart Myers[12] who pioneered the concept that financial investments generate real options and also coined the term "real options" in 1977. Stewart Myers argued that valuation of financial investment opportunities using the traditional DCF approach ignores the value of options arising in uncertain and risky investment projects. A decade later Myers took option analysis to the next level by applying the concept to value not only corporate securities but also corporate budget and investment decisions. He wrote, "standard discounted cash flow techniques will tend to understate the option value attached to growing profitable lines of businesses.[13] In other words, investments that do not pay off immediately but lay important groundwork for future growth opportunities are not recognized in the NPV framework. Their NPV is negative, but these investments buy the right to future cash flows, and those future cash flows must be included in the project appraisal. This research established the conceptual groundwork for the application of option pricing analysis outside of the world of finance.

Myer's work stimulated intense discussion, and in the early 1980s doubts regarding the applicability of traditional DCF for investment decisions related to risky projects increasingly surfaced. It was recognized that particularly the value of unforeseen spin-offs in R&D investments was not captured.[14] Return on investment (ROI) and DCF were blamed for hurdle rates exceeding the cost of capital. These high hurdle rates led to a decline in R&D spending, jeopardizing the competitive advantage of many sectors.[15] Specifically, corporate investment decisions were based on the same risk rate used throughout the business, even though the risks might vary between research, development, and commercialization.[16] Misuse of DCF was becoming responsible for the decline of American industry.[17]

Subsequently, Kester[18] translated the theoretical concept of "growth options" into a more strategic framework concept and ensured broader dissemination of the basic idea and concepts in a *Harvard Business Review* article. Pindyck[19] further expanded the notion of growth options by introducing irreversibility into the equation. While this is a key feature of all investment decisions, the NPV rule fails to recognize irreversibility as a cost, the opportunity cost of the money being invested, and the cost of giving up flexibility by committing resources irreversibly. Correspondingly, there must then be a value in keeping options open, that is, not exercising options, or in delaying the exercise until further information has arrived and uncertainty has been resolved. Dixit and Pindyck further elaborated this concept in their seminal book on the subject entitled *Investment Under Uncertainty*.[20] The title originally proposed was "The real option approach to investment." Shortly thereafter, in 1996, Trigeorgis[21] published a comprehensive review of the real option literature and its applications: *Real Options—Managerial Flexibility and Strategy in Resource Allocation*.

THE BASIC FRAMEWORK OF OPTION PRICING

An option is a right, but not an obligation. A call option gives the owner the right, but not the obligation, to buy the underlying asset at a predetermined price on or by a certain date. A European option has a fixed exercise date and can only be exercised on that date. In contrast, an American option can be exercised at any time either on or prior to the exercise date. A put option gives the holder the right, but not the obligation, to sell the asset at a predetermined price on or by a certain date. Acquiring the right on the option comes at a price, the option price or premium. The closer an option is to its exercise price, the more valuable it becomes. Exercising the right also comes at a price, the strike price. The strike price is the price at which the option owner can buy or sell the underlying asset. The value of the call option C is the difference between today's value of the expected future payoff S (that is, the value of the asset that will be acquired by exercising the option) and the costs K of exercising the option at maturity. The value of the put option P by analogy is the difference between the cost K of acquiring the asset and the price at which the underlying asset can be sold at maturity. Figure 1.4 depicts the standard payoff diagrams for call and put options and Equation 1.1 gives the mathematical formula for the value of a call (C) and a put (P).

$$C = \text{Max } [0, S - K]$$
$$P = \text{Max } [0, K - S] \tag{1.1}$$

The value of the call goes up as the value of the underlying asset goes up. The option holder benefits from the upside potential of the underlying asset. The value of the call approaches zero as the value of the underlying approaches the cost K of acquiring the option. If the asset value drops below

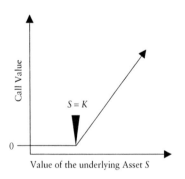
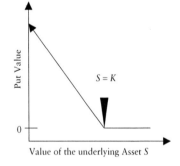

FIGURE 1.4 Payoff diagram for calls and puts

the cost K, the option value remains zero, and the owner of the option will not exercise the option, that is, not acquire the asset. The option expires worthless. The value of the put goes up as value of the underlying asset goes down. If the value of the asset S approaches the exercise price K, the value of the put approaches zero. If the value of the asset becomes greater than the exercise price K, the put option goes out of the money and its value diminishes. The owner will not exercise the put and the option expires worthless.

The value of the option at the time of exercise is driven by the value of the underlying asset, which is easily observable in the financial market. The price of the option today is determined by today's expectations on the future value of the underlying asset, that is, the stock. For financial options, these expectations derive from observing the random walk of stocks, the stochastic processes that stock values follow over time. Past volatility, it is assumed, is indicative of future volatility; the past upward drift is indicative of the future upward drift.

Thus, all one needs to know to predict the future stock price is the equation that describes the stochastic process. This stochastic process is assumed to be sustainable in the future along with the same characteristics that it has had in the past. The more volatile a stock tended to be in the past, the more volatile—so the assumption holds—it will be in the future. The more volatile a stock movement is, the higher the upside potential, that is, the likelihood that the value of the stock at the time of exercise will be much higher than the exercise price, creating more returns for the investor. For a stock with lower volatility that likelihood is smaller and the option price is lower. The strike price is pre-determined in the financial market, and most financial options offer a range of strike prices. Today's option price is determined by stock volatility and by the strike price; the higher the volatility, the lower the strike price, the higher today's price for acquiring the option as both parameters are expected to yield greater future payoffs.

Assuming investors are rational, the owner of an option will exercise that option only when the expected payoff is positive. Hence, by definition, the value of the option is always greater or equal to zero, never negative. An option with a negative payoff will expire unexercised, provided the investor is rational and is aware of the negative payoff. Both are obviously not always the case when it comes to real options. Value creation in option analysis stems from separating the upside potential from the downside risk.

When it comes to investments into real assets, it gets much more challenging to determine the exercise price, which is the costs and resources it may take to accomplish the task and complete the project, such as development of a new product or entrance into a new geographical market. Often, these costs are not known exactly but only as estimates or approximations.

The exercise price for real options entails any expense required to put the asset that will create the future cash flows in place. It includes, for example, paying a licensing fee to obtain a right to a mine or to a patent. It implies expenses to create the infrastructure for a distribution network in a new market.

This relationship between the asset value at the time of exercise and the exercise price defines the first real option investment rule: The option should be exercised once the value is greater than zero, that is, once the option is in the money. This guideline works fine in financial markets with observable stock prices, but it may be much more difficult to follow for real options when neither the expected asset value nor costs are certain or known. The world of real options is much closer, in the abstract, to the painting by Klee.

The relationship expressed in Equation 1.1 also provides other information that is sometimes even more useful: the critical value to invest. This is the payoff the future asset must generate under the working cost and uncertainty assumptions for the option to be in the money. For a financial option, the critical value to invest is reached when the exercise price of the option approaches the asset value S at the time of exercise. For a call option, if the asset value S drops below K, the option owner will choose not to exercise. For a put option, if the asset value increases beyond K, the option owner will also not exercise. In both cases, the critical value to invest by exercising the option has been reached. Likewise, there is a critical cost to invest for real options. It indicates the threshold, or maximum amount of money, beyond which management should not be willing to invest given the working assumptions on future payoffs. Any further commitment of resources would drive the option out of the money.

Obviously, both terms are two sides of the same coin. In some instances management may be very certain about the future market payoff of a novel product but may need guidance as to what the critical cost to invest is in order to keep the option on the project in the money. In other instances, management has only a fixed, budgeted amount available to invest, and needs to define a range of possible investment opportunities and the critical value those opportunities must create in the future—given their distinct technical risk profiles—to justify the investment now. Neither the critical value to invest nor the critical cost to invest are fixed thresholds but rather are highly dependent on the assumptions management makes as to when and with what probability future asset flows may materialize.

Let us clarify the notion of the critical value to invest with an example. Assume the option to invest in a project that will create an asset with a future revenue stream worth today $1000 million. The critical value to invest now into generating the asset with this future cash flow depends on the probability of success in obtaining the $1000 million, that is, on the risk associated with the project, as well as on the time frame when that cash flow starts materializing. Figure 1.5 depicts the critical value to invest today as a function of both parameters for an assumed asset value of $1000 million.

As the project becomes more risky, that is, as the probability to complete the project successfully declines to 30% ($q = 0.3$) and time to completion stretches out to five years, not more than $86 million should be invested now to prevent losses. Under these conditions, the value of the call option will be zero, and if more money than the $86 million is invested now the option will be out of the money. On the contrary, if management is 90% confident that the project can be completed within two years, it can invest $786 million now to preserve the in-the-moneyness of the option. The critical value to invest decreases as the probability q of success increases and as the time frame to completion shortens. Hence, the second, complementary real option investment rule is to go ahead with the exercise of the option if anticipated costs are less than the critical value to invest, and to abandon the project in all other cases.

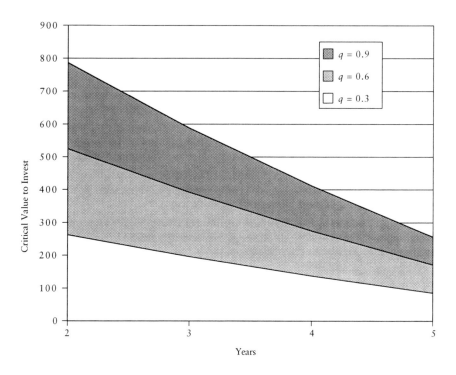

FIGURE 1.5 Critical investment value as a function of private risk and time to maturity

The challenge, of course, is to arrive at reliable assumptions as to how much value that future asset will generate. Joseph in Egypt and Thales in Greece had their own ways of having advanced knowledge of the future. Financial markets look back into the past to develop an understanding of the future. Here, financial option pricing is based on one basic and fundamental assumption: historic observations of stock-price movements are predictive for future stock-price movements. The past movements are fitted into a behavior that can be described as a process for which a mathematical formula is developed. This permits us to predict future movements and hence price the option. The challenge for real options is to find the process that also allows us to predict future asset value—or come up with an alternative solution.

THE BASICS OF FINANCIAL OPTION PRICING

Options, as we have seen, have been traded for centuries. The history of option pricing is much shorter, but nevertheless notable. To price an option today we need to know the value of the underlying asset, such as the stock, at the time of possible exercise in the future, the expected value. Thales did not know with certainty what the value of his olive press would be at the time of harvest, but he was certain it would be more than he was prepared to pay for them then. But then, this was also the only viable investment opportunity Thales faced, and being so sure about the upside potential, he went for it. Investors in stocks or in real assets face multiple investment opportunities, but they usually are not as gifted as Thales in foreseeing the future. Therefore, they rely on rudimentary tools to predict future values of the underlying asset—celestial insight is replaced by stochastic calculus, the foundation for financial option pricing.

Before Black-Scholes or the binomial option pricing model, the option price was determined by discounting the expected value of the stock at the expiration date using arbitrary risk premiums as a discount factor that were to reflect the volatility of the stock. Contemporary option pricing uses stochastic calculus that delivers a probability distribution of future asset values and permits us to use the risk-free rate to discount the option value to today. Central to this idea is the insight that one does not need to know the future stock price, but only needs to know the current stock price and the stochastic process of the parameters that drive the value of the stock going forward. This is referred to as the Markov property.

Andrej Andreyewitch Markov (1856–1922), a graduate of St. Petersburg University, pioneered the concept of the random walk, a chain of random variables in which the state of the future variable is determined by the preceding variable but is entirely independent of any other variable preceding that one. Markov is often viewed as the founding father of the theory of stochastic processes. He built his theory on distinct entities, variables. That way, the walk consists of distinct individual steps, just as Klee showed in his painting. Each step is conditional on the step taken before, but not on the one before that. What emerges is a chain of random values; the probability of each value depends on the value of the number at the previous step. The walker only goes forward, never goes back, and will never return to the step he just left. Each following step is conditional on the previous one; the path is determined by transition probability. The transition probability is the probability that step B is happening on the condition that step A has happened before.

Norbert Wiener (1894–1964) provided an additional, crucial extension to this concept. He transformed the Markov property into a continuous process, meaning there are no more single, distinct steps but an unbroken movement. This stochastic process is referred to as a Wiener process or Brownian motion. It describes a normal distribution over a continuous time frame that meets the Markov property, meaning each movement only depends on the previous state but not on the one prior to that. The Wiener process has an upward drift, meaning that if one were to draw a trend line through the up- and downward movements, over time, that trend line would go up. In addition, as time stretches out in the future, the size of the up- and downward movements increases, that is, the variance or volatility increases linearly with the time interval.

A look into a historic stock chart, in our example in Figure 1.6 the Nasdaq Industrial Index and the Nasdaq Insurance Index, both initiated on February 5, 1971, at a base of 100.00, illustrates what Markov and Wiener had been thinking about.

The indexes go either up or down; that movement only depends on the previous position, not on any position before, as the Markov property suggests. Over time, there is an upward drift, and the movement is continuous; there is no discontinuity, although you could argue that the latter is not entirely true. Stock exchanges tend to close in the evening and also over the weekends. Also, over time, the variance increases: The distance of the up- and downward movements towards the trend-line becomes more pronounced; the shaded area shows the growing cone of uncertainty as time stretches out. In a similar way, the real option cone, too, broadens going forward as management faces ever increasing uncertainty as the time horizon of

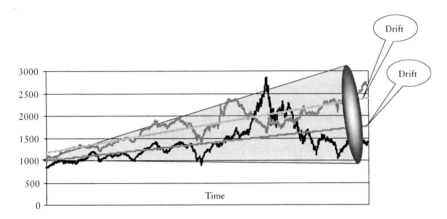

FIGURE 1.6 The option cone: Volatility, drift and stochastic processes of historic NASDAQ industrial and insurance indexes

planning and budgeting activities expands and future states of the world become less foreseeable and less defined.

A stochastic process, in other words, describes a sequence of events ruled by probabilistic laws. It allows foreseeing the likelihood of occurrence of seemingly random events. Having a reliable stochastic process that captures the range of possible future movements of the asset and ascribes a probability to each movement, puts us in the position to predict the future stock price with distinct probabilities. Knowing the future stock price, in turn, takes out the risk, and permits us to price today's value of the option using the risk-free interest rate as a discount factor. It allows the no-arbitrage pricing of the option on a stock today. The challenge is finding that reliable and predictable stochastic process, both for real options as well as for financial options.

Before we think about pricing a real option, let's quickly review the history of financial option pricing. Louis Bachielier (1872–1946)[22] was the first to come up with a mathematical formula, and the first indeed to price a financial option. Bachielier had enrolled as a student at the Sorbonne in Paris in 1892 after completing military service. He earned a degree in mathematics in 1895. Mathematics at the time focused mainly on mathematical physics, and Bachielier was exposed to the emerging theories of heat and diffusion as well as to Poincaré's breakthrough theories of probabilities. Probability as a mathematical subject was not formally introduced, however, until 1925. While taking classes at night at the Sorbonne, Louis Bachielier spent his days at the Paris stock exchange to make a living. It was the exposure to both of these worlds that led to the evolution of his ideas as to how to price options.

In 1900 he published his insights in his thesis "Theory of Speculation."[23] Bachielier introduced the idea of the normal distribution of price changes over time. He showed in his mathematical proof that the dispersion increases with the square root of time. In essence, he applied the Fourier equation of heat diffusion, with which he was familiar from his mathematical studies, to model historic price movements of the "rente" based on a data set covering 1894–1898. The "rente" was then the primary tool for speculation at the Paris bourse. Bachielier further extended these ideas by including a quantitative discussion of how this might also be applied to price calls and puts.

Bachielier does not mention Brownian motion, as this idea would not appear in Paris until 1902, but nevertheless Bachielier used the same concept of Brownian motions in his derivation of option pricing techniques. Brownian motions are the minute movements of atoms. The name refers to Robert Brown, a Scottish botanist who noticed in 1827 the rapid oscillatory movements of pollen grains suspended in water.[24] Ludwig Boltzmann was the first to connect these rapid movements and kinetic energy to temperature. He developed a kinetic theory of matter that was published in 1896.[25] His work was translated into French in 1902 and only then became available to Bachielier.

On a two-dimensional representation of Brownian motions, the movements are either up or down; the same applies to stocks. Stock prices really only have two behaviors: they can go up or down, and then up and down again. Over time and on average, they tend to go up more than down, creating an upward drift of the stock. The extent of those upward and downward movements determines the volatility of the stock and is different for each stock. Over time and with each step, the movements of the stock are captured by the binomial lattice tree that builds more and more branches as one looks further out into the future and the stock takes more steps. If one assumes that the stock price follows a continuous path (there are no discontinuities), the returns in one period are independent from the returns in the next period, and the returns are identically and also normally distributed, one fulfills all the assumptions required to utilize the Black-Scholes formula to price the option.

Louis Bachelier proposed the log-normal distribution as the appropriate stochastic process for financial stocks, and he came up with the earliest known analytical valuation for financial options in his mathematics dissertation. However, his formula was flawed by two critical assumptions: a zero interest rate, and a process that allowed for a negative share price.

Half a century later, in 1955, Paul Samuelson picked up the thread and wrote on "Brownian Motion in the Stock Market."[26] His work inspired Case Sprenkle to solve the two key problems in Bachielier's formula: He assumed that stock prices are log-normally distributed and also introduced the idea of a drift. Both helped to exclude negative stock prices. Both also helped to introduce the notion of risk aversion. Sprenkle's paper had been of useful assistance to Black and Scholes in solving their mathematical equations many years later.

In 1962, A. James Boness, a student at the University of Chicago, wrote a dissertation about "Theory and Measurement of Stock Option Value."[27] Boness introduced the concept of the time value of money in his option analysis. He discounted the expected terminal stock price back to today. As a discount rate, he used the expected rate of return to the stock. Boness was the first to come up with a mathematical formula for option pricing that incorporated key, now universally accepted assumptions: (i) stock prices are normally distributed (which guarantees that share prices are positive), (ii) the interest rate is a non-zero (negative or positive), and (iii) investors are risk averse.

Boness's pricing model served as the direct progenitor to the Black-Scholes formula. His approach allowed—as an acknowledgement of the risk-averse investor—for a compensation of the risk associated with a stock through an unknown interest rate that served as a compensation for the risk associated with the stock and was added to the risk-free interest rate. Fischer Black and Myron Scholes then eliminated any assumptions on the risk preference of the investors and delivered the proof that the risk-free interest rate is the correct discount factor, not the risk-associated interest rate. In 1973, they published their ground-breaking option pricing model. The equation derived from the Capital Asset Pricing Model (CAPM) by Merton. This model develops the equation to calculate the expected return on a risky asset as a function of its risk. At the time of the publication the authors did not realize that the differential equation they proposed was in fact the heat transfer equation, closing the loop to Bachielier. The Black and Scholes formula offers an analytical solution for a continuous time stochastic process, while the Cox-Ross and Rubinstein binomial option pricing model, published in 1979, delivers a solution for a discrete time stochastic process. The former requires a partial differential equation, the latter elementary mathematics.

Financial option pricing relies on two key assumptions. The first assumption is no arbitrage. Arbitrage refers to a trading strategy whereby the investor can create a positive cash flow with certainty at the time of settlements without requiring an initial cash outlay. In efficient markets, such arbitrage possibilities do not exist. As soon as the potential for a risk-free profit is recognized, multiple players in the market will bid for that asset and thereby cause the price of the asset to move in a direction that destroys the arbitrage possibility and re-establishes market parity.

The second fundamental assumption in financial option pricing is that there is a continuous risk-free hedge of the option. This hedge is created by borrowing and holding a part of the stock to replicate the option. Indeed, the key insight provided both by the binomial model and the Black-Scholes formula is that derivatives, such as options, can be priced using the risk-free rate. Risk is acknowledged not in the discount rate, but in the probability distribution of the future asset value. That key insight can be transferred to the application of real options, while the nature of the probability distributions may be very distinct in real options versus financial options. We will discuss some of the fundamental differences in the next chapter.

The Black-Scholes pricing method of financial options assumes a log-normal distribution of future returns in a continuous time framework. A diffusion process refers to continuous, smooth arrival of information that causes continuous price changes with either constant or changing variance. These price changes are normally distributed or log-normally distributed. In its basic form, the Black-Scholes formula values the European call on a non-dividend paying stock, but it can also be applied to other pricing problems.

The Black-Scholes formula is mostly known for its use in option pricing. However, it also has found application in portfolio insurance. Hayne Leland, a professor of finance at the University of Berkley in California, came up with the concept in September of 1976.[28] Leland in essence likened the basic idea of an insurance to a put option. It gives the put owner the right to dispose of an asset at a previously specified price. Applied to stock portfolios, this puts a floor to the potential losses from the portfolio, that is, providing an insurance. The upside potential of the portfolio remained preserved. At the core of the Black-Scholes formula lies the arbitrage argument, whereby the call option can be perfectly hedged by a negative stock position and therefore can be discounted at the risk-free rate.

Leland used the same concept but reversed it: He created a synthetic put option by hedging the stock with a risk-free asset. Selling stock and lending money, that is, buying government bonds at the risk-free rate as long as the payoff equals the payoff of a put, generates the put. The idea of a portfolio insurance was born; Leland took it to fund managers in the early eighties, and within a few years $100 billion dollars were invested in portfolio insurance. However, there was one problem with this concept. If stock prices fall, the value of the put on the stock goes up. To provide an effective insurance, that is, floor, a larger and larger position needs to be built to mitigate the risk, implying more and more stocks need to be sold, and more money must be lent by buying government bonds. If the entire market operates according to this principle, everybody ends up selling stocks, which is exactly what happened in the stock crash of 1987. That is why some argue that the portfolio insurance contributed to the crash of 1987.

The log-normal behavior of returns, on which the Black-Scholes formula builds, is of course just one type of behavior. It happens to fit reasonably well the behavior of stock prices. Other option pricing formulas have been developed to deal with returns that follow different stochastic movements such as jumps.

A jump process refers to the discontinuous arrival of information, which causes the asset value to jump. These processes are well described by a Poisson distribution. Both diffusion and jump processes, as well as combinations thereof, have been integrated in option pricing models: a pure-jump model,[29] the combined jump-diffusion model[30] that integrates the log-normal with the jump process, or the changing variance diffusion[31] that assumes that the volatility changes constantly. Margrabe[32] developed a pricing model for an Exchange Option, namely, the option to switch from one riskless asset, the delivery asset, to another one, the one to be acquired or optioned asset. His model is particularly useful in the pricing options for which the exercise price is uncertain. Margrabe also assumes a log-normal diffusion process for both the delivery and optioned asset. In addition, however, this model requires one to know how the two assets may be correlated. Both the strength of the correlation and its nature (positive versus negative) determines how the change in the volatility of one asset drives the value of another. The Margrabe exchange model has been used to price real R&D options in E-commerce.[33] The key advantage for such an application, compared to the Black-Scholes formula, lies in the basic assumption that both the future value of the asset as well as the costs are stochastic. Black-Scholes, on the contrary, assumes that the costs K are deterministic. Other authors have explored scenarios where future payoffs do not follow a log-normal distribution but are at risk of dropping to zero, that is, upon competitive entry. Schwartz and Moon[34] presented a real option valuation model based on a mixed-jump diffusion process, where the jump symbolizes the point in time when cash flows and asset values fall to zero. A further extension is the sequential exchange model postulated by Carr.[35] It calculates the value of a compounded option in which—as in Margrabe's model—both the future asset value and the costs behave stochastically, but it also provides an additional extension by further assuming that investment will occur in sequential steps that build on each other (compounded).

Despite all of these analytical models, many valuation problems for financial options still have no known analytic solution, such as the American put. Analytical models arrive at the expected value by solving a stochastic differential equation.[36] In order for this to work, one of course needs to know the nature of the stochastic process that fits the movements of the assets. This can be a challenge even for financial assets, and certainly is a significant challenge for real assets.

There are other methods that can be used to arrive at the expected value, numerical methods that allow us to ballpark the future value of the asset, such as a Monte Carlo simulation. Monte Carlo simulation was proposed by

Phelim Boyle in 1977.[37] It builds on the insight that whatever the distribution of stock value will be at the time the option expires, that distribution is determined by processes that drive the movements of the asset value between now and the expiration date. If such a process can be specified, then it can also be simulated using a computer. With any simulation, an asset value at the time of option expiration is generated. Thousands of simulations will create a distribution of future stock values, and from this probability distribution the expected value of the stock at the time of option expiration can be calculated. The more simulations are performed, the higher the accuracy of the method. The more accurate the result, the better the riskless hedge that can be formed, allowing us to use the expected value at the risk-less rate.

The binomial method was originally proposed by William Sharpe in 1978[38] but was made famous with the publication by John Cox, Stephen Ross, and Mark Rubinstein in 1979.[39] In the binomial model the probability distribution of the future stock price is determined by the size of the up- and downward movements at each discrete step in time. The size of these movements reflects the volatility of the stock prices in the past. Depending on the number of steps, the option cone evolves that gives the anticipated stock price at each node.

The binominal tree divides the time between now and the expiration date of the option into discrete intervals, marked by nodes, and so operates, just as Markov had done, with distinct time units. In each interval, or at each node, the stock can go either up or down, each with a probability q. Starting at time zero today, shown in Figure 1.7, which is node 0, those upward and downward steps over time create a tree, or lattice, of future stock prices. From node 0, the stock can go either up or down, hitting node 1 or 2. If it moves to node 2, it can then move to node 4 or 5, but not node 3. This is the Markov property: Each step is conditional on the previous step. As time goes on and more steps are taken, the variance or volatility increases and the option cone becomes broader and broader. After the first step, the variance is the difference between node 1 and 2. After six steps, the variance is between node 21 and node 27. Each of those nodes is a possible outcome when starting from node 0.

The binomial option also delivers a very intuitive and clear illustration of the no-arbitrage argument used to price the option at the risk-free rate. Instead of buying an option on a stock, the investor may also create a synthetic call by acquiring a mixture of some of the stock and borrow or lend money at the risk-free rate. This portfolio of stock and bonds is designed in such a way that it exactly replicates the future payoffs the investor would obtain from holding the option, given the volatility of the stock. If that is the case, then the price of the option today must be the same as today's price of the replicating portfolio—in accordance with the no-arbitrage argument. That

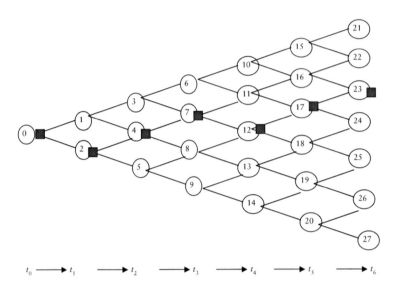

FIGURE 1.7 The binomial tree

price—in the absence of arbitrage—must then be the future expected payoff discounted back to today's value at the risk-less rate, the same price the investor would pay for the expected future payoff of the risk-less portfolio.

It is the concept of the replicating portfolio that led to the notion that real options can only be applied to investment projects for which a traded twin security can be found that exactly matches the risk and uncertainties of the project—at which point in most cases frustration sets in among practitioners. Another frustration that arises when attempting daily use of the real option framework derives from the sight of complex partial differential equations. These capture the assumed stochastic process of the underlying asset in an analytical solution but are hard, if not impossible, to convey as intuitive and meaningful insights to decision makers. The binomial model with a discrete time approach does not deliver an analytical solution but also does not require more than elementary mathematics and therefore is a very valuable alternative to option pricing.

The binomial option model further offers the following significant advantages:

- It is intuitive and transparent.
- It allows simple continuous time numerical approximation of complex valuation problems, also for scenarios for which no analytical closed form solutions exist.
- The option is priced without subjective risk preference of the investor.

NOTES

1. S.C. Myers, "Finance Theory and Financial Strategy," in D. Chew Jr., ed., *The New Corporate Finance*, 2nd ed., p. 119, (McGraw Hill, 1998).
2. I. Fisher, *The Rate of Interest: Its Nature, Determination and Relation to Economic Phenomena* (New York, 1907).
3. C. H. Loch and K. Bode-Gruel, "Evaluating Growth Options as Sources of Value for Pharmaceutical Research Projects, *R & D Management* 31:231, 2001.
4. C.H. Deutsch, "Software That Makes a Grown Company Cry," *New York Times*, Nov. 8, 1998.
5. T.S. Bowen, "Committing to Consultants: Outside Help Requires Internal Commitment and Management Skills," *InfoWorld*, 20:61, 1998; T. Ryrie, "What's ERP?" Chapter 70:46, 1999.
6. J. Moad, "Finding the Best Cultural Match for Software," *PC Week*, Sept. 8, 1997.
7. R.G. McGrath, "Falling Forward: Real Options Reasoning and Entrepreneurial Failure," *Academy of Management Review* 24:13, 1999.
8. E. Carew, "Derivatives Decoded," 1995.
9. D. Douggie, *Future Markets* (Prentice Hall, 1989).
10. F. Black and M. Scholes, "The Pricing of Options and Corporate Liabilities," *Journal of Political Economy* 81:637 1973.
11. R.C. Merton, "Theory of Rational Option Pricing," *Bell Journal of Economics and Management Science* 4:141, 1973; W.F. Sharpe, *Investments* (Prentice Hall, 1978).
12. S.C. Myers, "Determinants of Corporate Borrowing," *Journal of Financial Economics* 5:147, 1977.
13. S.C. Myers, "Finance Theory and Financial Strategy," *Midland Corporate Finance Journal* 5:5, 1987.
14. G. Mechlin and D. Berg, "Evaluating Research, ROI Is Not Enough," *Harvard Business Review* Jan.–Feb., 1980, 93–99.
15. R.H. Hayes and W.J. Abernathy, "Managing Our Way to Economic Decline," *Harvard Business Review*, Sept.–Oct. 1980, pp. 67–77; M. Porter, "Capital Disadvantage: America's Failing Capital Investment System," *Harvard Business Review*, Sept.–Oct. 65, 1992; C.Y. Baldwin and B.J. Clark, "Capital-Budgeting Systems and Capabilities Investments in U.S. Companies After the Second World War," *Business History Review* 68:73, 1994.
16. J.E. Hooder and H.E. Riggs, "Pitfalls in Evaluating Risky Projects," *Harvard Business Review*, Jan.–Feb. 63:128, 1985.
17. R. Hayes and D. Garvin, "Managing As If Tomorrow Mattered," *Harvard Business Review*, May–June, 71, 1982.

18. W.C. Kester, "Today's Options for Tomorrow's Growth," *Harvard Business Review*, March–April 18, 1984.
19. N.S. Pindyck, "Irreversible Investment, Capacity Choice and the Value of the Firm," *American Economic Review* 79:969, 1988a.
20. A.K. Dixit and N.S. Pindyck, *Investment under Uncertainty* (Princeton University Press, 1994).
21. L. Trigeorgis, *Real Options—Managerial Flexibility and Strategy in Resource Allocation* (MIT Press, Cambridge, MA, 1996).
22. For a more detailed historical description see, Murad S. Taqqu, "Bachelier and his Times: A Conversation with Bernard Bru," *Stochastic and Finance*, 2001 and references therein.
23. L. Bachielier, "Theorie de la speculation," *Annales Scientifiques de l'Ecole Normale Superieure* III–17:21(86) 1900. Thesis for the Doctorate in Mathematical Sciences (defended March 29, 1900). (Reprinted by *Editions Jacques Gabay*, Paris, 1995.) English translation in P. Cootner, ed., *The Random Character of Stock Market Prices*, pp. 17–78 (MIT Press, Cambridge, 1964).
24. R. Brown, "A Brief Account of Microscopical Observations Made in the Months of June, July, and August, 1827, on the Particles Contained in the Pollen of Plants; and on the General Existence of Active Molecules in Organic and Inorganic Bodies," *Philosophical Magazine* 4:161, 1828; B.J. Ford, "Brownien Movement in Clarkia Pollen: A Reprise of the First Observations," *The Microscope* 40:235, 1992.
25. L. Boltzmann, *Vorlesungen Äuber Gastheorie* (J.A. Barth, Leipzig, 1896.) *Ludwig Boltzmann (1844–1906)*, published in two volumes, 1896 and 1898. Appeared in French in 1902–1905, *Leçons sur la Theorie des Gaz* (Gauthier-Villars, Paris). Published in English by Dover, New York, as *Lectures on Gas Theory*, 490p.
26. P. Samuelson, "Rational Theory of Warrant Pricing," *Industrial Management Review* 6:13, 1967.
27. T. O'Brien and M.J.P. Selby, "Option Pricing Theory and Asset Expectations: A Review and Discussion in Tribute to James Boness," *Financial Review*, November 1986, 399–418.
28. H.E. Leland and M. Rubinstein, "The Evolution of Portfolio Insurance," in Don Luskin, ed., *Dynamic Hedging: A Guide to Portfolio Insurance* (John Wiley and Sons, 1988).
29. J.C. Cox and S.A. Ross, "The Valuation of Options for Alternative Stochastic Processes," *Journal of Financial Economics* 3:145, 1976.
30. R.C. Merton, "Option Pricing Where the Underlying Stock Returns Are Discontinuous," *Journal of Financial Economics* 3:449, 1974.

31. R. Geske, "The Valuation of Compound Options," *Journal of Financial Economics* 7:63, 1979.
32. W. Margrabe, "The Value of an Option to Exchange One Asset for Another. *Journal of Finance* 33:177, 1978.
33. J. Lee and D.A. Paxson, "Valuation of R&D Real American Sequential Exchange Options," *R&D Management* 31:191, 2001.
34. E.S. Schwartz and M. Moon, "Evaluating Research and Development Investments," in M. Brennan and L. Trigeorgis, eds., *Project Flexibility, Agency and Competition* (Oxford University Press, 2000).
35. P. Carr, "The Valuation of Sequential Exchange Opportunities," *Journal of Finance* 43:1235, 1988.
36. There are two other analytical methods: The lattice models avoided the requirement to solve a stochastic differential equation by specifying a particular process for the underlying asset price (a binomial process) and then using an iterative approach to solve the value of the option. The finite difference methodology involves replacing the differential equation with a series of difference equations. See J.C. Hull, *Options, Futures, and Other Derivatives* (Prentice Hall, 1997).
37. P.P. Boyle, "Options: A Monte Carlo Approach," *Journal of Financial Economics* 4:323, 1977.
38. W.F. Sharpe, *Investments* (Prentice Hall, 1978).
39. J.C. Cox, S.A. Ross, and M. Rubinstein, "Option Pricing: A Simplified Approach," *Journal of Financial Economics* 7:229, 1979.

CHAPTER 2

Taking an Idea into Practice

REAL OPTION CONCEPTS AND APPLICATIONS

Real option analysis values and rewards managerial insight and the resulting flexibility. Managers may delay an investment until further information is available to provide better insights into market conditions. They may change the scale of an ongoing project by either downsizing or expanding it. They may decide to abandon a project altogether. They may decide to exchange input resources, that is, switch from one energy form to another, or from one product output to another. They may also decide to structure an investment into a major new project in incremental steps, with an option to grow at each step, while at the same time obtaining valuable market and product information. Finally, they may want to stage a very risky investment into a new technology or into a new prototype incorporating multiple "go" and "no-go" decision points based on conditional probabilities of achieving certain milestones along the way.

The initial real option work focused on the value created by abandoning a project and liquidating the assets.[1] A project that can be abandoned, so the reasoning goes, is in essence an American put option on a dividend-paying stock: It gives management the right but entails no obligation to sell the asset at a salvage price, the exercise price, at any time, but it will forego the cash flows generated by the asset, equivalent to the dividend on a stock, as shown in Figure 2.1.

This managerial flexibility has value, and the value can be determined using option pricing theory. Management will make use of the abandonment option once market conditions have deteriorated and the potential value created by the asset, such as a production plant or an airplane fleet, over its remaining lifetime is lower than the value created by selling it. The value of the

33

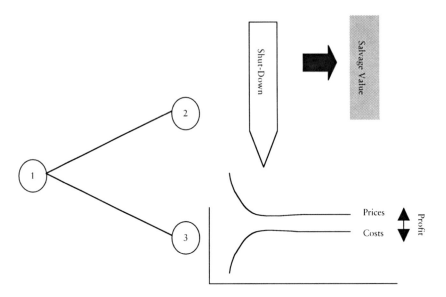

FIGURE 2.1 The abandonment option

put is the salvage price minus the costs incurred to exercise the option, such as transaction costs minus revenues foregone by selling the asset.

The first call on real assets to be priced was an investment in a natural resource project such as the exploration of an oil field or a mine.[2] Owning the mine provides the owner with a call option, the right, but not the obligation, to explore the mine. The value of the call on the mine depends on the costs and resources required to recover its contents but also on the revenue stream to be generated by future sales. The decision as to whether to initiate or continue exploration, to slow down exploration, or to shut down the mine altogether will be guided by management's expectations of future market conditions, as shown in Figure 2.2. The value of the option on the mine today reflects the degree of managerial flexibility in place to respond to future uncertainties in the optimum fashion.

This work also created the important insight that there is value in waiting. Traditional NPV analysis recommends investing as soon as today's value of expected future payoffs is bigger than today's value of the expected costs. In contrast, option analysis argues that there is value in waiting and deferring the investment decision until further information arrives to solve external market uncertainties, as shown in Figure 2.3.

Investing today in an uncertain future, where markets can be either great or bad, implies that resources are irreversibly spent while the payoff is uncertain. Deferring the investment until market uncertainty has been re-

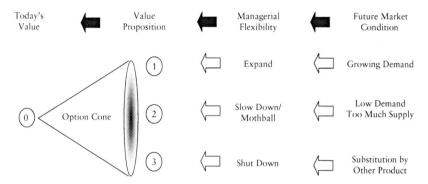

FIGURE 2.2 The real option cone for a mine owner

solved and then reserving the right, or the option, to invest only when market conditions are excellent, implies that the upside potential of the market can be taken advantage of while the downside risk resulting from bad market conditions is eliminated. Herein lies the value of waiting.[3] MacDonald and Siegel MacDonald[4] were the first to recognize the connection between irreversibility and uncertainty. They made the point that committing resources irreversibly into an uncertain future requires an option premium that compensates for the loss of flexibility in the face of uncertainty.

Majd and Pindyck[5] were the first to propose an option pricing model that includes the value created by managerial flexibility during the course of

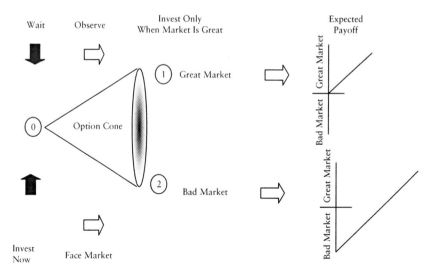

FIGURE 2.3 The value of waiting to invest

a prolonged staged investment project: Depending on new information arriving from the market, management can accelerate or slow down the project and also abandon it. Further, they pointed out that in such a sequential project each dollar spent buys the option to spend the next dollar, while cash flows only happen after the project is completed. This lays the conceptual groundwork for the compound option, which we will describe in more detail below. The important insights derived from the Majd and Pindyck study are the following: (i) Within a sequential project, the value of the investment program changes as a function of the value of the completed project, which is likely to fluctuate over a long "time-to-build" time period as well as the outstanding investment cost K required to complete the project. For each sequential phase the authors derive the critical project value of the completed project that needs to be met to justify going forward with resource investment into the next phase. (ii) This critical investment value of the completed project depends on the opportunity cost of money and increases with the assumed volatility of the completed project.

The work by Majd and Pindyck confirmed and extended the basic concept brought about by others earlier,[6] namely, that growing uncertainty increases the value of the call option and thereby the incentive to hold the option while decreasing the incentive to exercise it by investing. The most important insight of the Majd and Pindyck study is that time to build reduces the value of the payoff at completion, and that loss increases as the opportunity cost of delaying increases, further increasing the critical value to invest. Opportunity cost is, for example, foregone revenue: the longer it takes to complete the project, the more the potential revenue stream is foregone. For such a scenario, two main drivers of the option value emerge: the volatility or uncertainty of future cash flows, which increases the critical threshold to invest, and the rate of opportunity cost, which decreases it, as shown in Figure 2.4.

However, the effect of the opportunity costs also depends on the volatility. Time to build reduces the expected payoff at completion and creates opportunity costs, that is, revenue foregone due to the time it takes to complete the project. With low project volatility and high opportunity costs the incentive to invest declines. As project volatility increases, opportunity costs further increase and tend to lower the critical threshold to invest.

Depending on prevailing market conditions, managers routinely adjust the scale of an existing operation. For example, in a manufacturing plant there is flexibility to expand or to contract production to adjust to demand. Likewise, management can adjust the output of a mine or an oilfield to adjust to seasonal or macroeconomic changes in the market place. Brennan and Schwartz were the first to value the flexibility of being able to respond to those changes, and others extended that concept.[7] Expansion and con-

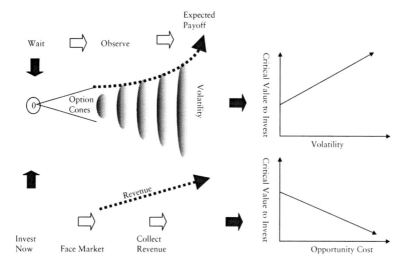

FIGURE 2.4 The critical cost while waiting to invest

tracting options relate not just to manufacturing or natural resource investments. Any joint venture that turns into an acquisition strategy qualifies as an expansion strategy. As empirical data based on the analysis of ninety-two joint ventures suggest, exercise of the option to expand from a joint venture into an acquisition is triggered by a perceived increase of the venture market value in response to product-market signals.[8] If management receives signals from the market to suggest significant growth in product demand and therefore an increase in the value of the venture, it becomes more inclined to expand the joint venture option into an acquisition.

Managers also have the flexibility to exchange one product for another, to alter input parameters, or to change the speed of production. This flexibility has been named the "exchange option." For example, oil refineries may produce crude heating oil or gasoline,[9] and the production output mix will be guided by what is perceived to be the most profitable mix. A plant that is allowed to implement production flexibility creates switching value. While management will not know which product will be most profitable in the future, a flexible plant creates the infrastructure to preserve future flexibility, thereby allowing management to respond to future uncertainties in the optimal fashion.[10] This is very similar to the real option we described earlier, involving heating oil and natural gas, encountered by the home owner.

The decision to enter new emerging markets involves considerable risk and uncertainty, and is likely to give a negative NPV in a traditional discounted cash flow analysis. However, this initial investment also lays the foundation for future market expansion, should the initial entry be successful.

Hence, the initial investment buys the corporation the option to grow, and the future market potential created by establishing an initial foreign subsidiary needs to be included in the original project appraisal. Several authors engaged in pioneering work related to value growth options between 1977 and 1988.[11] Practical examples include the investment in information technology infrastructure, R&D projects, or expansion into other markets that can be staged in segmental steps.[12] Anheuser Busch[13] notably created $13.4 billion in value in two years by expanding its investments by $1.9 billion. More than half of the value creation, namely 51%, is attributed to growth options that Anheuser acquired by obtaining minority interests in existing brewing concerns located in parts of the world with high growth rates for beer demand. Under the terms of the agreement, the local concern distributes Anheuser Busch products in these markets, effectively creating growth options for Anheuser Busch. The joint ventures allow Anheuser Busch to test and understand the local markets before committing larger investments toa more aggressive expansion strategy in those regions that prove most profitable.

The concept of compounded options is immediately attractive to an R&D project that comes in several phases, with each phase relying on successful completion of the previous phase. The investment will only be completed once all phases have been completed successfully, and only then can cash flows be realized. However, each completed phase contributes to the continuous value appreciation through two components: by reducing overall project uncertainty that is highest at the beginning,[14] but also by creating information, knowledge, expertise, and insight that may be transferable to other related projects, even if this one fails. Not surprisingly, therefore, compounded real options were quickly adapted in high-tech high-risk industries with a rich portfolio of R&D projects but also were adapted to applications in strategy and operations.[15]

EXTENSION AND VARIATIONS OF THE CONCEPTS—NEW INSIGHTS

As applications of real options spread, the basic concepts are fine-tuned. Novel option concepts continue to emerge, and existing paradigms are changed and extended. Initial option work studied mostly the impact of market uncertainty on option valuation and the timing and extent of investment decisions. The critical value to invest was defined by the cost of investment, the future asset value and the option premium, or the value of waiting to invest to reduce future uncertainty.[16] Trigeorgis[17] was the first to point out that a single investment project often entails several distinct real options creating scope for multiple option interactions. Once multiple options come into play, the value of each individual option tends to increase; but taken together, depending on the individual scenario, those embedded options may add up, synergize, or antagonize in terms of their contribution to the overall option value of the investment project.

While the concept of waiting and the value of sequential investment in the face of uncertainty has gained much attention, the notion that new information obtained through learning may also impact on the value of an investment is less explored.[18] This work opens a different perspective on option valuation. Option value derives from obtaining better information by delaying a decision, whereas, on the contrary, making the decision today could result in irreversible loss, an idea pioneered in the early seventies.[19] Arrow and Fisher then looked into the valuation of an irreversible investment decision, namely, the development of a piece of land that will forever change the natural features of an area. The value of the option derives from information that reduces the variability of the future payoff, creating the "quasi-option." In this framework, the option is on the expected value of reduced damage, relative to doing nothing. The option value reflects the value of delaying an irreversible investment that might be harmful and cause irreversible damage if additional information is expected in the future that resolves current uncertainty and has the potential to alter the course of this decision—thereby preventing that damage.

The intricate relationship between irreversibility and uncertainty has featured prominently in environmental economics since the early seventies. At that time two landmark publications appeared,[20] both of which emphasized the irreversibility effect of investment decisions. The standard example of the "irreversibility effect" is the construction of a dam that irreversibly floods and destroys a natural valley. In a more general context, this work, as well as more recent work building on the earlier insights,[21] extends the concept to scenarios in which irreversible decisions are made today even though preferences may change in the future. That change of preference may result from new, unanticipated information.

For example, the hazardous effects of lead on human health changed consumer preference for paints. The decision to incorporate lead into paints was made unknowingly and without anticipating that in the future the world would be aware of the fact that lead imposes a serious health hazard. A decision maker does not know how many possible future situations she may overlook, inadvertently. This situation is referred to as hard uncertainty.

Consider the binomial asset tree in Figure 2.5. The decision on the components of paint is made today, at node 1. In the future, lead may be

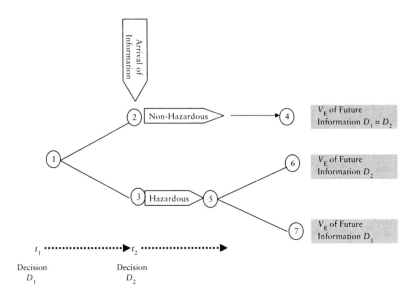

FIGURE 2.5 The quasi-option: facing hard uncertainty

nonhazardous (node 2), or hazardous (node 3). Suppose that the decision would be deferred to the later time point t_2. At t_2 it is known whether lead is hazardous or not. The quasi-option then values the information gain that leads to the decision at t_2, on the condition that no decision was made in t_1. In other words, waiting and deferring the decision to t_2 preserves the flexibility to wait for more information before choosing the paint component at t_2, and the option value is the value of this flexibility. In such a scenario the quasi-option is the gain from acquiring or obtaining information relevant to the state of the world in the decision-making process. If the lead turns out to be non-hazardous (node 2), the information gain for the decision is immaterial; the expected value of the information is the same irrespective of whether the decision was made at t_1 or t_2 (node 4). On the contrary, if lead turns out to be hazardous (node 3), the value of that information is material; it allows the decision maker who has deferred the decision until the arrival of information at time t_2 to make an informed decision (node 6), while the decision maker who has committed at t_1 now faces the consequences of his irreversible decision made in the face of uncertainty and the absence of information at t_1 (node 7).

In a corporate context, the time value of waiting is meaningful for monopoly options but needs to be revisited for shared options in a competitive environment. The value of waiting ignores and potentially compromises the value created by competitive positioning or preemptive moves that might in fact destroy the value of waiting. In 1994, Dixit and Pindyck took a first look at a duopoly situation with much simplified assumptions: The scenario is one in which there is a perpetual option, and both players have the same set of complete information. Lambrecht and Perraudin[22] extended the concept by introducing American put options as the payoff. They also assumed that the exercise price of the put was the transaction costs and known only by the players. The same authors provided an additional extension in a subsequent study.[23] Here, the value of the option to preempt a competitor was introduced. Again, the option was perpetual in nature, but the authors considered that each player had no knowledge of the critical value to invest of the other player. Further, the authors assumed that whoever was second lost the investment opportunity. Such a scenario is likely to play out only in industries with strong intellectual property positions. Adding another flavor to the competitive scenario, the market share lost by deferring an investment decision can be interpreted as a "competitive dividend," an opportunity cost foregone due to later market entry.[24] Not waiting, but investing early and thereby creating a preemptive position, on the other hand, adds to the dividend yield and hence reduces the critical value to invest. This additional dividend, the "competitive dividend," can be likened to the cash dividend that is reserved only for the stockholder but is lost by the option holder on the same stock.

Equally important is the distinction between market uncertainty and technical or private uncertainty, which relates to the internal capabilities and skill sets within any given firm to actually carry out successfully an innovation and implement it. Waiting to invest may resolve market uncertainty; it may even help to observe competitors solving some basic technical uncertainty. But the private, firm-specific source of technical uncertainty cannot be resolved without investing. Only by committing resources and actually initiating the project will the firm find out whether it has the skills to accomplish the goal.

Initial real option models also assumed that costs were deterministic, while, in practice, costs are uncertain most of the time, too. For example, consider a car manufacturer about to embark on building a new plant to manufacture cars. It will take about two years to complete the project, and during this time the costs for labor and materials may fluctuate considerably. Additional uncertainty may stem from changes in government regulations that may impose further construction and safety or environmental protection features that imply additional costs. The exact time frame needed to complete the work is also uncertain. The firm therefore faces significant cost uncertainties in undertaking the project. In 1993, Pindyck introduced cost uncertainty as a distinguishing feature of the real option framework.[25] He stated that each dollar spent towards completion really represents a single investment opportunity with an uncertain outcome, and that each dollar spent towards completion creates value in the form of the amount of progress that results. Further, once the new car production plant is completed, the asset is put in place and generates cash flows, but both demand and prices will change. During the lifetime of the plant, the demand for cars will fluctuate, as will the prices for the cars. Further, the firm will move along a firm-specific learning curve that permits unit cost to fall with experience and with output. Real option pricing models need to incorporate stochastic product life cycles and changing cost structures that are not necessarily log-normally distributed. Bollen provided the real option literature with such a life-cycle model of product demand and unit costs.[26]

Time to maturity is a key parameter that drives value in financial options. Rarely do real options resemble European options with fixed exercise dates. More often, the exercise time is unknown and very uncertain. For example, the time it takes to complete a major project, such as the construction of a high-rise tower, the design of a new airplane prototype, or a drug development project, is uncertain. A competitive entry may unexpectedly kill all or most of the option value, and the timing of such an entry is also uncertain. Uncertain time to maturity affects both the time and level of profitability.[27] Uncertainty surrounding the time needed to implement a project may provoke management to invest very early, especially if resolution of the timing uncertainty has a strong impact on the profitability of the project. Specific cases have been investigated in which the first to implement would be rewarded with a patent and hence could enjoy a monopoly situation for a limited period of time.

Future asset values are driven not just by product features and market demand, but also by distribution channels and marketing capabilities. These important yet uncertain parameters of future asset value were not included in the early option work. Another fundamental assumption of real option pricing of investment decisions is that these investments are irreversible, sunk cost.[28] However, in reality, an investment may not be entirely irreversible but may in fact be partially reversible.[29] Within any given firm that has multiple real options but limited resources, real option analysis has been used to prioritize among mutually exclusive R&D projects[30] as well as to assist in product portfolio management.[31]

Further, the notion that real assets do not move like Brownian motions but are subject to "catastrophic" events infiltrated much of the option work. It prompted the development of alternative models to incorporate those random events that—after all—are significant drivers of the asset value. Those random events could be internal discoveries, such as in an R&D project, or exogenous "catastrophic" events, such as the issue of a competitor's blocking patent. Those random events can be modeled as a Poisson process and linked to market data.[32] Others have enriched the option literature with Poisson or jump models that represent technology innovations, R&D innovations, or cost-reducing innovations.[33]

The application of real option valuation has been extended to value investments in intangible real assets such as the acquisition of knowledge and information, and intellectual property, which are sometimes referred to collectively as virtual options. Another line of research touches on organizational aspects of real option implementation, such as the ability of the organization to execute real options, specifically the abandonment option, as well as on the use of real option concepts to create and guide behavior.

COMPARATIVE ANALYSIS: FINANCIAL AND REAL OPTIONS

The conceptual analogy between financial options and real options is quite intuitive, and the table in Figure 2.6 summarizes the analogies that can be easily drawn.

It appears less obvious, however, that the mathematical concepts used to price financial options—with all the assumptions they rely on—will also be applicable to real options. The past decade has seen an explosion in real option developments far beyond the initial basic option concepts (wait/defer, abandon, switch, grow, expand/contract, compound). This work has delivered further important insights into the commonalities and differences between real options and financial options.

ANALOGIES: FINANCIAL OPTIONS—REAL OPTIONS

Financial Option	Variable	Investment Project/Real Option
Exercise price	K	Costs to acquire the asset
Stock price	S	Present value of future cash flows from the asset
Time to expiration	t	Length of time option is viable
Variance of stock returns	σ^2	Riskiness of the asset, variance of the best and worst case scenario
Risk-free rate of return	r	Risk-free rate of return

FIGURE 2.6 Financial versus real options

Financial options are available on a large and diverse group of underlying assets including individual stocks, stock indexes, government bonds, currencies, precious metals, and futures contracts. Real options deal with capital budgeting, investment decisions, and business transactions. The commonalities between the two include the following generic basics:

1. Investment in uncertainty
2. Irreversibility
3. The ability to choose between two or more alternatives

Investment decisions in both the financial and in the real world boil down to answering three key questions: Whether? When? How much? The dissimilarities between the two, however, outnumber the similarities by far, and they are quite fundamental. First, there are conceptual dissimilarities. Decisions must be made on real options even if not all of the uncertainty has been resolved. In contrast, for financial options, by the time the exercise date approaches, all variables required to make an informed decision are known. During the lifetime of an option, it easily moves in, out, and at the money. The financial option holder observes passively those movements. The real option holder, in contrast, has the flexibility and the capability—as well as the obligation towards her shareholders—to impact the movements of the underlying asset and thereby mitigate the downside risk while preserving or expanding the upside potential. This falls within the realm of real option execution. Hedging of real options is truly a challenge. This imposes restrictions as to how much of the downside risk can be truly limited, asking for prudent assumptions when framing the option analysis. Financial options have a known time to maturity, while real options most often do not. Mostly, there is no deadline for a decision to be made, and the time frame during which the opportunity is alive is often not known. For example, we cannot say for sure how long it may take to develop a prototype and we do not know when competitive entry will terminate our option externally and prematurely.

The source of option value is also different for financial and for real options. For financial options the value of the option is easily determined as the numerical difference between the upside potential and exercise price. For real options, part of the value arises naturally for a given firm as a result of core competence, existing market or technology position, possible barriers of entry including existing intellectual property, acquired knowledge and experience, technical expertise, or an existing brand name. Often, part of the value must be purchased by investments into R&D, intellectual property, technology development programs, infrastructure, contractual agreements with others including deals, leases, licensing agreements or outsourcing agreements.

The value of financial and real options responds differently to changes in certain parameters. For example, the time to maturation increases the value of the financial option. The intuition behind this is that, with larger time horizons, uncertainty and hence the upside potential increase. For real options, it depends on whether the option is proprietary or shared. Only in the former case may the option value increase with time. In the latter scenario, under competitive threats and at risk of losing market share by late entry, giving up preemptive and positioning value, and seeing a patent expire, the relationship between time to maturity and real option value is much more complex.

Financial option value increases with volatility, as higher volatility implies higher upside potential. This does not necessarily apply to real options; market volatility may increase the value of the option. However, if the main contribution to the option value comes from strategic preemption, demand uncertainty will actually pull the plug on the value of the option.[34] Increasing technical volatility, too, may well diminish the option value.[35]

Financial options can be leveraged, real options not so easily. Financial options are traded in centralized markets with complete information for all players, they are liquid, and their movements are continuous and can be observed at all times. The value of a real asset is hard to monitor continuously; past movements of the asset are not necessarily indicative of future value distributions. Real assets are liquid only very limited, and rarely traded. If so, the markets are decentralized, and information is asymmetric. This makes it conceptually harder to adapt the no-arbitrage argument to the real option world—but we ought not to forget that the DCF approach faces the same challenges.

In the real world, the value of the option can be defined as the difference between the maximum return from a flexible investment program versus the return from an inflexible program.[36] Such an analysis reveals the value of embedded options. For financial options, the strike price is fixed, while for real options it is often unclear at what cost the option acquisition will come. The value of the real option will also depend on how uncertain costs and uncertain future cash flows correlate. We will analyze this in more detail later.

Financial and real options also have distinct exercise rules. These rules are well defined for financial options. They reflect the underlying mathematics, which are equally well defined. For example, never exercise an American option on a non-dividend paying stock. As for real options, the exercise rules are equally well defined, but the branches of the binomial tree are multiple and intricately interwoven, making it more complex in defining how uncertainties and flexibility will influence the expected payoff. For real options the world is a lot fuzzier than for financial options, in which the asset value is clearly observable at the time of exercise, and time to expiration and exercise price are well defined. For real options, the time horizon tends to be much longer, and both exercise price and asset value are evolving over the time to maturity, which is uncertain. Realizing the value of a real option hinges on the ability to execute the option rationally. Financial options tend to be exercised by rational investors. As to the exercise of real options, organizational incentive structures, agency conflicts, and "emotional attachments" may stand in the way of rational exercise.

How then can the concepts of financial option pricing still be applied to real option pricing? Fundamentally, the price of an option reflects the expected future payoff of the underlying asset at the time of exercise. The expected future payoff is discounted back to today's time at the risk-free rate and gives today's option value. The procedure rests on the assumption that in complete markets the investor will find a traded security that exactly mimics the risk and uncertainties of the option payoff at any point in time between acquisition and exercise of the option. Using the twin security and a mix of either lending or borrowing money she can build a continuous replicating portfolio to hedge the option. If the option price is higher or lower than today's value of the future payoff, an arbitrage opportunity arises which—by definition—does not exist in complete markets.

When choosing a discount rate for a new investment project in order to determine its NPV, managers resort to—more or less—arbitrary risk premiums meant to reflect the risk of the investment project. The appropriate discount rate is the rate of returns an investor would expect from a traded twin security that carries the same risk as the project being valued. Now managers are offered the opportunity to supplement the NPV by a probability approach to investment valuation that works with risk-neutral probabilities and replaces the risk-adjusted discount rate with the risk-free rate. This is feasible even for non-traded investment projects for which no replicating traded security can be identified:[37] Treat the real option as if it were traded, just as a DCF-based analysis assumes that if the project were traded, the discount factor reflects the return investors would demand in the market. This is a fundamental assumption, but corporate managers have made it for years when applying DCF. Using real option pricing does not require a mental stretch beyond what is already implied and routine use in NPV-based capital budgeting approaches. Once one can accept that the fundamental argument used for many years in many corporations in their DCF analysis must also be valid for real option pricing, then the reminder of the rationale is straightforward:[38] The expected return the twin security offers equals the cost of capital for the real investment opportunity and is used to discount its value. An option on the twin security would be priced by building on the no-arbitrage or the risk-neutral argument at the risk-free rate. The option on the real asset must be priced exactly the same, otherwise an arbitrage opportunity would be created. Therefore, the use of the risk-free rate for risk-neutral payoffs of real options is in line with long-accepted concepts in corporate finance.

Freeing the application of real options from the need of a twin security has facilitated the application of the real option framework to an increasing variety of corporate investment decisions including those that may contribute to value creation but do not lead by themselves to cash-flow-generating assets. Those include, for example, real option analysis to value investments in employee education and training, in improvement of production processes or operational procedures, or in strategic positioning of a product, a brand name, or an entire firm.

The underlying asset on which the corporation acquires the real option are the future cash flows which are captured as certainty-equivalents, thereby separating risk from time value of money and making it possible to discount at the risk-free rate. When making the transition from a DCF-NPV to a real option approach, management must derive probability distributions for the future asset value, and map out the main drivers of uncertainty and how they might be impacted by managerial actions to mitigate risk. The binomial option pricing model represents a framework that helps in structuring this analysis and at the same time permits the option pricing.

In the DCF and NPV mindset, a single discount rate is usually instrumental to acknowledge risk. However, this approach assumes that the risk is constant for the course of the project, an assumption not justified in many real option projects. For example, in a drug development program, many managers will agree that the most risky part is the phase II clinical trial when the compound has to show clinical efficacy for the first time and the phase III clinical trial when it has to prove superior efficacy compared to existing therapies. The real option framework offers a more appropriate way of dealing with changing risk: the cash flows themselves are risk-adjusted for each phase of the project by introducing the probability of success. This leads to the concept of certainty-equivalent of cash flows, allowing the cash flows to be discounted at the risk-free rate.[39] In sum, real options have a complex response pattern to a variety of parameters. Which parameters will drive the value of a single corporate real option and how changes in those parameters will alter the value of the real option will depend on the relative contribution of individual drivers that constitute the overall option value.

As real options are used across industries, managers in conjunction with academic partners are likely to come up with appropriate option pricing techniques that work best for a given industry or a given firm, or a given scenario. In order to communicate real option value to investors and partners, there will, however, also be a need to achieve some standardization of the approach and tools used. Some fundamental features common to all real options will both facilitate and challenge the implementation of the concept internally and in communication with the outside world:

1. The value of the option is the expected value of the asset minus the price of acquiring the option and minus the price of exercising the option.
2. The correlation between asset value volatility and cost volatility defines the option value, not the absolute volatilities of either one.
3. Taking maximum advantage from optionality requires that option holders be capable of exercising their option—financially and organizationally.
4. Financial options do not discriminate: the same price and value is valid for every participant in the market. Real options, on the contrary, are individual. Acquiring the right on the same real asset will have different option values to different organizations, as skills, capabilities and, therefore, probability distributions and payoffs vary.

BLACK-SCHOLES FOR REAL OPTIONS—A VIABLE PATH?

Given the dissimilarities between real and financial options it appears at least risky, if not wrong, to use the Black-Scholes formula for real option pricing. A recent survey among practitioners in real options analysis across industries points out that the fundamental differences between real option and financial options are well recognized and actually prevent many from using the Black-Scholes formula.[40] Most interviewees mentioned the following reasons for not using the Black-Scholes formula:

- Real options are not necessarily European options with a determined exercise date.
- The basic and essential assumptions that returns on real assets are lognormally distributed are not applicable for most real assets.
- The Black-Scholes formula is perceived as a "black box" by senior management, which makes it difficult to understand the value drivers of a project and hence impedes buy-in into recommendations based on the formula. Deriving the "right" volatility is challenging, if not impossible.

Figure 2.7 summarizes some of the fundamental assumptions of the Black-Scholes formula that do not hold for real options.

Further, most of the time we do not know what the volatility of the underlying asset of our real option is, and we will often find it difficult to make assumptions about this parameter. Stock volatility of companies that oper-

❏ Project volatility is not constant over time.

❏ There is no definitive expiration date of the option.

❏ Both asset value as well as strike price (= development costs) behave stochastically.

❏ Returns are not normally distributed.

❏ The random walk of real assets is not symmetric; there are jumps.

FIGURE 2.7 Why Black-Scholes does not work for real options

ate in a similar business can serve as a comparable entity and have been used to determine the volatility of an investment project. This approach may be feasible and justified in some instances, but not as a general rule. An individual project that takes a company on a new, innovative path may have no proxies anywhere in the industry. Further, the nature of asset volatility will also impact how the volatility changes the option value: market uncertainty may in certain instances enhance the option value; technical uncertainty, however, may not. Further, even small alterations in volatility tend to have a substantial impact on the value of the option if one uses the Black-Scholes formula. Finally, investments in real options are characterized not only by asset volatility but also cost volatility. Black-Scholes, however, assumes costs to be constant and not subject to any risk or uncertainty. As for real options, the correlation between those two, rather than their absolute number, tends to determine the option value and hence the critical project value that must be realized to keep the option at the money, as shown in the example in Figure 2.8.

In this example, the volatility of the costs for a given investment opportunity is set constant at 0.643 or 64.3%. The critical project value to preserve the moneyness of the option is, as one would expect, a function of the expected costs, shown on the *x*-axis. As the correlation between asset and cost volatility changes from zero (no correlation at all) to 1 (perfect correlation), the slope of the curve changes significantly, and so does the critical project value. For example, if costs will be $8 million and asset and cost volatility do not correlate (0), the critical project value to preserve moneyness is $6.3 million. If the correlation is perfect, the critical project value drops to $1.8 million. If we were to do the same calculations for a lower cost volatility, say of only 34%, we would see again that the correlation between asset and cost volatility drives the critical project value. However, for a lower cost uncertainty, the impact of the correlation factor is different than for a higher cost volatility.

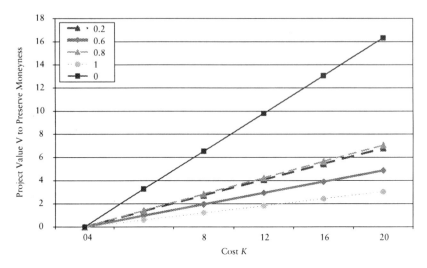

FIGURE 2.8 The critical investment value: Driven by the correlation between asset and cost volatility

What is the intuition behind the results of these calculations? Well, asset and cost uncertainty have opposite effects on the critical project value: asset uncertainty enhances the investment trigger as future cash flows are more uncertain. Cost uncertainty, on the contrary, reduces the investment trigger. With higher cost volatility there is more upside potential in that costs may be much lower than expected, so we should be prepared to invest more readily. When both are perfectly correlated, then the combined effect on the investment trigger will depend on which of the two is larger. If cost volatility is smaller than asset volatility, perfect correlation increases the critical project value required to preserve moneyness. In the opposite scenario (that is, cost volatility is larger than asset volatility), perfect correlation decreases the critical project value. A positive correlation provides a hedge, but also reduces the overall volatility and hence the value of the option. This example illustrates the sensitivity of option value to both cost and asset volatility. It also cautions us against the use of equations building on stochastic processes of both parameters if there is no clear understanding of either one and of how they correlate.

The use of the Black-Scholes formula requires that the underlying asset follow a continuous stochastic movement and that there be no jumps. If the Black-Scholes formula is applied to price real options that do have jumps, then the valuation tends to underestimate the value of deep out-of-the-money options, as the jump that could bring the option back into the money is in essence ignored in the Black-Scholes formula. Other option pricing models, such as Cox & Ross, would be more suitable for assets with jumps, though the inputs to these models are often difficult to estimate.

Black-Scholes not only requires knowledge of the volatility but also assumes that volatility does not change over time. This assumption often does not hold in the real world because most investment opportunities will change their risk-behavior over time. Again, other option pricing models, such as the Carr model that allows for changing variance, may be more appropriate and, indeed, have been used to price real options.[41] However, the Carr model requires a very explicit forecast as to how the variance is expected to change over time, and some decision makers may feel uncomfortable making those predictions and building major investment decisions on predictions of future variance changes.

Black-Scholes in its basic application is the pricing method for European call options, that is, exercise times are fixed and immediate, and can be pinpointed to a moment in time. Key to managerial flexibility, however, is that exercise of an option can take time, and that the time span is often unknown. For example, to realize the cash flows from a new plant, that plant needs to be built, and the time to completion of the construction is uncertain.

Black-Scholes assumes a log-normal distribution of the asset value. For real options, that assumption is unlikely to correctly represent the stochastic processes of the cash-flow–generating asset. Further, it is also unlikely that all the uncertainties that drive the value of the future asset, such as the exchange rate, the demand behavior, the uncertainty relating to the lifetime of the product, or the ability of the company to actually develop the product, behave in a log-normal fashion.

Finally, in certain industries, and specifically for high-risk projects, real options simply do not behave like financial options, as summarized in Figure 2.9.

❏ Increasing volatility does increase the value of financial options but not necessarily real option value.
  ❏ Market volatility does; technical volatility does not.
❏ Time to maturation does not increase option value.
  ❏ Patent expiration
  ❏ Threat of competitive entry
  ❏ Revenue lost due to late market entry

FIGURE 2.9 Real options behave different than financial options

THE BINOMIAL PRICING MODEL
TO PRICE REAL OPTIONS

Six years after Black and Scholes published their formula in 1979, Cox, Ross and Rubinstein (CRR) developed a simplified option pricing model, the binomial option pricing model.[42] The examples given in this book will use this framework. The beauty of the binomial model is its simplicity. It does not deliver closed form solutions but it omits the need for partial differential equations and relies on "elementary mathematics" instead. It does not require estimates of volatility; instead it uses probability distributions. It is based on a discrete-time approach, rather than continuous time. The discrete-time framework fits quite well with the real option world: while decisions can be made at any time, in practice, decisions are in fact made at discrete points in time, after certain information has arrived or after certain milestones have been completed.

The binomial option model assumes that in the next period of time, say until the next milestone is reached, the value of our asset either goes up or down, and then again goes either up or down in the succeeding period. Each happens with a probability q or $1 - q$, respectively, with q being ≤ 1. The value of a call on that asset will be the maximum of zero or $uS_0 - K$ in the upward state or, in the downward state, the maximum of zero or $dS_0 - K$, as shown in Figure 2.10.

What is the value of a call on this asset given that we do not know whether the asset will move up or down? The value of the call today is the value of today's contingent claim on the underlying asset and as such is driven by the volatility of the underlying asset. The value of the asset is a function of the probability q of achieving the best case scenario and $1 - q$ of achieving the worst case scenario, designated uS_0 and dS_0, respectively.

$$V = [q \cdot uS_0 + (1 - q) \cdot dS_0] \qquad (2.1)$$

Let us look at an example in Figure 2.11.

In the best state of nature the value of the cash-flow–generating asset will be $90 million tomorrow; in the worst state of nature, it will be only $30 million. The probability of the best state of nature to occur is 60%, while the probability of the worst case of nature to occur is 40%. It will take two years to build the asset, and only then will the cash flows materialize; it will cost $10 million worth of resources to create the asset. The value of the call on the asset tomorrow in the best case is then $80 million and $20 million in the worst case. The expected value at the time of exercise, considering the probability of each state of nature to occur, is then $66 million.

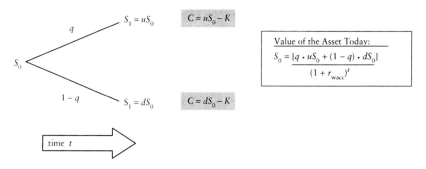

FIGURE 2.10 Asset value movements in the binomial tree

What is the value of the call today? We are confident based on our market research that the two figures capture the range of possible scenarios, the best scenario of $90 million and the worst scenario of $30 million. We also are confident that the chance of reaching the best state of the two worlds is 60%, and reaching the worst of the two worlds is 40%. Remember, in pricing the real option we make the assumption that a twin security exists in the market that captures exactly the risks and payoffs of the project and allows us to construct the risk-free hedge. Remember, too, that the same assumption is also made when discounting the future cash flows at the discount rate that captures the risk of the project, the risk premium. That discount rate is chosen to reflect the return an investor demands from the traded twin security that has the same risk and payoff profile as the project. So, if we do have a risk-free hedge from a portfolio of traded securities, we can work with the

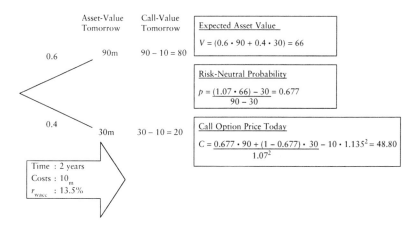

FIGURE 2.11 Call value in the binomial tree

risk-neutral probability to determine the expected payoff and discount the expected payoff to today's price using the risk-free discount rate. That then gives us the price of the option. The risk-neutral probability is a function of today's profit value. The mathematical formula to calculate the risk-neutral probability is:[43]

$$p = \frac{(r_f \cdot S_{expected}) - S_{min}}{S_{max} - S_{min}} \qquad (2.2)$$

r_f stands for the risk-free rate, which is the interest rate for treasury bonds, $S_{expected}$ denotes the expected value of the future asset, which is $66 million. S_{max} is the maximum anticipated asset value at the end of the next period, S_{min} the smallest anticipated asset value at the end of the next period. The risk-free probability p hence depends on market uncertainty (maximum and minimum asset value), as well as on the real probability q of succeeding in creating that asset value, as q feeds into the calculation of $S_{expected}$.

CRR defined p similarly: $p = (r_f - d)/(u - d)$. They arrived at this equation after constructing a risk-free non-arbitrage portfolio consisting of stocks and bonds that would replicate the option. The risk-free non-arbitrage portfolio made the option independent of risk and hence allowed risk-free valuation. As the authors wrote, "p is always greater than zero and smaller than one and so it has the properties of a probability. In other words, p is the value q would have in equilibrium in a risk-neutral world." p has the same quality if calculated with the formula provided in equation 2.2. Instead of using u for the upward movement and d for the downward movement, we use the maximum and minimum asset value to be expected at the end of the next period.

In our example, the risk-free probability p, assuming a risk-free rate of 7%, is 0.6770. p is then instrumental in determining today's value of the call using the following formula:

$$C = \frac{p \cdot S_{max} + (1-p) \cdot S_{min}}{1 + r_f^t} - K \cdot r_c^t \qquad (2.3)$$

Please note that we not only deduct cost K but also include the opportunity cost of money, assuming that this money could be put in the bank and could earn interest or is being borrowed for the purpose of this investment at the corporate cost of capital. In this example, we use as the opportunity cost the corporate cost of capital r_c. This gives us the current value of the call on this option as $48.80 million.

What is the critical cost to invest in this opportunity? The critical cost to invest is defined as the amount to be invested that drives the option at the money. If the critical cost to invest is exceeded, the option moves out of the money. The critical cost to invest is therefore calculated by setting equation 2.3 to zero and solving for K:

$$C = \frac{p \cdot S_{max} + (1 - p) \cdot S_{min}}{1 + r_f^t} - K \cdot r_c^t = 0$$

The critical value to invest, under all the given assumptions, is $47.85 million. If we invest more, at the corporate cost of capital, the option is out of the money.

Let us now see how the value of the option and the critical cost to invest change as we undertake a scenario analysis for the probability of success q as well as the maximum and minimum asset value (see Figure 2.12).

Not unexpectedly the value of our option is quite sensitive to the probability of success. The right diagram also shows that the critical investment value and the option are both a function of the probability of success q, all else remaining equal. The graphs clearly have a different slope. As the probability of succeeding increases, so does the critical value to invest. The intuition behind this is that, as the realization grows that a future payoff will in fact be likely, investment of more money becomes justifiable to create the future payoff. On the contrary, if the future payoff appears very risky, the investment trigger increases and the amount of resources to be committed declines. This was the key insight of the early real option work of Pindyck and Dixit: As uncertainty increases, the investment trigger rises as the option premium to be paid for committing resources in the face of uncertainty increases.

The left diagram illustrates the sensitivity of the option value to changes of the minimum or maximum asset value. Let us now see to which parameters the value of the call option is most sensitive by looking at the percentage change of the call value in relation to the percentage change of the

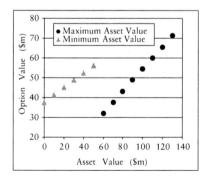
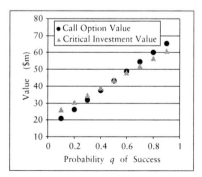

FIGURE 2.12 Call value and critical cost to invest as functions of asset value and private risk

probability of success q, the maximum value or the minimum value of the future asset (see Figure 2.13).

In our given example, the option value displays the highest sensitivity to changes in the maximum value and is least sensitive to changes in the minimum value. The option value is also sensitive to changes in q, the probability of succeeding. From this analysis we can derive the option space, the boundaries within which we feel comfortable the option will be ultimately located, given certain variation in the underlying assumptions. Assuming that each parameter can vary up to 20% of our current assumption and taking into account that those deviations are independent from each other and can hence go upward as well as downward, the option space becomes quite broad, as shown in Figure 2.14, with the option value being somewhere between $20 and $50 million.

This analysis illustrates the following two points. It is not so much the percentage deviation of either parameter but how they relate to each other that will determine the ultimate deviation in option results. We saw before that it is not the absolute volatility of costs or future asset value but the relative relationship between those two that drives the option value. This is consistent with the notion that the upward and downward swings determine the implied volatility of the underlying asset during this period. Even a comparatively small percentage change can have a significant effect on the ultimate option value and lead to a broad set of possible outcomes. As time progresses, uncertainty should be resolved and we should be able to refine

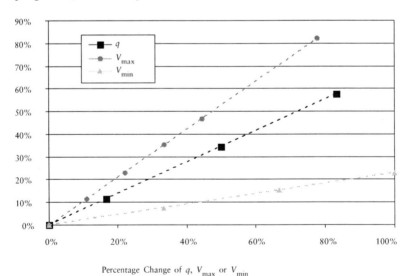

Percentage Change of q, V_{max} or V_{min}

FIGURE 2.13 Sensitivity of the option value

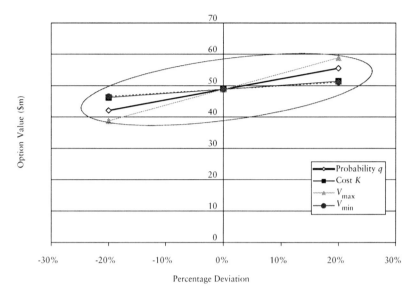

FIGURE 2.14 The option space

and narrow the option space. For the time being, we will have to accept those uncertainties; they serve us well as we attempt to identify the boundaries of the critical value to invest. Further, they provide very valuable guidelines as to which drivers of uncertainty impact sufficiently on future option values to warrant making investments in obtaining information to resolve uncertainties and better understand correlations between drivers of uncertainty.

How does the binomial option model look at risk and return? Let R denote the return. In the good state of the world, the return R at the end of the next period will be a multiple of the current value of the underlying asset. In the bad state of the world, the return R will go down and only be a fraction of the current value of the underlying $1/R$. Return is then defined as follows:

$$\text{Return for the upward state } R = S_1^+ / S_0$$
$$\text{Return for the downward state } 1/R = S_1^- / S_0 \tag{2.4}$$

We can also calculate the implied volatility. The implied volatility in the CRR binomial model is defined as:

$$\sigma_1 = \frac{ln\ R_1}{\sqrt{t_1}} \tag{2.5}$$

Let us now plot the return R against the risk-neutral probability of success and against the implied volatility (see Figure 2.15). The natural relationship between risk and return is preserved in the binomial option model: with increasing risk-free probability of success the expected return declines, while with increasing implied volatility, the expected return increases. Please note that the binomial model allows for calculating the implied volatility σ for each phase of the project. This has advantages specifically for sequential projects in which individual phases are subject to non-identical risk-profiles. Risk in the binomial model, as detailed before, is not adjusted for by the discount rate but by the probability of success.

The binomial model is based on the backward induction principle, a feature it shares with game theory. Because it is not a continuous but discrete-time model, it facilitates monitoring at each step what the option holder is doing, and what may happen in the environment. This is an excellent framework to use to analyze competitive scenarios. Other option pricing models that build on stochastic processes rely on the use of jumps to model those exogenous, game-changing events.

The binomial model delivers some important insights: first, it tells us the critical value to invest. This is the trigger point for the investment decision. Any investment exceeding the critical value to invest will—under the given assumptions—drive the option out of the money. The critical value to invest is not a cast-in-iron figure; it is a function of the probability of success, the future asset value and, to a smaller degree, the time of completion, as well as a function of the relationship in between those parameters. The value of this information lies in defining the safe boundaries of the option space that reflect the realistic range of assumptions. As the project proceeds and new information arrives to resolve market and technical uncertainty the assumptions become better defined, and so do the boundaries of the safe option space.

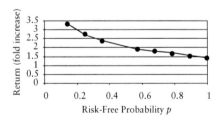
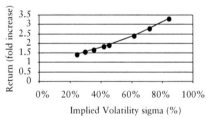

FIGURE 2.15 Return versus risk and implied volatility

Second, the option analysis tells us the value of the option and how it changes as key assumptions change, such as assumptions on future asset value, probabilities of success, time to completion, and costs. Again, the range of assumptions defines the boundaries of the option space. As uncertainty is resolved and assumptions become more refined, the value of the option narrows down. The investment rule is to invest in those options that provide the highest value, after making a careful comparison of all available options, which will lead us into portfolio analysis, to be discussed in more detail later. Finally, the model preserves the risk-return relationship, and this will be of special use when we use binomial option valuation in deal structuring.

The price of the option on a real asset derived by the binomial model reflects expectations about the future. To price a real option correctly, using the binomial model we will rely on an expected value that captures the uncertainties and risks associated with obtaining this value. To arrive at this expected value one will rely on basic assumptions that would also go into any NPV analysis: the best and the worst scenario, as well as the expected or most likely scenario. However, by including managerial flexibility in the valuation, it allows for incremental project appraisal with multiple "go" or "no go" decision points. In addition, the binomial option model illustrates how assumptions on the probability of success, maximum and minimum value, and the expected time frames impact on the option value. Thus, the real option analysis is an invitation to management to develop a good understanding of how uncertainty creates and diminishes option value, and to determine which parameters have the largest impact on the option space. The real option framework also raises red flags: it provides the critical value to invest, the threshold beyond which further investments would drive the option out of the money. Finally, it allows management to investigate how managerial actions enhance or diminish the option value by accelerating or delaying the project, by committing more resources and thereby enhancing the probability of success, by investing in expanding growth opportunities, or by saving investment costs by reducing the scope or shutting down. We will give examples of those scenarios later in the book.

One last word on the relationship of the binomial model and Black-Scholes: the binomial model converges into Black-Scholes as the time steps become smaller and their number increases. Under these circumstances, as the number of steps approaches infinity, the volatility of the asset movement is calculated based on the size of the upward movement per period and the number of steps over time. However, this also assumes that u, the upward movement, and d, the downward movement, are always the same in each period. This may not be the case for a real option, as we will see in later examples.

The past few years have witnessed an explosion in the academic literature exploring novel real option pricing concepts and approaches. Much of the work aims at closed form analytical solutions that in turn require simplified assumptions. Much of the work builds on Dixit and Pindyck's and other pioneering work and assumes that future returns on assets will follow a certain stochastic process, such as a Wiener process, that is, a log-normal distribution with a positive drift. In addition, some assume that costs are deterministic, that is, known and fixed at the outset, a condition hardly met by reality. The creativity in the approach is often compelling. However, as mathematical equations reach a certain complexity and require multiple assumptions about essentially unknown parameters, the practicality of the approach sometimes suffers. Some of the proposed option pricing models require specific software and extensive computation capacity.

Transparency of the approach and practicability may sometimes be more important than scientific accuracy. Further, the clear-cut graphical display of a "go" or "no-go" boundary tends to create the impression of a degree of scientific accuracy that is not entirely justified by the rough nature of the estimates that go into the analysis. In the real world, the goal is to work with as few assumptions as possible but develop a good understanding as to how the unknowns impact the ultimate outcome. Others have argued that the real limitation in real option analysis is not the framework but the fact that so few data and little knowledge of project parameters are available.[44] However, once the framework has been established, it becomes easy to investigate which parameters drive the value and the uncertainty. This insight, in turn, should create incentives to obtain better data and also help in identifying which data are most in need.

A methodology that is transparent, intuitive, and relies on algebra everybody understands and follows will be helpful when using real options on a daily basis without the need of bringing in an external specialist. Such a homemade analysis is also more likely to both create and communicate the insights as to how different possible but yet uncertain scenarios will play out in the financials of a given firm, and may create greater support to actually spend resources to narrow down the key parameters.

The organizational challenge will be to define and agree on the parameters that go into the option analysis. Multiple tools have been used in the past: interviews with key manufacturing personnel or engineers, Monte Carlo simulation, survey data, or stock volatility of comparable companies. For most companies, experience, internal evaluation, market research data comparables and traded securities combined will probably provide a good range of estimates for costs and future asset values that will be sufficient to price real options using a transparent mathematical approach. Notes Stephen Black from the PA Consulting Group in Cambridge, UK: "Simple financial models can capture the essence of option value by directly incorporating managers' existing knowledge of uncertainty and their possible decisions in the future. This approach avoids the dangers of complex formulae and unwarranted assumptions, and gives a lot more management insight than black-box formulae while creating less opportunity for academic publications."[45]

The Black-Scholes formula can still be applied when the assumptions fit in broad terms, for example, for European-type call options. The challenge has been for organizations to find the right figure for volatility. Management can rely on a qualified guess, use historical returns of comparable companies, or use a Monte Carlo simulation. The Black-Scholes valuation method is highly sensitive to the volatility; partial differential equations in general tend to be highly sensitive to individual volatilities as well as to correlations in between volatilities that feed into the equation. As such, we have seen how the correlation between cost and payoff volatility drives the value of the option. As for real options, the volatility of the asset, or its uncertainty, is more related to the ability of management to obtain information and to retain the flexibility to respond to it to mitigate risk. If management has no flexibility in responding to changing market conditions, there is no option value.

The binomial model, too, has limitations that should be mentioned. It can be very cumbersome to construct the binomial asset tree. This is especially true if multiple embedded options and their interactions need to be considered, when multiple sources of uncertainties feed into the assumptions, and when several time periods need to be considered. To some, the binomial option pricing model may look like a decision tree, and it is worth pointing out similarities and differences. As discussed earlier, real option pricing using the binomial model has its roots in financial option pricing. Decision analysis has evolved out of operations research and game theory. Both are indeed very similar in overall structure, and both aim at determining the expected value of the project. Both rely on mapping out all the options and all the uncertainties in a tree, both require and enforce complete information gathering, work with subjective probability measures, and benefit from scenario and sensitivity analysis. Both, too, work with discrete distributions and both work by backward induction and roll up the tree from the end. However, there are also some important features that differentiate the binomial model from the decision tree approach and make it a more feasible tool for investment project appraisal. Decision tree analysis discounts throughout the tree using a constant discount rate, usually a project specific discount rate or the average corporate cost of capital. The binomial tree, on the contrary, works with risk-neutral probabilities—which change as assumptions change and also are distinct for different branches of the tree or across different segments along one branch, acknowledging that the risk-profile of the underlying asset is not constant over time, that different managerial options within one tree have different risk profiles, too, and that managerial actions can be designed to mitigate those risks. Specifically by doing the latter, by ascribing value to managerial actions and flexibility, the binomial option tree builds on asymmetric payoffs, while the decision tree does not.

NOTES

1. J. Kensinger, *Project Abandonment As a Put Option: Dealing with the Capital Investment Decision and Operating Risk Using Option Pricing Theory*, working paper, 80–121 (Cox School of Business, October 1980); S.C. Myers and S. Majd, *Calculating Abandonment Value Using Option Pricing Theory,* working paper (Sloan School of Management, May 1983); S.C. Myers and S. Majd, "Abandonment Value and Project Life," *Advances in Futures and Option Research* 4:1, 1990.
2. M. Brennan and E. Schwartz, "Evaluating Natural Resource Investments," *Journal of Business* 58:135, 1985; D. Siegel, J. Smith, and J. Paddock, "Valuing Offshore Oil Properties with Option Pricing Models," *Midland Corporate Finance Journal*, Spring, p. 22, 1987.
3. M. Brennan and E. Schwartz, "Evaluating Natural Resource Investments," *Journal of Business* 58:135, 1985; R. MacDonald and D. Siegel, "The Value of Waiting to Invest," *Quarterly Journal of Economics* 101:707, 1986; J. Paddock, D. Siegel, and J. Smith, "Option Valuation of Claims on Physical Assets: The Case of Offshore Petroleum Leases," *Quarterly Journal of Economics* 103:479, 1988; J.E. Ingersoll and S.A. Ross, "Waiting to Invest: Investment and Uncertainty," *The Journal of Business* 65:29, 1992.
4. R. MacDonald, MacDonald and D. Siegel, "The Value of Waiting to Invest," *Quarterly Journal of Economics* 101:707, 1986.
5. S. Majd and R.S. Pindyck, "Time to Build, Option Value, and Investment Decision," *Journal of Industrial Economics* 18:7, 1987.
6. See Note 3.
7. M. Brennan and E. Schwartz, "Evaluating Natural Resource Investments," *Journal of Business* 58:135, 1985; L. Trigeorgis and S.P. Mason, "Valuing Managerial Flexibility," *Midland Corporate Finance Journal* 5:14, 1987; N.S. Pindyck, "Irreversible Investment, Capacity

Choice and the Value of the Firm," *American Economic Review* 79:969, 1988a.

8. B. Kogut, "Joint Ventures and the Option to Expand and Acquire," *Management Science* 37:19, 1991.

9. J.W. Kensinger, "Adding the Value of Active Management into the Capital Budgeting Equation," *Midland Corporate Finance Journal*, Spring, p. 31, 1987.

10. J.W. Kensinger, "Adding the Value of Active Management into the Capital Budgeting Equation," *Midland Corporate Finance Journal*, Spring, p. 31, 1987; N. Kulatilaka and A. Marcus, "General Formulation of Corporate Real Options," *Research in Finance* 7:183, 1988; W. Margrabe, "The Value of an Option to Exchange One Asset for Another," *Journal* of *Finance* 33:177, 1978.

11. S.C. Myers, "Determinants of Corporate Borrowing," *Journal of Financial Economics* 5:147, 1977; W.C. Kester, "Today's Options for Tomorrow's Growth," *Harvard Business Review*, March–April 18, 1984; N.S. Pindyck, "Irreversible Investment, Capacity Choice and the Value of the Firm," *American Economic Review* 79:969, 1988; L. Trigeorgis, "A Conceptual Options Framework for Capital Budgeting," *Advances in Futures and Options Research* 3:145, 1988.

12. S. Panayi and L. Trigeorgis, "Multi-Stage Real Options: The Cases of Information Technology Infrastructure and International Bank Expansion," *Quarterly Review of Economics and Finance* 38:675, 1998; H. Herath and C.S. Park, "Multi-Stage Capital Investment Opportunities as Compound Real Options," *Engineering Economist* 47:27, 2002; E. Pennings and O. Lint, *Market Entry, Phased Rollout or Abandonment? A Real Options Approach*, working paper (Erasmus University, 1998).

13. T. Arnold, "Value Creation at Anheuser-Busch: A Real Options Example," *Journal of Applied Corporate Finance* 14:52, 2001.

14. K. Roberts and M. Weitzman, "Funding Criteria for Research, Development and Exploration Projects," *Econometrica* 49:1261, 1981.

15. N. Nichols, "Scientific Management at Merck: An Interview with CFO Judy Lewent," *Harvard Business Review*, Jan.–Feb., p. 88, 1994; D.P. Newton and A.W. Pearson, "Application of Option Pricing Theory to R&D," *R&D Management* 24:83, 1994; D. Newton, D.A. Paxson, and A. Pearson, "Real R&D Options," in A. Belcher, J. Hassard, and S.D. Procter, eds., Routledge, London, 1996, 273; M.A. Brach and D.A. Paxson, "A Gene to Drug Venture: Poisson Options Analysis," *R&D Management* 31:203, 2001; H. Herath and C.S. Park, "Multi-Stage Capital Investment Opportunities as Compound Real Options," *Engineering*

Economist 47:27, 2002; G. Cortazar and E.S. Schwartz, "A Compound Option Model of Production and Intermediate Inventories," *The Journal of Business* 66:517, 1993.

16. A.K. Dixit and N.S. Pindyck, *Investment under Uncertainty* (Princeton University Press, 1994); R. MacDonald and D. Siegel, "The Value of Waiting to Invest," *Quarterly Journal of Economics* 101:707, 1986; S. Majd and R.S. Pindyck, "Time to Build, Option Value, and Investment Decisions," *Journal of Industrial Economics* 18:7, 1987.

17. L. Trigeorgis, "The Nature of Option Interactions and the Valuation of Investments with Multiple Real Options," *Journal of Financial and Quantitative Analysis* 28:20, 1993.

18. H.S.B. Herath and C.S. Park, "Real Option Valuation and Its Relationship to Bayesian Decision Making Methods," *Engineering Economist* 46:1, 2001.

19. K.J. Arrow and A.C. Fisher, "Environmental Preservation, Uncertainty and Irreversibility," *Quarterly Journal of Economics* 88:312, 1974; C. Henry, "Investment Decisions under Uncertainty: The Irreversibility Effect," *American Economic Review* 64:1006, 1974.

20. C. Henry, "Investment Decisions under Uncertainty: The Irreversibility Effect," *American Economic Review* 64:1006, 1974; K. Arrow and A. Fisher, "Environmental Preservation, Uncertainty and Irreversibility," *Quarterly Journal of Economics* 88:312, 1974.

21. M. Basili, *Quasi-Option Values—Empirical Measures*, working paper (University of Sienna, 1999); T. Graham-Tomasi, "Quasi-Option Value," in D.W. Bromley, ed., *Handbook of Environmental Economics* (Blackwell, Oxford, UK and Cambridge, USA, 1995).

22. B. Lambrecht and W. Perraudin, *Option Games*, working paper (Cambridge University, and CEPR, UK, August 1994).

23. B. Lambrecht and W. Perraudin, *Real Option and Preemption*, working paper (Cambridge University, Birkbeck College [London] and CEPR, UK, 1996).

24. L. Trigeorgis, *Real Options—Managerial Flexibility and Strategy in Resource Allocation* (MIT Press, Cambridge, MA, 1996).

25. R.S. Pindyck, "A Note on Competitive Investment under Uncertainty," *American Economic Review* 83:273, 1993.

26. N.P.B. Bollen, "Real Options and Product Life-cycle," *Management Science* 45:670, 1999.

27. A.E. Tsekrekos, "Investment under Economic and Implementation Uncertainty," *R&D Management* 31:127, 2001; T. Berrada, *Valuing Real Options When Time to Maturity Is Uncertain* (Third Real Option Group Conference, Cambridge, UK, 1999).

28. A.K. Dixit and R.S. Pindyck, *Investment under Uncertainty* (Princeton University Press, 1994).

29. A.A. Abel, A.K. Dixit, J.C. Eberly, and R.S. Pindyck, "Options, the Value of Capital and Investment," *Quarterly Journal of Economics* 111:753, 1996.

30. P.D. Childs, S.H. Ott, and A.J. Triantis, "Capital Budgeting for Interrelated Projects: A Real Options Approach," *Journal of Financial and Quantitative Analysis* 33:305, 1998.

31. O. Lint and E. Pennings, "An Option Approach to the New Product Development Process: A Case Study at Philips Electronics," *R&D Management* 31:163, 2001.

32. M.A. Brach and D.A. Paxson, "A Gene to Drug Venture: Poisson Options Analysis," *R&D Management* 31:203, 2001.

33. S.R. Grenadier and A.M. Weiss, "Investment in Technological Innovations: An Option Pricing Approach," *Journal of Financial Economics* 44:397, 1997; O. Lint and E. Pennings, "R&D As an Option on Market Introduction," *R&D Management* 28:279, 1998; E. Pennings and O. Lint, "The Option Value of Advanced R&D," *European Journal of Operational Research* 103:83, 1997; D. Mauer and S. Ott, "Investment under Uncertainty: The Case of Replacement Investment Decisions," *Journal of Financial and Quantitative Analysis* 30:581, 1995; H. Weeds, "Reverse Hysteresis: R&D Investments with Stochastic Innovation," working paper, 1999.

34. H.T.J. Smith and L. Trigeorgis, *R&D Option Strategies* (Fifth Real Option Conference, Los Angeles, 2001).

35. A. Huchzermeier and C.H. Loch, "Evaluating R&D Projects as Learning Options: Why More Variability Is Not Always Better," in H. Wildemann, ed., *Produktion und Controlling* (München: TCW Transfer Centrum Verlag, 185–197, 1999).

36. L.G. Chorn and A. Sharma, *Valuing Investments in Extensions to Product Lines and Services Offerings When Facing Competitive Entry*, draft 06/30/2001 (Fifth Real Option Conference, 2001).

37. R.A. Brealey and S.C. Myers, *Principles of Corporate Finance*, 6th Ed. (McGraw Hill, 1996).

38. Ibid.

39. J. McCormack and G. Sick, "Valuing PUD Reserves: A Practical Application of Real Option Techniques," *Journal of Applied Corporate Finance* 13, Volume 4, Winter 2001; T. Copeland and V. Antikarov, *Real Options: A Practitioner's Guide*, (Texetere, 2001: pp. 70–72).

40. A. Triantis and A. Borison, "Real Options: State of the Practice," *Journal of Applied Corporate Finance* 14:8, 2001.

41. L. Lee and D.A. Paxson, "Valuation of R&D Real American Sequential Exchange Options," *R&D Management* 31:191, 2001.
42. J.C. Cox, S.A. Ross, and M. Rubinstein, "Option Pricing: A Simplified Approach," *Journal of Financial Economics* 7:229, 1979.
43. L. Trigeorgis and S.P. Mason, "Valuing Managerial Flexibility," *Midland Corporate Finance Journal* 5:14, 1987.
44. T. Luehrman, "Investment Opportunities as Real Options: Getting Started on the Numbers," *Harvard Business Review*, July–August, p. 51, 1998.
45. S. Black, "Options for Change (Option-Pricing Theory)." A letter to the editor of *The Economist* (UK), September 4, 1999. Dr. Stephen Black, PA Consulting Group, Cambridge, UK.

CHAPTER 3

The Six Basic
Managerial Options

In this chapter we will start learning to use the binomial option model in practice. The initial applications focus on the valuation of the six basic managerial options that are summarized along with their real option counterparts in Figure 3.1. We will show how those basic options can be framed and valued using the binomial option model and also discuss how the model is useful in looking at option interaction.

The Option to Defer	Wait until further information reduces market uncertainty.
The Option to Abandon	Dispose of an unprofitable project.
The Option to Switch	Change input/output parameters or modus operandi.
The Option to Expand/Contract	Alter capacity depending on market conditions.
The Option to Grow	Entertain future-related opportunities.
The Option to Stage	Break up investment into incremental, conditional steps.

FIGURE 3.1 The basic real options

THE OPTION OF WAITING TO INVEST

The deferral option, or option of waiting to invest, derives its value from reducing uncertainty by delaying an investment decision until more information has arrived. A mining company with proprietary rights to a given mine may want to delay exploring the mine once price uncertainty has been resolved and the cost of recovering the contents of the mine is well covered by the anticipated revenue stream coming from the sale of the metal. The owner of the mine pays a license fee for the mine or a property tax, which is the price to keep the option alive and exercise it once market conditions allow the upside potential to be realized. Translated into financial terms, the mine owner has a perpetual American call option: He is the option owner and can exercise at any time in perpetuity, without any expiration date.

A drug maker may want to delay the decision to build a new manufacturing plant for a newly approved drug until a better understanding of the market performance of the compound has developed and therefore to outsource manufacturing in the meantime. The decision as to whether or not to build a new manufacturing plant will depend on what path offers the better option value today. It is driven by assumptions about key uncertainties related to product performance, pricing, market penetration, and competitive entry. A carmaker may want to delay the decision to build a new plant for a new model until a better understanding of the market performance of the product has developed and to outsource manufacturing in the meantime. These managers hold what in financial option terminology is called a Parisian barrier option.

The Parisian barrier option was created by Mark Chesney and colleagues in Paris and was first described in 1997.[1] A barrier option is an option in which the payoff to the option owner not only depends on the value of the underlying asset or stock at the maturity date—as it does for European options—but also on whether the asset has reached during the lifetime of the option a certain, pre-defined threshold, the barrier. If the stock does cross that threshold prior to the expiration date of the option, the option expires. A Parisian barrier option, on the contrary, does not lose its value once the threshold has been crossed. The Parisian barrier option expires and loses all option value only if that pre-determined lower or upper threshold is crossed for a prolonged period of time.

So, regarding the car manufacturer who holds a perpetual Parisian barrier option, he will exercise the option and build the manufacturing plant for the new car model once the lower barrier for demand has been crossed for a prolonged period of time. Alternatively, if the demand falls below a certain threshold for a prolonged period of time, the Parisian barrier option to build the manufacturing plant will expire worthless, and the plant will not be built.

The option is path-dependent, meaning that the payoff depends on the realized asset path that has to cross a certain level, and it is Parisian because the level has to be sustained for some time before the option is exercised. Management wants to make sure that demand does not hit a certain peak just once, but rather will be sustainable at a minimum level, the lower barrier. The option expires if the price of the underlying asset remains below some level(s) continuously over a specified period of time, the "window."

In this example, the car manufacturer aims at resolving market uncertainty by waiting. Technical uncertainty, on the contrary, can only be partially resolved by waiting. If the technical uncertainty is entirely private in nature, that is, rests within the firm and is driven by the internal technical talent and ability to succeed, it cannot be solved by waiting. Only by investing in research and development work will management find out whether a new technology is feasible and whether the new car prototype can be built. Some components of technical uncertainty may be resolved by waiting. For example, if management contemplates building a novel prototype that relies entirely on the use of solar energy, it may want to wait for other firms to develop solar technology for different applications. Once the basic feasibility of solar energy to drive machines has been established, management may then go ahead and approve a pilot project to investigate whether the concept of solar energy can be adapted to cars. Also, management, depending on its attitude towards risk and innovation and its trust in the innovative skills of its workforce, may want to act as a follower and permit its competitor to be the leader. For an innovative internal development program, there may be value in waiting to learn from observable results such as those produced by basic feasibility studies undertaken by the competitor.

Having this kind of managerial flexibility implies value to the firm. Giving up this flexibility by committing to an investment, on the other hand, implies opportunity costs. Dixit and Pindyck were the first to point out the interactions between the irreversibility nature of investments in an uncertain future and the timing of those investments. They also analyzed the qualitative and quantitative consequences of those interactions. Specifically, they derived the important insight that committing to an investment implies giving up managerial flexibility and hence killing the option to invest. Management should be willing to pay a premium, the option premium, for giving up this flexibility. This premium, added to the net present value, raises the critical trigger to invest.

We will now value the option to wait or deferral option as a stand-alone entity. However, we acknowledge that the value of waiting ultimately has to be viewed in the context of overall corporate strategies and may be diminished or destroyed by the value a company creates from a competitive position or a preemptive strategy that does not allow for waiting. We will investigate in later chapters how these options interplay and derive an optimum investment strategy for more complex scenarios. The value of the deferral option is highest for monopoly options but declines for shared options.

Let us consider the example of the car manufacturer somewhat further. Assumptions that drive the investment decision relate to future market size as well as to the costs of building the plant. Costs also include opportunity cost; the money needed for the plant could be earning interest, at the very least, if the plant were not built. The money might be borrowed at a price. The money may be invested into alternative projects whose option values then also need to be considered. This scenario leads us to consideration of interactive options and ultimately to portfolio management. Not building the plant will require that manufacturing be outsourced and result in higher variable costs than in-house production. Management believes that two years from now it will have a much better understanding of the market and that this additional time should allow a better-informed decision on building the plant, which will depend on the market for the new car. What is the value of the option to defer the decision for two years? More importantly, under which scenarios is the option in the money? What triggers the investment in a new plant, and when does the option to defer move out of the money? The goal of the option analysis is to provide decision boundaries, which create optimal decision guidelines under a range of what-if scenarios.

For a practical example, let us assume the following:

* Building the plant will cost somewhere between $30 million and $50 million.
* The opportunity costs are 7%.
* Within two years management will know in what direction the market is going to move: the product will make no more than $50 million in the worst case scenario and up to $120 million per annum in the best case scenario.
* Outsourcing of the production will incur an extra cost between 10% and 20% of revenues.

These assumptions translate into a binomial asset tree, as shown in Figure 3.2.

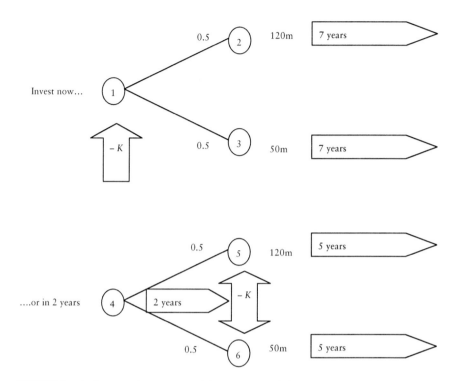

FIGURE 3.2 The binomial asset tree of the option to defer

Management can build the plant now and will receive the full revenue stream, somewhere between $50 million and $120 million for seven years. Management can defer the decision for two years and then decide what the best way forward is, depending on the then-prevailing revenue stream. It would then invest only if the present value of revenue foregone due to outsourcing is higher than the anticipated investment costs to build the plant. What is the value of deferring the decision for two years until market uncertainty has been resolved?

We assume the likelihood for the best and worse case revenue scenario of future revenue streams to be 50% each. We assume the product to be on the market for seven years and the outsourcing margin to range between 10% and 20%. We first calculate the value of the option to invest now. We determine the present value at node 2/3 of the revenue foregone over seven years due to outsourcing under the best and worst case scenarios as well as the expected value

TABLE 3.1 The asset value of investing now

	Present Value of the Asset		Expected Value
Margin (%)	50 ($ millions)	120 ($ millions)	($ millions)
10	26.48	63.56	45.02
15	39.72	95.34	67.53
20	52.97	127.12	90.04

of that figure. These cash outflows are discounted at the corporate cost of capital (15%) over the seven-year period. The data are summarized in Table 3.1.

Investing in the plant implies that management will save the outsourcing costs. Not investing implies the outsourcing costs are revenue foregone.
The value of the call option is driven by the amount of money saved on outsourcing costs by investing in the plant. These savings are calculated as the
product of the anticipated outsourcing margin, denoted as $x\%$, and the best
or worst case payoff scenario. The exercise price for the call option is the investment costs K required to build the manufacturing plant. From there derives the value of the call, which is always equal to or larger than zero:

$$C = \text{Max}(0, \frac{p \cdot x \cdot V_{max} + (1-p) \cdot x \cdot V_{min}}{(1+r_f)^2} - K \cdot (1 + r_{wacc})^2)$$

p, as explained before, denotes the risk-free probability and is calculated
using the formula provided in Chapter 2, equation 2.2, with V_e denoting the
expected asset value, V_{min} the value to be achieved in the worst case scenario,
and V_{max} the value to be reached in the best case scenario:

$$p = \frac{(r_f \cdot V_e) - V_{min}}{V_{max} - V_{min}}$$

For the 10% outsourcing margin and a risk-free rate of 7%, p then becomes

$$p = \frac{(1+7\%) \cdot 45.02 - 26.48}{63.56 - 26.48} = 0.59$$

Hence, the value of the call for K of $30 million or K of $50 million for a
10% outsourcing margin is:

$$C_{30} = \text{Max } 0, \frac{0.59 \cdot 63.56 + (1 - 0.59) \cdot 26.48}{1.07^2} - 30 \cdot (1 + 7\%)^2$$

$$= \text{Max } (0, \ 7.21) = 7.21$$

For an investment cost K of \$30 million, the value maximizing decision is to build the plant.

$$C_{50} = \text{Max } 0, \frac{0.59 \cdot 63.56 + (1 - 0.59) \cdot 26.48}{1.07^2} - 50 \cdot (1 + 7\%)^2$$

$$= \text{Max } (0, \ -10.12) = 0$$

For an investment cost K of \$50 million the value maximizing decision is not to build the plant.

We calculate the option value for a K of both \$30 million and \$50 million and for a range of outsourcing margins between 10% and 20%. Figure 3.3 summarizes the results.

The option to invest today is out of the money if the plant costs \$50 million and the outsourcing margin is 10%. The option to invest today moves in the money as costs for the plant approach \$30 million, or as the outsourcing margin climbs above 10%. What is the critical cost to invest under these conditions? The critical cost to invest is defined as the cost $K^{\diamond}$ that moves the option out of the money, that is, the option value approaches

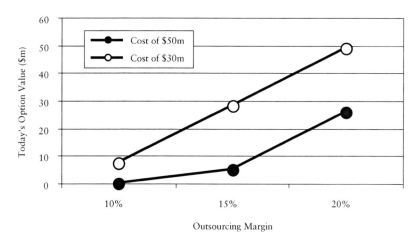

FIGURE 3.3 The option value of investing now

zero. We calculate $K^\diamond$ by setting the call option equation to zero and solving for $K^\diamond$ using the solver or goal seek function in the Excel spreadsheet:

$$C = \frac{p \cdot x\% \cdot V_{\max} + (1-p) \cdot x\% \cdot V_{\min}}{(1 + r_f)^2} - K^\diamond \cdot (1+r)^2 = 0$$

For example, for an outsourcing margin of 10%, we obtain the following equation:

$$C = \frac{0.59 \cdot 63.54 + (1 - 0.59) \cdot 26.48}{1.07^2} - K^\diamond \cdot (1 + 7\%)^2 = 0$$

Solving that equation for $K^\diamond$, we obtain $36.24 million. Figure 3.4 summarizes the results for the critical value to invest for the range of outsourcing margins.

If management defers the investment decision for two years, it will then have a much better understanding of the market acceptance of the product. Much of the market uncertainty will have been resolved, and management can make a much-better-informed decision as to whether or not to build the plant depending on the then-available sales data. If the good state of nature has materialized and product acceptance is high, management would then build the plant. If the bad state of nature has materialized and product acceptance is low, management would continue to outsource the manufacturing of the product and abandon the idea of building a new plant. The decision scenario is summarized in the binomial asset tree shown in Figure 3.5.

If in two years from today the product generates $120 million per year (node 6), management will determine whether it would be better off to pay the outsourcing margin on this revenue stream or whether it would be better off to build the plant by paying the investment costs K. Similarly, if the

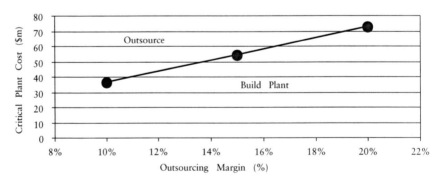

FIGURE 3.4 The critical threshold to invest

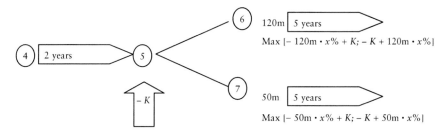

FIGURE 3.5 The binomial asset tree for the deferred decision

product creates only $50 million in annual revenues (node 7), management will make the same calculation and determine the value maximizing, cost-minimizing path forward.

Table 3.2 shows the value of the revenues foregone for the remaining five years at nodes 6/7 under the different scenarios as well as the expected value, assuming a 50% probability for each market payoff scenario. Assume it will cost $50 million to build the plant. If revenue streams are $120 million at a 15% distribution margin, the present value of the revenue foregone will be $72.83 million, and the better, cost-minimizing and value maximizing decision would be to build the plant. Management would invest $50 million but save $72.83 million in outsourcing costs (i.e., –$57 million + $72.83 million > –$72.83 million + $50 million). If, however, revenues are only $50 million, the present value of the revenue foregone would be $30.34 million at a 15% outsourcing margin, and management would be better off not spending the present value of $57 million for the plant (i.e., –$57 million + $30.34 million < –$30.34 million + $57 million). We determine the optimum decision at each node for each scenario and, under the assumption that the best and worst revenue scenarios are equally likely, we then calculate the expected value created (by cost minimization). Table 3.3 summarizes the data.

The data for expected value as well as the best and worst case go into the calculation of the risk-free probability p for each node under

TABLE 3.2 The asset value of investing later

Margin (%)	Present Value of the Asset		Expected Value
	50 ($ millions)	120 ($ millions)	($ millions)
10	20.23	48.55	34.39
15	30.34	72.83	51.59
20	40.46	97.10	68.78

TABLE 3.3 Cost savings when deferring the decision to invest

Margin (%)	Best Case Revenue		Worst Case Revenue		Expected Value	
	K = 50m ($)	K = 30m ($)	K = 50m ($)	K = 30m ($)	K = 50m ($)	K = 30m ($)
10	9.23	13.88	37.55	14.44	23.39	14.16
15	15.05	38.16	27.44	4.33	21.25	21.25
20	39.32	62.43	17.32	5.79	28.32	34.11

each scenario. This then allows us to calculate the value of the option at node 4:

$$C = \frac{p \cdot V_{max} + (1 - p) \cdot V_{min}}{(1 + r_f)^2}$$

Figure 3.6 depicts today's value of the option to invest (or not) in two years. This graph delivers some interesting insights: First, the option of making the decision in two years is always in the money. The intuition is that management will in two years from now have more information, less uncertainty, and be in a much better position to identify the best, value-maximizing, cost-minimizing path forward because it then had full knowledge of the prevailing market conditions. The value of the option to wait is rooted in the

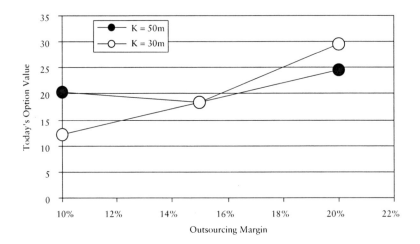

FIGURE 3.6 The option value of investing in two years

asymmetry of the payoff that results from obtaining further information and making the decision after uncertainty has been resolved.

Second, the option value is lowest for the 10% outsourcing margin under the low-cost scenario. In this scenario the cost saving differential between the two managerial strategic options in the best and worst case revenue scenarios is the smallest. The option value is highest for the highest distribution margin and lowest plant costs, as the cost-saving differential between the two strategic options is largest, that is, $56 million. Having managerial flexibility in this instance is thus of greatest value to the firm.

It may be counterintuitive at first glance to see the value of the option going up with increasing outsourcing margins, that is, revenues foregone. But we need to remember that we value managerial flexibility and the ability to choose the cost-minimizing path. Therefore, it makes sense that for the low outsourcing margin of 10% the option value is higher for high plant costs than for low plant costs. By deferring the decision, management saves higher costs by not building the plant if expected costs are high compared to if they are low.

What now is the value of deferring the decision? It is the value of the option to invest in two years minus the exercise price. The exercise price of deferral is the revenue foregone due to outsourcing for the time the decision is deferred, that is, two years. For example, if the plant costs are $50 million and the outsourcing margin is 10%, the value of investing now is 0 and today's value of the option to invest in two years is $15.24 million. By deferring, we incur over a period of two years (the deferral period) a loss of revenues foregone due to outsourcing, that is, 10% of the expected two-year revenue stream. At node 4, this amounts to $13.82 million, the exercise price for the option to defer. In today's value, discounted for another two years at the corporate cost of capital, this amounts to $10.45 million. The value of the option to defer is thus $15.24 million – $0 million – $10.45 million = $1.42 million.

Table 3.4 summarizes the present value of revenues foregone due to outsourcing during the deferral period of two years for the different outsourcing

TABLE 3.4 The opportunity cost of deferring the decision

Margin (%)	50 ($ millions)	120 ($ millions)	Expected ($ millions)
10	8.13	19.51	13.82
15	12.19	29.26	20.73
20	26.26	39.02	32.64

margins and revenue scenarios. From there we can calculate the value of the deferral option under all scenarios, as summarized in Figure 3.7.

For the low-cost ($K = 30$) assumption, the deferral option value increases as the outsourcing margin increases. Here, the exercise price grows slower than the future asset value as the outsourcing margin increases. On the contrary, for the high-cost scenario, the reverse situation applies: Here, the exercise price grows faster than the future asset value as the outsourcing margin increases. For all but one scenario, the option to defer is in the money. The option to defer is out of the money for the high cost and high outsourcing margin. Management must now find out which of the scenarios is most likely, but given that in five out of six investigated scenarios the option to defer is in the money, that might appear to be the value-maximizing path forward, unless, of course, the probability of the out-of-the money scenario is more likely than all the other five scenarios to occur.

What are the boundary conditions that define when management is better off to defer the decision or not? In other words, what is the critical threshold for the deferral option to move in and out of the money? The deferral option is at the money as soon as the differential between today's option value to invest in two years C_2 minus the revenue foregone (RF) through outsourcing during the deferral period equals exactly today's option value to invest today C_1. If the former is larger than the latter, the deferral option moves into the money.

We therefore have to solve the equation $C_2 - RF = C_1$. We can either look for the outsourcing margin that under a given cost scenario defines the critical threshold between deferring and investing now, or we can alter the outsourcing margin and solve for each condition for the critical plant cost K that defines the boundary between investing now and deferring.

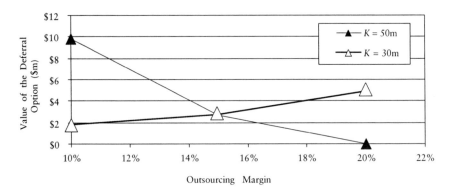

FIGURE 3.7 The option value to defer

For example,

$$p_2 \cdot \text{Max}[10 \cdot V_{max} - K; K - 10 \cdot V_{max}] + (1 - p_2) \cdot \text{Max}[10 \cdot V_{min} - K;$$
$$K - 10 \cdot V_{min}] - PV\ RF =$$
$$p_1 \cdot \text{Max}[10 \cdot V_{max} - K; K - 10 \cdot V_{max}] + (1 - p_1) \cdot \text{Max}[10 \cdot V_{min} - K;$$
$$K - 10 \cdot V_{min}]$$

We use the goal seek or solver function in Excel to accomplish this. Figure 3.8 summarizes the results. Shown is the critical plant cost K that defines the boundary between investing now and investing in two years for a range of outsourcing margins, assuming a deferral period of two years.

Above the solid line, management is better off to defer the decision and pay the exercise price by outsourcing manufacturing. Below the trend line, management is better off to invest in the plant now. Given the exercise price of paying for outsourcing and the anticipated costs of the plant, there is no value created by waiting for market uncertainty to be resolved.

As the outsourcing margin goes up, management would only be better off to defer the investment decision if the expected costs of building the plant also increase substantially. For a 20% outsourcing margin, for example, the plant should be in excess of $84.3 million to justify a deferral of the decision. On the contrary, for a 10% outsourcing margin, management is better off to defer the decision, unless the plant can be obtained for less than $34.7 million.

We can further broaden the option space by considering that the best and worst case scenarios may not be equally likely as assumed so far. Management may feel inclined to assume that the likelihood for the best case

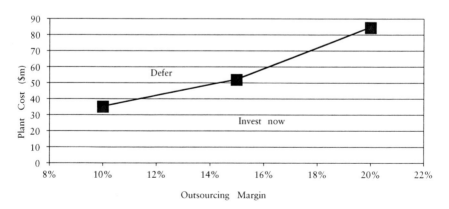

FIGURE 3.8 The decision line: Invest now versus defer

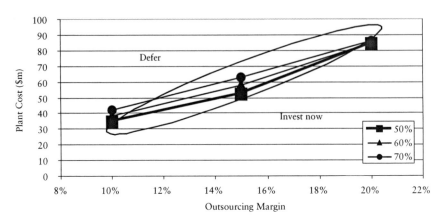

FIGURE 3.9 The option space: Invest now versus defer

scenario of an annual revenue of $120 million to materialize is somewhere between 50% and 70%. This assumption creates an upward drift of the option space, as shown in Figure 3.9.

The option space extends as the assumptions broaden, but it also helps management to define the critical zone where a deferral versus invest now decision is not clear-cut. For conditions that lie in that zone, a more careful and considerate analysis is needed to establish with greater confidence the best path forward. Management may want to contemplate investing in active learning in order to reduce the uncertainty and better refine and reduce the option space.

Management may also want to consider whether to determine for which length of time revenues need to exceed the worst case payoff scenario or reach the best case payoff scenario in order to justify the expenses for building a plant. If, for example, sales do reach peak levels of $120 million, but do not sustain that level consistently, then the option to build the plant may quickly move out of the money again. In this analysis the real option scenario turns into the valuation of a Parisian barrier option.

THE OPTION TO ABANDON

The option to abandon is a put option, the right to dispose of a stock or an asset and to recover the salvage value once market conditions change or market expectations remained unfulfilled. In essence, the put option is a hedge against an economic downturn. The option to abandon a project and liquidate its assets was one of the first real options to which option pricing theory was applied.[2] The sale of an asset compensates for losses and permits investment in new assets or more valuable real options.

For example, the manager of the car manufacturer might include the salvage price of the plant into the current decision scenario. Let us assume that the plant can be sold in two years from now for $20 million. Management would only make use of the abandonment option when sales are slow and resources put into building the plant do not pay off compared to the distribution percentage paid to a third party. Figure 3.10 depicts the binomial asset tree.

At the decision node 2 and 3, management will compare its options and choose the path forward that maximizes value. It will either accept revenues foregone due to outsourcing and gain the salvage value for the plant, or it will keep the plant, foregoing the salvage money but saving the outsourcing margin. The option to abandon expires worthless with the option value zero in all cases where, due to the outsourcing margin, the value of the revenue stream foregone is larger than the salvage value. In all other instances, the expected payoff at node 2 or 3 is the difference between the salvage value obtained and the present value of the revenue stream foregone due to the outsourcing margin and drives the put value.

For example, if revenues were to reach $120 million, the value of the revenues foregone due to the distribution margin of 10% for the expected five years of outstanding revenue stream is $48.55 million. A salvage price of $25 million would not recover the revenues foregone, and management would keep the plant, so the value of the abandonment option is zero. On the other hand, if revenues are only $50 million, the present value of the outstanding revenue foregone due to a distribution margin of 10% is $20.23 million. In that instance, cashing a $25 million salvage price for the plant

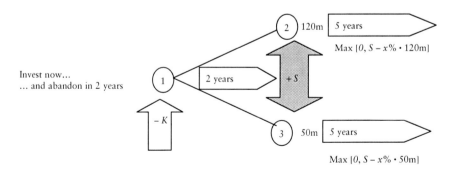

FIGURE 3.10 The binomial asset tree of the option to abandon

would be the better decision. In this scenario, the option to abandon the plant is of value.

The revenue foregone due to the outsourcing margin represents the exercise price to be paid when exercising the abandonment option. The formula for calculating the value of the put on the plant is

$$P = \frac{p \cdot [\max(0, - V_{max} \cdot x\% + S)] + (1 - p) \cdot \max[0, - V_{min} \cdot x\% + S]}{(1 + r_f)^2}$$

The put option is in the money only for the small distribution margin of 10%, and it moves out of the money at higher distribution margins of 15% or 20%. We calculate the critical salvage value that needs to be recovered to move the abandonment option into the money by setting the above equation for the put option equal to zero and solving for S. The results are shown in Figure 3.11.

As the outsourcing margin increases, the critical salvage value required to move the put option into the money also grows. How does the inclusion of the abandonment option alter the original investment decision of building the plant now? Well, with the investment into building the plant, the option to abandon the plant is acquired and may as well be included in the original project appraisal by adding the abandonment option value to the value of the option to invest now. Figure 3.12 shows the results.

Open symbols represent the value of investing now without the abandonment option; closed symbols show the value of the investment including

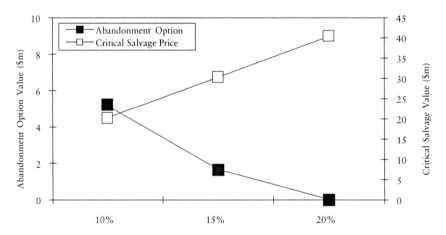

FIGURE 3.11 The abandonment option value and critical salvage value

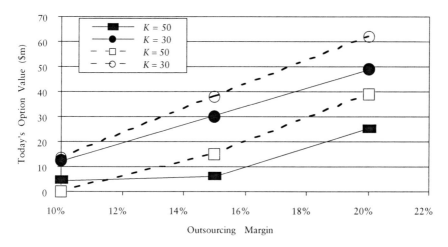

FIGURE 3.12 The option value to invest now under inclusion of the abandonment option

the abandonment option. Inclusion of the abandonment option moves the option to invest in the plant now into the money in all examined scenarios. That, however, does not necessarily imply investing now is still the best of all managerial choices. We still need to compare the value of investing now including the option value to abandon in two years with the option to defer the decision for two years. If the former is greater than the latter, we will invest now, and we will defer otherwise. Under the current assumptions, there is only one scenario in which the deferral option is of higher value than the option to invest now and abandon when market conditions are not supportive, namely, when plant costs are $50 million and the outsourcing margin is 10%.

We can summarize the analysis by stating that if the option to abandon the plant in two years is included, there is no value in deferring the decision under the current set of assumptions. Are there any circumstances that would make the option to defer more valuable than the option to invest now with the possibility of abandoning the plant against salvage value in two years? What, in other words, are the boundary conditions that separate investing now with the option to abandon from deferring for two years for the range of outsourcing margins? To answer this question, we need to define for which plant cost K the option to invest now and potentially abandon at a salvage price equals the investment to defer and pay for the outsourcing margin in the meantime. This is achieved by setting the two equations equal

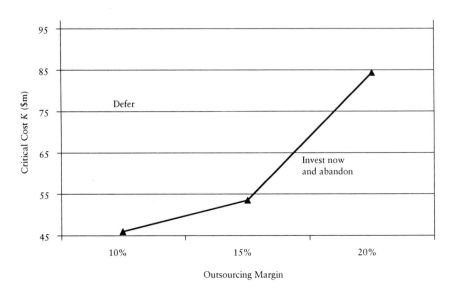

FIGURE 3.13 The decision line: Invest now and abandon versus defer

and solving for the cost K. Figure 3.13 shows the result for the range of outsourcing margins, and for a salvage value of $35 million.

The line separates the two strategic alternatives. Below the line, management is better off to invest now with the option to abandon if market conditions are unfavorable. Above the line, management is better off deferring the decision for two years. The salvage price has very little impact on the boundary that separates both decisions. That impact completely vanishes as the outsourcing margin increases.

THE OPTION TO CHANGE SCALE: EXPAND OR CONTRACT

The option to change scale acknowledges managerial flexibility to alter capacity in order to respond to changing market conditions. This can lead to a project being downsized, expanded, or narrowed in its focus. The option to expand or contract recognizes that management alters the scale and rate of resource expenditure once market conditions change. The option to grow implies that an investment can be staged into a sequence of incremental steps that build on each other, with each step contributing to growth.

For example, an existing airline company may consider expanding by increasing the frequency of flights on established routes or by adding new connections to its existing network. Similarly, a manufacturing plant manager may contemplate a new investment to expand capacity because there is a chance that consumer demand for that specific product will pick up. Likewise, a flexible manufacturing plant may have the option to reduce capacity.

For a moment, we return to the car manufacturer as an example. Management may have the option to acquire a smaller plant now for $30 million, which would be suitable to satisfy the production needs if demand is low. This plant could be expanded for an additional expense of $25 million in two years if demand moves above the $50 million revenue threshold and reaches the $120 million volume level. Figure 3.14 depicts the binomial asset tree.

If revenues remain low, management will not expand the plant. The value of that option becomes zero. If, however, revenues climb beyond $50 million, management may see value in expanding the plant, as demand beyond $50 million will have to be outsourced at a given outsourcing margin. The decision will be made in two years. At that time market uncertainty will have been resolved and management will be in the position to make an informed decision on the expansion strategy. What is the value of the option to expand? If market conditions are bad and revenues do not exceed $50 million, management has no need to outsource, and will not incur any outsourcing costs. If market conditions are good, management will cover demand up to $50 million and outsource beyond that, incurring outsourcing costs over the anticipated remaining lifetime of five years for the product. The present value of those costs is calculated for the range of outsourcing margins. The expected outsourcing costs at today's value reflect the market risk. Management assumes that the bad and the worst case demand scenario are equally likely. Table 3.5 summarizes the data.

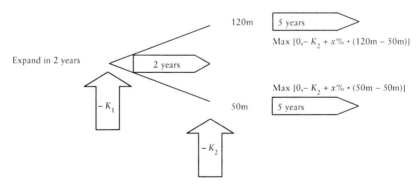

FIGURE 3.14 The binomial asset tree of the option to expand

TABLE 3.5 The asset value of expanding

Margin (%)	Present Value of the Asset		Expected Value
	50 ($ millions)	120 ($ millions)	($ millions)
10	0.00	28.32	14.16
15	0.00	42.48	21.24
20	0.00	56.64	28.32

The maximum value created by expansion is the cost saved by not paying the outsourcing margin for the residual five years of product life, and it ranges between $28.32 million and $56.64 million in asset value two years from now. The minimum value is zero, and the expected value ranges between $14.16 million and $28.32 million. Those data give rise to a risk-free probability of 0.5375 in all three scenarios. For each scenario, management will determine the value-maximizing or cost-minimizing path. For example, the value of the call on the expansion option for the 10% outsourcing margin and an expansion cost of $30 million becomes:

$$C_{10\%} = 0.5375 \cdot \text{Max} (0, 28.32 - 30) + (1 - 0.5375) \cdot \text{Max} (0, 0 - 30)$$
$$= 0.5375 \cdot \text{Max} (0, -1.68) + 0.4625 \cdot \text{Max} (0, -30)$$
$$= 0.5375 \cdot 0 + 0.4625 \cdot 0$$
$$= 0$$

The general formula to calculate the call option for different outsourcing margins is:

$$C = \frac{p \cdot \text{max}[0, x\% \cdot (V_{max}) - K2] + (1 - p) \cdot \text{max}[0, x\% \cdot (V_{min}) - K2]}{(1 + r_f)^2}$$

Management also likes to understand the critical cost to invest into the plant expansion under the different outsourcing margins. The critical cost to invest in expansion is reached when the expansion option moves out of the money. We calculate it by setting the equation for the expansion call option to zero and solving for the critical cost $K2$. Figure 3.15 shows the value of the expansion option as well as the critical value to invest in expansion for the range of outsourcing margins and a maximum revenue of $120 million as well as an expected lifetime of five years after expansion.

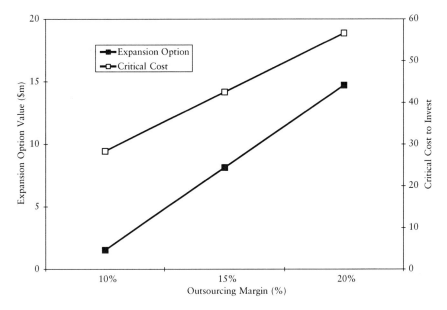

FIGURE 3.15 The expansion option value and critical cost to invest in expansion

THE OPTION TO SWITCH

A financial switch option is a path-dependent derivative on one underlying stock: The pay-off of the switch option depends on pre-defined barriers, a lower barrier and an upper barrier. The switch option becomes activated every time the stock hits the barrier; it becomes de-activated if the stock hits the other barrier. The payoff at the time of exercise is a function of the value of the underlying asset if the option is activated at the time of exercise, and a lower function if the option is deactivated at the time of exercise. The switch option is never zero, and it is never canceled. With increasing volatility of the underlying asset, the switch option has higher chances of being both reactivated and de-activated.

The real option to switch captures the managerial flexibility to alter the modus operandi of any given business. This includes exchanging input or output parameters, volume, processes, and global locations. Brenner and Schwartz pioneered the option to switch in the mining industry by analyzing the closing and opening of the mine as the two switching extremes of operations.[3] Similarly, Dixit examines the value of having managerial flexibility to enter or exit any given market as a switching option.[4] Kulatilaka explores the option to switch between two different energy forms in running a plant.[5] Often, switching refers to a technology; for example, one technology may be more cost effective in high-demand states, another more cost effective in low-demand states.[6]

Having the flexibility to exchange or switch between technologies creates value, as it permits management to respond to future uncertainties in an optimal fashion. Integrating flexibility in real estate development, for example, allows switching in the future between different uses, such as rental apartments and condominiums, office and retail space.[7] Creating operational flexibility that facilitates wide-ranging use of assets in place generates a real option to switch. The value of this flexibility increases as the correlation of the returns between different uses as well as the costs to redevelop and change between uses decrease. The switch option value lowers the critical threshold to invest and also affects the timing of the investment decision.

The operator of a service institution as well as a manufacturing plant may be faced with the option to switch scheduling priorities in order to avoid or better manage queuing problems. Priorities would be based on the expected inventory cost in terms of what is in the queue and the expected price of the product or service. Other examples of switch options relate to managerial flexibility to choose among several inputs. For example, a chicken producer may value the flexibility to switch between different feed sources, while an electric utility company may value switching between fuel sources, just as the homeowner does. Likewise, the manager of a manufacturing plant may have the flexibility to change the plant's output, for example, from one car model to a different one or to the production of lawn-mowing machines. The option to switch may also refer to managerial flexibility to expand or to contract capacity and produce efficiently at different demand levels.

The basic component of the switching option that drives its value includes the costs saved or additional cash flows generated by having the ability to respond to future uncertainties and change a cost-driving operational parameter. The exercise price is the additional investment required today to establish the enabling technology that will allow management to switch. In addition to these one-time costs, there may be a "switching-fee," an additional cost that occurs anytime management does switch in between parameters. We can view these fees as a maintenance cost to the option that keeps the option alive.

We will introduce the basics of the switching option with a very simple example. Imagine a home-builder who considers equipping a new home with either a gas or an oil furnace; both may be equally costly to install, but the value driver will be uncertain gas and oil prices in the future. At an additional cost, say of $8,000, the homeowner can install a dual fuel burning furnace that allows him to switch. This furnace is expected to last 20 years; the expected lifetime of the switch option is hence 20 years.

The value of the option is driven by the additional costs, the exercise price of the option, but also by the homeowner's demand over time and the anticipated price differential between the two energy sources over the expected life-expectancy of the furnace. The homeowner does not need to know or predict future prices, but he wants to think about the current prices. In other words, he needs to know how the volatility of the price of either energy form will behave, how those volatilities relate to each other, and what the best and worst case scenarios of the average annual price differential might look like. If both gas and oil are likely to go up at the same rate, the option to switch will be of little value, as the price differential between those two energy forms will be zero. The larger the price differential between the two energy forms is, the more value the homeowner will be able to extract from the flexibility to switch between both energy forms. Let us assume that in the worst case scenario the price differential will be no more than 1% while in the best case scenario that differential goes up to 50%. We also assume that each scenario is equally likely, that is, $q = 0.5$. Figure 3.16 depicts the scenario in a binomial tree.

We assume an annual demand of 10,000 units, no matter what energy form, for the next 20 years and a current price of $1.50 per unit for the currently cheapest energy form. The value of the switch option is driven by the amount of cost savings the homeowner realizes by always choosing the cheapest energy source. We therefore need to determine the value of the average future price differentials, assuming that the homeowner acts rationally and will always choose to switch to the cheapest energy form. We also assume initially that there will be no additional costs in switching; all the homeowner has to do is "switch" a button. The exercise price for the switch option is the cost K of $8,000, the premium the homeowner has to pay for the furnace with integrated energy-switching features. The value of future

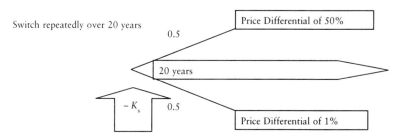

FIGURE 3.16 The binomial asset tree for the option to switch

TABLE 3.6 The asset value of switching

Present Value ($)	Price Differential (%)
79,335.92	50
63,468.74	40
47,601.55	30
31,734.37	20
15,867.18	10
7,933.59	5
1,586.72	1

average price differentials is more difficult to predict. The homeowner studies how prices for both energy sources have behaved in the past (that is, their volatility) and also needs to know how those past price curves correlate with each other. If one energy source tended to be cheaper than the other at most time points and if a price increase in one energy source was regularly accompanied by a price increase in the other energy source, there may be little value in the switching option. Only when prices tend to move in opposite directions (that is, are negatively correlated) would there be an opportunity to benefit from switching.

The homeowner starts by assuming a range of possible average price differentials from 1% in the worst case scenario and 50% in the best case scenario, using the current price of $1.50 per unit as a basis. He calculates the present value of those price differentials assuming an annual demand of 10,000 units over a period of 20 years. Table 3.6 shows the results.

Then the homeowner assigns a range of probabilities q from 10% to 50% for both the best case scenario (that is, the largest price differential of 50%) and correspondingly probabilities $1 - q$ for the worst case scenario (that is, the smallest price differential of only 1%) to occur. Those probabilities drive the expected value of the price differential today. This then makes it possible to calculate the risk-free probability p and subsequently the value of the call on the switch option for an exercise price of $8,000. The data are presented in Table 3.7

TABLE 3.7 The option value of switching

q	0.5	0.4	0.3	0.2	0.1
Expected Value	$40,461	$32,686	$24,911	$17,137	$9,362
p	0.536	0.429	0.322	0.215	0.108
Call	$35,294	$26,974	$18,655	$10,336	$2,017

The option will be in the money under all those scenarios under the given cost assumptions. Obviously, the homeowner can now also calculate the critical cost to invest under the given scenarios that would move the option out of the money, and should prevent him from purchasing the more expensive furnace with the switching option. The critical cost to invest is reached for each scenario once the value of the option approaches zero. We set the equation to calculate the call to zero and solve for the critical cost K.

$$C = \frac{p \cdot V_{max} + (1 - p) \cdot V_{min}}{(1 + r_f)^t} - K = 0$$

So far, the homeowner assumes that there is no additional cost for switching, and that he can switch all the time effortlessly. We will now introduce switching costs per switch, say, for additional maintenance and cleaning of the furnace. Assuming an annual extra expense for switching ranging between $200 and $3,000, depending how often per year the owner may want to switch, we observe how the option to install the switching option at $8,000 moves out of the money. Increasing annual switching costs and decreasing probabilities q to realize an average price differential of 50% per annum over the next 20 years both work together to drive the option out of the money, as shown in Figure 3.17.

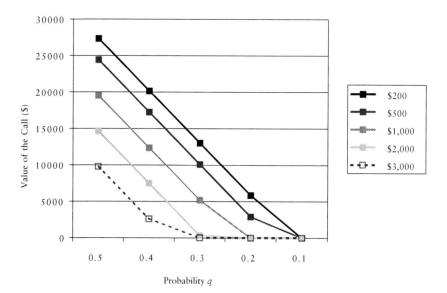

FIGURE 3.17 Sensitivity of the switch option value to switching costs

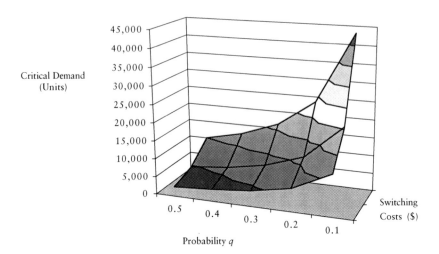

FIGURE 3.18 Sensitivity of the switch option value to demand

If demand were to drop from the currently anticipated 10,000 units per annum, how would the value of the call option change, and what is the minimum critical demand per year for the option to be in the money? Figure 3.18 shows the results. As the probability for high volatility market conditions and hence larger switching benefits declines and as switching costs increase, the unit energy demand must go up to keep the switching option at the money.

The value of the switching option comes from the flexibility to manage uncertainty and respond to unknown future market conditions. The value reflects cost savings for the homeowner who has the flexibility to change from one energy form to another. Introduction of switching flexibility affects the value of other options we have analyzed so far: the timing of the investment, the value to defer, and the value to abandon. We will study option interaction in later sections of this book.

THE OPTION TO GROW

A company acquires a growth option by making an initial investment in a new market, a new product line, or a new technology. Such an investment often requires more initial outlays than the expected revenue would justify. In other words, the NPV gives a negative result. However, the value of this investment opportunity comes from creating future growth opportunities. If the new market proves profitable, the initial outlay can be expanded into a broader geographic area. If the new product line is successful in a pilot market area, production and launch can be expanded. If initial experience in a pilot plant with a new production technology decreases costs and increases efficiency, the technology can be implemented throughout the entire corporate enterprise.

Growth options create infrastructure and opportunities for future expansion and hence are of strategic value. They are sequential options that link distinct growth and expansion steps but always preserve managerial flexibility to embark on the next expansion step, depending on prevailing market conditions. Even if the pilot project turns out to be a complete flop, the company will gain experience and insights that may be of value for the planning or implementation of other growth options in the future.

Growth options exist in every industry, but they may be especially important for high-tech, high-risk endeavors. Growth options have been valued for biotech companies,[8] for the development and implementation of new software,[9] or for an entire Information Technology infrastructure, including the consideration of competitive scenarios drawing on game theory.[10] Benaroch and Kauffman[11] apply the binomial and Black-Scholes models to evaluating IT investment, with a real case study on the Yankee-24 electronic banking network.

Imagine a company that faces the opportunity to invest in a new enterprise-wise software that enables it to improve, simplify, accelerate, and integrate its entire manufacturing, inventory, and ordering system. Implementation of the system would provide substantial cost savings for the ongoing operations but those cost savings are unlikely to justify the implementation costs. On the other hand, at an additional expense, the system could be upgraded to interface with customers and provide a web-based tracking opportunity for customers to track their orders or place orders on the Internet. Such a service would provide the company with a strong competitive advantage and could help in maintaining and even increasing the customer base, which in turn would help to justify the investment in the infrastructure.

One way of finding out whether this rationale makes sense is to conduct a pilot project restricted to a certain geographical area. The investment costs for the pilot project would be $30 million, compared to $250 million for the full-blown project. If the pilot project works well, the anticipated cost savings are $40 million in two years from now; if it works badly, no more than $15 million could be saved. Management anticipates that there is a 70% chance that things will work out well, but a 30% chance that they will not. If the pilot project is a success, then the company will install the software enterprise-wide at an additional cost of $220 million. It will take three years to implement the follow-up project. Cost savings on an enterprise-wide basis would be $400 million in the best case scenario and $80 million in the worst case scenario. The probability for the best case is 70% and for the worst case 30%.

Let us start the project appraisal with an NPV analysis:

Pilot Project: $\dfrac{0.7 \cdot 40 + 0.3 \cdot 15}{1.15^2} - 30 = -5.43$

Follow-up Project: $\dfrac{0.7 \cdot 400 + 0.3 \cdot 80}{1.15^3} - 220 = -20.12$

The combined NPV is –$24.15 million.

The NPV analysis clearly suggests rejecting this project. The real option analysis provides a different perspective on the valuation. Let's frame the situation with a binomial asset tree, shown in Figure 3.19.

Management would only decide to move forward with the project if the outcome of the pilot project is favorable. It would not exercise the option to invest an additional $220 million if the pilot project suggests that expected cost savings would not exceed $80 million.

The expected value of the follow-up project at node 4 is

$$V_{E4} = 0.7 \cdot 400 + 0.3 \cdot 80 = 304$$

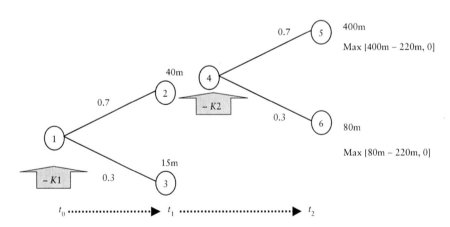

FIGURE 3.19 The binomial asset tree of the growth option

The risk-free probability p at node 4 is thus

$$p = \frac{(1 + 7\%) \cdot 304 - 80}{400 - 80} = 0.7665$$

The value of the call at node 4 is then at a risk-free rate of 7%.

$$C_4 = \frac{0.7665 \cdot 400 + (1 - 0.7665) \cdot 80}{1.07^3} - 220$$

$$= \frac{306.06 + 18.69}{1.07^3} - 220$$

$$= 265.53 - 220$$

$$= \$45.53 \text{ million}$$

With a 70% probability of success, the company will reach node 2 and thereby acquire the call option, starting at node 4, to expand the software implementation to the entire enterprise; that option is worth $45.53 million. With a probability of 30%, cost savings during the pilot phase will not exceed $15 million, and enterprise-wide implementation of the software will not be pursued. Thus, by investing in the pilot project, management initiates an NPV negative project worth –$5.43 million but also acquires an expansion option worth $45.53 million. The expanded NPV then becomes $40.10 million and is clearly positive. Management should go ahead and initiate the pilot project.

The option perspective provides the key insight that management has the flexibility to respond to the experience gained during the pilot project at time point t_1. If the pilot project does not work out, there will be no follow-up project and the downside risk is hence limited. The negative NPV of $5.3 million for the pilot project is the price management has to pay to acquire the growth option in the form of the follow-on project.

THE COMPOUND OPTION

Major projects often unfold in a series of subsequent steps, with each step relying on successful completion of the preceding one, and with management keeping the option to evaluate the project at each sequential step. Other than a growth option, the payoff for a compound option will only materialize after completion of all steps. Investments into technology platforms, into early-stage research projects such as investments in new technologies or new prototypes, and into late-stage R&D such as prototype development fit the criteria for a compound option very well. But also an investment in a new IT infrastructure, a novel distribution network, and an e-commerce strategy are ideally valued as compound options.

The commonalities among this range of projects is the nature of staged investments in uncertainty as well as two main sources of risk: (i) the private or technical risk that relates to the ability of the firm to actually carry out successfully the project and (ii) the market or non-private risk that refers to future demand uncertainty and is determined by the competitive landscape, by product features, and by product requirements as imposed by the consumer. The critical threshold or critical cost to invest is determined in part by both. The key flexibility features to come with a sequential project include the choice of timing (of the level of expenditures and speed of spending) in addition to the choice of abandoning the project after information on each milestone is obtained.

A compound option is an option on an option. By investing and completing each step management buys the option, but not the obligation to take the project to the next level. Geske was the first to price a compound option.[12] He valued the call option on a stock as a call option on a call option of the firm's assets. While Black-Scholes also valued the same call option, provided it was European, Geske's analysis provided an important extension: it made it possible to price the call for changing volatility of the stock. Changing volatility of the stock may result from the volatility of the underlying asset to change, or from the firm's leverage to change. Rubinstein further extended Geske's concept of a compound option by generalizing the formula to allow for pricing of a call on a put, a put on a call, and a put on a put. He also considered the situation of continuous payout on the assets.[13]

In the financial world, compound options are applied extensively in fixed income and currency markets. Here, the downside protection provided by the option is only limited and the buyer of the compound option is thus unwilling to pay more than a reduced initial premium.

As for real options, the sequential option resembles mostly a variation of the compound option, namely, the installment option. The option price is paid sequentially and in installments over time. At each installment the option owner decides whether to pay the installment, thereby exercising the option and acquiring the right to continue the option. If the option owner decides against paying the installment, the entire installment option will expire, and the option owner relinquishes all previously paid installments. However, as for real options, the option owner may recover some residual value from the previous installments even when failing to complete all installments with the creation of a marketable asset. This residual value entails, for example, learning, knowledge acquisition, or a proprietary technology that could be licensed out for applications in non-core business areas.

Cortazar and Schwartz[14] adopted the concept of a compound option to real assets to determine the best procedure in a manufacturing context. They valued the option to change output when production costs per unit are fixed but future product prices are uncertain and follow a stochastic process. The firm has the option to build up inventory within a two-staged production process, and this step separates the two phases of the compounded option. The authors show that as price volatility increases (that is, uncertainty and interest rates increase), the incentive to complete the first production stage at fixed costs and building inventory before going into the second production phase also grows.

A good example of a compound option situation in the real world is a pharmaceutical drug development program. Usually, such an adventure starts with an investment into pre-clinical research that produces a molecule. Completing this step successfully gives the option owner the right, but not the obligation, to take the molecule to the next stage, which is an initial clinical trial involving normal volunteers, a phase I trial. Completing this step successfully, that is, by showing that the molecule is safe, allows the option owner to proceed to the next step, a phase II clinical trial, and so forth, until the molecule is filed for market approval with the Federal Drug Administration (FDA). Such an investment program gives management the flexibility at each step to consider whether to take the program to the next level. This implies that resources need not be committed to the entire seven-year program but can be applied in incremental steps. This kind of flexibility represents in essence a series of call options that build on each other and is best viewed as a compound option or a sequential option.

If one either assumes or knows the stochastic processes that costs and returns of the future asset will follow, then closed-form solutions provided by different real option valuation methods can be considered: the Black-Scholes formula that assumes deterministic costs, the Margrabe exchange model that assumes both costs and future returns to be stochastic and that they are exchanged for the asset once it is developed, or the Carr sequential option.

If those stochastic processes are unknown, the binomial option model offers a valid alternative to price the compound option. Let's start by framing the binomial asset tree, as shown in Figure 3.20.

The decision points are given almost naturally with the various phases of the program. For each phase, the probability of success, q, the time to completion, and the expected costs need to be assessed. To find the value of

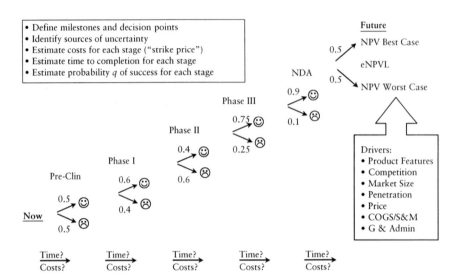

FIGURE 3.20 The binomial asset tree of the compound option

the asset at all points during the evolution of the program we start with the ultimate node, in this example the approval of the drug. Only at this stage, when the product finally reaches the market, will its value become apparent. Several parameters such as overall market size, market penetration, costs, and pricing will drive the scenario analysis, leading to a best and a worst case scenario. Assuming probabilities for those scenarios to occur, one can then calculate the expected case. We assign a probability of 50% to the best and worst case scenarios.

The value at the end of the tree is the present value of future asset flows at that point in time. This figure drives the value of the asset going backward to today through all preceding nodes. It also drives the option value at all nodes in the binomial tree. Using estimates of probabilities of success, we calculate backward the expected value of the asset at each preceding node in the tree, discounting at the appropriate corporate discount rate that reflects the weighted cost of capital (WACC). The rationale for this procedure is as follows: After launch, the future asset value is driven by market risk. Therefore, the corporate cost of capital is appropriate to discount the asset value throughout the entire development program to today. During the development, however, the future asset is in addition subject to technical uncertainty, the private risk the company faces in developing the drug. We account for this not by a risk premium added to the corporate discount rate but by using corporate benchmarks to estimate probabilities of success for each of the development phases.

Let us now walk through the real option pricing procedure using the example given in Figure 3.21. Assume, in the best case scenario, that the drug will generate total sales over its estimated lifetime of 10 years with a net present value at the time of launch of $520 million. In the worst case scenario, the drug will generate no more than $24 million. Management believes each scenario to be equally likely. This gives an expected value at the time of launch of $272 million.

In the penultimate node, the expected value is the product of the probability of completing the next phase, namely FDA approval, successfully (that is, 90%) times the expected asset value after approval (that is, $272m), discounted back at the corporate discount rate of 13.5% over the estimated length of this period, yielding $216 million. The maximum asset value at the penultimate node is defined as the maximum asset value after

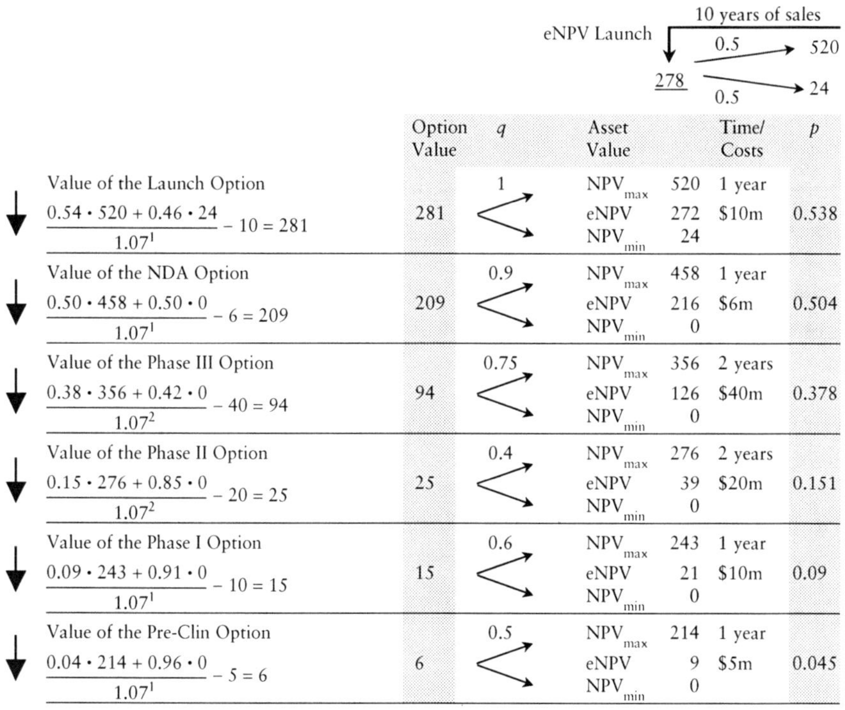

	Option Value	q	Asset Value		Time/Costs	p
			eNPV Launch $\nearrow^{0.5}$ 520	10 years of sales		
			278 $\searrow_{0.5}$ 24			
Value of the Launch Option $\frac{0.54 \cdot 520 + 0.46 \cdot 24}{1.07^1} - 10 = 281$	281	1	NPV_{max} eNPV NPV_{min}	520 272 24	1 year $10m	0.538
Value of the NDA Option $\frac{0.50 \cdot 458 + 0.50 \cdot 0}{1.07^1} - 6 = 209$	209	0.9	NPV_{max} eNPV NPV_{min}	458 216 0	1 year $6m	0.504
Value of the Phase III Option $\frac{0.38 \cdot 356 + 0.42 \cdot 0}{1.07^2} - 40 = 94$	94	0.75	NPV_{max} eNPV NPV_{min}	356 126 0	2 years $40m	0.378
Value of the Phase II Option $\frac{0.15 \cdot 276 + 0.85 \cdot 0}{1.07^2} - 20 = 25$	25	0.4	NPV_{max} eNPV NPV_{min}	276 39 0	2 years $20m	0.151
Value of the Phase I Option $\frac{0.09 \cdot 243 + 0.91 \cdot 0}{1.07^1} - 10 = 15$	15	0.6	NPV_{max} eNPV NPV_{min}	243 21 0	1 year $10m	0.09
Value of the Pre-Clin Option $\frac{0.04 \cdot 214 + 0.96 \cdot 0}{1.07^1} - 5 = 6$	6	0.5	NPV_{max} eNPV NPV_{min}	214 9 0	1 year $5m	0.045

FIGURE 3.21 How to calculate the compound option value

launch, discounted back to the time of FDA filing. For the best case scenario, we thus assume 100% probability of technical success as well as the best market scenario. Thus we discount $520 million at 13.5% for one year, giving $458 million. The minimum asset value at the FDA filing stage and at all stages prior to that is zero. At those points in time, there is always a chance of technical failure that will prevent product launch.

In a similar fashion, we calculate back the expected maximum and minimum asset value for each preceding node across the entire binomial tree. This gives us the asset value of today, prior to embarking on the pre-clinical R&D program, taking into account future market scenarios as well as our assumptions on probabilities of success, costs, and time frames. The probabilities of success are either internal estimates or industry benchmarks. Sensitivity analysis will reveal how sensitive the value of our option is to those parameters.

To now determine the value of the option on this program at each node in time we first calculate the risk-free probability using the known equation:

$$p = \frac{(1 + r) \cdot V_e - V_{min}}{V_{max} - V_{min}}$$

V_e denotes the expected value, V_{max} and V_{min} the maximum and minimum value, respectively. For example, after completion of the initial step in the sequential tree, that is, the pre-clinical program, the expected value of the asset is $9 million. The maximum asset value is $214 million, which assumes 100% of technical success and the best case market scenario. The minimum asset value after completion of the pre-clinical program is zero, that is, the research has failed. Hence, the risk-free probability at node 1 is:

$$p_1 = \frac{1.07 \cdot 9 - 0}{214 - 0} = 0.045$$

The risk-free probability is different at each stage and increases from now going forward until FDA approval. This reflects that the technical probability of success changes during each stage and that the overall cumulative probability of success increases as we proceed successfully from one phase through the next. Even if the probability of success for each stage would decline over the lifetime of the project, with, say, a 90% chance of finding a candidate pre-clinical program down to a 10% chance of getting the drug approved at the FDA, the cumulative probability would still increase, and so would the risk-free probability, as shown in Figure 3.22.

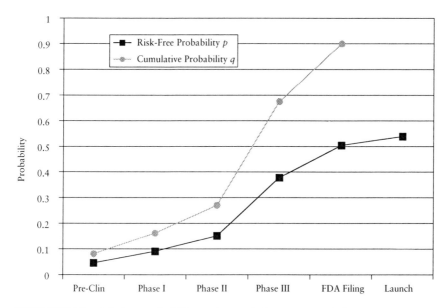

FIGURE 3.22 The risk-free probability and cumulative project risk for a pharmaceutical drug development program

The value of the call option at each node is then calculated using Equation 2.3 introduced in Chapter 2:

$$C = \frac{p \cdot V_{max} + (1 - p) \cdot V_{min}}{(1 + r_f)^t} - K$$

An NPV valuation would take the expected case scenario, discount it back at the corporate discount rate, and deduct the present value of all cash flows required to generate the asset. A risk-adjusted NPV valuation would take into account the technical probability of success. Figure 3.23 shows the option value, the NPV, and the risk-adjusted NPV for the given scenario.

The critical cost K to invest today is a function of the probability of success of the first step, the pre-clinical phase, but also a function of the overall cumulative probability of success. As such, the critical value to invest is even more sensitive to increasing probability of success in any of the later stages, as shown for this example in Figure 3.24.

The critical cost to invest in the pre-clinical stage of the drug development program increases with the probability of success for the pre-clinical

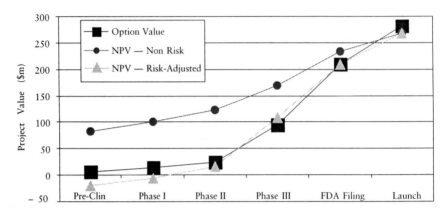

FIGURE 3.23 Three approaches to appraising the drug development program

stage. However, it increases even further and with a steeper slope once the probability of success for phase II increases. This observation implies that any investment undertaken today to increase the probability of success in later stages will pay off. It also implies that any investment undertaken today to increase the predictive value of future probabilities of success also has option value. Those investments are learning options, and we will discuss them in a later chapter of the book.

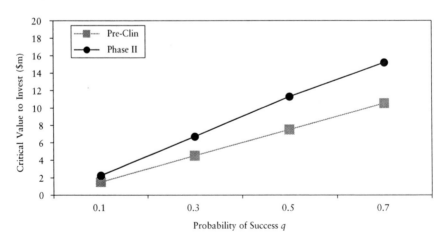

FIGURE 3.24 The critical value to invest as a function of private risk

SYNOPSIS

The simple case examples of basic options have illustrated the complexity that can arise as a result of multiple embedded options that are mutually exclusive or interact in an additive or synergistic fashion. While there is a need to think those interactions through and model them explicitly, there is also a trade-off decision to be made: being complete versus remaining transparent. It is crucial to the overall analysis to embrace the foreseeable interactions, but also to judge how material these interactions will be to the overall decision. It is equally crucial to identify the key interactions and action scenarios that will actually drive the overall option value and hence the decision, and to embrace those interactions and the resulting complexity. However, it is also key not to become paranoid or obsessed about a level of detail that will not be material to the overall option value.

The second insight from the few simple case studies presented in this chapter is that the value drivers for real options are really very distinct from those for financial options, and the following points illustrate this in more detail:

1. The riskiness of the asset drives option value for both financial and real options. However, for real options it is not the riskiness per se but the ability of management to adequately respond to it in order to enable the organization to take full benefit from the upside potential that results from the asset volatility.
2. Management's ability to respond to the riskiness is also determined by the arrival of information. Both dimensions drive the real option value.
3. The value of the option finally depends on managerial ability to exercise, and exercise may include abandoning a project.

NOTES

1. M. Chesney, M. Jeanblanc-Pique, and M. Yor, "Brownian Excursions and Parisien Barrier Options," *Advances in Applied Probability* 29:165, 1997.
2. John Kensinger, *Project Abandonment As a Put Option: Dealing with the Capital Investment Decision and Operating Risk Using Option Pricing Theory*, working paper, 80–121 (Cox School of Business, October 1980); S.C. Myers and S. Majd, *Calculating Abandonment Value Using Option Pricing Theory*, working paper (Sloan School of Management, May 1983).

3. M. Brenner and E. Schwartz, "Evaluating Natural Resource Investments," *Journal of Business* 58:135, 1985.
4. A. Dixit, "Entry and Exit Decisions under Uncertainty," *Journal of Political Economy* 97:620, 1989.
5. N. Kulatilaka, "The Value of Flexibility: The Case of a Dual-Fuel Industrial Steam Boiler," *Financial Management* 22:271, 1993.
6. L. Trigeorgis, *Real Options—Managerial Flexibility and Strategy in Resource Allocation* (MIT Press, Cambridge, MA, 1996); T. Copeland and V. Antikarov, *Real Options—A Practitioner's Guide* (Texetere, 2001).
7. P.D. Childs, T.R. Riddiough, and A. Triantis, "Mixed Uses and the Redevelopment Option," *Real Estate Economics* 24:317, 1996.
8. R.E. Ottoo, "Valuation of Internal Growth Opportunities: The Case of a Biotech Company," *Quarterly Review of Economics and Finance* 38:615, 1998.
9. H. Erdogmus, *Management of License Cost Uncertainty in Software Development: A Real Option Approach* (Fifth Real Option Conference, Los Angeles, 2001).
10. K.X. Zhu, *Strategic Investment in Information Technologies: A Real-Options and Game-Theoretic Approach*, unpublished doctoral dissertation (Stanford University, 1999).
11. M. Benaroch and R.J. Kauffman, "A Case for Using Real Options Pricing Analysis to Evaluate Information Technology Project Investments," *Information Systems Research* 10:70, 1999.
12. R. Geske, "The Valuation of Compound Options," *Journal of Financial Economics* 7:63, 1979.
13. M. Rubinstein, "Double Trouble," *Risk Magazine* 4:73, 1992.
14. G. Cortazar and E.S. Schwartz, "A Compound Option Model of Production and Intermediate Inventories," *Journal of Business* 66:517, 1993; H. Herath and C.S. Park, "Multi-Stage Capital Investment Opportunities as Compound Real Options." *Engineering Economist* 47:27, 2002.

CHAPTER 4

The Value of Uncertainty

The general assumption in financial option pricing is that enhanced volatility enhances the value of the option. For financial options, a series of "Greeks" are tools that can be used by analysts to describe and understand the sensitivity of the financial option to key uncertainty parameters. These include vega, delta, theta, rho, and xi. These parameters capture the sensitivity of the option to the uncertainty in time to expiration, changing volatility of the future value of the underlying asset, to the exercise price, the risk-free rate or historical price volatility of the underlying. They also help financial agents to create hedging strategies that minimize the risk caused by changes in the variables that drive the value of the option.

For real options, the relationship between option value and uncertainty is less clear cut. Uncertainty and risk can not only enhance but also diminish the value of the real option. We have already discussed the effect of private or technical uncertainty on the value of the compounded option. We have seen that with increasing probability of success the option value rises and the critical cost threshold decreases. In this instance, increasing the uncertainty of technical success clearly diminishes the value of the real option.

There are multiple drivers of uncertainty for real options, and the option value displays distinct sensitivities to each of them. Further, depending on how many sources of uncertainty any given option is exposed to, those sources of uncertainty may have additive, synergistic, or antagonistic effects on the option value and the critical cost to invest. We will discuss four main sources of uncertainties in this chapter:

- Market variability uncertainty: Uncertainty regarding the product requirements the consumer will expect from future products
- Time of maturity uncertainty: Uncertainty related to the time needed to complete a project (call option)

- Time of expiration uncertainty: Uncertainty related to the viability of the product on the market (put or abandonment option)
- Technology uncertainty: Uncertainty related to the arrival of novel, superior technologies

We will show how these sources of uncertainty can be modeled in the binomial model and how they may impact the option value in our examples.

MARKET VARIABILITY UNCERTAINTY

Huchzermeier and Loch[1] were first to show that an increase in volatility does not per se imply an increase in real option value, which differs from the situation found in financial option pricing. Market payoff volatility does, but private or technical variability or market requirement variability does not. The basic concept is outlined in graphical forms in Figure 4.1, which has been adapted from the authors' work.

Once a firm initiates a new product or service development program, it faces a significant degree of technical or private uncertainty that will only be resolved over time as the product or service is being developed. Initially, the firm is also uncertain about what level of performance features the final product or service will meet. Management and engineers or marketing personnel are likely to have some beliefs, though, as to the probability to reach different levels of performance of the product or of the service to be implemented. The product or service then enters a market that may either be highly sensitive to performance criteria (scenario A) or minimally sensitive to performance criteria (scenario B). In scenario A, incremental increases in product or service performance are rewarded by large increases in payoffs.

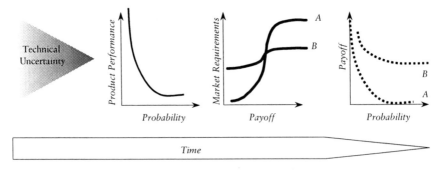

FIGURE 4.1 Market variability reduces option value. Source: Huchzermeier and Loch

In scenario B, even significant improvements of product or service performance criteria will only yield incremental additional payoffs.

The degree of technical or private uncertainty, the degree of product performance uncertainty, and the degree of market requirement uncertainty drive the shape of the ultimate payoff function. A high market uncertainty (scenario A) will result, everything else remaining equal, in a much more uncertain and volatile payoff function. With a very small probability, management can expect a significant payoff; with much higher probabilities, the expected payoff for scenario A levels off very quickly. On the contrary, the payoff function of scenario B with little market requirement uncertainty is much less volatile. With a higher probability, management can expect to realize the maximum payoff, and with increasing certainty there is only a small decline in the expected payoff.

We will now model market variability uncertainty in a binomial model. Let's assume that a pharmaceutical company has a portfolio of four different pre-clinical products for different disease indications. For each product, scientists and clinical researchers can define reasonably well five classes of distinct product performance categories, designated 1 to 5, by looking into efficacy, side-effects of the compound, interaction with other drugs likely to be taken by the same patient population, convenience in administering it for patients and doctors, and ultimately the cost-benefit profile. Scientists and clinicians can further predict with reasonable confidence for each product the likelihood of meeting each of the product performance criteria. The four products address different disease indications. In each disease indication the therapeutic market looks different. Specifically, in each market, the future acceptance and ultimately the market share of the product will display distinct and different sensitivities to the product performance of the future drug. The various scenarios are depicted in Figure 4.2.

For example, in an already crowded market of hypertensive drugs, incremental product performance will not impact much on overall market share. However, if the product turns out to be very superior and offers significant cost savings, it can capture a significant share of a big market (product scenario 1). The second product targets a market where there is no satisfactory treatment yet. The technical uncertainty of developing the product may be higher, but the market payoff function is largely independent of incremental improvement in product performance along the categories outlined above. The product will capture a significant market once its clinical efficacy is proven and it is approved; further improvements along any of the other product performance categories will have only incremental if any effect on market share (product scenario 2). The volatility between the best and the worst product performance category is very small. Yet another

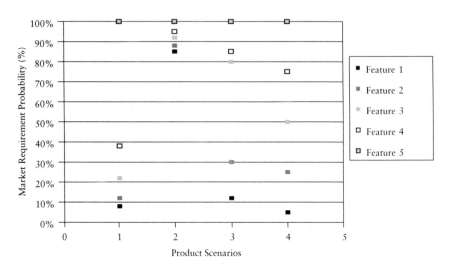

FIGURE 4.2 Product market variability scenarios

compound targets a market where any incremental improvement in the side-effect profile and drug-interaction profile is likely to help capture a significant fraction in a currently fragmented market, while further improvements are unlikely to result in major increases in market share (product scenario 3). Finally, let's assume there is a fourth product where each step in product improvement will result in incremental steps in more market share (product scenario 4).

The market requirement variability is clearly distinct for each product (Figure 4.2). We will now examine how this plays out in the option valuation. In order to get a good understanding of the isolated effect of market requirement variability on the option value of each of these investment projects, we assume initially that all other key drivers of option value, including future asset value as well as private or technical uncertainty to develop the four different products are the same. We will in a later chapter (Chapter 7) relax these assumptions and vary the technical risk as well as the market size to find the right investment decision for this product portfolio. We also assume for each product and for each product feature the same technical probability of success of 20%. In other words, our pharmaceutical firm is equally capable of developing all five product features for all four products. As a result, we eliminate any effect that technical uncertainty may have on actually succeeding in product development.

Product 1 has the largest variance for market requirements: incremental product improvement leads to significant increases in market share. Product

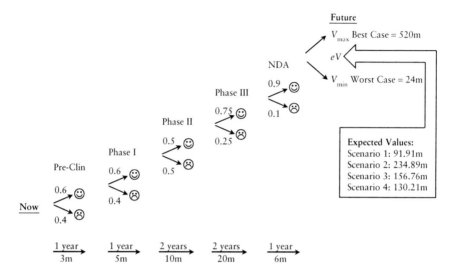

FIGURE 4.3 The binomial asset tree of the compound option under market variability

2 has the smallest market requirement variability: small product improvements will have only little impact on overall market share. Product 3 has less market requirement variability than Product 4. How does the market variability affect the value of the option on the drug development program? We work with the same assumptions as in Chapter 3 regarding costs, time to development, and overall technical risk. Figure 4.3 summarizes the binomial asset tree.

The expected value at time of launch is different for each of the product scenarios and reflects the assumptions on market variability. The expected value at the time of launch is determined by both market uncertainty as well as market requirement variability. Figure 4.4 summarizes the steps

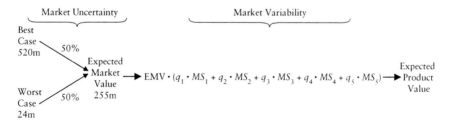

FIGURE 4.4 How to calculate the asset value under market uncertainty

taken to calculate the expected product value at the time of launch for each product.

The expected market value is based on managerial assumptions of the best case and worst case scenario and the probability assigned to each to occur, amounting in our example to $255 million. This figure also went into the initial compounded option analysis of this drug development program in Chapter 3. To arrive at the expected product value at the time of launch we multiply the expected market value (EMV) by the technical probability q_x of implementing the product feature that will allow capturing the market share assigned to this product feature (MS_x). This gives us the expected product value (EPV) at the time of launch for each of the four products.

For example, for product 1, the expected product value is:

$$EPV_1 = \$255 \text{ million} \cdot$$
$$(0.2 \cdot 8 + 0.2 \cdot 12 + 0.2 \cdot 22 + 0.2 \cdot 38 + 0.2 \cdot 100)$$
$$= \$91.91 \text{ million}$$

For product 1, there is a 20% chance for each to achieve incremental product improvements that will help to capture 8%, 12%, 22%, 38%, and ultimately 100% of the market. This translates into an expected value at launch of $91.91 million. For product 2, however, each improvement step with a 20% chance of success will advance the overall market share from 85% to 88%, 92%, 95%, and ultimately 100%, yielding an expected market value of $234.89 million. We calculate the EPV for each product at the time of launch. The maximum asset value at the time of launch for each product is $520 million, assuming that all product features are met and that the full market can be captured. Likewise, the minimum asset value assumes that there is no market variability, and the minimum market value will be captured, that is, $24 million at the time of launch and zero at any time prior to the time of launch.

As in our basic compound option model, we take the expected product values back to the pre-clinical stage of development, applying the same probability of success as before (Chapter 3). We calculate p for each product scenario and stage of development as before $(p = [(1 + r) \cdot EPV - V_{min}] / [V_{max} - V_{min}])$ and then determine the value of the call for each stage under each product scenario. Figure 4.5 depicts the results and also shows again, for comparison, the value of the option for the product, ignoring market requirement variability (dashed line and solid symbol).

The fundamental insight provided by this analysis is that market requirement variability reduces the value of the investment option: the higher the variability, the lower the option value. That effect is most pronounced when a

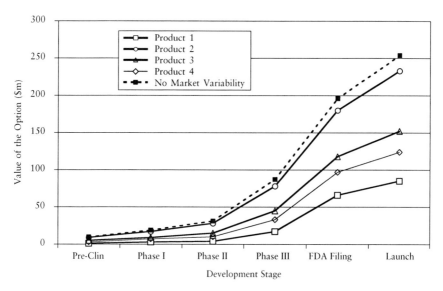

FIGURE 4.5 Value of the compound option under market uncertainty

comparison is made between the option values of product 1 and product 2. The highest option value is seen in the absence of market variability.

This notion is contrary to the general assumption that increasing uncertainty increases the value of your option. It points to the importance of differentiating the sources of uncertainty and their value on the asset and hence on the option. While increased market payoff uncertainty increases the value of the option, market requirement variability, as previously pointed out by Huchzermeier and Loch, does not.

In essence, the more a given set of product features drives diverse payoffs, the smaller the likelihood of reaching a certain fraction of the market becomes. For example, with 60% probability, product 1 will meet three product hurdles and thereby have 22% of the market. With the same probability, product 2 reaches three product hurdles, but by then already captures 92% of the market.

The analysis also promotes another question: How sensitive is the value of the option to a change in market variability when it is at the money, for example, at the pre-clinical stage of drug development, compared to when it is deep in the money, for example, at launch? Clearly, Figure 4.5 suggests that the absolute impact of market variability uncertainty increases sharply as the four product options move deeper into the money as they progress successfully through the development stages.

Figure 4.6 examines this in more detail. It displays the change of option value under increasing market variability as a percentage of base-line value in the absence of market variability for the investment opportunity. Shown are the data for the option value in the pre-clinical stage, when the option is either out of the money or at the money, as well as for the launch stage, when the option is deep in the money. The four product scenarios are arranged on the x-axis in such a way that the variability decreases from left to right, that is, highest for product scenario 1 and lowest for product scenario 2.

The data suggest that market variability consistently has a greater relative impact on the percent change of option value for an option at the money (product in pre-clinical stage, round symbols) compared to an option deep in the money (product at launch, square symbols). As market uncertainty declines, moving from left to right on the x-axis, that differential also declines.

This insight is important in developing an understanding as to when market uncertainty becomes an important driver of option valuation. Such an understanding in turn becomes important for management in defining the conditions when there is value in resolving market variability uncertainty, that is, by making investments in active learning. For an investment option that is deep in the money, resolving market uncertainty is not so critical. For an option that is at the money, reducing the uncertainty surrounding market requirement variability is much more crucial. If management believes that market product requirements display little volatility (product scenario 4),

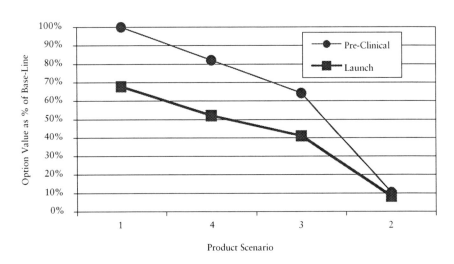

FIGURE 4.6 Loss of option value with increasing market uncertainty

there is little value in resolving any residual uncertainty for options that are either deep in the money or just at the money. On the other hand, if market requirement variability is perceived to be very high, then management may want to invest resources in learning and defining the market variability, specifically for investment options that are only at the money.

REAL CALL OPTIONS WITH UNCERTAIN TIME TO MATURITY

Real options, other than financial options, often suffer from the random nature of the time to maturity of an investment. It is unclear for projects of a diverse nature how long it may take to complete them so that they create revenue streams for the organization. It is equally unclear, for the majority of real asset values, how long they will generate a profitable revenue stream, with potential competitive entry or future technology advances not yet resolved.

In the introductory chapter we saw that some of the value of a financial option is derived from the time to maturity: the farther out the exercise date is the more valuable the option becomes, everything else remaining equal. For a real call option, that is not true. The farther out the time to maturity is, the farther away the future cash flows generated by the asset to be acquired are, and hence the smaller the current value. This simply acknowledges the time value of money. In addition, a key difference between real and financial options is that financial options are monopoly options, while real options are often shared. Competitive entry may prematurely terminate a real option. Further, for real options, we often do not know exactly what the time to maturity is, as development times to implement and create real assets are uncertain.

Some of the time uncertainty is technical or private in nature. For example, for a new product development program, management will only have an estimate as to how long it may take for scientists and engineers to come up with the first prototype if all goes smoothly. Bumps that delay the development are likely, and potentially less likely are "eureka" moments that advance and speed up the development.

What effect does uncertain time to maturity have on the option value? How sensitive is the value of a real call option to time volatility? To draw the comparison to a financial option: This decision scenario represents a call option on a dividend-paying stock; the call owner obtains the dividend only when he exercises the option and acquires the stock. While the advice to American call owners is never to exercise, this guidance changes if the option is on a stock that pays a dividend. The best time to exercise an American call option on a dividend-paying stock is the day before the dividend is due.

Maturity, in the world of real options, is private, and there is no hedge. The closest we come in financial options to the problem of unknown maturity is an American option with random maturity. Here, the value of the option is always smaller than the value of the weighted average of the standard American call, an insight Peter Carr gained in his 1998 paper.[2] The intuition behind Carr's conclusion is that an American option with random maturity really is nothing other than a portfolio of multiple calls with distinct maturities. The owner of the option will exercise the entire portfolio at the same exercise time, and therefore the value of the call must be less than for a randomized option, while the critical value to invest is higher.

The random maturity lowers the value of the option and reduces the trigger value.[3] In fact, as time to maturity becomes highly uncertain, the critical threshold to invest approaches the level an NPV analysis would yield, killing in effect the option value of waiting. The size of the impact of uncertain time of maturity will depend on the distribution of maturity, mean, and variance. The higher the volatility, (that is, the more uncertain the time to maturity is), the more the lower and the upper border of the option space converge, until they finally collapse at the NPV figure. For real options, the uncertainty of the maturity time stems from a variety of sources, the most obvious being competitive entry that kills significant option value.

Assume that management has an opportunity to invest $100 million in a new product line that has a probability of 50% to create cash flows with a present value of $500 million for the expected lifetime at the time of product launch. In the worst case scenario, the present value of those revenue streams at time of product launch will be only $200 million. Management envisions four scenarios as to the time frame necessary to complete the development of its new product line, as summarized in Figure 4.7.

Please note that we do not include in the analysis that the time to maturity will also affect the revenue stream: the sooner the product reaches the market, the more cash flow will be generated. To strictly investigate the effect of time uncertainty we assume that the amount of cash flow generated will not change as a function of the timing of product launch. Table 4.1 summarizes the basic parameters to calculate the call option. We give the value of the call assuming a certain time to maturity of four years.

As time is uncertain, there is for each of the four scenarios a distinct probability to complete the program and launch the product at any given time. For example, for scenario 1, the probability to complete after 2 years, 3 years, 4 years, 5 years, or 6 years is 20% for each. On the contrary, for scenario 2, the likelihood to complete the project in 2 years is only 3%, while

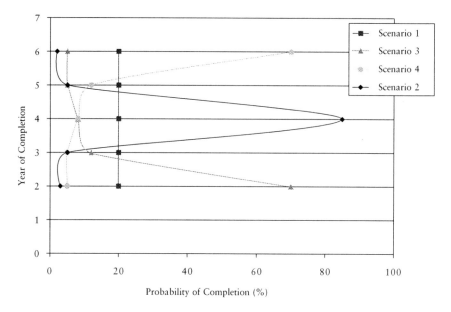

FIGURE 4.7 Time to maturation scenarios for a new-product development program

at a probability of 85% the product will be completed after four years. To acknowledge uncertainty of time to maturity in the calculation of the option value for the four different scenarios, we need to incorporate the probability function of completion when discounting the option value to today's

TABLE 4.1 The basic call option parameters—without time uncertainty

Basic Option Parameters	
WACC	13.50%
Risk-Free Rate	7%
q	0.5
Expected Value	350
Max Value	500
Min Value	200
Cost	100
p	0.581666667
t (years)	4
Call	185.70

time. The formula below shows the calculation: The probability q to complete the project for each time scenario t_2 to t_5 goes into the denominator to acknowledge the expected time to completion when discounting the option value:

$$C_x = \frac{p \cdot V_{max} + (1-p) \cdot V_{min}}{q_{t2x}(1+r)^2 + q_{t3x} \cdot (1+r)^3 + q_{t4x} \cdot (1+r)^4 + q_{t5x} \cdot (1+r)^5}$$

This gives us the following results for the call option for each time scenario as summarized in Table 4.2.

There is a substantial difference in option value between the four scenarios investigated. This is to a large degree explained by the fact that the expected time to completion for each scenario is different, thus yielding significant sooner or significant later cash streams that will alter the option value simply because of the time value of money. Table 4.3 summarizes the expected time to completion for each scenario.

By fixing the expected time to completion to four years but varying the variance, we eliminate the effect of the time value of money and see the effect of time volatility. Figure 4.8 depicts on the left panel four different time scenarios, all of which have an expected time to completion of four years, and on the right panel the corresponding value of the call options.

The effect of increasing the volatility of time to maturity is small but noticeable. The value of the call option is highest in the absence of time uncertainty (scenario 5) and lowest if the variance of the time to maturity ranges between 1 and 7 periods (scenario 4). Note that the analysis has not included the effect of uncertain time to maturity on the opportunity cost of capital. However, the analysis also shows that time uncertainty has a significant ef-

TABLE 4.2 The option value under time uncertainty

	Value of the Call Option			
Timing Scenario	1	2	3	4
Call Value ($ m)	184.40	185.90	212.48	159.68

TABLE 4.3 Expected time to completion under four product development scenarios

	Expected Time to Completion (years)			
Timing Scenario	1	2	3	4
Expected Time	4.00	3.98	2.63	5.37

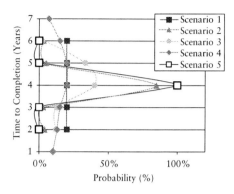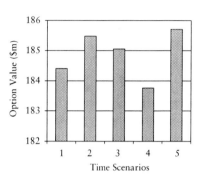

FIGURE 4.8 Time uncertainty and option value

fect on option value only if it alters the expected time to completion or maturity time.

Time to maturity not only impacts on option value, but also on the critical cost to invest: The farther out the cash flow stream, the smaller its today's value, and hence the sooner the option is out of the money. The higher the uncertainty as to when cash flow will materialize, the lower investment costs should be not to move the option out of the money. Similarly, the higher the uncertainty surrounding time to maturity or project completion, the higher the critical asset value needs to become to justify investing the anticipated costs without moving the option out of the money. Figure 4.9 shows for the five different timing scenarios and an expected asset value of $350 million the critical cost to invest. If management were to invest more than the critical cost, the investment option would move out of the money.

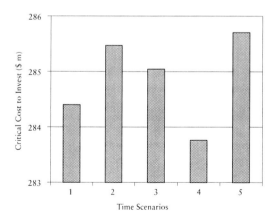

FIGURE 4.9 The critical cost to invest under time uncertainty

In the absence of time to maturity uncertainty (scenario 5), the critical cost to invest is highest. As the volatility of timing increases, the critical cost that management should be prepared to invest in the project declines. It is lowest for scenario 4, which has the highest time to completion volatility.

Previously, when looking at the effect of market variability, we saw how the sensitivity of the option value changes depending on whether the option is at the money or deep in the money. We will now investigate the sensitivity of the call option to time uncertainty depending on whether the option is at the money or in the money. In the example given in Figure 4.10, we reduce the maximum asset value from $500 million (see Table 4.1) and allow it to vary between $200 million and $300 million. We first calculate the value of the option for this range of best case scenarios under each time uncertainty scenario. The results are summarized in Figure 4.10.

The time uncertainty scenarios are arranged in such a way that the time volatility declines from left to right. At a maximum asset value of $200 million, the option is just at the money for all time uncertainty scenarios; at a maximum asset value of $300 million, the option is deep in the money. For all best case market payoff assumptions, a decline in time volatility (moving

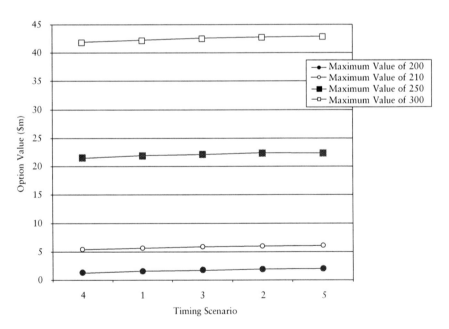

FIGURE 4.10 Option value sensitivity to time uncertainty for at- and in-the-money options

from left to right on the *x*-axis) appears to do little to the overall option value.

We now examine the effect of time uncertainty in more detail by looking at the change in option value for each of the future payoff scenarios as a percentage of the base-line option value under no time uncertainty (scenario 5). Figure 4.11 summarizes the data.

High time uncertainty changes the option value significantly for an option that is at the money. For example, for a maximum future payoff of $200 million the option value under high time uncertainty in scenario 4 is reduced by 34% compared to the option value under no time uncertainty. For a less volatile scenario, such as scenario 2, the value difference for an at the money option is only 4.4%. As the expected future payoff increases and the option moves more and more into the money, the option value becomes less sensitive even to significant time uncertainty. At a future payoff of $300 million, with the option deep in the money, even high time uncertainty (scenario 4) does little to change the value of the option. The option value under high time uncertainty (scenario 4) is reduced by 2.2% compared to the conditions

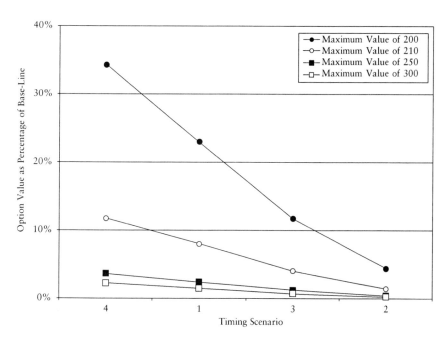

FIGURE 4.11 Option value loss under time uncertainty for at- and in-the-money options

without time uncertainty. As time volatility declines, moving on the x-axis from left to right, its impact on option value becomes less and less material, irrespective as to whether the option is at the money or deep in the money.

What is the implication for management? Time uncertainty becomes more critical to understand and control as the option is at the money than for a call option deep in the money. However, time uncertainty is not very material as long as the expected time to maturation does not change. Management may want to invest in learning and controlling time uncertainty for call options at the money but should be less inclined to do so for call options deep in the money, unless the expected time to maturity can be shortened to capture the time value of money and/or some preemptive value.

REAL PUT OPTIONS WITH UNCERTAIN TIME TO MATURITY

Uncertain time to maturity may also refer to the length of time a real put option is viable for the holder of an asset for which market conditions deteriorate. For example, the sudden entry of a competitor may terminate or significantly diminish the current cash flow from an existing asset prematurely or alter its value considerably. This situation is comparable to an American put on a dividend-paying stock.

The company receives a constant dividend, namely, the cash flows generated by the asset. However, it is unclear when the asset may move out of the money and the revenue stream dies off or reaches such a low level that the operation becomes unprofitable. How do we value real put options when time to maturity is unknown, or at least very uncertain?

Let's start with a simple example. Management owns an asset that creates $200 million in value. Management believes that a competitive entry will happen, but the time frame is uncertain. If it happens, the maximum value to be generated from the existing asset may still stay at $200 million in value in the best case scenario, or drop to $30 million in the worst case scenario. Each scenario is equally likely (i.e., q is 50%). Management can abandon fixed assets related to the product against a salvage price of $130 million as soon as a competitive entry becomes certain. This price reflects management assumptions about the outstanding value of the fixed assets over their remaining lifetime. What is the value of this put option?

Initially, we determine the put option value by assuming that the anticipated competitive entry and decline will happen with certainty four years from now. The exercise price for the put is today's value for the revenues foregone over the remaining lifetime of the asset. The value of the underlying asset is the salvage price management expects to receive when selling the asset. In this scenario we are valuing a put with a determined asset value but uncertain exercise price. The equation to calculate the value of the put is:

$$P = \frac{S_v - [p \cdot K_{max} + (1 - p) \cdot K_{min}]}{(1 + r)^t}$$

with S_v denoting the salvage value of $130 million and K_{max} and K_{min} denoting the maximum and minimum revenue stream foregone when exercising the put option on the asset, equivalent to the exercise price. Table 4.4 shows the basic put option parameters and the put value for the basic scenario.

We now introduce uncertainty to the time of maturity. We use the same assumptions as for the call option in the previous section. These assumptions reflect management's beliefs as to when the drop in asset value will occur. These sets of assumptions yield, as shown before, a disparate set of expected times to maturity, shown on the left panel of Table 4.5, and a mean time to maturity set fixed at four years (mean) but with smaller or larger variance. To acknowledge uncertainty of the time to maturity we calculate the value of the put option—as was done before for the call option—by incorporating the probability q for each time scenario t_2 to t_5 using the following formula:

$$P = \frac{S_v - [p \cdot K_{max} + (1 - p) \cdot K_{min}]}{q_{t2}(1 + r)^2 + q_{t3} \cdot (1 + r)^3 + q_{t4} \cdot (1 + r)^4 + q_{t5} \cdot (1 + r)^5}$$

Using this formula, we arrive at the following values for the put option under the different timing conditions, summarized in Table 4.5.

TABLE 4.4 The basic put option parameters—without time uncertainty

WACC	13.50%
Risk-Free-Rate	7%
q	0.5
Expected Value	115
Max Cost K	200
Min Cost K	30
Salvage Value	130
p	0.54735
t (years)	4
Put	$5.30

TABLE 4.5 The value of the put option under time uncertainty

Expected Time of Maturity (years)				Expected Time to Maturity (years)				
1	2	3	4	1	2	3	4	5
4.00	3.98	2.63	5.37	4.00	4.00	4.00	4.00	4.00

Value of the Put Option				Value of the Put Option				
1	2	3	4	1	2	3	4	5
5.28	5.31	5.80	4.82	5.28	5.30	5.29	5.27	5.30

The way this scenario is set up for the put option, both the asset value (that is, the salvage value) and the exercise price (that is, the present value of the revenue stream) are subjected to the time uncertainty, as management will make the decision to abandon the project at the time point of competitive entry, and that time point is subject to uncertainty. This set up is different from the previous example, which looked at the value of the call option under time uncertainty. There, the timing of the exercise price (that is, the commitment of the investment costs K) was fixed and not subject to uncertainty.

This explains why we do not see for this put scenario the same degree of change in value of the put, as the expected time to maturity changes between 2.63 and 5.37 years (left panel, Table 4.5 above). This reflects that time uncertainty in this scenario is the same for both asset value as well as exercise price, and is therefore perfectly correlated. A positive correlation, as we have discussed in Chapter 2, provides a hedge but reduces overall volatility and thereby the option value. As with the call option, we note for the put option that the value decreases the farther out the time to maturity lies. We further see qualitatively that uncertainty in the timing of expiration has the same effect on the put option as on the call option: The more certain the time is (scenario 5), the higher the value of the put option; the more volatile the time is, the lower the value of the put option (scenario 4). The quantitative difference, however, is less pronounced for the put option in the chosen set up than for the call option in the previous example as cost and asset volatility are perfectly correlated.

We will now introduce an example in which the salvage price is fixed today but the exercise price is subjected to uncertain time to expiration. Imagine that management has the option to abandon the asset today against a salvage price of $130 million. Management has some beliefs as to when competitive entry will occur, leading to the projected decline in asset value, but there is uncertainty about the exact timing. As done previously with the call option example, we will ignore the effect that uncertain timing has on the revenue stream to separate out market uncertainty from timing uncertainty in the valuation of this put option.

The value of the put option for this set up is calculated using the following equation:

$$P = S_v - \frac{p \cdot K_{max} + (1 - p) \cdot K_{min}}{(1 + r)^t}$$

Table 4.6 summarizes the basic option parameters as well as the value of the put option for a time to expiration fixed at four years.

We now study the effect of uncertain time to maturity by expanding the formula for the put for this set up, as shown in the following equation:

$$P = S_v - \frac{p \cdot K_{max} + (1 - p) \cdot K_{min}}{q_{t2}(1 + r)^2 + q_{t3} \cdot (1 + r)^3 + q_{t4} \cdot (1 + r)^4 + q_{t5} \cdot (1 + r)^5}$$

Management's beliefs as to the timing scenarios are the same as shown for the call option, which gives rise to the following put option values, summarized in Table 4.7. As we have seen for the value of the call option under uncertain time to maturity, we also see for the put option in this set up that

TABLE 4.6 The basic put option parameters—with fixed expected time to maturity

Basic Put Option	
WACC	13.50%
Risk-Free-Rate	7%
q	0.5
Expected Value	115
Max Cost	200
Min Cost	30
Salvage Value	130
p	0.5474
t (years)	4
Put	$36.13

TABLE 4.7 The value of the put option under increasing time volatility

Expected Time of Maturity (years)					Expected Time to Maturity (years)				
1	2	3	4		1	2	3	4	5
4.00	3.98	2.63	5.37		4.00	4.00	4.00	4.00	4.00
Value of the Put Option ($m)					Value of the Put Option ($m)				
1	2	3	4		1	2	3	4	5
36.55	36.06	27.33	44.68		36.55	36.20	36.34	36.76	36.13

the value of the option is most sensitive to changes in the expected time to expiration. However, contrary to what we have seen with the call option, the value of the put option in this set up declines as the expected time to expiration shortens.

For example, with an expected time to expiration of 2.63 years, the value of the put option is $27.33 million, while for an expected time to expiration of 5.37 years, the value of the put option is $44.68 million. For a short expected time to maturity the value of the asset is higher simply because of the time value of money. So, giving it up against the salvage price implies a smaller payoff. As time moves on, today's value of the asset declines, and the payoff from salvage at a price fixed today goes up. What is the intuition? Remember, we assume the overall cash flow that management expects still to be generated by the fixed assets to be at best $200 million and at worst $30 million. It is unclear, though, whether this cash flow will be generated over an expected time of maturity of 2.63 years (scenario 3) or over 5.37 years (scenario 4). In scenario 3, the time value of revenues foregone today, at the time management contemplates salvaging the fixed assets against $130 million, is $102.67 million; in scenario 4 it is $85.32 million. The value of abandoning the fixed assets today is smaller if revenues foregone can be cashed out quickly, while an asset with a protracted but low revenue stream has a higher abandonment option value.

Also, for this put option set up, the effect of time volatility is opposite that which we saw for the call option, as shown in the right-hand panel of Figure 4.8. Remember that here the expected time to expiration is fixed at four years, but the volatility varies. With certain time to maturity of 4 years (scenario 5, right-hand panel), the value of the put is lowest. As volatility of timing increases, the value of the put also increases. It is highest for scenario 4, which captures the most volatile timing assumptions. The call option, as we have seen before, behaves in an opposite manner: the less volatile the timing to maturity becomes, the more the call option increases in value.

TECHNOLOGY UNCERTAINTY

Many firms not only have to question the timing and sizing of their investments in new-product development but also examine carefully in what technology to invest at what point in time, given that technologies in most industries undergo rapid advancements. A computer maker will have to consider which technology to implement in his latest models and whether he may be better off waiting another year or two, until an even better technology becomes available for his products. On the other hand, discoveries happen randomly, and regularly there is little or no correlation between the resources put into research and the creation of an asset that will result in a profitable cash flow. As Weeds points out:[4] "When the firm exercises its option to invest in research it gains a second option, that of making the discovery itself, whose exercise time occurs randomly rather than being a single date chosen explicitly by the firm." This situation of technical uncertainty may provide an additional incentive to defer an investment.

Let's examine how such a scenario can be modeled in a binomial option model. We assume that a firm faces the decision either to adopt an existing technology today for its next generation of products, or to wait until the new technology arrives at a yet unknown time. Management assumes that the firm can use either the existing technology 1 or a future technology 2 whose arrival date is uncertain. Once the current technology 1 is adopted, the firm foregoes the option to adopt any new technology for a period of three years. This time frame reflects management's assumptions about development times as well as product life expectancy in a competitive market.

Technology 1 is already developed and in place; there is no technical risk associated with the implementation of technology 1. Technology 2, however, still needs to be implemented and there is some uncertainty as to whether the firm will be able to do so.

For now we do ignore the competitive environment for this decision, but we will relax this assumption later. Whether management is better off to implement technology 1 now or to wait for technology 2 is likely to be influenced by management's beliefs about the following parameters:

* The importance of the new technology for sustaining or expanding existing market share.
* The costs and time frame of implementing the new technology.
* The private probability q of being successful in implementing the new technology.
* The opportunity cost foregone due to waiting for the arrival of technology 2 if technology 1 is not implemented.

We will provide a binomial model that allows incorporating and varying all these parameters. Figure 4.12 shows the binomial framework.

Management initiates an intensive discussion internally with engineers, scientists, and the product development team, as well as the marketing team, and also spends resources on primary and secondary market research and some competitive intelligence to better define the environmental conditions for this investment decision. As a result of these initiatives, the company comes up with the following set of consensus assumptions.

Management assumes three different probability distributions to predict the arrival of technology 2. At yet uncertain costs, management will have the option to acquire technology 2 (node 1). The probabilities of success in implementing the technology and integrating it in the new product are still ill defined (node 2 and 3). However, if the company succeeds in implementing technology 2, there are three distinct probability distributions that depict the future market payoff (node 4 and 5). For the currently available technology 1, management believes that a product containing technology 1 will be less competitive and less likely to gain significant market share, but will also be cheaper as well as quicker to develop and bring to market. Management believes that it will cost $50 million to implement technology 1, that there will be no technical risk (technology probability of 100%; $q_6 = 1$), and that it will be able to develop and launch the product in one year. Management assumes three basic scenarios to reflect product penetration using the currently avail-

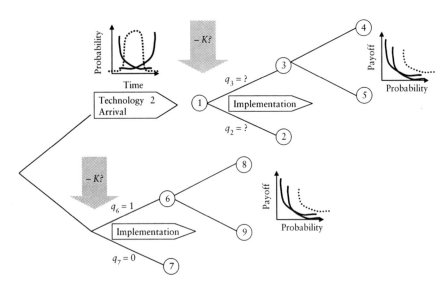

FIGURE 4.12 The binomial asset tree for technology uncertainty

able technology 1, each of which is equally likely ($q = 0.333$). These scenarios are driven by other uncertainties such as the competitive environment and overall global economic situation that affect demand. Management also assumes that peak market penetration will be reached in year 6 and decline thereafter. The overall market size lies somewhere between $500 million in annual revenue as the best case scenario and $200 million in revenue as the worst case scenario for the product. The probability q for the best case scenario is 0.7, and 0.3 correspondingly for the worst case scenario. Table 4.8 summarizes management's assumptions about market penetration scenarios for a product containing technology 1 and future revenue streams.

The expected value generated from the asset in year 1 is the present value of these revenue streams weighted for their probability of occurrence (that is, 0.7 for the best case (BC) scenario, 0.3 for the worst case (WC) scenario, and 0.333 for each of the market penetration scenarios (S1, S2, S3).

$$V_{exp} = [\ 0.7 \cdot (0.333\ BC - S_1 + 0.3333\ BC - S_2 + 0.333 \cdot BC - S_3) + 0.3 \cdot (0.3333\ WC - S_1 + 0.3333 \cdot WC - S_2 + 0.33333 \cdot WC - S_3)]$$

TABLE 4.8 Basic market uncertainties: Penetration scenarios and future revenue stream scenarios for a product with technology 1

	Market Penetration		
Time of Entry (years)	1 (%)	2 (%)	3 (%)
1	5	3	1
2	8	5	2
3	15	8	4
4	20	10	8
5	27	15	10

Revenue Stream Scenarios		Year 2	Year 3	Year 4	Year 5	Year 6	q
Best Case	Scenario						
	1	25	40	75	100	135	0.333
	2	15	25	40	50	75	0.333
	3	5	10	20	40	50	0.333
Worst Case	Scenario						
	1	10	16	30	40	54	0.333
	2	6	10	16	20	30	0.333
	3	2	4	8	16	20	0.333

TABLE 4.9 The call option value for
technology 1 in the absence of private risk

Probability of Technical Success	100%
Expected Value	$90.96
V_{max}	$129.95
V_{min}	51.98
p	0.58167
Call	$20.60

The maximum asset value is derived from assuming that the overall
market size will be the best case scenario (i.e., $500 million); the minimum
asset value correspondingly derives from assuming that the worst case market size will materialize. For each, the revenue streams for the different scenarios with their corresponding probability of occurrence (0.3333) will be
added up. These assumptions translate into the following parameters, shown
in Table 4.9 for the call option on investing into technology 1, assuming
there is no risk of technical failure.

For the arrival of technology 2, management envisions three different
timing scenarios. Those assumptions are summarized in Figure 4.13, with
the time of arrival on the x-axis and the probability of arrival on the y-axis.
The probability of actually succeeding in implementing the new technology
for its product is thought to range between 50% and 85%.

Management further assumes that the overall market size for the product, $500 million in the best case scenario and $200 million in the worst case
scenario, will be independent of its decision to implement technology 1 or
technology 2. Management also assumes that the probability of reaching the
best case scenario is 70%, while the probability for the worst case scenario is

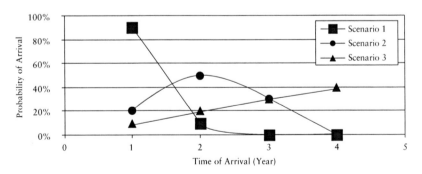

FIGURE 4.13 New technology arrival scenarios

30%. However, the market penetration is thought to be more aggressive for a product with technology 2, yielding ultimately a higher revenue stream. There is no expectation that the market potential will expand with the new technology. Table 4.10 summarizes managerial assumptions and the anticipated revenue streams resulting from launching a product with technology 2.

The expected value generated from the asset in year 2 is—as was outlined above for the technology 1 product—the present value of these revenue streams weighted for their probability of occurrence (that is, 0.7 for the best case scenario, 0.3 for the worst case scenario, and 0.333 for each of the market penetration scenarios).

$$V_{exp} = [\ 0.7 \cdot (0.333\ BC - S_1 + 0.3333\ BC - S_2 + 0.333 \cdot BC - S_3) + 0.3 \cdot (0.3333\ WC - S_1 + 0.3333 \cdot WC - S_2 + 0.33333 \cdot WC - S_3)]$$

The expected value of the future asset to be generated by technology 2 is in addition a function of the timing and probability of technology 2 arrival, the technical probability to succeed in implementing it, and the future market payoff scenarios. We multiply the expected value as calculated above

TABLE 4.10 Basic market uncertainties: Penetration scenarios and future revenue stream scenarios for a product with technology 2

Time of Entry (years)	Market Penetration		
	1 (%)	2 (%)	3 (%)
2	15	5	3
3	25	10	5
4	35	15	8
5	45	25	12
6	50	35	18

Revenue Stream Scenarios		Year 2	Year 3	Year 4	Year 5	Year 6	q
Best Case	Scenario						
	1	75	125	175	225	250	0.333
	2	25	50	75	125	175	0.333
	3	15	25	40	60	90	0.333
Worst Case	Scenario						
	1	30	50	70	90	100	0.333
	2	10	20	30	50	70	0.333
	3	6	10	16	24	36	0.333

by the probability of technical arrival. We acknowledge the probability distribution of technology 2 arrival by discounting for the respective number of years at the corporate cost of capital.

The expected value, assuming 100% technical success, is $206.83 million. In scenario 1, there is a 90% probability for the new technology to arrive in year 1 and a 10% probability for it to arrive in year 2. The expected value hence is:

$$EV_1 = \frac{0.9 \cdot 206.83}{1.135^1} + \frac{0.1 \cdot \$206.83 \text{ million}}{1.135^2} + \frac{0 \cdot 206.83}{1.135^3} + \frac{0 \cdot \$206.83 \text{ million}}{1.135^4}$$

$$= \$180.06 \text{ million}$$

The maximum asset value is derived from assuming that the overall market size will be the best case scenario (that is, $500 million), that technology 2 will arrive instantly and be implemented within 2 years, and that the technical probability of implementing it is 100%. The minimum asset value correspondingly derives from assuming that the worst case market size will materialize. The technical success probability is lowest (50%) and it may take as long as four years for the technology to arrive. For each, the revenue streams for the different scenarios with their corresponding probability of occurrence (0.3333) will be added up.

This calculation gives the following results for the expected value under the three different technology arrival scenarios for four different sets of assumptions about the technical probability of success, assuming that each of the market payoff scenarios will materialize at an equal probability of 33%. The results are summarized in Table 4.11.

TABLE 4.11 Asset value and risk-neutral probability p under private risk and uncertain technology arrival timing

Probability of Technical Success	100%	85%	75%	50%
Expected Value				
Scenario 1	$180.06	$153.05	$135.05	$90.03
Scenario 2	$159.16	$135.29	$119.37	$79.58
Scenario 3	$142.62	$121.23	$106.97	$71.31
V_{max}	$252.23	$252.23	$252.23	$252.23
V_{min}	$30.40	$30.40	$30.40	$30.40
p				
Scenario 1	0.8606	0.7110	0.6112	0.3618
Scenario 2	0.7315	0.6012	0.5144	0.2972
Scenario 3	0.6307	0.5155	0.4387	0.2468

Those data translate into the following call valuations, as summarized in Figure 4.14. The solid line indicates the value of the call of investing in technology 1. It defines the boundary below which investing in technology 1 is the better option for management.

This basic set up now gives management a tool for investigating how changes in the basic assumption affect the value of each option as well as their relation to each other. Specifically, it defines under which set of assumptions waiting for the arrival of technology 2 is the more valuable option.

The declining option value for technology 2 under the various arrival scenarios, but for the same probability of technical success, mostly reflects the fact that the expected time of technology arrival is distinct: 1.1 year for scenario 1, 2 years for scenario 2, and 3.10 years for scenario 3. The declining option value is thus likely to reflect the time value of money. To obtain a better understanding of the impact of technology arrival volatility, we will now set the expected time to be fixed but increase the variance. Figure 4.15 gives two scenarios and the respective call value.

In scenario 1, the technology arrival has a higher volatility than in scenario 2; both have an expected technology arrival time frame of 2.5 years. Under scenario 1 the value of the call option is higher. Hence, increasing the technology arrival uncertainty increases the value of the option. The intuition

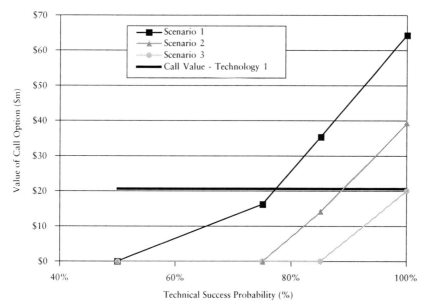

FIGURE 4.14 Call option value under private risk and uncertain technology arrival timing

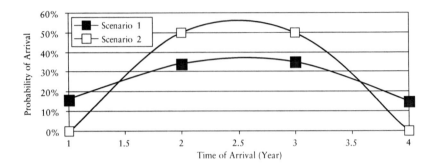

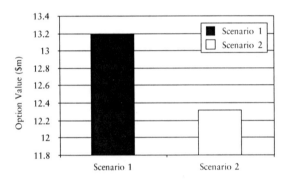

FIGURE 4.15 Call option value under increasing technology uncertainty

is that, with increasing arrival volatility, the potential upside (that is, early arrival of the new technology) also increases, yielding a higher option value.

NOTES

1. A. Huchzermeier and C.H. Loch, "Evaluating R&D Projects as Learning Options: Why More Variability Is Not Always Better," in H. Wildemann, ed., *Produktion und Controlling* (München: TCW Transfer Centrum Verlag, 1999, 185–197).
2. P. Carr, "Randomization and the American Put," *Review of Financial Studies* 11:597, 1998.
3. T. Berrada, *Valuing Real Options When Time to Maturity Is Uncertain* (Third Real Option Conference, 1999).
4. H. Weeds, "Reverse Hysteresis: R&D Investments with Stochastic Innovation," working paper, 1999.

CHAPTER 5

A Strategic Framework for Competitive Scenarios

GAME THEORY AND REAL OPTIONS

Much of the original success and application of the real option concept was driven by the insight that traditional NPV analysis undervalues embedded growth options. In fact, the DCF methodology was accused of inviting management to use hurdle rates exceeding the cost of capital. According to the reasoning at the time, this drove many attractive but very risky investments into negative NPV figures and discouraged management from investing in innovative but risky projects. Ultimately, a decline in R&D spending was lamented and it was feared that the decline jeopardized the competitive advantage of U.S. industry across many sectors.[1] Misuse of DCF, in short, was made responsible for the decline of American industry.

Subsequently, McDonald and Siegel, Dixit and Pinyck, Majd, and others generated the insight that—on the other hand—NPV valuation motivates making investments in very uncertain and risky projects too early and ignores the premium that should be paid for committing and thus giving up flexibility, the option premium. And yet, as of today, the body of the real option work is biased towards the analysis of decision scenarios in which the owner of the option is in a monopoly position. Here, by definition, strategy has no role, and the actions of the monopolist do not impact on price or on market structure. Obviously, few scenarios in the real world meet these criteria.

The majority of managerial decisions are influenced by strategic considerations that include possible competitive entry or the value of preemption. Creating or having flexibility in these situations can be of great value to any given firm. How can one identify the right timing of an investment? When can one afford to delay without losing a valuable strategic position or market share? And when does one have to invest early and accept the higher risks in order to create a strong strategic position? How does one value an option when time to maturity is uncertain, that is, when a competitor enters and kills the option?

These questions touch on the valuation of shared options, options that emerge and expire and alter in value as competitors enter or exit the market place and change the market dynamics, as well as options that are designed to affect the competitor's behavior.

A key tool to use for competitive and strategic analysis is game theory. It examines questions of strategic advantage and preemption. Married with real option analysis, it allows us to derive insights as to how those strategic considerations are altered by both technical and market uncertainty.

There are four basic categories of games: static and dynamic games, with complete or incomplete information. In a static game, both players act simultaneously and choose their strategies from a set of feasible actions. In a complete information scenario, the payoff functions of each player are common knowledge. In mathematical terms, such a scenario is characterized by a Nash equilibrium. Here, none of the players wants to change the predicted strategy, which creates an inefficient situation best described by the prisoner's dilemma. Figure 5.1 shows an example of a prisoner's dilemma.

Firm A has the opportunity to invest in a new technology that would create a new software. It knows of at least one other player in the industry, firm B, which has the same investment opportunity. Firm A does not know firm B's strategy. If A invents a technology it will capture a market payoff of 5 if firm B also invents the same or a similar technology. If B chooses to withdraw and will not invent, firm A can enjoy a payoff of 10. If firm A does not invent, but B does, firm A is left with a payoff of 5. If it does not invent and B also does not invent, both will have a payoff of 10. There is no advantage to either decision for firm A.

In a dynamic game with complete information, one player acts first; the second player observes and then acts. Each player realizes his payoffs after

Firm A

		Invent	Do Not Invent
	Invent	5	5
Firm B	Do Not Invent	10	10

FIGURE 5.1 Prisoner's dilemma

all players have completed their actions. If incomplete information is introduced to these scenarios, then each player has exact knowledge about his own payoffs but not about the other player's payoffs. Such a situation is described as Bayesian. For example, each player is unlikely to know the exact production or distribution costs of the competitor. In a static scenario, players act simultaneously (static Bayesian), and each player follows his own beliefs about the other player's payoff when defining his actions.

In a dynamic game with incomplete information, we have what game theorists call a perfect Bayesian equilibrium. Each player has assumptions and beliefs regarding the payoffs and potential future actions of the other player. At each point in time, each player decides and his next step is based on those beliefs. He goes for what appears to him to be the optimal strategy. Each player realizes the ultimate payoff only after all players have completed their moves. Figure 5.2 displays a sequential game.

Firm A decides first to either invent or not to invent. Firm B then follows and either withdraws or invents, too. Each firm's moves are guided by their respective assumptions about the firm's internal capabilities and their beliefs about the capabilities and future actions of the other player. The ultimate payoffs will materialize only after all players have completed their respective moves.

The origins of game theory date back 2,500 years, and they lie in Chinese philosophy.[2] Knowledge in ancient Chinese philosophy was defined as the ability to map out a strategic situation, to envision how things will develop,

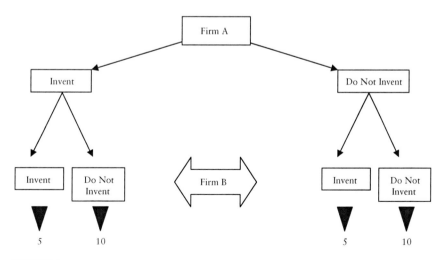

FIGURE 5.2 A dynamic game with incomplete information

and to "take care of the great while the great is still small." This approach, applied in ancient China to war tactics, was coined backward induction by game theorists. It refers to the ability to control future developments not only by understanding or foreseeing the dynamics but also by being able to control the dynamics. As the reader will appreciate, this concept of backward induction is well applied in the binomial option model. The only difference is that the intent from a managerial perspective is not always to control, but often just to respond and adopt in a value-preserving or value-enhancing fashion.

Let's adopt the sequential game framework for a compound option: Each step forward in a sequential compound option is conditional on the then-prevailing situation as well as managerial expectations of future developments. Management will assess the technical success of product development so far but also incorporate into any decision the current competitive environment as well as managerial anticipation as to what actions competitors may take, how governmental regulations may change, or how consumer demand may alter, and how these events would impact on the future market environment.

At each step management may decide to abandon, accelerate, or defer the decision and wait for further information to arrive, or for its competitor to yet complete another step. Likewise, management may choose actions purely to signal commitment in an attempt to deter competitors from taking certain steps.

The threat of competitive entry creates a trade-off decision between wanting to preserve flexibility in the face of uncertainty on one side and recognizing the need to invest early in order to create a strong competitive position. The initial work focuses on scenarios that play out in two distinct time periods.[3] Spencer and Brady[4] investigate in a duopoly situation the value of deferring compared to the strategic value of investing early. The authors develop a model to determine the timing of committing to an output decision and thus giving up flexibility as a function of uncertainty. Smit and Ankum,[5] in fact, made the first connections between the real option concept and game theory. They pioneered the pricing of the option to defer an investment or to expand under perfect competition, which by definition implies complete information. In essence, one must weigh the option to wait against the option to invest now to preempt and thereby create a first mover advantage and deter competitive entry. Specifically, the authors investigate the value of deferring the decision to expand production facilities against the risk to miss out on a revenue opportunity if demand rises to a level that cannot be satisfied with the existing production facility.

Other authors, including Smets[6] and Leahy[7] as well as Fries, Miller and Perraudin,[8] have studied the same problem but have used a continuous time framework to analyze option values in a perfectly competitive industry equilibrium. Smit and Trigeorgis[9] looked at strategic investments under competitive conditions using a binomial tree.

All of this work assumes both full information for each player as well as non-cooperative games. Lambrecht and Perraudin[10] were first to introduce incomplete information. In their option games, two players face interdependent payoffs but have asymmetric information, with each player knowing only his own cost structure and investment trigger, his critical cost to invest. The timing decision is uncertain. In other words, the authors model a Bayesian-Nash equilibrium in a real option framework. They also work on the assumption, similar to the strategic growth option we discussed earlier, that the investment is designed to create a strong preemptive position, thereby allowing patenting the invention and creating a monopoly situation for a limited period of time.

Empirical evidence supports the notion that in a highly competitive environment firms tend to make investments that preempt others from entering the same market. A survey conducted in the early '90s in the United Kingdom, for example, showed that managers often employ a diverse range of preemptive strategies in high-risk industries where a substantial amount of resources goes into research and product development.[11] Similarly, the acquisition of a technology platform company, instead of obtaining a license to certain aspects of the technology, can be driven by the need to deter competitors from accessing the same technology through similar licensing agreements. These investments are irreversible and the payoffs uncertain.

Lambrecht and Perraudin investigate how in a game-theoretic scenario incomplete information paired with the desire to create a strong, preemptive position destroys significant real option value. The authors argue that under incomplete information two competing firms have no understanding of the other firm's investment cost related to a new product development that provides an incentive to delay the investment. On the contrary, if the two firms were to have complete information about the other firm's investment costs and seek to preempt the competitor, this would result in lowering the threshold for investing and ultimately in destroying the value of the option to wait.

Lambrecht and Perraudin thus find that the average strategic trigger increases with uncertainty under incomplete information. In line with the classic option theory of Brennan and Schwartz or Dixit and Pindyck, an option premium is to be paid for keeping the option alive and waiting for uncertainty to be resolved. However, under competitive conditions, the investment trigger is much less sensitive to uncertainty and rises far less with increasing uncertainty. Competitive pressures, in other words, lower the critical hurdle to invest compared to a monopoly situation. The value of preemption is strongest in industries that create a strong position through patent position. In other instances, building a distribution channel may provide an equally strong preemptive position that is subject to erosion, although the precise timing and extent of that erosion may not be known.

Weeds examines a scenario similar to that of Lambrecht and Perraudin:[12] Two firms have the opportunity to invest in competing research projects. The winner will be awarded the patent, the loser will gain nothing. She argues that with the initiation of the investment by one firm, the competing firm sees the value of its option to defer the decision declining. With the investment there is a probability that a patentable discovery will be made. However, as discovery is accidental and not necessarily determined by the amount of resources or the time put into the research process, the risk of preemption is reduced. In fact, the competing firm may be reluctant to engage in a "race for patent" and defer the decision to invest. But it may observe its rival and come back into the patent race at a later time point. Weeds compares the decision to a long-distance race in which the runners run for a substantial part of the way in a pack, until shortly before the end the future winner breaks away. Such a behavior would argue for the notion that, even under competitive scenarios with the option to preempt, the value of the option to defer can be preserved.

Kulatilaka and Perotti[13] looked at the value of growth options under imperfect competition. They argue that an investment in a new technology, entering a new market, building a competitive distribution network, acquiring proprietary market knowledge, and customer access buy capabilities that strengthen the firm's positioning and facilitate opportunities to take much better advantage of future growth possibilities. For example, by investing in an information collection system on customer purchase habits and in building a very effective distribution system, Wal-Mart created a very strong capability, unmatched by its competitors at the time, that facilitated its rapid expansion throughout the U.S. The investment was irreversible, but the timing of it also created a strong competitive advantage and paved the way for future growth options. Investment in the same infrastructure at a later time point would likely have diminished the growth opportunity or killed it forever if snatched by a competitor. Taking advantage of a better position can take different directions: it may imply having a more efficient cost structure, a better distribution network, or a superior product. Each of those features provides the firm with an additional strategic value.

The analysis of Kulatilaka and Perotti suggests that under imperfect competition with asymmetric information, the effect of uncertainty on the relative value of strategic positioning through growth options is ambiguous and largely depends on the preemptive effect the investing firm believes to be achievable. If the preemptive effect results in a higher market share and also in a greater convexity of the ex post profit curve, the value of waiting to invest increases with greater uncertainty. However, the value of the growth option increases even more, making the option to invest in a pilot project more attractive than the option to wait as uncertainty increases. In other words, by incurring the opportunity costs associated with early commitment and acquisition of a time advantage the firm buys a strategic growth option, such as a dominant market position and a larger market share. The firm would forego this growth option by deferring the investment decision to solve uncertainty. So increasing uncertainty in a situation of irreversible investment with strategic behavior accelerates investment. The authors arrive at this conclusion because the returns of the first mover follow in their model a more convex function than those of the second mover, in line with standard economic analysis.

Some of these growth options, such as the Wal-Mart example, may exist only for a certain window of time and expire if not exercised during this time frame. This concept is related to the idea of core competence[14] or the notion of building a core capability by a platform investment.[15] Similarly, Zhu[16] looks at the value of competitive preemption and technology substitution in a game-theoretical model. His analysis also indicates that under competitive conditions the threshold to exercise the option rather than waiting declines. This promotes aggressive investment behavior but also reduces the value of the option.

The nature of information, too, is critical for the behavior of players in a game-theory scenario and therefore also for option analysis.[17] With symmetric information, the value of the American option is not changed. On the contrary, under asymmetric information the value of the investment opportunity really equals what in financial terms is called a pseudo-barrier option: The option is being exercised once a pre-determined barrier level is reached. The difference between the exercise trigger of both options, the pseudo-barrier option and the American option, is the cost of preemption the player has to pay to account for information asymmetry. For a player who expects a small loss in market share if she does not preempt, it is likely to be desirable to defer the investment decision if some of the prevailing uncertainty can be resolved. On the contrary, if management expects a large loss of market share and thereby perceives the value of preemption as high, the player might be tempted to invest early and therefore exercises her option early even if a significant amount of uncertainty remains unresolved at the time of exercise. The critical value to invest will differ for these two scenarios.

Grenadier[18] studied in the real estate market continuous-time leader-follower games in which each firm chooses a strategic trigger point for investment. He shows that if one assumes an industry equilibrium, the value of today's assets is driven not just by current supply and demand, but also by the pipeline of previous and ongoing constructions, creating a path dependency of the real option value. This pipeline of previous constructions, the "committed capacity" and the timing of projects under development, as Grenadier points out, drive the decision of any player in this industry to invest today in projects that will take some years to finish. Today's value of these projects depends on the market conditions prevailing upon completion. Today's decision of each individual player to enter the market and engage in the construction of new buildings is driven by today's assumption and information about the market dynamics. Future prices, on the contrary, will be a function of market clearance. Specifically, Grenadier also shows that the value of the option to wait goes out of the money under competitive pressure. Future prices of the real estate units are driven by the completed supply but also by the time of entry into the construction pipeline of future units. The important insight derived from Grenadier's study is that it, in fact, explains why we often observe waves of over-construction followed by waves of insufficient supply of real estate. Once there is unsatisfied demand for real estate, novel players are attracted by the market and enter based on the firm's individual assumptions of future rental prices and costs of construction. Entry into the market, therefore, is driven by assumptions about committed capacity and about the future equilibrium price, discounted back to today. Given that new players will be tempted to enter the market as long as they envision unsatisfied demand, the industry as a whole will always aim at equilibrium. To the individual firm, the value of the asset today is the present value of future cash flows upon completion minus the loss of value from the future increase in market supply delivered by pipeline constructions and future entries into the market minus the expenses to complete the construction. Because of the competitive nature of the industry, the best any firm can do is to invest when this equation is zero. This is the most important insight from the Grenadier study. As he notes, investing earlier or later than this drives the option out of the money; the competitive pressure destroys the value of the option to wait.

Most of these studies assume stochastic processes (such as log-normal behavior of returns and of underlying risk factors) and employ partial differential equations to solve for the critical value to invest, assuming a stochastic behavior for costs and for the expected value. We will adopt those concepts but use the binomial model to investigate competitive scenarios.

THE OPTION TO WAIT UNDER COMPETITIVE CONDITIONS

We start by examining the option to defer under competitive conditions. Intuitively and as suggested by the academic research reviewed above,[19] the value of waiting to invest is likely to decline if such a deferral not only permits but possibly invites a competitor to enter first and capture market share. Further, many large-scale projects take significant time to complete. An R&D program to develop a new drug takes up to seven years, building a major shopping mall or a high-rise office tower may require two years, and the construction of an underground mine may last five or six years. During those time frames, market conditions between initiating the project and completing it can fluctuate greatly. The drug manufacturer can face competitive entry of another compound equally effective for the same disease, the owner of the office towers may face an economic downturn or see other office towers rise in the same neighborhood, repressing future rents, and the mine company may face a downturn of natural resource prices.

To give an example, let's return to the car manufacturer introduced in Chapter 3. Assume that management has made a commitment to invest $100 million to develop a new prototype of a car. This new model can not only run with conventional gas but also use emerging alternative sources of energy. Management knows that its closest competitor also considers developing a car with similar features. Management is unsure how demand for the new car will unfold and whether or not it should also commit to an additional investment of $30 million or up to $50 million to build a manufacturing plant for the new car model. By deferring the decision to build the plant for two years after product launch, management will be in the position to observe market demand and identify the value-maximizing path forward: If demand is high, the plant will be built; if demand is low, management will outsource manufacturing. However, management also believes that its decision to build or not to build the plant will send a strong signal to its competitor and is likely to influence how its competitor will approach the entire product development program. After intense internal discussions and some secondary market research, the senior management team comes up with the binomial tree shown in Figure 5.3 to depict the various option scenarios management envisions.

If management decides to defer the decision to invest in the manufacturing plant now (node 1), its competitor could interpret that as a signal that management has little confidence in the market for the product and more confidence in the competitor's product. The competitor might be inclined to continue (node 2) or even accelerate (node 3) his own program. Alternatively, the competitor may consider that our management team has additional proprietary information about either technical feasibility or market conditions that prevent it from investing now. The competitor may now decide, too, to defer. Let us further assume that the probability of the competitor to pursue is 80%, while the probability that he will defer is 20% ($q_1 = 0.8$; $q_8 = 0.2$).

If the competitor were to continue with the program (node 2), he is likely to be able to produce at lower costs and therefore create a competitive advantage by giving part of that cost reduction to the customer. This, our

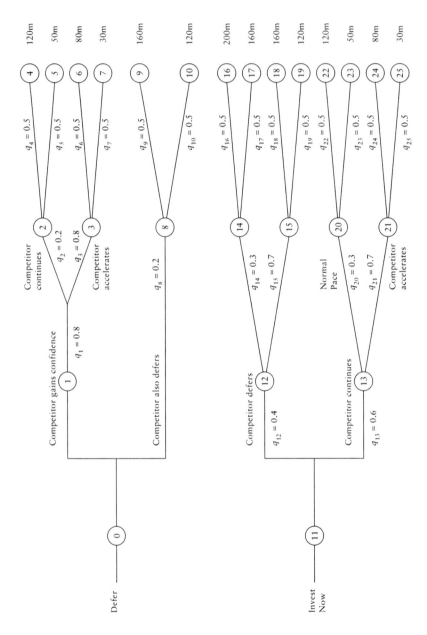

FIGURE 5.3 The binomial tree for the option to wait under competitive conditions

management team estimates, will result in a 10% loss of its own market share and also force them to offer the product at a price reduced by 5% compared to the price originally envisioned. Management assumes it will generate in the best case scenario $120 million and in the worst case scenario $50 million in annual revenue over a total of five years (node 4/5). Management assumes a 80% chance that the competitor may in fact accelerate his own program (node 3; $q_3 = 0.8$). If that is the case and the competitor reaches the market even quicker, management expects that its own revenues could fall to $80 million in the best case and $30 million in the worst case scenario (node 6/7). If the competitor were also to defer the decision (node 8), market conditions would not change. Our management team would keep the additional 10% market share and offer its product at the planned price. In this scenario, management expects annual revenues of $160 million in the best case and $120 million in the worst case (node 9/10) over a period of five years.

If, on the other hand, our management team decides to go ahead as planned and does not defer (node 11), its competitor may either defer or continue with its plan without change. Our management team assumes that there is a 40% chance that its competitor may defer ($q_{12} = 0.4$). If the competitor defers, there is a 30% ($q_{14} = 0.3$) chance that our car manufacturer—independent of market conditions—will increase its market share by 10% and also be able to offer its product at a 5% higher price, thereby creating an additional upside potential totaling $200 million in annual revenues, while also improving the worst case scenario to $160 million over seven years. As before, the probability of a best and a worst case scenario occurring is 50% each ($q_{16}/q_{17} = 0.5$). There is then also a 70% chance that such a deferral will not improve the market outlook ($q_{15} = 0.7$), leaving annual revenues at $160 million for the best case scenario and $120 million for the worst case scenario for the seven years of product lifetime (node 18/19).

Our management team further believes that with a likelihood of 60% ($q_{13} = 0.6$), its competitor will continue the program. If so, there is a 30% chance that it will continue at the current pace ($q_{20} = 0.3$), and a 70% chance that it will accelerate the program ($q_{21} = 0.7$). If the competitor continues at the same pace, there will be no change in the overall strategic conditions, and our expectations as to the final payoff functions are unchanged: $120 million revenue in the best case scenario and $50 million in the worst case scenario (node 22/23). If the competitor accelerates and enters the market first, then the outcome for our management team will be as discussed above for nodes 6 and 7, that is, the best case scenario will be no better than $80 million and the worst case scenario will be $30 million.

What shall our management team decide? Which of the options is the most valuable one?

We will approach the problem in three simple steps:

1. Calculate the option to invest in two years under competitive conditions.
2. Calculate the option to invest now under competitive conditions.
3. Calculate the value of the option to defer as the difference between option value 1 and option value 2.

Step 1

Under the deferral scenario starting at node 0, management hence has committed to the $100 million but defers the decision to build the plant at an additional cost of $30 to $50 million until market uncertainty has been resolved. The option value of deferring the decision for two years is driven by two components:

1. The signaling effect of delaying the decision to build the new plant on its competitor that has the potential to change market dynamics and thereby the asset value underlying the call on the entire development program, including the already committed $100 million to build the new prototype.
2. The value of resolving market uncertainty by deferring the decision to commit between $50 million and $30 million to build the plant and thereby choosing in two years from now the optimum value-maximizing path forward by either outsourcing or by building the new plant, depending on product demand.

Deferring the option to invest in the plant buys the contingent claim on the future revenue stream under the different competitive scenarios emerging from node 0 minus the revenue foregone due to outsourcing or the investment costs of building the plant later, whichever is the least expensive. This translates into the following data for the maximum and minimum as well as the expected asset value and the risk-neutral probability at nodes 2 and 3 for a range of distribution margins and for a presumed plant cost of $50 million, shown in Table 5.1.

The exercise price is the $100 million development costs. From there the value of the call option at nodes 2 and 3 is derived, shown for a plant cost of $50 million in Table 5.2 The value of the option to defer at node 0 is further driven by a 20% chance that the competitor may also defer (node 8). In this case management assumes that it will enjoy, with a 50% probability, the best case market payoff of $166 million in annual revenues (node 9) and with 50% probability the worst case market payoff (node 10) of $120 million in annual revenues. This gives rise to the following data for the best and

TABLE 5.1 The asset values at nodes 2 and 3 of the binomial asset tree

	Node 2			
	PV of the asset		Expected Value	
Margin (%)	50 ($)	120 ($)	($)	p
10	188.65	452.76	320.70	0.59
15	174.11	422.63	298.37	0.59
20	159.57	408.58	284.08	0.59
	Node 3			
	PV of the asset		Expected Value	
Margin (%)	30 ($)	80 ($)	($)	p
10	113.20	301.84	207.52	0.58
15	104.46	278.57	191.51	0.58
20	95.74	255.31	175.52	0.58

TABLE 5.2 The option values at nodes 2 and 3 of the binomial asset tree

Option Value at Node 2		Option Value at Node 3	
Margin (%)	$K = 100 + 50$ ($)	Margin (%)	$K = 100 + 50$ ($)
10	182.77	10	77.48
15	161.99	15	77.48
20	148.70	20	77.48

worst case market payoff scenarios as well as the expected case for the range of assumed distribution margins and also permits us to calculate the value of the option at node 8, shown in Table 5.3 for a $50 million plant cost.

We can then proceed to calculate the option value to defer at node 0. The best case scenario asset value is the expected value at node 1, which in turn is determined by the probability q of 20% of achieving the expected payoff at node 2 ($q_2 = 0.2$) or probability q_3 of 80% of achieving the expected value at node 3. So, for example, for the 15% distribution margin the best case asset value is $298.37 million, the expected value at node 2 for 15% margin, as shown in Table 5.1. The worst case value is similarly the expected value at node 3, and this is for a 15% distribution margin, the $191.51 million, as shown in Table 5.1. This gives an expected asset value at node 1 for a 15% distribution margin and $50 million projected plant costs of $0.2 \cdot 298.37 + 0.8 \cdot 191.51 = 212.89$. The data are summarized in Table 5.4.

TABLE 5.3 The asset and option value at node 8

	PV of the asset		Expected Value	
	Node 8			
Margin (%)	120 ($)	160 ($)	($)	p
10	452.76	603.68	528.22	0.76
15	422.63	582.77	502.70	0.74
20	408.58	564.04	486.31	0.73

Option Value at Node 8	
Margin (%)	$K = 100 + 50$ ($)
10	375.80
15	352.07
20	336.82

TABLE 5.4 The asset value at node 1

	PV of the asset		Expected Value
	Node 1		
Margin (%)	V_{max} ($)	V_{min} ($)	($)
10	320.70	207.52	230.16
15	298.37	191.51	212.89
20	284.08	175.52	197.24

The expected value at node 0 is correspondingly derived from the probability at node 1, assumed to be 80% for the competitor to go ahead and 20% at node 8 also to defer the decision ($q_8 = 0.2$) now. The expected value at node 0, V_{0E}, then becomes for the 15% distribution margin:

$$V_{0E} = 0.8 \cdot 212.89 + 0.2 \cdot 502.70 = 270.85$$

Correspondingly, we calculate p using the standard formula:

$$p = \frac{(1 + r) \cdot V_{0E} - V_{min}}{V_{max} - V_{min}}$$

$$p = \frac{(1 + 7.5\%) \cdot 270.85 - 212.89}{502.70 - 212.89} = 0.27$$

TABLE 5.5 The option value at node 0

	Option Value at Node 0		
Margin (%)	Expected Value ($)	p	$K = 100 + 50$ ($)
10	289.77	0.273	153.99
15	270.85	0.270	136.39
20	255.05	0.266	121.69

The value of the call option at node 0 for the option to invest in two years from now under competitive conditions for a plant cost of $50 million and a 15% outsourcing margin is calculated as follows:

$$C_1 = \frac{p \cdot V_{max} + (1 - p) \cdot V_{min}}{(1 + r_f)^2} - 100 \cdot (1 + r_{WACC})^2$$

For example, for a 15% distribution margin the value of the call, assuming that development costs of $100 million have already been committed:

$$C_1 = \frac{0.27 \cdot 502.70 + 0.73 \cdot 212.89}{1.07^2} - 115.56 = 136.39$$

The option to invest $100 million now and defer the decision to invest $50 million two years after product launch under competitive conditions is worth $136.39 million.

Table 5.5 summarizes the results for all distribution margins. The option at node 0 is in the money for all scenarios. This analysis concludes step 1.

Step 2

In step 2, we determine the value of the option to invest now under competitive conditions. Like always, we roll up the binomial tree backwards and start by calculating the asset values as well as the option values for node 14 and 15, which allows us to calculate the option value at node 12. Table 5.6 summarizes the data and the procedure. Remember, under this scenario the total costs of $100 million for prototype development and $50 million for building the plant are committed at node 11.

We then in a similar fashion calculate asset value and option value at nodes 20 and 21 and subsequently at node 13, as summarized in Table 5.7.

TABLE 5.6 How to calculate asset and option value at node 12

Node 14

| | PV of Asset | | Expected | |
Margin (%)	160 ($)	200 ($)	Value ($)	p
10	627.07	783.84	705.45	0.838
15	592.23	740.29	666.26	0.838
20	557.39	696.74	627.06	0.838

Node 15

| | PV of Asset | | Expected | |
Margin (%)	120 ($)	160 ($)	Value ($)	p
10	470.30	627.07	548.68	0.762
15	444.18	592.23	518.20	0.763
20	418.05	557.39	487.72	0.763

Node 12

| | Expected | | |
Margin (%)	Value ($)	p	K = 150 ($)
10	595.71	0.585	357.75
15	562.62	0.585	328.24
20	529.52	0.585	298.73

148

TABLE 5.7 How to calculate asset and option value at node 13

Node 20

Margin (%)	PV of Asset		Expected Value ($)	p
	50 ($)	120 ($)		
10	195.96	470.30	333.13	0.591
15	185.07	444.18	314.62	0.591
20	174.18	418.05	296.11	0.591

Node 21

Margin (%)	PV of Asset		Expected Value ($)	p
	30 ($)	80 ($)		
10	117.58	313.53	215.55	0.583
15	111.04	296.11	203.57	0.582
20	104.51	278.70	191.60	0.582

Node 13

Margin (%)	Expected Value ($)	p	$K = 150$ ($)
10	250.83	0.540	59.98
15	236.89	0.540	47.02
20	222.96	0.540	34.06

TABLE 5.8 Expected asset and option value at node 11

	Node 11		
Margin (%)	Expected Value ($)	K = 150 ($)	p
10	388.78	188.31	0.515
15	367.18	168.22	0.515
20	345.58	148.13	0.515

To then determine the option value today, at node 11, we proceed as for node 12 or 13. The expected value of the asset at node 11 derives from the expected values at nodes 12 and 13 at their respective probability of occurrence, that is, 40% for node 12 and 60% for node 3. The maximum asset value at node 11 is the expected value at node 12, and the minimum asset value is the expected value at node 13. Table 5.8 shows the results.

Step 3

We can now compare today's value of the option to defer the decision for two years with today's value of the decision to invest now; Figure 5.4 summarizes the data.

Under all scenarios investigated, the option to invest now is always more valuable than the option to invest in two years; the value of deferring the decision therefore is zero under the current assumptions. This insight is hardly surprising; it is in fact very consistent with much of the standard economy theory and with previous real option analysis.

However, there are also real-life examples of situations in which even under competitive scenarios the option to wait can be of great value. For example, there are companies that have entered a market as a follower and outperformed the first movers, challenging the notion that first-movers regularly capture long-term market value. The most famous examples include the competition between Betamax and VHR for the VCR market. Betamax arrived first, but when it arrived the VCR quickly took over the market. The main competitive advantages for VHR included its larger recording capacity (two hours versus one hour for Betamax) and its ability to quickly establish close links with the emerging video-rental retail industry. These advantages resulted in the creation of very effective barriers of penetration

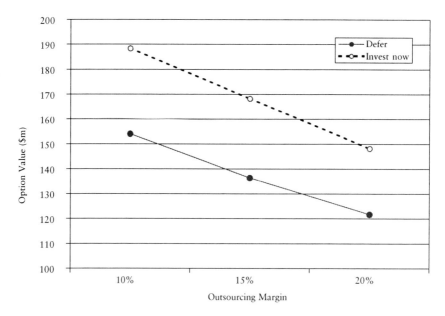

FIGURE 5.4 The value of the option to invest now or to defer

for Betamax.[20] The second well-known example is the success of Excel software, also not a pioneer, but a follower. The first spreadsheet software on the market when it arrived in 1979 was called VisciCell and had been developed by Dan Bricklin and Bob Frankston. Visci-Cell was quickly replaced by the IBM software Lotus 1-2-3, which in turn had to make room for Microsoft's Excel. Excel has since then held a dominant market position, even though it was the third to enter the market.

Let's revisit our assumptions and now suppose that our competitor may enter the market first once we defer the decision. This will give our management team an excellent opportunity to observe the market reaction to the new product and learn from what is observed. The engineers in our car company will utilize the information to refine the prototype and ultimately come up with a much-improved model in a market that has already been introduced to the concept of a duel-fuel car.

Our management team goes back to the drawing board and comes up with a revised version of the binomial tree, shown in Figure 5.5, that reflects the other set of assumptions.

Let's assume that, in fact, by deferring the decision, our car manufacturer will enter the market as follower, but also capture a higher market

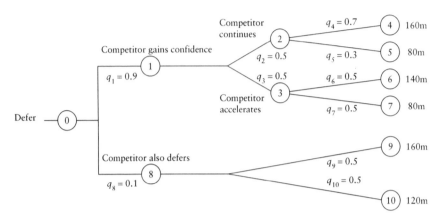

FIGURE 5.5 The binomial asset tree for the deferral option

share at a higher price for a better product, yielding in the best case scenario up to $160 million in revenues (node 4). At the same time, because the firm now enters with a better product, management also feels safe to assume that the worse case scenario will be no less than $80 million (node 5), and that the probability for this to occur can be reduced from currently 50% to 30%. Further assume, that even if the competitor accelerates (node 3), management believes that the improved product will have a better market outlook with $140 million in the best case scenario and $80 million in the worst case scenario (nodes 6/7). Management further believes that a decision to defer will actually provide an incentive for the competitor to go ahead and therefore increases the probability of competitive entry to 90% (node 1).

How will this affect the option to defer even under competitive conditions?

Under these circumstances, there is value in waiting to invest. Figure 5.6 illustrates the value of today's option to invest now and the value of today's option to invest in two years.

If the management team believes that deferring the investment decision allows learning and advances competitive positioning in the market even as a late entry, it will postpone the investment. This may be specifically the case in competitive situations with asymmetric information and high payoff uncertainty. Option analysis makes it possible to determine under which other set of assumptions waiting is the more valuable path. Once the binomial tree and the matching Excel sheet are built, assumptions are easily changed to construct the option space.

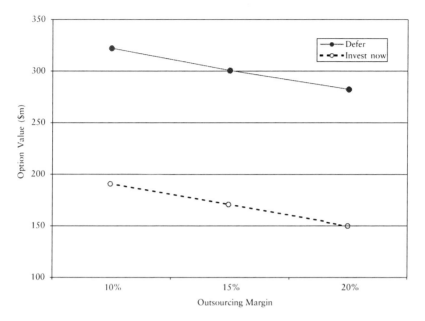

FIGURE 5.6 The option values of investing now or deferring

THE OPTION TO ABANDON UNDER COMPETITIVE CONDITIONS

In Chapter 3 we introduced the option to abandon; in Chapter 4 we investigated the sensitivity of the abandonment option to time uncertainty. We will now provide a framework to analyze the abandonment option under competitive conditions. We return to the example introduced in Chapter 3 but make the following additional assumptions: we assume that the product will give in the absence of competition a steady revenue stream of $50 million per year in the worst case scenario and of $120 million in the best case scenario. We further assume that there is a probability that a competitor will enter during the anticipated remaining seven-year life span of the product and that competitive entry will reduce market share over time.

In this scenario, uncertainty relates to the probability of competitive entry as well as to the timing of competitive entry. Both will affect the future product demand for our manufacturer. By abandoning the plant against the salvage price, management will occur outsourcing costs to cover product demand. The value of this put option increases as the salvage price increases and as the revenue foregone due to outsourcing declines. If product demand becomes sufficiently low, the salvage price for the plant will become higher than the outsourcing costs management will incur to cover outsourcing of product manufacturing. In a setting of asymmetric information, management has no insight or advanced knowledge of the competitive moves. It feels, however, based on its own understanding of the market, confident in predicting how competitive entry is likely to alter the market dynamic and how it will affect the company's market share and revenue stream from the asset. Management believes that two different scenarios, the best and the worst case, capture the dynamics and range of possible losses due to competitive entry. Those scenarios are displayed in Figure 5.7.

Management has no good understanding as to when competitive entry may occur but would like to develop some understanding as to how the option to abandon the manufacturing plant against a salvage price changes in value for a broad set of assumptions. Management assumes that it will be able to sell the plant for $15 million to $35 million. The value of the abandonment option is a put option, and it is calculated using the following equation whereby S_v denotes the salvage value, while V denotes the value of outsourcing costs incurred once the plant is salvaged.

$$P = S_v - \frac{p \cdot V_{max} + (1-p) \cdot V_{min}}{(1+r_f)^t}$$

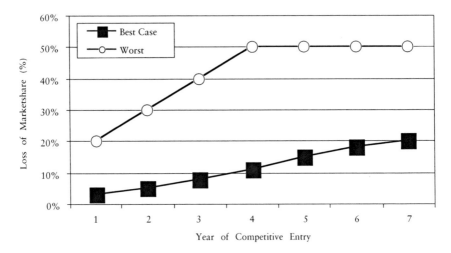

FIGURE 5.7 Market conditions under competitive entry

The challenge in determining the option value is that both V_{max} as well as V_{min} are a function of the probability distribution of timing of competitive entry. We calculate the abandonment option for the best and worst case scenarios assuming a range of salvage values between $25 million and $45 million, competitive entry in year 1, and a range of probabilities for that competitive entry to occur. Figure 5.8 shows the set-up of the binomial tree in the upper panel and the value of the abandonment option as a function of competitive entry in the lower panel.

If the competitor enters, product demand will decline, and so will the revenue stream foregone due to outsourcing, which will make it less attractive to

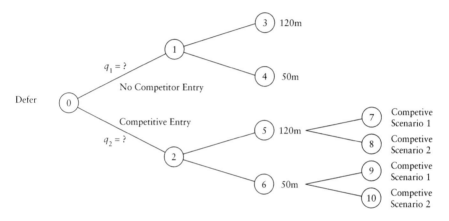

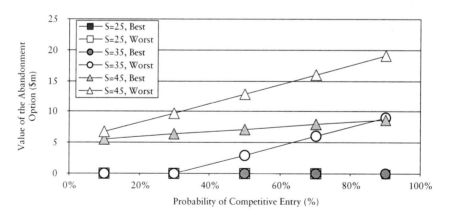

FIGURE 5.8 The binomial asset tree and option value for the abandonment option under competitive conditions.

keep the plant. First, the *PV* of those revenue streams foregone under competitive entry are calculated. We assume a minimum annual cash flow of $50 million and a maximum cash flow of $120 million per year. These are threatened by either one of the competitive scenarios, scenario 1 or scenario 2. We also assume each scenario to be equally likely; this gives rise to an expected value of cash flows (nodes 5 and 6, Figure 5.8) that remains subject to outsourcing. If the competitor fails to enter, product demand will remain constant for the next seven years and give rise to a constant stream of revenues foregone due to outsourcing (nodes 3 and 4). The option value to abandon is hence driven by the residual cash flow that goes into outsourcing under competitive and non-competitive conditions as well as the likelihood of competitive entry (q_2).

The value of the abandonment option is most sensitive to the salvage price, but with increasing salvage price the sensitivity of the abandonment option to the probability of competitive entry also increases for the worst case market scenario. This result confirms our intuition. The put option increases in value as—for a fixed exercise price (that is, the salvage price)—the value of the underlying asset declines, increasing the payoff for the put owner. The put option is a hedge for a downturn in the market.

However, we may want to consider that the salvage price to be obtained by management will reflect the fair market value of the plant. If the product market becomes more segmented due to competitive entry, this is likely to also impact on the salvage price management will be able to realize. In other words, if the plant offers no manufacturing flexibility and can only be used to produce a single product for which competitive entry is foreseen, the salvage price is likely to decrease with deteriorating market conditions. If indeed the salvage price is subject to the same volatility as the outstanding revenue stream, and if those volatilities are positively correlated, the value of the put option will decline. If, on the other hand, both are subjected to distinct uncertainties that are negatively correlated, the value of the put could increase. For example, as the probability of competitive entry increases and as the competitor eats more and more market share she may become very interested in acquiring the manufacturing plant to cover her own growing product demand. Both salvage price and revenue foregone to outsourcing are subject to the same uncertainty, competitive entry, but this uncertainty will play out differently for the two components of the abandonment option and increase its value.

The management team of the car manufacturer also wants to develop an understanding of how sensitive the abandonment option is to the year of competitive entry. We show such a scenario analysis for the salvage value of

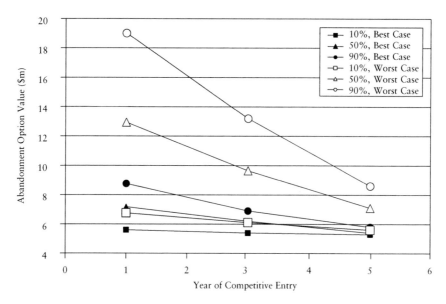

FIGURE 5.9 Sensitivity of the abandonment option value to probability and timing of competitive entry

$45 million and the best and worst case market loss scenarios and a range of probabilities for competitive entry in year 1, 3, or 5 in Figure 5.9.

The analysis shows that the value of the abandonment option is most sensitive to the probability of competitive entry in the worst case scenario, and increasingly so for early competitive entry. The analysis further documents that the value of the abandonment option rapidly declines as the year of competitive entry is delayed, and more so, the higher the likelihood of competitive entry is.

What is the value of the analysis? In a situation of asymmetric information, it indicates the impact various drivers of uncertainty have on the value of the option, in this case the abandonment option. The analysis therefore guides management as to which of the uncertainties might be worth resolving in order to facilitate good decision making. Management may want to consider investing into obtaining competitive intelligence. If so, such an endeavor should focus in narrowing down the uncertainty around salvage value of the plant and timing of competitive entry.

THE OPTION TO PREEMPT—A COMPETITIVE RACE

Competitive conditions play a significant role in a firm's incentive to innovate as one way to preempt.[21] The R&D pipeline for example is a major source of value for pharmaceutical firms as it is perceived and valued by financial analysts as future growth options. Empirical analysis in fact shows that the contribution of growth options to the stock price ranges between 70% and 92% for R&D-intense industries such as pharmaceuticals, information technology, or electronics, whereas this contribution is significantly less, between 38% and 62%, for transportation, chemical, or electric power industries.[22] In other instances, building a distribution channel may provide an equally strong preemptive position that is, however, subject to the uncertain timing of erosion. Investments in preemptive strategies are irreversible and the payoffs uncertain.

The value of preemption is strongest in industries that create a transient monopoly strong position through patent protection. In the pharmaceutical industry, without the option to patent a molecule, there would be no drug development program. There might not even be a pharmaceutical industry. An analysis by Kamien and Schwartz[23] pointed out that as long as the National Institutes of Health failed to grant exclusive rights on inventions, no pharmaceutical drug reached the market that was based on NIH inventions. After that policy changed, within a period of 10 years more than seventy drug discoveries were made with NIH support. Patents provide an incentive to enter the market and at the same time create a barrier to entering a market, even if not commercialized. According to Bart Lambrecht,[24] patents are "strategic real options."

Assume that a firm is engaged in a new product development that—if successful—should give rise to a very competitive product in the software market. There are several other players that are trying to achieve the same goal. It is generally assumed that the firm that enters the market first will create the standard and—by distribution networks and other means—create a strong market position that is likely to be further amplified by a networking effect.

In a binomial tree, such a scenario can be depicted as shown in Figure 5.10.

In this competitive race, there are two phases. The success in the first phase determines who gets to play in the second phase. Only the winner will be entitled to dominant patent protection and has the opportunity to explore the market. Three factors appear critical in succeeding in the first phase, all of which are private in nature: the technical talent available to the organization that drives the technical success, the probability of discovery, and the time needed to bring it all to a successful end. Whoever is not first will lose all.

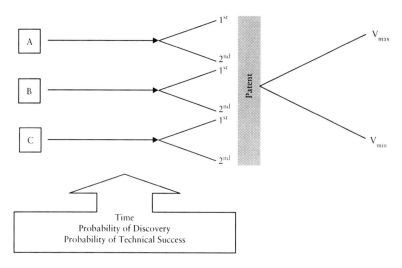

FIGURE 5.10 The preemption scenario

This and similar scenarios have been investigated in the real option framework before, and we have already alluded to this work in the introductory section of this chapter. We will briefly summarize the main insights in the following lists.[25]

Lambrecht and Perraudin's analysis suggests that

* The option moves out of the money faster with increasing uncertainty and under incomplete information.
* With competitive pressure, the option becomes less sensitive to uncertainty and option value rises less with market payoff uncertainty.
* Competitive pressure lowers the threshold to invest.

Weeds argues for a competitive scenario with the option to preempt by obtaining patent protection.

* There is an incentive to delay the investment, observe the competitor, and return to the race for the patent in a later stage.
* The rationale is that discoveries are accidental and not correlated with the input committed to the research. Thus, a firm may be better off by learning from passive observation and preserving its position by reduced investment, but come back into the race with a very aggressive strategy for winning the race over the final yards.

Kulatilaka and Perotti finally compare the scenario to a Stackelberg growth option and argue that

* The incentive to invest decreases with increasing uncertainty.
* In a competitive scenario with incomplete information, the incentive to invest is guided by the firm's perception of the preemptive effect it may exercise.
* Under uncertainty in a competitive scenario, the value of preemption grows more than the value of the option to defer.

In financial terms, this scenario fits a binary barrier option. It is an option with two outcomes only: an all or nothing option. Merton proposed a closed-form solution for a very similar option in 1973, the down-and-out European option. Cox and Rubinstein published in 1985 yet another closed-form pricing formula for a single barrier option.[26] They recommended using this kind of option to value a bond that comes with a safety covenant. Rubinstein and Reiner[27] then proposed in 1991 a pricing technique for the binary barrier option based on a binomial tree valuation.

Investors in financial securities who expect some future information to change the value of the underlying asset and also expect this information to arrive within a pre-determined time frame can actually hedge their option by a time-dependent barrier or knock-in option. Real option risk management will rely on defining alternative or intervention strategies.

We will build a binomial option model in an attempt to replicate some of these scenarios and to provide a framework to investigate the impact of changes in the value drivers on the option value of different sets of managerial flexibility.

We are assuming a three-player game, and we look at the game from the perspective of our hero firm A. Firm A has the opportunity to develop a novel software that allows wireless access to the Internet. There are at least two other players that have the same opportunity. The scenario is characterized by asymmetric information: Each player only knows his own internal technical capability budget and resource structure, and there is very limited sharing about technology developments or success at trade shows, via press releases, or through other means.

Firm A operates from the binomial option tree perspective and assumptions that are summarized in Figure 5.11. Firm A believes that its software engineers will be capable, at a probability of 70%, to develop the software within a little less than 22 months. Management further believes that competitor C has only a 50% chance and will take at least 27 months. Competitor B, on the other hand, is perceived to be a very close rival and as com-

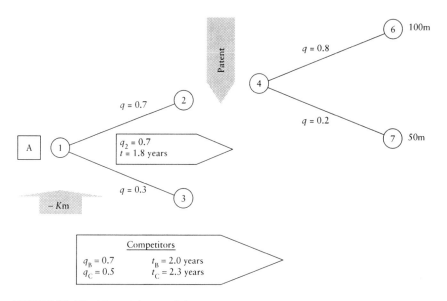

FIGURE 5.11 The binomial tree of the preemption option

petent to develop the product as firm A itself, but is likely to take a little more time (that is, 5 months longer). Management has no doubts about the attractiveness of the future payoffs. In the best case scenario, it assumes that it will capture a $100 million market, and the probability is 80%. There is only a small chance of 20% that the market will be less lucrative at a $50 million payoff. Costs are anticipated to be $30 million.

These assumptions translate into the following real option pricing. The expected value at node 4 is

$$V_{e4} = 0.8 \cdot 100 + 0.2 \cdot 50 = \$90 \text{ million}$$

From the perspective of node 1, this is the maximum asset value (node 2). The minimum asset value (node 3) is zero. This materializes only if a competitor is able to develop the software and patents the invention first. Then firm A has no chance to protect its inventions and no chance to commercialize the product. The only residual value in this scenario could be derived from the learning experience and knowledge collection, which we will, however, ignore for now. At a technical probability of 70% to complete the development program successfully and in time, before the competitor does, the expected value of the asset at node 1 is

$$V_{e1} = 0.7 \cdot 90 + 0.3 \cdot 0 = \$63 \text{ million}$$

This translates into the following calculations for p and for the value of the call at node 1:

$$p = \frac{1.07 \cdot 63 - 0}{90 - 0} = 0.749$$

$$C_1 = \frac{0.759 \cdot 90 + (1 - 0.750) \cdot 0}{1.07^{1.8}} - 30$$

$$= 29.68 \text{ million}$$

The value of the call option is deep in the money for firm A.

At this stage of the project the call option is most sensitive to management's assumptions about the technical probability of success and the timing in the first phase of the project in relation to management's beliefs about the outlook of those drivers for its competitors B and C. Changes in those assumptions have the potential to kill the option for A. Specifically, in the given set up with a patent barrier, timing is the most critical issue. Assume that management believes that there is a chance that firm B may actually develop the product faster.

Figure 5.12 shows a few scenarios of how management could envision the time of completing the invention to unfold for firm B.

How does this impact on the value of the investment opportunity for firm A? Clearly, now there is a remote chance that B will get to the patent office first. How do we incorporate this into our binomial model? We have to

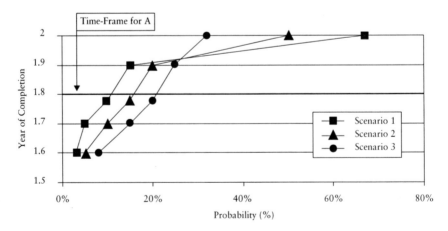

FIGURE 5.12 Timing scenarios for the rival product

allow for another driver of success or failure, in addition to the technical probability of succeeding, that we will term timing probability. It is externally driven by managerial beliefs about the timing of its competitors and it reduces the overall probability of firm A to emerge as a winner in the first stage of the project. We thus have to add it to the overall probability of failure, or subtract it from the overall probability of success. Therefore, it alters the expected value of the project, but not the maximum or minimum asset value, as these will materialize for whoever the winner is. It will also, by changing the expected value at node 1, change the risk-free probability p, and through p affect the value of the call option on this investment opportunity.

For example, for the timing scenario 1, the cumulative probability for B to walk through the door of the patent office first is 18%. Therefore, the probability for A to get there first is reduced by 18%, and we add this to the technical probability of success for A. This gives an overall probability for A to not only succeed technically but also in time to

$$q \text{ technical} + q \text{ timing} = 70 - 18 = 52$$

The expected value for node 1 becomes:

$$V_{e1} = 0.52 \cdot 90 + (1 - 0.52) \cdot 0 = 46.80$$

This alters the risk-free probability:

$$p = \frac{1.07 \cdot 46.80 - 0}{90 - 0} = 0.5564$$

The value of the call option then becomes:

$$C = \frac{0.5564 \cdot 90 + (1 - 0.5564) \cdot 0}{1.07^{1.8}} - 30 = 14.33$$

We summarize those changes in Figure 5.13. All anticipated time-to-completion scenarios for competitor B reduce the value of the investment option for firm A. Scenario B3, in fact, drives the option out of the money for firm A.

If the management of firm A believes that its assumptions about the early success of company B are reliable, it will then be interested in gaining an understanding as to how it could potentially accelerate its own program to beat B under the set of timing assumptions for B. Most likely, the more A wants to accelerate its own program, the more expensive the development

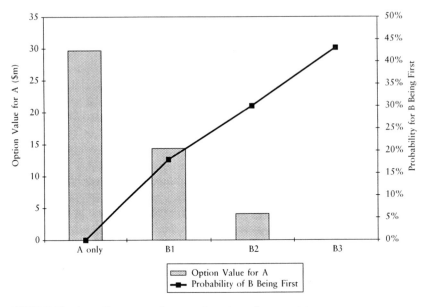

FIGURE 5.13 The call option value as a function of competitive entry

will become. After consulting with its engineers, management has the following beliefs as to how additional resource input would translate into time savings, shown in Table 5.9.

These costs and time savings affect the value of the investment opportunity for the basic scenario that excludes the probability of competitor B entering prior to firm A, as well as for all those scenarios in which competitor B has various degrees of probability to enter around the time or just before firm A plans to. In the first instance, A incurs more costs but also enjoys the anticipated revenue stream earlier. In those instances where there is increasing probability of B entering just around the time A hopes to enter, firm A enhances its probability to beat firm B but also occurs an additional cost.

For example, if B's timeline to completion follows scenario 3, there is a cumulative chance of 43% that it will get to the patent office before A does.

TABLE 5.9 The costs of accelerating product development

	Time Savings		
	1	**2**	**3**
Costs (m)	2	5	10
Time Savings (Years)	0.05	0.1	0.2

If A spends $2 million and accelerates its program by 0.05 years and arrives at the patent office in 1.75 years, it can beat B if B does not enter before 1.78 years from now. There is still a cumulative chance of 23% that B will enter prior to 1.75 years. If A is prepared to spend an extra $5 million or $10 million, it can get to the patent office in 1.70 or 1.60 years from now, respectively. The chances for B to enter just before that are 15% and 8%.

These dynamics are captured in the option valuation. If B follows scenario 3 and the management team of A does decide not to accelerate, the value of the investment opportunity to A becomes zero, down from $29.68 million if B with certainty were not to complete its program before two years from now. In this scenario, A faces a technical probability of 70% to succeed against a 43% probability of B succeeding first. The residual probability of A not only to succeed but also be first drops to 27%. The expected value therefore declines to $V_e = 0.27 \cdot 90 + 0.73 \cdot 0 = \$24.3$ million. While the maximum and minimum asset values remain at $90 million and $0 million, respectively, p drops to 0.2889:

$$p = \frac{1.07 \cdot 24.3 - 0}{90 - 0} = 0.2889$$

Therefore, the value of the call option declines to zero:

$$C = \text{Max} \left(0, \frac{0.2889 \cdot 90 + (1 - 0.2889) \cdot 0}{1.07^{1.8}} - 30\right)$$

$$= \text{Max} \, (0, \ 26.00 - 30)$$

$$= \text{Max} \, (0, \ -3.99)$$

$$= 0$$

Figure 5.14 summarizes the results for the option value under all the different program acceleration scenarios firm A has the flexibility to entertain. The data provide the following insights: The management team of firm A can rescue the option value of its project under the most aggressive assumptions for competitor B timelines (B3) by providing more resources. If A invests $2 million and accelerates 0.05 years, the value of the investment opportunity grows from zero to $8.21 million. Investing $5 million and $10 million and thereby accelerating its own program by 0.1 and 0.2 years further increases the value of the investment opportunity to $18 million and $20 million, respectively. If management tends to believe in less aggressive timelines for its closest competitor B (that is, scenario B_1 and B_2), investing $10 million to accelerate the internal program by 0.2 years suppresses option value compared

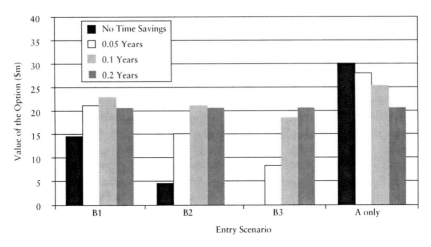

FIGURE 5.14 The call option value of preemption: Program acceleration under competitive threat

to investing just $5 million. This reflects the small probability of 3% and 5%, respectively, for B to enter prior to 1.7 years, but the relatively high cost for A to battle that small probability. If there were no risk of competitive entry of B prior to A (scenario A), investment in an accelerated program destroys option value: The time value of money by bringing the product to market earlier does not recover the costs associated therewith.

In principle, in a situation with high competitive pressure and a risk of losing the entire investment opportunity by not being the leader, there is an incentive to invest early and aggressively to maintain the investment opportunity. However, management's incentive to invest is likely also to be influenced by managerial expectations about other drivers of uncertainty, most notably the ability to complete the project successfully and the future payoff scenarios. Within the given setting, where the patentability of the invention creates a "natural" barrier between technical uncertainty and market payoff, we can now investigate the impact of each uncertainty on the managerial decision to commit more resources in order to accelerate the program.

We will initially examine how sensitive the option to accelerate is to the assumed probability of technical success, and we look at a technical probability of 70%, 50%, and 40% presented in Figure 5.15.

The x-axis in each panel shows the best case scenario followed by the three acceleration programs A could entertain. As the technical probability of success q_t drops to 40%, shown in the lower panel, the notion of competitor B arriving first at the patent office, even at the smallest probability investigated of 3% in 1.6 years from now, drives the option value for firm

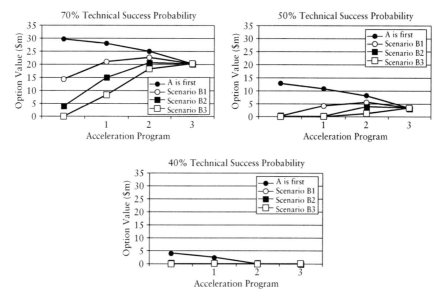

FIGURE 5.15 Scenario analysis for the preemption option

A to zero. In fact, we can calculate for the low technical probability of success the likelihood of competitive entry that must not be exceeded in order for the option to remain alive for the management team of firm A. This is the critical probability of competitive entry that under the given cost and payoff assumptions kills the option for the firm.

We do this by setting the equation to calculate the call option equal to zero and solving for the probability q of competitive q_C entry using the solver function in Excel:

$$C = \frac{p \cdot V_{max} + (1 - p) \cdot V_{min}}{1.07^{1.8}} - 30$$

For our example:

$$C = \frac{p \cdot 90 + (1 - p) \cdot 0}{1.07^{1.8}} - 30$$

$$C = \frac{\left(\dfrac{1.07 \cdot V_e - 0}{90 - 0}\right) \cdot 90 + \left(1 - \dfrac{1.07 \cdot V_e - 0}{90 - 0}\right) \cdot 0}{1.07^{1.8}} - 30$$

With $V_e = (q_t - q_C) V_{max} + (1 - q_t - q_c) \cdot V_{min}$, i.e., in our example

$$V_e = (0.7 - q_c) \cdot 90 + (1 - 0.7 - q_c) \cdot 0$$

Figure 5.16 summarizes the data for a range of technical probabilities to succeed for firm A.

Once the technical probability to succeed drops below 35.2% for firm A, the option moves out of the money, irrespective of the competitive conditions. At any probability of technical success higher than that management can define the boundaries for the likelihood of competitive entry that would kill the option. For example, at a technical probability of success of 50% and the likelihood of competitive entry of more than 15%, the option moves out of the money.

This analysis suggests that for high-risk investment projects, a small amount of competitive pressure may be sufficient to discourage management from investing. However, under these circumstances the option to learn and participate in a growth option by engaging in a joint venture may still be in the money. Such an agreement is likely to require a smaller exercise price and to reduce future payoffs, but will still preserve the moneyness of the growth option. We will introduce real option valuation for R&D joint ventures in Chapter 8.

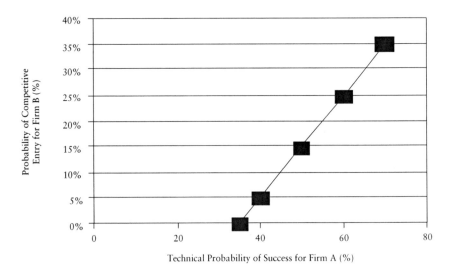

FIGURE 5.16 The decision line under private and competitive risk: Preempt or do not preempt

We now move on and examine for these probabilities of competitive success the boundary conditions for which the "rescue" option of the project by aggressive commitment of resources to beat the competitor is in the money. This is achieved by setting the equation for the call option to zero and solving for the critical cost K under the different scenarios.

For example, for a technical probability q_t of success of 60%, the critical probability q_c for a competitor to be first is 24.8%. The value of the call is zero at a cost K of $30 million. At an additional cost of $K^\diamond$, firm A can accelerate by 0.2 years and beat the competitor, restoring the overall probability of success to 60%. The value of the call is then:

$$C = \frac{p \cdot V_{max} + (1-p) \cdot V_{min}}{1.07^{1.6}} - K - K^\diamond$$

$$= \frac{p \cdot 90 + (1-p) \cdot 0}{1.07^{1.6}} - 30 - K^\diamond$$

$$= \frac{p \cdot 90}{1.07^{1.6}} - 30 - K^\diamond$$

p is defined as follows: $p = \dfrac{r_f \cdot V_e - V_{min}}{V_{max} - V_{min}}$

Therefore, p becomes: $p = \dfrac{(1+r) \cdot V_e - 0}{90 - 0}$

V_e derives from the technical probability q_t and the probability q_c of a competitor to enter.

$$V_e = (q_t - q_c) \cdot V_{max}$$

For our specific example:

$$V_e = (0.6 - 0.248) \cdot 90 = 0.352 \cdot 90 = 31.68$$

$$p = \frac{1.07 \cdot 31.68 - 0}{90 - 0} = 0.37664$$

The value of the call is zero for these parameters. If acceleration results in beating the competitor we can eliminate q_c out of the equation. V_e then becomes:

$$V_e = 0.6 \cdot 90 = 54$$

p changes from 0.37664 to 0.642, and the value of the call increases from zero to $21.85 million. Accelerating the program and thereby eliminating the probability q_c from the call equation is worth a maximum investment of $21.85 million. This is the critical cost to preempt. If it costs firm A more to accelerate the program by 0.2 years and beat competitor B, it should not do it; the option is out of the money.

Obviously, the critical cost to preempt also depends on the expected time frame to which the program will accelerate, simply because of the time value of money. Any acceleration not only preempts the competitor but also creates an earlier revenue stream, which on its own is of value.

We summarize the critical cost to preempt for firm A for the option to accelerate by 0.1 by 0.2 years in Figure 5.17.

The combined analysis defines the option space for the management of firm A. The major drivers of uncertainty for the first stage of the investment project are the internal probability of success and the likelihood of a competitor being first. Both uncertainties drive the value of the option and determine the critical cost to invest, as summarized in Figure 5.18.

Obviously, the final payoff function that will only materialize for the winner in the second stage of the investment project will have an additional impact on the options dynamics. An increase or decrease of either the maximum or minimum value of future payoffs will have two effects.

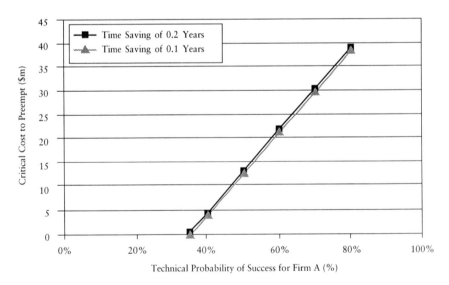

FIGURE 5.17 The critical cost to preempt under private risk

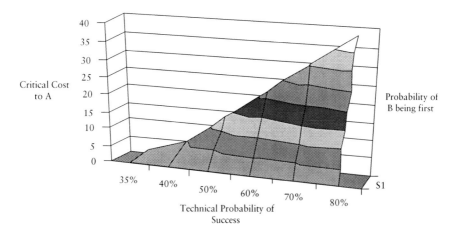

FIGURE 5.18 Sensitivity analysis: The critical cost to preempt under private and competitive risk

1. It will increase or decrease the expected value for phase 2, which becomes the maximum asset value for stage 1. It will thus enhance or lower the expected values in phase 1 and thereby impact the overall option value, but also raise or reduce the critical cost to invest under competitive pressures.
2. If those market assumptions are not just private assumptions made by firm A but are public information and the beliefs are shared among all three firms participating in this race, higher expectations regarding future payoffs are likely to intensify the competitive pressure, while declining expectations are likely to release the competitive pressure.

NOTES

1. R.H. Hayes and W.J. Abernathy, "Managing Our Way to Economic Decline," *Harvard Business Review*, September–October, 67, 1980; R. Hayes and D. Garvin, "Managing As If Tomorrow Mattered," *Harvard Business Review*, May–June, 71, 1982; M. Porter, "Capital Disadvantage: America's Failing Capital Investment System," *Harvard Business Review*, September–October, 65, 1992; C.Y. Baldwin and B.J. Clark, "Capital-Budgeting Systems and Capabilities Investments in U.S. Companies after the Second World War," *Business History Review* 68:73, 1994.

2. See for example, S. Tzu, *The Art of War* (Oxford University Press, 1988).

3. For review, A.K. Dixit and R.S. Pindyck, *Investment under Uncertainty* (Princeton University Press, 1994).

4. B.J. Spencer and J.A. Brander, "Pre-Commitment and Flexibility: Applications to Oligopoly Theory," *European Economic Review* 36:1601, 1992.

5. T.J. Smith and L.A. Ankum, "A Real Options and Game-Theoretic Approach to Corporate Investment Strategy under Competition," *Financial Management* 22:241, 1993.

6. F. Smets, *Exporting versus FDI: The Effect of Uncertainty, Irreversibility and Strategic Interactions*, working paper (Yale University Press, 1991).

7. J.V. Leahy, "Investment in Competitive Equilibrium: The Optimality of Myopic Behavior," *Quarterly Journal of Economics* 108:1105, 1993.

8. S. Fries, M. Miller, and W. Perraudin, "Debt Pricing in Industry Equilibrium," *Review of Financial Studies* 10:39, 1997; L. Trigeorgis, *Real Options—Managerial Flexibility and Strategy in Resource Allocation* (MIT Press, Cambridge, MA, 1996; Chapter 9).

9. H.T.J. Smit and L. Trigeorgis, *Flexibility and Competitive R&D Strategies*, working paper (Erasmus University, 1997).

10. B. Lambrecht and W. Perraudin, *Option Games*, working paper (Cambridge University, and CEPR, UK, August 1994); B. Lambrecht and W. Perraudin, *Real Option and Preemption*, working paper (Cambridge University, Birkbeck College [London] and CEPR, UK, 1996).

11. D.S. Bunch and R. Smiley, "Who Deters Entry? Evidence on the Use of Strategic Entry Deterrents," *Review of Economics and Statistics* 74:509, 1992.

12. H. Weeds, "Strategic Delay in a Real Options Model of R&D Consumption," *Review of Economic Studies*, in print, 2002.

13. N. Kulatilaka and E.C. Perotti, "Strategic Growth Options," *Management Science* 44:1021, 1998.

14. G. Hamel and C.K. Prahalad, *Competing for the Future* (Harvard Business School Press, 1994).

15. C.Y. Baldwin and B.J. Clark, "Capital-Budgeting Systems and Capabilities Investments in U.S. Companies after the Second World War," *Business History Review* 68:73, 1994; B. Kogut and N. Kulatilaka, "Capabilities as Real Options," *Organization Science* 12:744, 2001.

16. K.X. Zhu, *Strategic Investment in Information Technologies: A Real-Options and Game-Theoretic Approach*, unpublished doctoral dissertation (Stanford University, 1999).

17. P. Botteron, M. Chesney, and R. Gibson-Asner, *An Application of Exotic Options to Firm's Strategic Delocalisation Policies under Exchange Rate Risk* (Real Option Group Conference, Cambridge, 1998).
18. S. Grenadier, "Valuing Lease Contracts. A Real-Options Approach," *Journal of Financial Economics* 38:297, 1995; S. Grenadier, *Game Choices. The Intersection of Real Options and Game Theory* (Risk Books, London, 2001).
19. N. Kulatilaka and E.C. Perotti, "Strategic Growth Options," *Management Science* 44:1021, 1998; B. Lambrecht and W. Perraudin, *Real Option and Preemption*, working paper (Cambridge University, Birkbeck College [London] and CEPR, UK, 1996); S. Grenadier, *Game Choices. The Intersection of Real Options and Game Theory* (Risk Books, London, 2001); H.T.J. Smit and L.A. Ankum, "A Real Options and Game-Theoretic Approach to Corporate Investment Strategy under Competition," *Financial Management* 22:241, 1993; H.T.J. Smit and L. Trigeorgis, *Flexibility and Competitive R&D Strategies*, working paper (Erasmus University, 1997).
20. Harvard Case Study, "Betamax-VHS"; T. Cottrell and G. Sick, "First Mover (Dis)advantage and Real Options," *Journal of Applied Corporate Finance* 14 (2), 2001; A. Graham, "The Place of Reason in the Chinese Philosophical Tradition," in R. Dawson, ed., *The Legacy of China* (Cheng and Tsui, Boston, 1964, pp. 28–56).
21. D.S. Bunch and R. Smiley, "Who Deters Entry? Evidence on the Use of Strategic Entry Deterrents," *Review of Economics and Statistics* 74:509, 1992.
22. H.T.J. Smit, *Empirical Characteristics of Growth Options* (Presented at the Real Option Group Conference, Cambridge, 1999).
23. M. Kamien and N. Schwartz, *Market Structure and Innovation* (Cambridge University Press, 1982).
24. B. Lambrecht, "Strategic Sequential Investments and Sleeping Patents," in M. Brennan and L. Trigeorgis, eds., *Project Flexibility, Agency and Competition* (Oxford University Press, 2001).
25. B. Lambrecht and W. Perraudin, *Real Option and Preemption*, working paper (Cambridge University, Birkbeck College [London] and CEPR, UK, 1996); H. Weeds, *Reverse Hysteresis: R&D Investments with Stochastic Innovation*, working paper, 1999; H. Weeds, "Strategic Delay in a Real Options Model of R&D Consumption." *Review of Economic Studies*, in print, 2002; N. Kulatilaka and E.C. Perotti, "Strategic Growth Options," *Management Science* 44:1021, 1998.

26. J. Cox and M. Rubinstein, *Options Markets* (Prentice-Hall, Englewood, NJ, 1985).

27. M. Rubinstein and E. Reiner, "Breaking Down the Barriers" *Risk Magazine* 8:28, 1991; M. Rubinstein and E. Reiner, "Unscrambling the Binary Code" *Risk Magazine* 9:37, 1991.

CHAPTER 6

Adding Option Value by Intervention

Real options value managerial flexibility in response to future uncertainties. Managerial flexibility entails all measures that add value to ongoing operations or improve decision making on future operations such as the option to position, the option to improve a product, and the option to accelerate or delay time to market of a product or service, as well as the option to invest in learning.

Financial option pricing, as pointed out in Chapter 1, is based on the observable market price of the stock and on the assumption that historic movement is indicative for future movement. For real options, assumptions about future payoffs of any given asset are subjective estimates. There is a value-adding incentive to reduce uncertainty for those estimates, and from this derives the value of the option to wait for the arrival of new information. Management, however, may not just allow for passive learning by observing the market but may also reduce uncertainty by investing in an active learning process that reveals valuable information now. Either way, management adds value by enabling the organization to make a more informed decision on accepting, accelerating, staging or rejecting an investment opportunity.

Management may also want to explore whether a strategic move may create value by supporting an existing product through strengthening the positioning of the underlying technology. Those investments are unlikely to create positive payoffs on their own but will create value for the firm by preserving an existing market stake. Obviously, the assumptions as to how good the protective effect will be and how much the revenue stream can be conserved will drive the value of these options as well as the critical value to invest in strategic moves of this nature.

Management may consider the development of improved second- or third-generation products to fight loss of market share from competitors but then in that case also risks cannibalization of its own first-generation products. Managerial beliefs regarding the timing and effect of competitive entry on its current position, the costs of developing improved products, and the future payoffs of those products compared to future payoffs of the first-generation product will have to go into the option analysis. Finally, management may consider speeding up an ongoing product development in order to win a competitive race and preempt. Managerial beliefs as to how important it will be to enter the market first, how advanced its competitors are and how successful they will be in bringing their product to the market, and how the future payoff may evolve will drive the value of this option.

THE OPTION TO LEARN

The incentive to invest in active learning increases as the value of the information increases, which in turn is reflective of the perceived risk. Risk aversion and information value are two sides of the same coin. When management faces the option to invest in a new technology with uncertain benefits and effects on firm value there is a strong incentive to entertain an active information-gathering exercise.[1] Likewise, a firm contemplating the acquisition of another firm initiates a costly process of due diligence to reduce uncertainty and risk associated with such a step. If the learning experience is advanced only by actively engaging in the project, the desire to learn turns into an incentive to accelerate the commitment.[2] In this sense, the investment in the very early R&D phases of a new product development program also qualifies as a learning experience: The investment is necessary to obtain initial, basic information on technical feasibility; by the same token, it is already the first stage of a sequential investment program. The investment in the information-gathering exercises derives value by reducing technical uncertainty or private risk and advancing the program. The presumed market opportunity and payoff function at product launch drives the critical cost to invest in the first phase of the product development program—the information gathering exercise.

McCardle, Roberts, and Weitzman published their thoughts at a time when uncertainty and risk were perceived as negative and acknowledged for by increasing the discount rate in the NPV appraisal. Management must make the investment now, but the future value of the asset is uncertain. Management receives a range of signals now as to what that future value might be, but those signals are not clear; they are clouded by noise. Uncertainty derives from the reception of noisy signals as to the future states of the world. It affects the managerial ability to make a good decision, and therefore uncertainty is penalized in the DCF framework by applying a higher discount rate.

The real option framework does not penalize uncertainty as long as it is paired with flexibility. However, real option analysis does not value uncertainty that derives from noise. Therefore, also in the real option framework, there is an incentive for investing in costly acquisition of information or in a learning option if that facilitates a more refined, more reliable assessment of the future payoff. The organization seeks to protect itself against acquiring an option that is out of the money or forgoing an option that is deep in the money. The effect of noise on the acquisition and exercise of real options is ambiguous. Noise can lead to a more aggressive exercise of a real option than when the true asset value can be perfectly observed. Noise diminishes the quality of information obtained from observation and thereby reduces the incentive and value to wait. Noise, on the other hand, can also encourage delaying the acquisition or exercise of a real option more than a real option analysis based on the true asset value would suggest. For example, a firm may be reluctant to take a position as market leader—although the real option is deep in the money—because it is concerned that its steps will reveal very valuable demand and price information to its competitors, who may utilize it to generate a second mover advantage, thereby reducing the noise for its competitor at no cost.

We can draw yet another parallel to the natural sciences: Biology, physics, and engineering have spent much effort and thought in assessing how to understand a process that cannot be observed directly. In the medical sciences, an entire field is dedicated to deriving, developing, and interpreting surrogate markers that make it possible to understand and predict an underlying disease process that cannot be observed directly. This is a substantial part of the hype and attraction ascribed to modern molecular techniques designed to decipher individual genetic codes. The better the quality of the marker and its reliability, the more valuable is the surrogate marker. Noisy signals do little to resolve the uncertainty. Hence, there is value in reducing the noise.[3]

Imagine that you were to buy a piece of antique furniture from an art dealer unknown to you. Imagine further that you are not an expert about antique furniture. Depending on the sales price proposed to you by the dealer and your determination to acquire the piece at any price, you may or may not be inclined to obtain the independent appraisal of a qualified antique expert to reduce the noise you are facing as you make this purchase decision. Antiques, just like real assets, are traded in decentralized, incomplete markets, which brings noise to the valuation process. The real asset value cannot be perfectly observed by all market participants; the true value of the asset remains clouded by noise. An independent appraisal delivers a second data-point and reduces the noise somewhat. This is of value to you, the buyer of the antique, and that value is reflected in the amount of money you are willing to pay for the independent review, or the acquisition of the learning option.

Similarly, there is value for a firm in reducing the noise surrounding the future payoff or technical uncertainty of the investment project to be initiated today. The value of the learning option lies in the value it adds to better decision making. With learning, the real option value of the investment opportunity moves towards the NPV value as learning refines uncertainty and helps in defining the best option path forward.

Learning options come in two flavors: They facilitate a more reliable prediction of the true future asset value or they actually change the value by affecting the probability of success. The first entails, for example, primary market research; interview data are gathered in order to deliver a more reliable prediction of future market size. The second involves a set of experiments that will improve the experimental set up in subsequent product development phases and thereby enhance the probability of success. It entails, for example, launching a product in a test market and learning from the observation about product improvement or changes in product features that would alter the success of the product. It may also entail an investment in an additional series of experiments designed to reduce uncertainty surrounding the technical feasibility of an innovative novel product, be it a new software program, a new service, a new gadget, or a new drug. Obtaining information to make better predictions and obtaining information to change probabilities of success are both learning experiences.

Like a deferral option, the learning option facilitates identifying the best path forward after uncertainty has been resolved. This may seem contradictory to the basic concept of option valuation: The option value is supposed to go up with increasing uncertainty. However, this is only true if the option can be exercised after the market value has been observed, a scenario applicable to financial options. Here, the option owner clearly will not exercise an option that is out of the money.

As for real options, the value of the underlying asset cannot be readily observed and part of the exercise price often needs to be paid in advance, when the value of the underlying asset is still evolving. For example, management needs to invest in R&D and obtain experimental results before it will understand the technical probability of success. This investment will then buy the option or the right to engage in a new product development program with an uncertain market payoff. If the technical probability of success for the R&D phase is zero, the option is out of the money. Management has no way of having advanced knowledge of the probability of success; it has to pay the entire R&D costs to find out.

Once the firm has committed its resources to a specific R&D program, it has forgone the flexibility and lost the option value. Therefore, in the real option framework, there is also a benefit in obtaining a reliable and precise understanding of the future value of the underlying asset prior to exercising the option.[4] This benefit drives the value of the learning option, the critical cost to invest in obtaining information in order to reduce future uncertainty. If a learning experience reduces the uncertainty of technical success in a drug development program, it enhances the value of the option and lowers the critical value to invest. It may invite management to accept a more aggressive and costly development program in order to exercise a real option with a high probability of success.

The value of learning by reducing technical uncertainty depends on two key drivers:

* The reliability of the information received through learning in relation to the costs incurred for learning.
* The impact of learning on managerial decision making.

In some ways, the learning option is to managers what a diagnostic test is to physicians. The value of the medical test to the doctor depends on how reliably it can predict or exclude a disease. It also depends on what impact the information received from the test will have on the treatment decision of the physician, that is, are there any therapeutic options available at all? If so, is there more than one way of treating the disease in question, and if so, does the diagnostic test result decide which treatment option to choose, and if so, how does the cost of the diagnostic test relate to the additional benefit for the patient derived from receiving one treatment versus another?

Real option value is never absolute; it is always option value that is related to a specific organizational entity. This is very true, too, for the learning option. The value of information to any given firm may depend on the degree of risk aversion cultivated within the firm, as well as the organizational culture of decision making.[5] Traditional beliefs in the academic literature entail that a risk averse organization is much more motivated to reduce uncertainty by obtaining information than one that is risk neutral and therefore is also willing to pay more for information. Others have disputed that risk aversion and the value of information correlate in a monotonous fashion. Hilton identified four dimensions that impact on the value of information, including the structure of the decision, the environment in which the decision is being made, and the initial beliefs and prior knowledge of the decision maker, as well as the specific features of the information system. These components all drive the value of the real option to acquire information, but they do not act synergistically.

To return to the analogy of the physician who is about to order a diagnostic test: If there is just one drug available, even for a risk-averse physician there is very little value in ordering a diagnostic test. If reimbursement and regulatory constraints prevent reimbursement and the patient is not able to finance the best therapeutic choice from her own resources, the decision environment also reduces the value of the information to be obtained. If the physician has seen the condition many times before and feels confident about making an accurate diagnosis in the absence of the specific test, he may also be inclined not to purchase the additional piece of information. As an aside, in a similar manner, a corporation with a significant set of organizational experience and knowledge in one specific area may refrain from obtaining additional information because it feels confident that it can judge the risk of a new opportunity based on a rich fund of past experience. Here, the corporation predicts—just as the financial markets do when pricing financial options—future project volatility based on historical comparables. Obviously, there are risks inherent in such an approach: An organization's overconfidence in past experience and internal judgment can lead to organizational blindness. Forgoing the opportunity of open-minded information gathering and learning may effectively prevent the organization from picking up discrete signals that will ultimately challenge the validity of historic assumptions and jeopardize the entire framework of the real option analysis and valuation. The path-dependency of passive learning that includes learned and trained behaviors and ingrained organizational routines narrow organizational perceptiveness and thus constrain the radius of future activities. Finally, features inherent in the information itself, including its reliability, accuracy, and timing, will also guide the value of information.

The real option value of passive learning, simply by observing the market and deferring the investment decision, has been studied before.[6] Martzoukos[7] has pointed out more recently the path dependency of active learning options: Management can invest now at time zero in learning about the future market size. Acquired knowledge, in this instance, affects subsequent actions and investment decisions. It reveals the true value of the asset and guides managerial decision as to whether to proceed or to abandon. Management can also take learning actions at the time of exercise simply by observing the asset value evolve. In this instance, the payoff may be different from the expected one; management may find out that it exercised an option out of the money or much deeper in the money than expected. Martzoukos also defined the boundary conditions of active learning about market uncertainty: These are determined by the critical project value. If learning will not alter the managerial decision because the anticipated market payoff is either too good or too bad, there is no value in investing in learning. Under these conditions the option to defer the decision and wait is more valuable than the option to invest in active learning. In other words, the value of information acquisition is greatest in the boundary space that separates the option to invest from the option to abandon the investment, as shown in Figure 6.1.

Here, the option owner is indifferent between the two paths forward. Any piece of reliable information or learning is capable of swinging the balance to one or the other side. The value of the learning or information acquisition option decreases as the option owner moves out of the boundary space towards one or the other side of the separation line.

In more generic terms, the value of the option to learn is driven by the exercise price, that is, the cost of learning, the level of certainty that is created by learning, and how this translates into improved decision making and thus creates value. Hence, a learning option that results in more reliable prediction of future outcomes of uncertainty is approached and valued in the binomial model very much like a deferral option, with the exception that

- Learning is not for free but needs to be acquired.
- Management can decide on what aspects or drivers of uncertainty the learning experience should focus on.

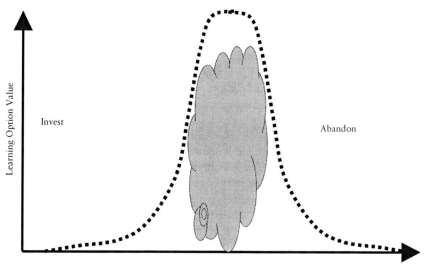

FIGURE 6.1 The value of the learning option

* There is either no time delay or less time delay involved for active learning.
* Passive learning and investing ex post is more reliable; active learning ex ante will not provide a 100% security as learning ex post does.

The Value of Learning by Reducing Noise

We will investigate the value of learning, that is, reducing noise about the technical probability of success in the compounded option of a drug development program. When first introducing the compound option of a drug development program in Chapter 3 we documented the sensitivity of the critical cost to invest to the technical probability of success. Equally, we can document how the value of the option increases as private or technical uncertainty decreases and the likelihood to succeed increases. This is exemplified in Figure 6.2. Here we show the effect of increasing the probability of succeeding for the Phase II clinical trial on the value of the option to embark on the pre-clinical program or to embark on the Phase II clinical trial.

Most likely, management will apply a range of technical success probabilities rather than having exact advanced knowledge of a specific figure: If there is little organizational experience with a novel technology, the likelihood of succeeding could be anywhere between 10% and 90%. If, on the other hand, the firm has already collected some experience with a specific technology, management may feel confident in assuming a more narrow range of technical success probabilities, say between 40% and 50%. In the first scenario, the option will be out of the money easily; in the second scenario, the option will be in the money. Noise reduces the expected value of the asset. Noise therefore also influences exercise policies by altering the option value. A high level of noise moves the option out of the money.

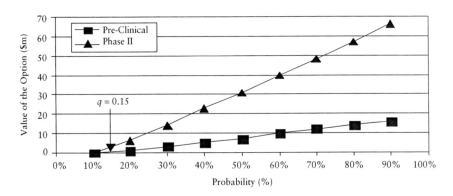

FIGURE 6.2 The compound option value under private risk

We base the initial scenario on the same set of assumptions as were detailed in Chapter 3. The value of learning emerges from allowing management to better predict outcome and therefore improve the quality of the decision, that is, choose for each predicted probability scenario the path with the highest option value. If learning were to increase the reliability of the prediction to succeed or fail, management would have a better understanding of the option value and the critical cost to invest. The benefit of learning would be to protect management from driving the option out of the money by over-investing. All management needs to know is whether the technical probability of success is sufficiently high so that under the current cost assumptions the investment opportunity is in the money. If that is the case, management will invest. If not, management will abandon.

The value of the abandonment option, or the put, is the exercise price, that is, the sunk cost saved ex ante for the drug development program through Phase II by making the informed decision not to invest in the project. The anticipated costs for this project up to the completion of Phase II are $12.5 million. In an R&D budgeting portfolio scenario, this investment project was to compete against other R&D investment options. Investing in this project would likely imply forgoing another investment opportunity. Not investing in this project and saving the $12.5 million in projected costs for an alternative investment—in the context of an R&D project portfolio—then likewise also implies that the salvage value is not $12.5 million but the value of the investment option that will be pursued at the expense of the one currently under consideration. For example, if the $12.5 million could also buy an investment opportunity with a real option value of $20 million, then the salvage value for this project is no longer $12.5 million but $20 million.

Figure 6.3 shows the value of the investment option at the pre-clinical stage as a function of the probability to successfully complete the Phase II trial assuming a total cost of $12.5 million to complete the program through Phase II. At a 56.7% technical success probability of Phase II, the option moves in the money. If the salvage value were to increase to $20 million by including option value of another opportunity forgone when investing into this project, the investment hurdle for this project increases, implying that either the expected market payoff or the required technical success probability had to increase to move the option into the money.

What is the value of learning for the R&D investment option? Assume management has the opportunity to invest in a learning exercise that could reduce some of the uncertainty surrounding the outcome of the Phase II clinical trial. Figure 6.4 depicts the binomial asset tree for the managerial strategy as impacted by such a learning experience.

At node 1, management has the option to invest resources, the costs K of learning (K_l), in a learning experience which will with unknown probability

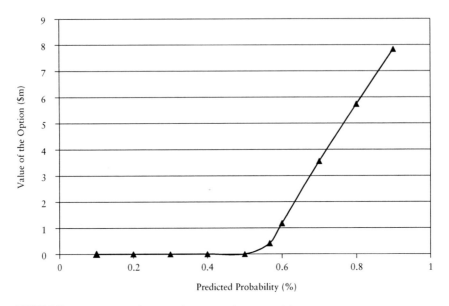

FIGURE 6.3 The option value as a function of private risk

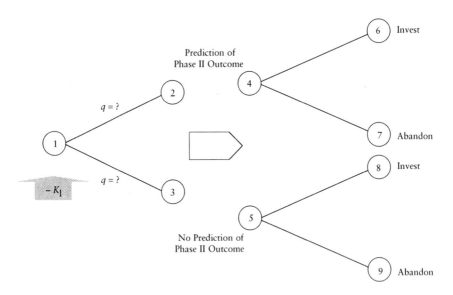

FIGURE 6.4 The binomial asset tree of the learning option

allow management to predict the outcome of the Phase II clinical trial (node 2) or fail to do so (node 3). In the first case, the outcome of the learning experience (nodes 2/4 in Figure 6.4) will facilitate an informed managerial decision to invest (node 6) or to abandon (node 7). If learning fails (node 3) management can either invest or abandon but has to rely on internal assumptions. Suppose internal assumptions are very vague and clouded by significant uncertainty such as that the likelihood of technical success for Phase II is ranged anywhere between 10% and 90%. The expected value of the opportunity now, at the inception of the R&D program that will ultimately lead to the Phase II clinical trial, under this range of success probability scenarios with a best case future market payoff (see Chapter 3) of $520 million and a worst case payoff of $24 million, ranges between $2 million and $19.18 million, as summarized in Table 6.1.

The minimum and maximum value at node 8 is the lowest and highest asset value achievable, depending on the technical success probability, that is, $2 million and $19.18 million. The expected values at node 8, assuming each technical success scenario is equally likely, is $10.64 million. These figures give rise to a risk-free probability of 0.546 and, at a budgeted cost of $12.5 million, an option value 0. Given the noise surrounding the technical likelihood of succeeding at node 3, in the absence of learning, or if learning fails, the option is out of the money and management is better off to abandon the idea.

Assume now that the learning expense will reliably predict the probability of failure of the Phase II trial (node 2). This allows management to choose the value-maximizing path forward with certainty: If the predicted probability of success is sufficiently high for the budgeted costs to keep the investment option in the money, management will invest in the project (node 6). If the predicted probability of success is too low and drives the option out of the money under the current cost assumptions, management will abandon the project and preserve the $12.5 million projected costs (node 7). For each technical probability scenario, as identified by the learning experience, management would always be able to identify the best, that is, value-maximizing, path forward. Table 6.2 summarizes the results.

TABLE 6.1 The expected value at node 8 under a range of technical risks

Technical Uncertainty	10%	20%	30%	40%	50%	60%	70%	80%	90%
Node 8 Expected Value	($)	($)	($)	($)	($)	($)	($)	($)	($)
	2.00	4.26	6.39	8.52	10.65	12.78	14.91	17.05	19.18

TABLE 6.2 The value-maximizing path after learning

Technical Uncertainty	10%	20%	30%	40%	50%	60%	70%	80%	90%
Node 6 Expected Value	($) 2.00	($) 4.26	($) 6.39	($) 8.52	($) 10.65	($) 12.78	($) 14.91	($) 17.05	($) 19.18
Node 7 Expected Value	12.50	12.50	12.50	12.50	12.50	12.50	12.50	12.50	12.50
Managerial Choice	12.50	12.50	12.50	12.50	12.50	12.78	14.91	17.05	19.18

The expected value then, assuming that each technical success probability is an equally likely outcome of the learning experience, is $14.05 million. The minimum and the maximum value, again assuming that each technical probability scenario is an equally likely outcome of the learning experience, is the minimum and maximum possible value under all scenarios, that is, $12.5 million and maximal $19.18 million. These input parameters give rise to a risk-free probability of 0.758 and a value of the investment option of $15.03 million at node 4, compared to an option value of zero at node 5. To calculate the value of the learning option we need to move backwards to node 1. Assume it will cost $5 million to undertake experiments that will predict the outcome of the Phase II trial. This is the exercise price of the learning option. Assume further that those experiments have a 70% probability of giving a meaningful learning experience that reliably predicts the outcome of the Phase II trial. At node 1, then, the maximum asset value to be achieved is the expected value at node 4, $14.05 million. The minimum asset value is the expected value at node 3, when the learning experience fails to predict outcome (Figure 6.4). This gives rise to an expected value of $12.34 million and at an exercise price of $5 million of $7.34 million. The learning experience creates an option value of $15.03 million. Clearly, if the learning experience would provide that kind of reliable decision guideline, the value is significant.

If, in the absence of learning, management can pinpoint the technical probability of success between 30% and 60%, the option value of investing is still zero. If under these circumstances a learning experience would exactly predict the technical probability of success as being 30%, 40%, 50%, or 60%, it would again permit management to identify the best path forward and bring the value at node 4 to $12.57 million, the value added to the investment opportunity by learning. In this scenario, the amount of uncertainty to be reduced by learning is less than in the previous scenario. Therefore, the value of the learning experience is also less, that is, $13.45 million versus $15.03 million. Does that mean management should be prepared to invest $15.03 million in learning? No, of course not. The resources saved by not exercising an out-of-the money option define the lower boundary of the learning option. Or, in other words, the resources required for ex post learning constitute the lower boundary of the learning option, in this example $12.5 million. The upper boundary of the learning option is the total value created from learning, which is $15.03 million in our first example. Those two boundaries define the value of the learning option to $2.8 million. Management should not spend more than $2.8 million to obtain ex ante information. This assumes that the learning experience will be successful and deliver the information, that is, the probability at node 2 in Figure 6.4 is set at 100%. If the likelihood of the learning experience to deliver meaningful results declines, say to 70%, then the value of the learning option obviously also declines. In this scenario, there is a 30% chance that the learning experience will not deliver a meaningful result (node 3). This diminishes the value of learning and reduces the critical cost to invest in the learning option to $2.1 million.

If, on the other hand, in the absence of learning, management expects the probability of success for the Phase II trial to be between 60% and 90%, it would decide to move on with the project. A learning experience that would not challenge this assumption but only reduce the volatility by pinpointing the exact probability to be 60%, 70%, 80% or 90% would not add any value and not alter the managerial decision. The learning option value is zero.

So far we have assumed that the learning experience will deliver reliable results. However, the value of the learning option is also driven by its predictive power, which may not be 100%. How does lack of reliability play out in the value of the learning option?

Look at the binomial tree shown in Figure 6.5. If the learning experience results in 50% certainty that the project can be successfully developed through the Phase II clinical trial, the investment of $12.5 million will acquire a follow-on option of $87 million, the value of the investment opportunity prior to initiating Phase III and following completion of Phase II (node 2). With a 50% certainty, that assumption is wrong, and the investment of $12.5 million buys nothing (node 3). The expected value is hence 0.5 · $87.5 million or $43.75 million (node 1). If management decides to abandon the project, it will thereby save the budgeted costs of $12.5 million, the salvage value, and protect the firm against acquiring an option out of the

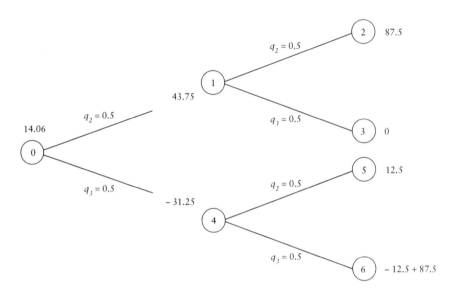

FIGURE 6.5 The binomial asset tree of the learning option I

money (node 5). There also is a 50% chance that it will forgo the opportunity to acquire an option worth $87.5 million with an initial investment out-
lay of $12.5 million (node 6). The expected value hence is 0.5 · $12.5 million
+ 0.5 · ($12.5 million – $87.5 million) or –$31.25 million.

Is it worth investing in a learning option that cannot deliver more reliable information? At node 0, acquiring the learning option creates in the
best case a value of $43.75 million. In the worst case, the learning experience
delivers unreliable information that misleads management so that it does not
acquire an investment option that is deep in the money. This will cost management an opportunity value of $31.25 million. The expected value is 0.5 ·
$43.75 million – 0.5 · $31.25 million, i.e., $14.06 million. The risk-free
probability derives from here as 0.617, and the value of the learning option
at node 0 is $15.04 million for a 50/50 certainty level.

If the result of the learning experience is only 20% reliable, then, for
each path forward (that is, investing or not investing), there is an 80%
chance of making the wrong decision. A 20% certainty that the project will
be successful implies that 8 out of 10 times the decision will be wrong and
the investment is out of the money. A 20% certainty that the project will be
a failure implies that in 8 out of 10 cases management will forgo the opportunity to acquire a follow-up option worth $87.5 million by investing

$12.5 million. The value of the call at a 20% certainty level is out of the money.

Assume now that the learning experience will predict success or failure with 80% certainty. If the prediction is successful, investing in the program buys the option worth $87.5 million with 80% certainty. In 2 out of 10 cases, that option will not materialize and the $12.5 million investment buys nothing. The expected value at node 1 then becomes: $0.80 \cdot \$87.5$ million + $0.2 \cdot \$0$ million = $70 million. If the learning experience excludes success with 80% certainty, management would abandon the project and be right in doing so in 8 out of 10 cases. In 2 out of 10 cases that decision would forgo the opportunity to acquire an option worth $87.5 million. The expected value hence becomes: $0.8 \cdot \$12.5$ million $- 0.2 \cdot \$87.5$ million, i.e., $-\$5$ million. As both outcomes of the learning experience are equally likely, the expected value now, at node zero, is $0.5 \cdot \$56$ million $- 0.5 \cdot \$5$ million, i.e., $33.75 million. This gives at a risk-free rate of 7% a risk-free probability of 0.548 and drives the value of the call to $36.11 million.

We calculate the value of the learning option at node zero as a function of the reliability provided by the learning experience. Figure 6.6 summarizes the results.

In fact, we can calculate the certainty level the learning exercise has to deliver for the learning option to be at the money at node 0. This is the certainty level that needs to be achieved to drive the value of the learning option at node 0 to zero. We calculate that, using the solver function in Excel, to be 28.57%.

The value of learning is the difference in option value at managerial certainty without learning compared to managerial certainty with learning. In other words, if management is already very certain about the prediction, say 60% that the project will either fail or succeed (low noise level), the incremental value created by incremental increase in certainty is small. If a learning

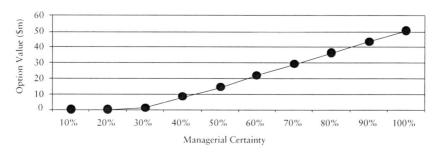

FIGURE 6.6 The learning option value as a function of learning reliability

experience decreases the noise and provides a certainty level of 70%, the incremental option value achieved is $29.09 million – $22.07 million or $5.2 million. However, if management is very uncertain and much noise clouds the prediction, then there is significant potential for value creation by gaining confidence in the prediction through learning.

Learning to Change the Probability of Success

Assume now that management can invest in a learning experience that will actually change the probability of success in Phase II of the drug development program. This would be a pilot program designed to deliver important clues on technical feasibility. Those clues will assist in shaping the actual R&D program and contribute to its success. An example of such a learning experience in the context of a drug development program is conducting additional pre-clinical tests with high predictive value that do not—per se—add to the development program. These could entail additional feasibility studies in animals or in cellular models.

If the learning exercise succeeds, in that it provides valuable information, it will impact on the value of the investment option in Phase II as well as all preceding phases. It will therefore also alter the critical cost to invest in the drug development program in all phases preceding Phase II. Further, it will change management's decision to invest at all or to abandon. If the learning exercise fails, it will not alter the probability of success, and management is left with the choice to make the decision to invest or abandon based on the original assumptions.

The learning exercise is restricted to reducing uncertainty of the private risk, the technical probability to succeed. We therefore assume that the learning exercise does not affect market uncertainty; assumptions about the best and worst payoff and the probability q of reaching one versus the other remain unchanged. However, the expected value of the asset prior to launch, when it is strictly a function of the technical probability to succeed, will be changed by the outcome of the learning exercise. The set up is summarized in the binomial option tree shown in Figure 6.7.

Management currently assumes a 60% likelihood of technical success for Phase II. The learning exercise can either challenge that assumption for the better or worse (node 4) or fail to produce any conclusive answer (node 5). If at node 4 the outcome of learning is an enhanced probability of success, management will invest (node 6) and face a $520 million payoff in the best case scenario (node 10) or $0 million in the worst case scenario (node 11) if the project fails at a later stage. If at node 4 the outcome is a reduced

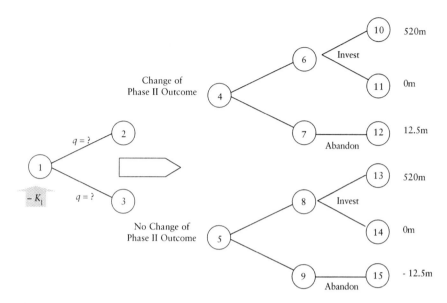

FIGURE 6.7 The binomial asset tree of managerial options under learning

probability of success, management may be inclined to abandon the project and will save $12.5 million in investment costs (node 12). Table 6.3 summarizes the expected managerial choice for investment and abandoning at various probabilities of success ranging from 20% to 90%.

We assume that once the learning exercise is completed and management knows the probability of success for Phase II, it will decide for the value-maximizing path forward, that is, abandon if prudent and invest if promising. Hence, we derive the expected value from the maximum value

TABLE 6.3 The asset value at node 4 under private risk

Technical Success	20%	30%	40%	50%	60%	70%	80%	90%
Value at Node 6	($) 4.26	($) 6.39	($) 8.52	($) 10.65	($) 12.78	($) 14.91	($) 17.05	($) 19.18
Value at Node 7	12.50	12.50	12.50	12.50	12.50	12.50	12.50	12.50
Managerial Choice at Node 4	12.50	12.50	12.50	12.50	12.78	14.91	17.05	19.18

and assign equal probabilities of 0.125 or 12.5% to each of the eight technical probability scenarios examined. This amounts to $14.24 million. The maximum asset value is the maximum value to be achieved under all possible scenarios of technical success, that is, $19.18 million if the technical success is 90%. The minimum asset value, again over the range of possible outcomes for technical success, is correspondingly $12.5 million. These input data make it possible to calculate the value of the call at node 4:

$$p_4 = \frac{1.07 \cdot 14.24 - 12.5}{19.18 - 12.25} = 0.4097$$

$$C_4 = 0.4097 \cdot 19.18 + (1 - 0.4309) \cdot 12.5 = 15.24m$$

We now move on to value the lower arm of the binomial tree. This captures the scenario that the learning exercise fails to provide a conclusive answer. In this case management will rely on its own assumptions, that is, a 60% probability of success for Phase II. We have previously determined the asset value at node 8 for this scenario to be $12.78 million. There is a 40% chance that the product will fail in Phase II; the option will then be out of the money, and the $12.5 million incurred costs are lost, the value at node 15 in Figure 6.7 is then –$12.5 million. This leads to an expected value at node 5 of $2.67 million. We now look at the first node in the binomial tree and determine its value. Figure 6.8 summarizes the above analysis.

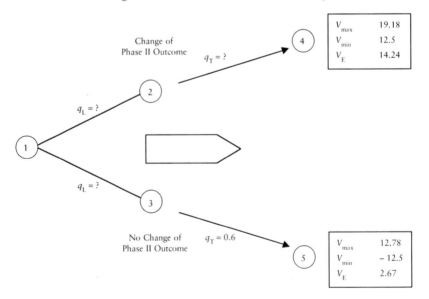

FIGURE 6.8 The binomial asset tree of the learning option II

TABLE 6.4 The option value of learning at node 1 as a function of risk reduction through learning

qL		10%	30%	50%	70%	90%
V_{max}	$14.24					
V_{min}	$2.67					
V_{exp}		$3.83	$6.14	$8.45	$10.77	$13.08
p		0.123	0.337	0.551	0.765	0.979
Call at Node 1		$4.09	$6.57	$9.05	$11.52	$14.00

The expected value at node 4 and at node 5, $14.24 million and $2.67 million, respectively, become the maximum and minimum asset value at node 2 and 3, respectively. The expected value at node 1 depends hence on the probability q_1 that the learning exercise will actually deliver a reliable result and alter the outcome of the Phase II trial. We show the value of the learning option as a function of increasing probability to deliver conclusive results in Table 6.4.

With increasing likelihood of the learning exercise to alter the outcome of Phase II, the value of the call option increases. Please note that this is irrespective of the nature of that change. Even if the outcome of Phase II would—as a result of the learning exercise—be downgraded from the working assumption of 60% success to 20% success, that result, if reliable, is very valuable to management. It would allow management to ex ante decide not to move forward with the drug development program, but either save the investment costs of $12.5 million or invest them in another project. Management would not learn ex post, upon completion of Phase II, that the trial had failed.

PASSIVE AND ACTIVE LEARNING UNDER COMPETITIVE CONDITIONS

The value of the learning option, similar to that of a medical diagnostic test, is driven by the impact it has on managerial decisions. Only if a diagnostic test has the potential to change the treatment decision will it be of value to the physician. Similarly, only if the outcome of the learning experience has the potential to change a managerial decision will it be of value. We will now investigate the value of a learning option under competitive conditions that alters the payoff function. Initially we will investigate the value of the option to defer and learn passively and then move on to study the added value of active learning in a competitive scenario.

In Chapter 5 we saw the potential benefit of passive learning for a new product development program. We also recognized that deferring and learning passively from observation also implies a certain risk of incurring enhanced opportunity costs under competitive threat. Deferring the decision results in later market entry that may cause loss of market share or of a competitive position and destroy option value. We will now examine how a scenario of competitive threat impacts on the option to defer and learn passively versus the option to invest early and also invest in active learning.

A publishing firm contemplates developing an electronic book. There is significant uncertainty as to the market acceptance of such a product, as well as uncertainty as to the probability of technical success. The management team has a set of beliefs regarding its own internal development time line, cost structure, and probability of success. Further, there is substantial concern that the closest rival may contemplate a similar project. In the absence of reliable competitive intelligence, management has to build its decision on internal assumptions and beliefs. A binomial asset tree shown in Figure 6.9 is helpful in framing the various possible scenarios.

Management assumes it will take two years from project inception to product launch, cost $60 million to develop the program, and the probability of success is estimated to be 70% (node 4; $q_4 = 0.7$). The ultimate market payoff is thought to be between $150 million and $60 million (node 8 and 9, respectively) with each scenario being equally likely ($q_8 = q_9 = 0.5$).

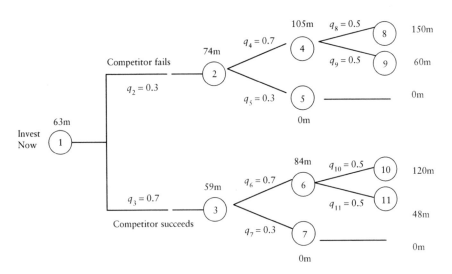

FIGURE 6.9 The investment option under competitive conditions

Management further believes that there is a 70% chance ($q_3 = 0.7$) for its rival publishing house to also engage in a similar project and to succeed and enter the market simultaneously but target a slightly different market initially. Our management team therefore believes that simultaneous competitive entry by the rival will reduce its market share by 20%. Under these assumptions the expected payoff will decline to $120 million in the best case and $48 million in the worst case scenario (nodes 10 and 11, respectively).

The expected payoffs at node 4 and 6 reflect managerial assumptions of the best and worst market payoff, both are assumed to be equally likely under compete and non-compete conditions ($q = 0.5$), yielding an expected value of $105 million and $84 million, respectively (node 4 and node 6). There is a 30% chance of failing both under compete and non-compete conditions (nodes 5 and 7), respectively, yielding to zero payoffs. The expected payoffs at nodes 2 and 3 then become $74 million and $59 million, respectively.

With a likelihood of competitive entry of 70%, the expected value at node 1 becomes $63 million. The maximum value to be achieved under these sets of assumptions is $74 million at node 2, and the minimum value at node 3 is $59 million. This gives rise to a risk-free probability p_1 for these sets of assumptions.

$$p_1 = \frac{1.07 \cdot 63 - 59}{74 - 59} = 0.601$$

The value of the call at node 1 for an anticipated development time frame of two years until product launch and an exercise price of $60 million then becomes:

$$C_1 = \frac{0.601 \cdot 74 + (1 - 0.601) \cdot 59}{1.07^2} - 60 = 5.37$$

Management would now like to obtain an understanding of the sensitivity of the option value to the probability of competitive entry as well as to the extent of market share loss. Specifically management wants to know under what set of assumptions the option moves out of the money. As part of this sensitivity analysis, the success probability for the competitor is decreased to 50% and increased to 90%, while the anticipated loss in market share ranges now from 15% in the best case to 55% in the worst case scenario. For each of those conditions the option value is calculated. Those data are summarized in Figure 6.10.

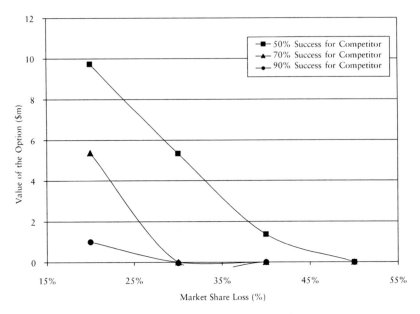

FIGURE 6.10 Option value as a function of competitive threat

As the probability of competitive entry increases from 50% to 70% and 90%, a loss of 43.6%, 29.2% and 21.3% market share, respectively, is sufficient to drive the option value to zero. In other words, if management is expecting as much as a 21% loss in market share due to a competitor, it will be better off to abandon the project if it expects the competitor to enter with high probability. However, if that probability drops below 90%, management may still find option value in investing in the project.

How sensitive is the value of the investment option to predictions of the best and the worst market payoff scenario to occur? Figure 6.11 shows the results assuming the competitor fails or assuming he succeeds and captures 20% or 30% of the market share.

Looking at these data, management realizes that small deviations of the plan and underestimation of its competitor could move the option out of the money rather quickly. Under these considerations, management contemplates two alternative strategies:

1. Defer and observe market acceptance of the electronic book by letting its competitor move first.
2. Invest in active learning and—depending on the learning outcome—pursue the program aggressively.

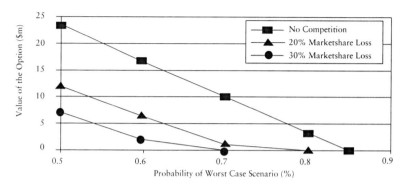

FIGURE 6.11 Sensitivity of the option value to the worst case market scenario

Those strategic options and managerial beliefs about the potential outcome are depicted in the binomial asset tree shown in Figure 6.12.

If management defers and the competitor moves on and launches in two years from now (node 3), management would learn about the market acceptance within the first six months of its competitor's product launch, as well as about the basic feasibility of the technology. If its competitor succeeds and market acceptance is good, management would then initiate the internal program (node 8). Management would expect that the product would have some superior features that would permit market success even as a follower, minimizing the downside market risk in the worst case scenario to $100 million while preserving an upside potential of $120 million (nodes 12/13). Management further feels confident enough to increase the overall technical probability of success to 0.9 (q_{10}), as it will be able to learn from the competitor's product. If the competitor's product does badly, and there is no market acceptance of the product, management would abandon the project (node 9). There would be no sunk cost and no value created.

There is a 30% chance that the competitor will not enter the market, either because the product development fails or because the competitor defers. If management moves forward (node 2), there will be no learning experience despite deferring the decision. Hence, both the assumptions on technical success probability and on ultimate market payoff are as uncertain as they are now. The technical probability of success is 70% (node 4), and the market payoff can range between $150 million and $60 million (nodes 6 and 7, respectively).

Alternatively, management could invest in an active learning exercise now (node 14) that would hedge some of the market uncertainty. There would be an additional expense of $3 million ($-K$) for market research including prototype testing, and the product launch would be delayed by three months. Depending on the outcome of this pilot project, management would accept the product

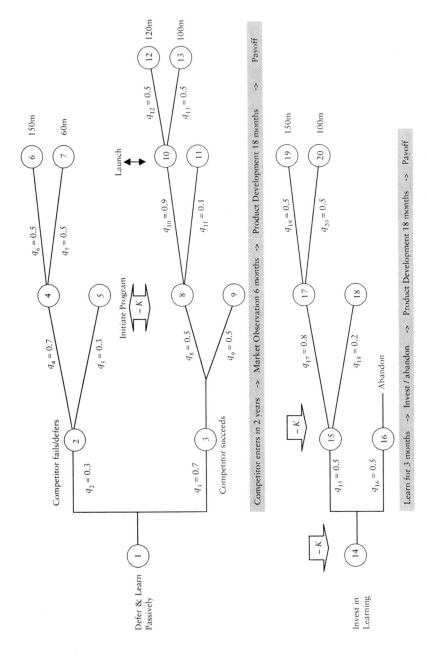

FIGURE 6.12 The binomial tree of managerial options: Invest in learning or learn passively by deferring

(node 15) and move forward if market payoff ranges between $150 million and $100 million (nodes 19/20) and abandon the project otherwise (node 16). The pilot project will also allow management to make better predictions about the technical success, which is likely to be 80% once the initial prototype has been built (node 17). There remains a 20% chance of failure (node 18).

What is the better strategic option under these assumptions, and how would a change in assumptions alter the best path forward? We provide the calculations for the initial assumptions in the revised binomial tree in Figure 6.13.

Please note that at nodes 9 and 16 the minimum value is the abandonment value, i.e., 0. This assumes that if the project fails, there will be no residual value for the organization from the investment. If management feels that even in the event of failure the organization will extract additional insight, knowledge, or data from the experience, that residual value would replace the current salvage value of zero.

The maximum value at node 8 is the expected future payoff from nodes 10/11 minus the anticipated costs of $60 million. The maximum value at node 15 is the expected future value from nodes 17/18 minus the anticipated product development costs of $60 million. Under the current assumptions the value of active learning today at node 14 is $12.96 million.

At node 1 management decides to defer and learn passively. From then on, there are two possible outcomes, shown in more detail in Figure 6.14: the competitor enters and management will learn (node 3), or the competitor fails and management has no opportunity to learn (node 2).

For node 3, the expected value derives from the expected value at node 8 and node 9. At node 8, the expected value is the present value of the expected value from nodes 10 and 11 minus the expected costs of $60 million, i.e., $39 million. At node 9 the project will be abandoned and the expected value is zero. Given that each scenario is assumed to be equally likely ($q_8 = q_9 = 0.5$) the expected value at node 3 hence is 19.3m. For node 2, the expected value derives from nodes 4 and 5 and amounts to $74 million minus the expected costs of $60 million, i.e., $14 million. The expected value at node 2 will materialize six months before the expected value at node 3 will, which needs to be considered when calculating the value of the call. We therefore discount at the corporate WACC the expected value at nodes 2 and 3 back to the time at node 1, yielding $10.48 million for node 2 and $9.25 million for node 3. At a probability of 0.7 for the competitor to enter and the scenario following node 3 to materialize, the expected value for node 1 hence becomes $9.62 million, the risk-free probability is 0.845, and the value of the call at node 1 is $8.99 million (Figure 6.13). Strategy 2, ending at node 14, on the other hand, gives an option value of $12.96 million and is the more valuable path forward.

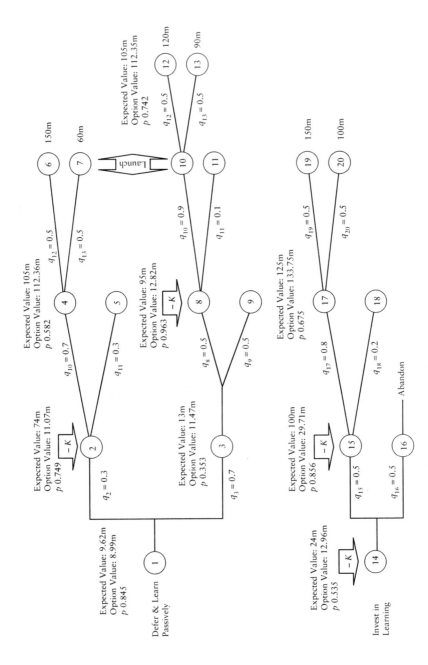

FIGURE 6.13 Asset and option values for the strategic options

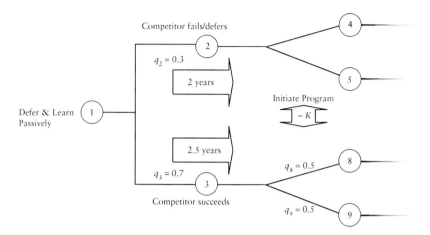

FIGURE 6.14 The binomial asset tree for the option to defer and learn passively

Management would like to develop a better understanding as to what drives the value of each option path, and under what circumstances both options are equally valuable. In mathematical terms, management needs to identify what conditions make the equation shown in Figure 6.15 equal to define the option space.

Intuitively, the probability of competitive entry and the extent of market share loss on the left side (nodes 2 and 3) as well as the probability of the learning exercise to deliver a result that meets the requirements for proceeding with the project or in failing to do so will drive the balance of the equation. On the right side, important drivers also include how much a successful learning exercise will actually increase the upside potential at node 15 by reducing the private or technical risk (node 17) and the assumptions for the final market payoff at nodes 19 and 20, as shown in Figure 6.13.

We first look at the sensitivity of the option to learn actively at node 14 to the likelihood of the learning experience to be successful (node 15) and to

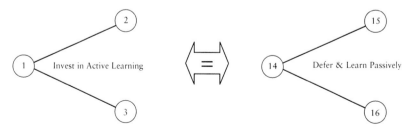

FIGURE 6.15 The decision equation

actually decrease the private risk (node 17). The data are summarized in Figure 6.16.

Keeping the probability for technical success or private risk constant at 80%, the probability for the learning experience to be successful (node 15) is increased at incremental steps of 1% (solid squares). Keeping the probability of success for the learning experience at node 15 constant at 50%, the solid triangles depict how the value of the option at node 14 changes as the likelihood of technical success increases in incremental steps from 80% to 95% at node 17.

The value of the learning option is most sensitive to the ability of the learning exercise to actually help in increasing the technical probability of success (node 17). It is much less sensitive to the probability of success or failure of the learning experience itself at node 15. This is evident from the slope of both curves. Figure 6.17 summarizes the percentage change in option value as a result of incremental 1% increases in the probability of success for learning and the technical probability of success.

We can now also show the value of the option as a function of changing probabilities in both node 15 and node 17 and calculate for all probability scenarios the conditions under which for the current market payoff assumptions the value of learning actively equals exactly the value of deferring and investing later. The dashed line in Figure 6.18 depicts the border

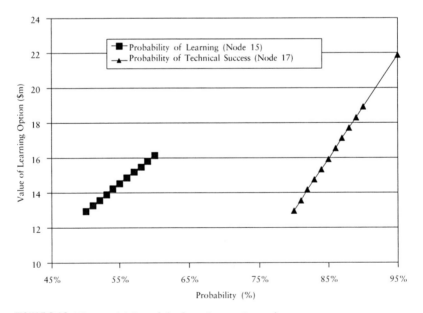

FIGURE 6.16 The sensitivity of the learning option value

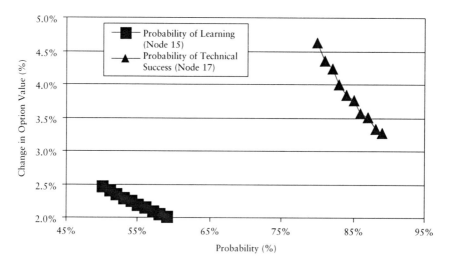

FIGURE 6.17 Changes in option value caused by incremental changes in private risk or learning success

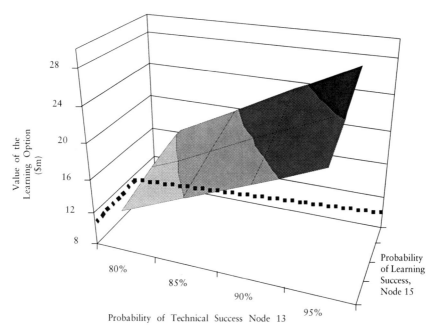

FIGURE 6.18 Value of the learning option as a function of private risk reduction and learning success

between deferring (area below the dashed line) and investing in learning (area above the dashed line) for a range of probabilities of technical success (x-axis) and learning success (z-axis).

Management would also like to develop an understanding as to how sensitive the value of the learning option is to the ultimate market payoff assumptions. This is analyzed for the basic set of assumptions, i.e. probability at node 15 of 50% and at node 17 of 80%. See Figure 6.19.

A 1% increase in both minimum and maximum market payoff results in an increase of option value of $0.47 million, compared to a $0.60 million increase in incremental option value for each percentage increase of the technical probability of success and a $0.32 million incremental increase for each percentage increase in probability at node 15.

What must happen in order for the option to wait and defer (node 1) to be as valuable as the option to learn actively (node 14)? First, waiting must be worthwhile, that is, management must be rewarded by learning from waiting. The way the current scenario is set up, passive learning is linked to the competitor entering. If the competitor fails to enter, management does not have the opportunity to learn much. In this case (node 2) management will invest with a two-year delay. The risk of not learning anything by delaying but instead losing time value of money is 30%. The potential upside of learning

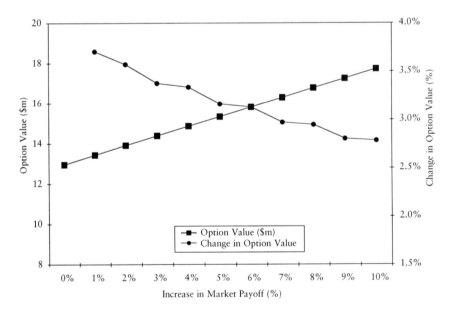

FIGURE 6.19 Value of the learning option as a function of market payoff

has to compensate for this risk. Either the minimum or maximum expected payoff at nodes 6 and 7, respectively (Figure 6.12) must increase to compensate for the time value of money. If the competitor enters, management will learn about technical feasibility and about market acceptability leading to more confident assumptions on the likelihood of developing the product (q_{10}) and also more refined assumptions as to the market size at nodes 12 and 13. Passive learning will help the organization to devise the proper product development strategy so that the likelihood of success at q_{10} is 90%. Additional improvements may come from developing a better product that will still capture significant market share at node 12 or by accelerating the product development time. Even if competitive entry would not result in market share loss and preserve the estimated $150 million asset value as best case scenario at node 12 and limit the worst case scenario to $90 million, the option value at node 1 is, with $11.89 million, still less than the option to invest in active learning. In other words, under the basic set of assumptions that give a value of $12.96 million for the option to invest in active learning and proceed with the program now, competitive entry without the risk of losing market share will not rescue the option to learn passively.

If there is no risk for market share loss under competitive entry as the players address different market segments and if by deferring and passive learning the technical probability of success can be increased to 95%, the value of the option at node 1 becomes $13.19 million and hence the better choice. Alternatively, if there is no risk of market share loss and the development time can be shortened by 33% to one year, the value of the option at node 1 becomes $12.69 million, still less than the option value for the alternative strategy.

Alternatively, management may want to know what the benefit of the learning experience has to be at minimum to justify the expense. If the learning exercise fails to limit the downside of the market risk, currently assumed to be no less than $100 million, the value of the option at node 14 declines quickly, as shown in Figure 6.20 with the solid squares. Solid triangles represent the option value at node 1.

If the learning experience fails to limit with certainty the downside market risk to $79.1 million as the worst case scenario, the option to defer and learn passively becomes more valuable. If the active learning experience fails to eliminate the downside private risk of technical failure in product development, then, too, there is rapid loss in the value of entertaining an active learning experiment. Figure 6.21 depicts the steady decline in option value at node 14 as the learning exercise fails to limit the downside risk of technical failure to 20%.

How does the option space for the strategy to defer versus active learning look like now? Table 6.5 summarizes the results of the sensitivity analysis and the resulting strategic recommendation.

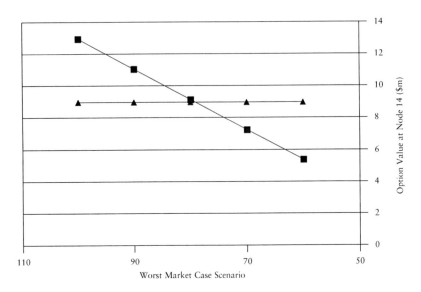

FIGURE 6.20 Value of the learning option at node 14 as a function of worst case scenarios

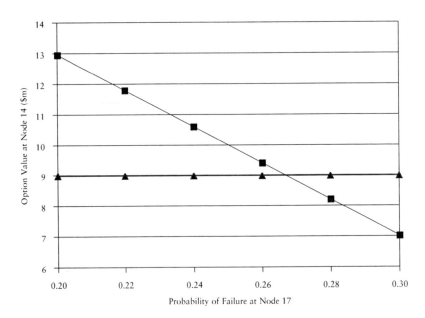

FIGURE 6.21 Value of the learning option at node 14 depending on the probability of failure at node 17

TABLE 6.5 The option space: Strategic recommendations for uncertainty scenarios

Assumptions for Learn Actively Strategy	*p* Node 15: 0.5 / P Node 17: 0.8 / Payoff: 100–150m / Option Value: 12.96	*p* Node 15: ≤ 0.337 / P Node 17: 0.8 / Payoff: 100m–150m / Option Value: ≤ 8.97	*p* Node 15: 0.5 / P Node 17: 0.8 / Payoff: < 79.1m–150m / Option Value: < 8.99	*p* Node 15: 0.5 / P Node 17: ≤ 0.733 / Payoff: 100m–150m / Option Value: ≤ 8.98
Assumptions for Defer & Passive Learning		**Option Recommendation**		
20% Loss of Market Share; 90% Technical Probability; 1.5 years Time of Development 70% Probability of Competitive Entry	Learn Actively Option Value 8.99	Defer & Learn Passively	Defer & Learn Passively	Defer & Learn Passively
No loss of Market Share under Competitive Entry	Learn Actively Option Value 11.89	Defer & Learn Passively	Defer & Learn Passively	Defer & Learn Passively
No Loss of Market Share + Technical Success Probability of 95%	Defer & Learn Option Value 13.19	Defer & Learn Passively	Defer & Learn Passively	Defer & Learn Passively
No Loss of Market Share & Reduced Development Time to 1 year	Learn Actively Option Value 12.69	Defer & Learn Passively	Defer & Learn Passively	Defer & Learn Passively

THE VALUE OF IMPROVING VERSUS TIMING

In new product development, especially in situations involving a competitive race, management is often required to make a trade-off decision between accelerating the time to market of the new product in order to secure a strong market position and gain rapid market penetration, on one side, or allowing more time for product improvements, on the other side. This decision becomes especially difficult at the boundary space of both options, namely when the need to accelerate time to market jeopardizes the success of the product. Accelerating program development can, for example, decrease the probability of technical success, as important development steps have to be taken very quickly. Alternatively, the firm may focus on basic product features and may not be able to take the time to address critical market requirements for the product.

A comparable scenario has been investigated in a recent publication by Lint and Pennings.[8] The authors look at the new product development process at Philips Electronics. They separate the launch phase of a new product to be developed from the R&D phase that leads to its development. The launch of the product in their interpretation equals an American perpetual call option with no limitation in the exercise time. The value of the product at each time prior to launch is derived from the expected value post launch, just as we have seen when looking at the pharmaceutical R&D project as a compounded option in Chapter 3. The value of this option during the R&D phase changes as new information on technical success, market requirements, or competitive entry arrives, permitting management to abandon, delay, accelerate, or mothball the project.

Lint and Pennings value this product development option as a forward start American call option. A financial forward start option is paid for now but will not start before some time in the future. Usually, forward start options are at the money when they are issued. The value of a forward start option on a non-dividend paying stock is the same as the value of an at-the-money regular option with the same time to maturity.[9] We will now provide an option valuation framework based on the binomial option that permits comparing the option to accelerate time to market versus the option to improve, and thereby also delay market entry under a variety of uncertainties.

A firm contemplates the development of a novel product for its retail customers. Figure 6.22 summarizes the basic managerial assumptions in a binomial asset tree. It will cost $100 million and take about two years to get to the market. The expected payoff is $200 million in the best case and $150 million in the worst case (nodes 9/10). Engineers estimate the technical probability of success to be 80%. In an attempt to send a strong signal to the

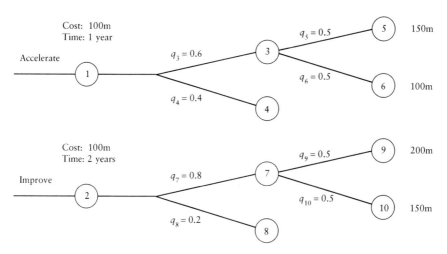

FIGURE 6.22 The binomial asset tree of the option to improve versus to accelerate

market and its competitors, management would rather see a first version of the product evolve much quicker, that is, in one year. This product may have less refined features and therefore is expected to enjoy a reduced market payoff. Market adoption will be slower and penetration less impressive than an upgraded version of the same product is expected to achieve. The maximum payoff of this product version will not be more than $150 million, and in the worst case it will be only $100 million (nodes 5/6). As development steps have to be accelerated and certain probing and testing exercises will be omitted entirely, the engineers feel that for such an accelerated program the technical likelihood of succeeding is no more than 60% ($q_3 = 0.6$). As emphasis is on speed, maximum resources will be mobilized, and it will cost as much to develop an inferior, less-developed and less-refined product more quickly as it would cost to produce a more-refined product in a longer period of time. The exercise price for this strategy therefore is also assumed to be $100 million. The challenge for senior management is to identify the best path forward, both for non-compete and compete conditions.

What is the value of each managerial option, what are the key sensitivities, and what are the conditions that separate the two paths forward? We will answer this for the basic set of assumptions first, then provide some scenario analysis and ultimately also investigate how a competitive threat may alter the decision.

As to the value of the call option at node 1, we start at the end of the binomial tree and work our way backwards.

The asset value at node 3 is the expected value of future payoffs, that is,

$$V_3 = q_5 \cdot V_5 + q_6 \cdot V_6$$

$$V_3 = 0.5 \cdot \$150 \text{ million} + 0.5 \cdot \$100 \text{ million} = \$125 \text{ million}$$

The value at node 4 is zero, that is, the project failed. Hence, at a technical probability of success of q_4 equal to 60% the expected value at node 1 is $75 million. This allows calculating the risk-free probability p at node 1:

$$p_1 = \frac{1.07 \cdot V_{E1} - V_4}{V_3 - V_4}$$

$$p = \frac{1.07 \cdot 75 - 0}{125 - 0}$$

$$= 0.642$$

The value of the call for a time to maturity of one year and a cost outlay of $100 million today, which accrues at the corporate cost of capital for one year to $113.5 million, then becomes:

$$C_1 = \text{Max}\ (0, \frac{0.642 \cdot 125 + (1 - 0.642) \cdot 0}{1.07^1} - 113.5)$$

$$= \text{Max}\ (0, -33.25)$$

$$= 0$$

The value of the call on the investment opportunity to accelerate the program is deep out of the money.

On the contrary, applying the same calculation scheme to value the call at node 2, we obtain $17.34 million. Under the current set of assumptions, clearly the option to accept a longer time frame for product development but develop an improved product with higher market potential is the more valuable path.

Management next needs to define the most important drivers of uncertainty for each strategy as well as the boundary conditions that separate one strategy from the other as the more valuable strategy. We look at the sensitivity of each option to market uncertainty first.

We saw before that the sensitivity of options to drivers of uncertainty depends on whether the option is at or deep in the money. To ensure comparability of each option to market uncertainty at nodes 3 and 7, respectively, we define the conditions when the technical probability of success moves either option at the money. For the call at node 1, the technical probability of success has to increase from the current prediction of 60% to 84.95% to move the call option at the money. For the call at node 2, a technical probability of success of 69.4% is sufficient to preserve the moneyness of the option. We now investigate how an incremental change of 1% towards the best market scenario, currently assumed to be 50%, impacts the value of the option at node 1 and at node 2. Figure 6.23 summarizes the results.

In absolute terms, each incremental increase in market payoff probability towards the best case scenario delivers more option value to node 1 than to node 2. The percentage change of option value, however (right panel), is the same.

Under the basic set of assumptions with a technical success probability of 80% and an equal probability for the best and worst case market payoff scenario of 50%, the call at node 1 moves at the money if the expected payoff for the minimum and maximum asset value each increase by 41.5% to $212 million for node 5 and $142 million for node 6, respectively. For node 2, the ultimate payoff can drop by 13.2% for the maximum and minimum assert value, that is, to $174 million and $130 million at nodes 9 and 10, respectively, to move the option at the money. For those basic conditions we investigate how an incremental increase of 1% of the maximum and minimum payoff alters the option value when both options are at the money. Figure 6.24 summarizes the data; the call at node 2 is more sensitive to changes in total market payoff than the call at node 1.

Finally we look at the sensitivity of each call to changes in the technical probability of success under conditions in which both options are at the money. Assuming a market probability of 50% for the best and worst case scenario and a final market payoff of $212 million and $141 million for call 1, and $175 million and $130 million for call 2, respectively, we increase the

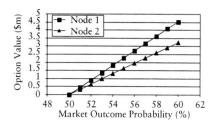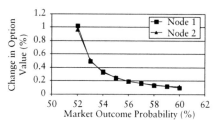

FIGURE 6.23 Option sensitivity to market risk

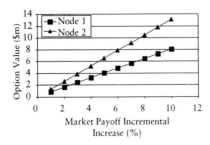 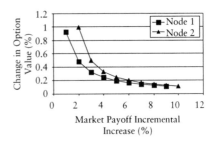

FIGURE 6.24 Option sensitivity to market payoff

basic technical probability of success of 60% for call 1 and 80% for call 2 in increments of 1%. Figure 6.25 summarizes the data.

Under these conditions, both calls display equal sensitivity to a percent increase in technical probability of success (right panel), while the incremental absolute increase in option value, shown in the left panel, is higher for the call at node 1.

What are now the boundary conditions that separate whichever of the two product development strategies is of higher value? The call at node 1 is deeply out of the money. We require a 41.25% increase in expected market payoff to move this call at the money under the current probability and cost scenarios. To achieve the same value as call 2, the payoff at nodes 5 and 6 has to increase by 63%. Clearly, if management feels that the technical probability of success at node 4 could increase to 70% or even 80% and also the probability for the best market scenario to materialize could increase from currently 50% at node 5 to more, the required payoff at nodes 5 and 6 would not have to increase as much to make the option at node 1 as valuable as the option at node 2, namely $17.96 million.

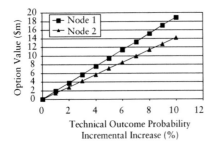 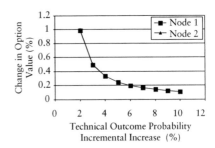

FIGURE 6.25 Option sensitivity to private risk

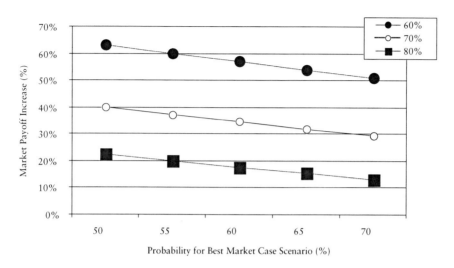

FIGURE 6.26 The decision line: Accelerate versus improve under private and market risk

Figure 6.26 summarizes the scenario analysis. For three different probabilities of technical success at node 3, namely 60%, 70%, and 80%, and as a function of the likelihood that the best market payoff scenario will materialize (on the x-axis), it is shown how much the overall expected market payoff has to increase so that the option value at node 1 is the same as the option value at node 2. The three solid lines separate the different investment strategies for the three different assumptions about private or technical risk. Above each line it is better to go for the accelerated program; below each line it is more valuable to go for the longer product development program that delivers an improved product.

How will the two options compare to each other if the improved product that reaches the market after a one-year delay will not capture more market share than the accelerated product that would enter one year earlier? Here we look at the option value for node 2 for a best case market payoff of $150 million and a worst case of $100 million. For a technical probability of success of 80% and equal likelihood of best and worst case market scenario, that option is now out of the money at node 2. Figure 6.27 summarizes how the option at node 2 moves at the money for a range of technical probabilities at node 7 as a function of the expected payoff (solid line), and defines the boundary conditions between "improving" (above the line) and "accelerating" (below the line).

How will competitive entry alter the dynamics of the two strategic options, accelerating product development versus improving product features?

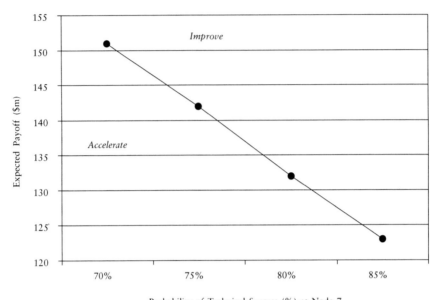

FIGURE 6.27 The decision line accelerate versus improve

Obviously, this again depends on the assumptions: the probability of competitive entry, the timing and the anticipated loss in market share and which of the two product development strategies is more at risk under various competitive entry scenarios. Assume that competitive entry will happen within a year, and the product will be in exact competition with the product an accelerated development strategy would produce. Under these circumstances, the market penetration and market share will be reduced, making strategy 1 an even less desirable path forward. Even if an improved product has outstanding product differentiation characteristics, there is a good chance that prior competitive entry will reduce the market potential for the improved version as well. If the improved product fails to capture at minimum $132 million of market value after launch, the investment opportunity is out of the money. If a competitor is expected to enter the market in two years with an advanced product that has a good chance of reducing market share to less than $132 million, management better reconsider its investment options. A complementary example for a preemptive investment scenario has been discussed in Chapter 5.

NOTES

1. K. McCardle, "Information Acquisition and the Adoption of New Technology," *Management Science* 31:1372, 1985.
2. K. Roberts and M. Weitzman, "Funding Criteria for Research, Development and Exploration Projects," *Econometrica* 49:1261, 1981.
3. D. Epstein, N. Mayor, P. Schonbucher, E. Whalley, and P. Wilmott, "The Value of Market Research When a Firm is Learning. Real Option Pricing and Optimal Filtering," in L. Trigeorgis, ed., *Real Options and Business Strategy. Applications to Decision-making* (Risk Books, 2001).
4. P.D. Childs, S.H. Ott, and T.J. Riddiough, "Valuation and Information Acquisition Policy for Claims Written on Noisy Real Assets." *Financial Management* 30:45, 2001.
5. J. Gould, "Risk, Stochastic Preference and the Value of Information," *Journal of Economic Theory* 8:64, 1974; R. Hilton, "Determinants of Information Value." *Management Science* 27:57, 1981; M. Willinger, "Risk Aversion and the Value of Information," *Journal of Risk and Insurance* 56:320, 1989; L. Eeckhoudt and P. Godfroid, "Risk Aversion and the Value of Information," *Journal of Economic Education* 31:382, 2000.
6. S. Majd and R.S. Pindyck, "Time to Build, Option Value, and Investment Decisions," *Journal of Industrial Economics* 18:7, 1987; E. Pennings and O. Lint, "The Option Value of Advanced R&D," *European Journal of Operational Research* 103:83, 1997.
7. S.H. Martzoukos, "Real R&D Options with Endogenous and Exogenous Learning," working paper 01–07, 2001.
8. O. Lint and E. Pennings, "An Option Approach to the New Product Development Process: A Case Study at Philips Electronics," *R&D Management* 31:163, 2001.
9. J.C. Hull, *Options, Futures and Other Derivatives* (Prentice Hall, 1997).

CHAPTER 7

Real Option Analysis—A Support Framework for Corporate Strategy

Strategy, according to the *Oxford Dictionary*, is a plan intended to achieve a particular purpose, such as the planning of movements of armies in a battle of war. The origin of the word is Greek; *strategia* refers to the office of the general. Strategy is science and art, and it involves three components: resources, understanding of a situation, and a goal. From these three components the strategic plan is derived. Strategy addresses uncertainty, irreversibility, and flexibility. The cornerstones of real option analysis are uncertainty, irreversibility, and the managerial flexibility to respond to future changes. Rumelt[1] noticed some time ago a growing closeness between strategic management research and economic theory; the main goal of real option analysis is to align corporate strategy with financial markets[2] in times of great uncertainty and complexity.

Several concepts and frameworks feature in the strategic management literature to assist management in drawing the road map for future value creation. Real options are an excellent analytical tool to integrate internally project management, budget decisions, and overall corporate strategy, while also establishing the link to internal and external uncertainties. Key ingredients for reliable and helpful real option analysis include a very good understanding of corporate capabilities and resources, the competitive environment, and market dynamics. Strategy requires predictions about the future, and so does real option analysis, but in the words of Niels Bohr, the Danish physicist: "Prediction is very difficult, especially about the future." Or, as Eugene Ionesco, the Romanian-born, French writer states: "You can only predict things after they have happened." Still, patterns of the past provide comforting guidance; they serve to collect data, as projections for future what-if scenarios, and as such deliver the scaffold for planning.

A look at the strategic management literature suggests that strategic management concepts undergo decadal changes.[3] The seventies valued market growth and favored the emergence of large, diversified multinational conglomerates. The strategic management literate witnessed the creation of the Boston Consulting Group Growth Share matrix and subsequent to that a strong focus on the portfolio approach to management. The eighties, under the influence of dramatic conglomerate failures, invited a more comprehensive analysis of competitive forces that shape business decisions and business survival: they became the decade of Porter's five forces. The nineties replaced strategic focus on differentiation and cost leadership by a new emphasis on quality. As businesses that focused on total quality management failed, during the last decade of the past millennium continued renewal, core competence, and time and network building emerged as driving strategic forces that led to business success.

Each of these concepts reflects economic systems, society, culture, and the realization that the existing mainframe paradigm failed to work in a changing environment. Each new concept provides a new perspective on how to approach value creation for the firm, and what it may entail. Real option analysis works well within all those strategic frameworks. This chapter will discuss how the real option framework can be integrated into, support, and benefit from some of these concepts. We will touch on three main ideas: the notion of core competence of an organization, the balanced scorecard, and portfolio management.

THE BALANCED SCORECARD

Kaplan and Norton[4] introduced the balanced scorecard to managerial thinking in the early nineties. The balanced scorecard marries financial with organizational performance. The authors propose a causative link between monitoring and evaluation of daily business operations and overall strategic achievements as well as financial performance. The creation of the balanced scorecard was driven by the ambition to offer an alternative perspective to organizations that overemphasized short-term financial performance. The balanced scorecard introduces four dimensions of performance measurement and their mutual interplay: Financials, Learning, Processes, and Customers (Figure 7.1). The ability of the organization to learn continuously and manage and improve processes and procedures is key to customer satisfaction and loyalty. Enhancing both customer satisfaction and retention will ultimately also improve financial performance.

There are some obvious overlaps between the balanced scorecard and the real option framework: (1) Enforcement and communication throughout

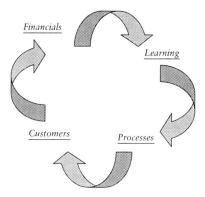

Financials

Learning

Customers

Processes

FIGURE 7.1 The balanced scorecard concept

the organization is key to the successful implementation of the balanced scorecard, an idea also common to the real option framework. 2) Measurement of past performance, as was pointed out when Kaplan and Norton[5] recently revisited the topic, has consequences far beyond reporting on the past: It creates focus for the future and communicates important messages to all organizational units and employees. In other words, it shapes corporate strategy, bottom-up and top-down. Ultimately, the scorecard aims at helping with the alignment of management processes and systems to corporate strategy.[6] The balanced scorecard increasingly emerges as a strategic management system to institutionalize cultural values and structures. If tightly linked with traditional organizational processes and procedures, such as compensation, budgeting, and resource allocation, it becomes a strategy scorecard. Paired with real option analysis, the loop to alignment with financial markets is closed.

Enforcement of communication throughout the organization as well as gathering historical data on benchmarks and performance generates the empirical platform to identify, create, and value emerging real options. Firms that have performance measures in place and are diligent in observing and measuring them will not only learn very quickly about their resources, skills, and capabilities but also use the wealth of data that is generated to make predictions related to private risks with less noise and thereby deliver a more reliable and valuable real option analysis. They also will have processes and procedures in place to monitor the drivers of private risk and will realize when trigger thresholds to delay, accelerate, abandon, expand, contract or switch are hit. Furthermore, they will be able to link internal data with value creation in the market. The real option framework serves well to provide the roadmap back and forth from strategy to organizational performance via financial performance and back to strategy, as shown in Figure 7.2.

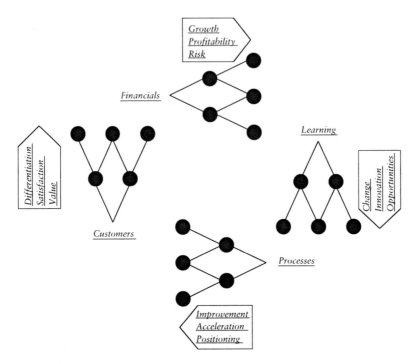

FIGURE 7.2 The integrated real option scorecard

The balanced scorecard turns into an integrated real option scorecard. Financials, Learning, Processes and Customers are broken down into components; value creation and risk-exposure of those components are mapped out and analyzed, drivers of uncertainty and their impact on overall value contribution will be understood and guide adjusting and redesigning the parameters the scorecard should capture.

A key challenge in implementing the balanced scorecard, as pointed out recently by Peter Brewer,[7] is translating strategic statements into specific scorecard measures that serve to connect strategy and performance measurement. The real option framework could serve well as an analytical tool to link strategy, performance measure, and financial management. It can assist in defining performance measures that actually drive uncertainty and value creation, while at the same time benefiting from the data gathered to refine assumptions underlying the real option valuation.

In fact, there are numerous key success factors that apply to implementing both the balanced scorecard and the real option framework. Both concepts also offer similar organizational benefits to ultimately drive the strategic success of the corporation.

Both concepts help management to communicate the company's vision and mission and link performance measures to mission and strategy. An organization that excels in one capacity will be able to create real option value in an area where others fail or will derive less value from the same opportunity.

Both rely on the involvement of employees in defining the parameters for performance and using the measured data stemming from operations, logistics, human resources, and finance as input parameters for private risk, speed, time to development, and competitive strength to assess real option valuation.

Both benefit from a focus on the essentials. It is easy to get lost in a real option jungle by finding more and more sources of uncertainty and discovering more and more options that are beyond the organizational ability to execute. Equally, a scorecard approach that pays equal attention to vital performance measures and less important parameters diverts focus and may fail to capture the essence.

Both are optimally utilized if closely linked to corporate strategy and vision. The performance measures used in the scorecard should be key to implementing corporate strategy. Having those measures installed, in turn, delivers the basic organizational data to perform a reliable real option analysis.

Implementation of both concepts benefits if it is endorsed as a strategic, corporate initiative throughout the entire organization rather than a project with limited applicability. Both also benefit from strong links to outcome: value creation is a strong feedback mechanism for performance measures and exercise of real options. Both finally rely on creating an incentive and compensation structure that is aligned: Performance measures need to tie in with the scorecard to be reinforcing, honest, and motivational. Real options will only be exercised rationally and will be value maximizing if execution is rewarded and not penalized, not even for the abandonment option.

The success of both tools for continuous organizational improvement, strategy enforcement and value creation, relies on daily use of each one. Real options require continuous monitoring of the environment to adjust risks and uncertainties, alter option triggers, and exercise the option if the trigger is hit. Likewise, the balanced scorecard will only work effectively if it becomes deeply engrained in daily management activities.

Both concepts also benefit from continuous efforts to improve and adapt to individual and changing organizational needs and changing strategies. Figure 7.3 provides the conceptual outline as to how the balanced scorecard and the real option framework can work together to support a strategic vision.

Assume that a firm attempts a change in strategic vision from a mass production approach to a more tailored, customized product portfolio. It is motivated to make that move because a more detailed analysis of its profit structure has shown that the most profitable customers are those that value

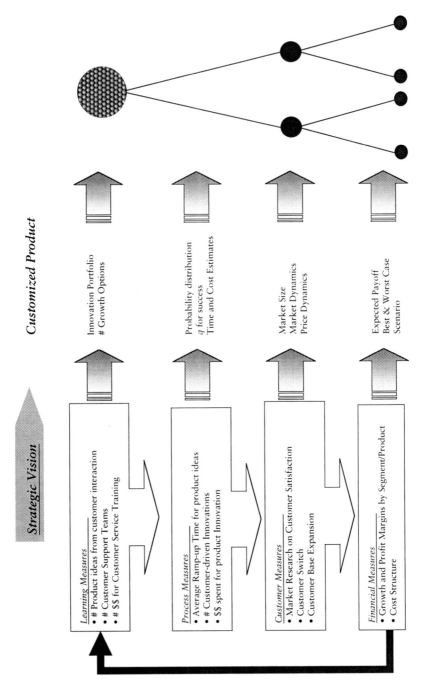

FIGURE 7.3 Strategic vision—an integrated real option scorecard approach

tailored product design. Learning measures designed to focus the organization on making that transition could entail the amount spent on the training of customer service employees, the number of customer support teams built, and the number of product ideas or improvement suggestions collected through the improved and more direct interaction with the customer. Those ideas may constitute the pool of product ideas from which future growth options arise. Each dollar spent for training and education of the customer support team (the exercise price) can be related to the number of product ideas created, and more importantly, the number of executed growth options derived from the idea portfolio.

As process measures, the firm may contemplate gathering data about how long it takes to transfer a product idea into a tangible improvement of an existing product or new product, and how often a growth option is successfully executed. Gathering these operational metrics will help the firm in the future to derive internal benchmarks on the probability distribution of customer-derived product ideas to advance into novel products or product features, what the time of maturation for those options is, and what the exercise price, that is, costs involved, may be.

Customer measures along these lines could entail primary market research on customer satisfaction and data collection on keeping or losing customers, as well as expansion of the customer base. Each performance measure will help refine market uncertainties: the best and worst case market scenarios as well as market and size dynamics over time.

Financial measures, finally, will include repeated over-time assessment of profit and cost function of the organization, and these data will help the organization to arrive at reliable estimates for expected payoff as well as exercise prices.

From here, the loop can be closed back to the beginning. Is the strategic vision turning into reality? Does the expense in employee training pay off by increasing customer satisfaction, stabilizing the customer base or even expanding it, and leading to more innovative product ideas that result in executable growth options? And does the entire exercise pay off financially by leading to an expansion of the most profitable customer segment?

CORE COMPETENCE

The concept of core competence as a firm foundation for corporate success evolved in the late eighties in response to increasing financial pressures exercised by institutional investors. In an environment of aggressive mergers and acquisitions, the notion that a firm's unique resources and capabilities were the key factors in achieving and maintaining competitive advantage gained much attention and support in the early nineties.[8]

The resource-based view of the firm emerged in response to Michael Porter's concept of the competitive forces that shape corporate payoff and ultimately strategy. Porter put the corporation in the midst of a power struggle where it is exposed to pressures from buyers, supplier power, barriers to entry, the threat of product substitution, and competitive pressure that dictated the overall profit potential of a given industry as well as the profit performance of the individual corporation. In the real option framework, these components drive the external, non-private uncertainties that put the value of the real option at risk but by the same token also create the upside potential.

The resource-based view of the firm[9] offers a complimentary perspective on corporate strategy. It argues that the firm's collective tangible and intangible assets and resources create the foundation for a specific set of competencies that cannot be easily imitated and therefore constitute the basis for sustainable competitive advantage. Conceptually, these ideas had their roots in work done by Selznik and Penrose,[10] who proposed the notion that the unique set of a firm's capabilities drive the competitive advantage. In the real option framework, this collective organizational ability, tangible and intangible resources that include financial resources, skills, knowledge, intellectual property, organizational processes and procedures, drive the organizational ability to cope with uncertainties. Both components, external uncertainties or forces and internal capabilities, drive the real option equation, as symbolized in Figure 7.4.

Core competence—through the real option lens—entails the entire body of organizational capabilities that creates option value and allows responding to future changes. Core competence adds value to a real option, for example, by allowing an organization to ascribe a higher probability of technical success and shorter development time frame to a new product development program—based on internal know-how and established processes, thereby potentially driving an investment option at or in the money that remains out of the money for a less capable organization. Somewhat indirect empirical support comes from several sources that identify the diversification discount.[11] The market value of diversified firms, which by intuition are less likely to have had the chance of developing core competencies, is less than the sum of market value of individual firms that operate with exclusive focus in similar businesses. This phenomenon may point to the alignment of financial markets to corporate strategy via the real option framework. Financial markets, intuitively, may acknowledge that diversified

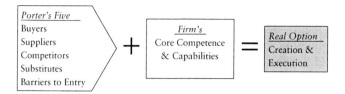

FIGURE 7.4 The real option framework at the interface of industry dynamics and corporate competencies

operations with less core competence and fewer key capabilities pay a higher exercise price to execute their real options and thus create less value than focused firms with a more specialized but relevant skill set.

Firm-specific resources or capabilities include skilled, qualified, and motivated personnel, in-house knowledge of technology, and established processes and procedures as well as trade contracts.[12] These resources evolve and grow through organizational learning and are intricately linked to the evolution of the firm and its traditional playgrounds in terms of products, markets, and technologies.[13] It is the combined organizational knowledge, skill set, and experience that permit a given firm to offer products of better quality, at cheaper prices, with more reliability, and within a shorter time to market.

In addition, there are organizational skills and competence, acquired over time by learning and growing experience, to deal with uncertainties and environmentally imposed changes and challenges. Henderson and Cockburn,[14] for example, have suggested—based on a comparative analysis of the corporate competences of ten leading pharmaceutical firms—that organizational competence explains variances in research productivity across firms, ultimately creating competitive advantage.

Each capability has a value-added impact on the real option valuation as it drives the assumptions on costs, probability of success, time frames, and market share that go into the analysis. Therefore, the same market opportunity has a different real option value to different firms. Further, since firms operate with different skill sets, the execution capabilities of real options differ and lead to different payoffs. This, in turn, impacts the learning experience an organization gains when executing a real option and guides how the organization will analyze and value similar real options in the future.

Hamel and Prahalad,[15] building on and extending the view of the resource-based firm and emphasizing the idea of the competitive advantage that derives from internal resources, have pointed out that a firm capable of not just reacting to but in fact shaping the environment is positioned best to benefit from future uncertainties. Such a firm, in real option terminology, is capable of identifying and maximizing the upside potential of current and future emerging options by managing all available resources to build competitive flexibility. This, in turn, enables the organization to create and also execute real options where others fail to do so.

More recent literature also focuses on the organizational ability to create, maintain, and protect knowledge, which is perceived as a key competitive advantage. Leonard-Barton[16] suggested eight strategies that facilitate organizational learning, sharing and retention of knowledge. These include learning from the market, a key element of option analysis. In addition, establishing internal communication channels and creating room for shared problem solving and for experimenting also feature prominently on her list of key success factors. The latter, room for experimenting, is captured nicely in the real learning option. Shared problem solving, on the other hand, is mandatory to arrive at cross-organizational consensus estimates for risks and uncertainties underlying the real option analysis and valuation. In fact, building on the early work of Nelson and Winter,[17] some have suggested that the ability of firms to create and, more importantly, to recombine and transfer knowledge internally constitutes the basis for the evolution of multinational corporations.[18] This ability creates the competitive advantage that allows firms to operate across countries.

The basic ingredients of an organizational architecture that facilitates effective accumulation and sharing of expertise, knowledge, and information will—if implemented well—undoubtedly assist in bringing together the collective organizational wisdom that drives many of the assumptions that guide a real option analysis valuation and execution. Other sources of competitive advantage include the managerial systems and problem-solving strategies established within any given firm. These capabilities dictate the success of the firm to access and integrate external knowledge and transform it into competitive capabilities and products.

Internal capabilities and competencies of this nature have a tangible effect on the firm's performance and on the outcome of the real option analysis. For example, the pharmaceutical company Merck has been praised for its capabilities in clinical trial design and trial management.[19] The firm designed, planned, executed, and communicated with regulatory authorities about a multitude of clinical trials. This has led through a successive build up to a wealth of cumulative organizational experience about this critical step of drug development. This collective organizational wisdom impacts on real option analysis at several levels.

The firm created over time a large internal dataset from both completed as well as failed clinical programs. This is a corporate treasure that facilitates making key assumptions for option analysis such as the likelihood of success, the timelines for different steps in the development program, the likely costs involved, and a good understanding of regulatory challenges. Merck can make those assumptions based on past experience, and be quite confident about the assumptions. Merck also reduced the uncertainty caused by noise which, as we discussed before, does not add to real option value. Further, the organization can assign higher probabilities of success to the final regulatory step in the product development program, which will contribute to increases in option value and the critical cost to invest. The organization may be able to shorten development time by good trial design and a strong focus on key deliverables, thereby reducing time to maturation, and thus increasing the real option value to the organization. In addition, the organization may have procedures in place to efficiently execute the trial program, thereby reducing the exercise price, increasing real option value as well as freeing resources to invest in other growth options.

An organization less skilled or apt may still envision the real options but fail while executing them. Organizational learning, be it project-specific passive learning by waiting for information or by active investment and experimentation, or collective learning over time about improving organizational experience, skills, tacit knowledge, and organizational processes and procedures, is a key ingredient in building core competence and enabling the organization in the identification and execution of real options.

The concept of core competence has attracted much attention and interest, but many managers find it hard to adopt it for their organizations. In-house knowledge of technology processes and designs, for example, are frequently cited as important firm competencies.[20] Because such technology capabilities often arise only with accumulated experience and are based on embedded or highly tacit knowledge, they are largely immobile and difficult for other firms to easily acquire or imitate.[21]

The difficulty, for managers, however, remains in defining what exactly a core competence should be for a given organization. The quick, but not necessarily right or helpful answer lies in filling the paradigm with firm-specific and pragmatic content. A core competence is what made you succeed, a non-competence is what made you fail. That may be helpful when doing a post-mortem analysis, but such a definition will provide little guidance in identifying competences key to the success of the firm in the future, and helping build them. Then core competence as a strategic management tool becomes a "mirage."[22]

Real option analysis, instead of delivering yet another mirage, will actually help in putting boundaries and tangibility on the core competence mirage. Core competence makes an opportunity into a real option at the money or deep in the money for a given business. Other organizations with different organizational skills and experience will fail to create that moneyness when going after the same opportunity. A core competence is what drives the value of the opportunity into the money because internal skill sets and capabilities reduce the technical uncertainty, shorten the time to market, trouble the competitive environment, and permit execution of the real option.

Real options link core competence to capabilities to financial valuation. Let us discuss this with an example. In a recent article Nolan argues that data competence is a core competence of nurse leaders in the information age.[23] The primary nurse, in the case of an acutely ill patient, has comprehensive knowledge of the patient and his care. With the help of information technology, the same nurse can access a wealth of clinical and statistical data, the collective wisdom of patient care. The author argues in a hypothetical example that a data-competent nurse can integrate available exogenous information on patient care and financial data to guide management decisions on patient care.

Key to the idea of competitive advantage through core competence is the ability of the organization to reduce uncertainty by increasing flexibility. This may entail the ability to reduce fixed costs by creating economies of scope and by sharing resources.[24] This notion is also at the very heart of real option analysis. However, some scholars have also pointed out an important trade off: the path-dependency of core competence. The more specialized and adept an organization becomes, the less capable it may be in preserving opportunistic fitness—at the end of this path waits the core competence trap. "While a firm's distinctive capabilities facilitate innovation, they have a flip side called core rigidities that hamper development."[25] Core competence then becomes a double-edged sword when organizational skills and specialized capabilities transform into inertia and create core incompetence,[26] or a real anti-option. The established set of core competence is unsuitable to create real option value from emerging opportunities. The real organizational challenge then becomes creating and sustaining the dynamic core competence.[27]

Again, real option analysis may be a valuable tool to succeed on this path. While management cannot easily switch from the established set of core competences to a new one that better fits the current market requirements, it can invest in fundamental organizational capabilities that will enable it to make flexible responses in the future. From this perspective, core competence entails the set of capabilities that prepares a firm in the best possible way to respond to future uncertainties.[28]

The value of real options is very sensitive to the strength of corporate competencies; real options provide a link between assets, resources, organizational capabilities, and core competencies. Real option analysis will assign value to unique and to flexible core competencies; the right mixture of both will ensure sustainable dynamic core competence.

Some have argued that today's business environment is characterized by very efficient markets, in capital as well as in products or talents, that will not tolerate idle disparities of corporate performance.[29] In such an environment, the ability to anticipate future changes (that is, foresight) is viewed as a very valuable corporate asset and indeed core competence.[30]

Along these lines, Hamel and Prahalad made the point that the real mission of industry foresight starts with the question "what could be?" and then works backward to what must happen today to make that future happen tomorrow. Here lies another strong parallel to real option analysis and the binomial framework: We also start way out in the future and work our way back to today to identify the value of the future world. We identify what must happen now to make the future happen, what endangers the path into that future, and what an alternative future may then look like. It is foresight informed by insights that derive from picking up today's signals of future scenarios.

Corporate capabilities describe in sum the way of doing business. They entail knowledge assets, including patents, brand names, and reputation, as well as organizational assets such as culture, capability of information sharing and processes of decision making, as well as technologies and procedures in place. The value of investing in intangible assets such as business processes and procedures, employer training and education, positioning and early stage R&D to create core capabilities is well recognized by U.S. firms. At the end of the last decade, U.S. firms spent approximately $1 trillion per year on these items, compared to $1.2 trillion of investments that went into tangible assets within the manufacturing sector alone.[31] How then can real option analysis assist in shaping strategic intent, identifying required capabilities and core competence and closing the gap between the current skill set and the one required in the future?

Consider the example of a computer manufacturer who may find out from a detailed market survey and internal analysis of his customer segments that the most profitable customers consist of a selective group that places much more importance on the flexible and individualized design of computer features rather than overall price. A general flow chart for building transferable as well as flexible corporate core competence is outlined in the diagram in Figure 7.5. It consists of the following key steps: Identify and quantify the value of product flexibility, map out the required capabilities, focus on those capabilities that emerge as value drivers in the real option valuation, adjust organizational processes, perform performance review, and

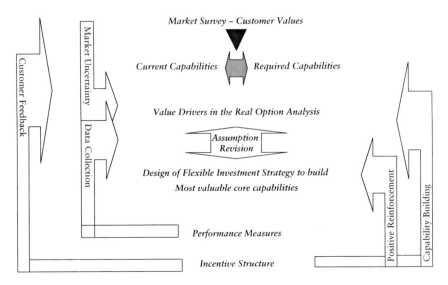

FIGURE 7.5 Flow chart to build corporate capabilities integrating the real option framework

create incentives in line with revised product strategy, monitor success based on market data and customer feedback.

To better and more effectively address this customer group and also expand market share within this customer segment, management devises a set of core capabilities that are viewed as critical to the success. These include a modular production process with maximum flexibility, sufficient inventory capacity to facilitate quick and flexible assembly of individual modules, and a responsive and efficient customer service department to pick up trends and customer demands proactively, as well as an efficient and reliable distribution network. These organizational capabilities are very distinct from those required for a production process that focuses on product competition through price: economies of scale through a simplified mainstream assembly-line process, just-in-time relationships with suppliers and buyers, and low inventory.

Management envisions a multi-step cross-functional and cross-organizational strategy that should ultimately lead to building the new set of required capabilities and provide growth of the most profitable customer segment. This strategy addresses three major components of the firm: organization, its culture and procedures, and operational processes as well as technology. Each of these components can be further broken up in several sub-components that need to be addressed, as shown in Figure 7.6.

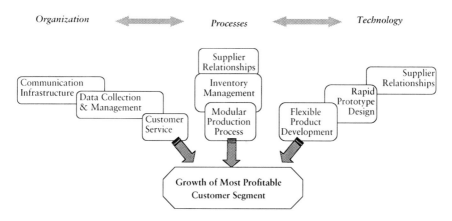

FIGURE 7.6 A three component approach to increase profitability

In order to define the best investment strategy, value and risk drivers need to be defined. Management needs to understand the added value and cost implications for each of these items as well as their contribution to the real option valuation of the entire project. Then the process of organizational change to build new sets of core capabilities will be initiated.

Assume that an internal survey combined with market research produces the following information: Because of the current design of the production process and inventory management, 10% of the most profitable customer segment are not served in the most optimal fashion. Failure to deliver desired custom-designed products within acceptable time frames has led to cancellations or withdrawals of 5% of these customers, costing the firm $4 million in product revenues per month on average and building up an increasingly negative brand name and reputation that will make it more and more difficult to attract new customers. This in turn suppresses the firm's growth rate in this most profitable customer segment. There is a risk that the current trend worsens, and in the worst case scenario, management envisions accumulating annual losses of market share in this customer segment of up to 20%, leading to significant revenue loss of approximately $80 million per year over the next seven years and even more pronounced declines in overall profitability of the firm by 5%, which will undoubtedly attract the attention of Wall Street and be penalized in the market.

To reverse the trend, management envisions major improvements in three core areas: customer service, production processes, and new product development (Figure 7.6). Building more core competence in the customer service department is likely to result in a better, proactive understanding of changing trends in the customer base and will allow in the future somewhat improved product development and production planning. After an initial learning curve of 12 months, inventory management should improve, reducing working capital requirements by 15%. This leads to cost savings of $5 million per year without compromising the quality of the newly built improved service.

Production processes need to be changed to a more modular procedure. This will require an initial cost outlay of $5 million and also enhance the cost of production by $0.3 million annually.

Finally, management envisions a new initiative in product development designed to focus on prototype developments that incorporate modular production processes. The envisioned benefit is two-fold: rapid response to changing customer demands, thereby helping to sustain and expand market share in the most attractive customer segment. In the worst case scenario, this should help to sustain market share, while product prices could be enhanced to compensate for highly desirable product features, resulting in additional annual revenue starting in two years from now, which is—over a period of five years—valued at $50 million of additional asset value. In the best case scenario, the market could be grown over time, leading to an overall additional asset value of $80 million in the best case. The new product development initiative should also create a more efficient, cost-effective modular production process that would ultimately reduce the variable cost outlay, also starting in two years and—over a period of five years—resulting in cost savings of $5 million. These assumptions translate into the following binomial asset tree shown in Figure 7.7.

Without reversion of the trend, management sees its current option in place on future revenues at risk. In the best case scenario, the present value of $336 million could be lost; in the worst case $560 million could be lost. The expected value at risk amounts to $479.36 million.

Improving the current customer service is expected to take one year to complete and require an investment of $5 million. Management expects that this improvement will be successful at a probability of 90% ($q7 = 0.9$), and that it will result in cost savings over a period of six years of a minimum of $30 million and a maximum of $48 million, with equal probability for each scenario ($q9 = q10 = 0.5$). Management also believes that this program will assist in retaining customers and reducing the number of orders that will be withdrawn. Management expects that with a probability of 40% at the best case, 30% of customers can be retained, and with a probability of 60% in the worst case, 20% of the customers will be retained. This secures revenue

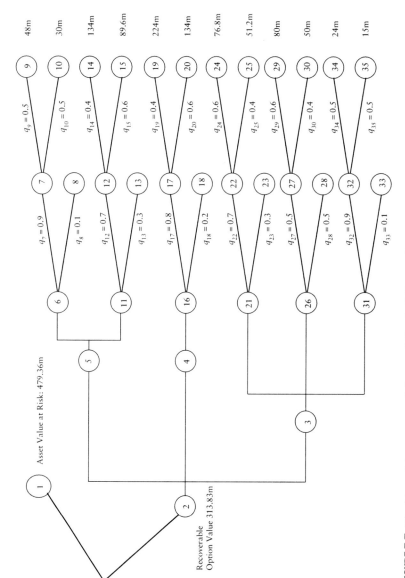

FIGURE 7.7 The binomial asset tree of the capability building option

streams worth $134.4 million in the best case scenario and $89.6 million in the worst case scenario (nodes 14 and 15, respectively).

Management further assumes that this part of the customer service and training program has a success probability of 70% ($q12 = 0.7$). The maximum value at nodes 7 and 12, respectively, is the expected value derived from customer retention and cost savings, that is, $35 million and $107 million. The minimum value at node 8 and node 13, respectively, is zero when the trading and education program fails to succeed, with a likelihood of 10% for node 8 and of 30% for node 13, respectively. Under these assumptions the value of the call at node 6 and node 11 is $37.56 million and $88.53 million, respectively. Both options will be acquired with the initial investment outlay at node 5; at a budgeted cost of $5 million the value of the call at node 5 then becomes $113.09 million.

Changes in the production process will come at a total cost of $7.1 million (present value), but management believes that those changes will ultimately facilitate retaining in the best case 50% of the customers at risk of switching at a probability of 40%, and in the worst case retain 30% of customers with a probability of 60%. This translates into retained revenue streams of $224 million (node 19) or $134 million (node 20). This gives a call value at node 17 of $175.05 million and at nodes 4/16 of $145.72 given a 20% chance that those measures may fail (node 16).

Finally, management contemplates an initial investment of $50 million in order to create a new product development initiative designed to come up with fast prototype developments (node 3). This initiative will not materialize until three years from now, but then has the potential to secure up to 90% of the current customers that remain at risk of switching despite the improvements in customer services and production processes. This will preserve $76.8 million in the best case scenario (60% probability) and $51.2 million in the worst case scenario (40% probability) of revenues currently at risk (nodes 24/25). It creates an option value of $71 million at node 22. The probability of the product development program being completed successfully and being able to make this contribution to customer retention is estimated to be 70% (node 22). This gives rise to an option value at node 21 of $49.85 million.

Management further assumes that the new product development initiative will permit bringing products that are in better alignment with changing customer demands much quicker to the market and thereby expects this initiative to also expand the customer base by another 5% to 10% at the most at a probability of 60%. This would result in an additional revenue stream of $80 million in the best case scenario and $50 million in the worst case scenario (nodes 29 and 30, respectively). The likelihood of this component of the new product development initiative to succeed is estimated to be 50% ($q27 = q28 = 0.5$).

Finally, management envisions cost savings coming out of the product development initiative simply by allowing for more flexibility in the production process. These savings will more than outweigh the envisioned increased production costs that result from changing the production processes (Part B of the program) which have been included in the option valuation at node 16 as a component of the exercise price. Those cost savings will be in the worst case scenario $5 million per year, starting in year 4, and in the best case scenario $8 million per year. Each scenario is equally likely ($q34 = q35 = 0.5$), and the likelihood of completing this part of the new product development initiative is 90% ($q32 = 0.9$). This gives an option value at node 31 of $18.78 million. The initial investment outlay of $50 million acquires all three options; the value of the call at node 3 then becomes $55 million. Taking all options together, the value at node 2 is $313.82 million. How does this compare to the expected value of $479.36 million at risk?

THE OPTION VALUE OF POSITIONING

In the strategic management literature, positioning refers to the ability of a firm to increase its organizational effectiveness by placing or rearranging its resources. Ideally, positioning increases the efficacy of any given firm in relation to that of the competitor, who is ideally weakened or put into disarray by these strategic moves. Whether in table games such as chess, in a wartime situation, or in business strategy, moves that create a positional advantage are of value. For a firm, they refer to economies of scale, to network effects of a specific technology, to patents, a brand name, ownership of a distribution channel, or special supply contracts. Investments that create or emphasize positional advantages have option value, even if they do not create cash flow by themselves. Indirectly, through the positional advantage, they contribute either to cost savings, that is, reducing the exercise price of the option, prolonging the life-time of the asset, or enhancing payoff.

Rita McGrath refers to investments designed to strengthen a firm's position as "amplifying pre-investments."[32] One example given by the author includes investments in lobbying at regulatory or government authorities to facilitate the creation of a favorable regulatory environment that will accept products in development.

Positioning also entails investments in a proof of concept for any given technology or product. For example, a car manufacturer may spend resources

for excessive car safety testing in extreme environmental conditions. The results of these tests can be utilized in commercials and other forms of adver-
tising and help to create or sustain a reputation for safety that preserves
market share. Such a reputation would position not just the model for which
those tests have been done but would extend to the entire product line. Similarly, a drug manufacturer may engage in a series of clinical trials to prove
an additional benefit of a marketed compound related to the underlying
technology employed in the design of the compound. If such a trial is done
with leading medical authorities in the field, the results will have additional
credibility and impact. This may assist the sales force of this particular company in convincing physicians to use this drug instead of the competing
compound.

Positioning options create value in many ways: by securing network positions or distribution channels, by promoting rapid product adoption or
sustaining demand by promoting brand-name and strengthening reputation.
The value of the option is driven by several factors:

- Maintenance of current market position
- Deterrence of competitor
- Expansion of current market position
- Costs of positioning

If the positioning value extends to an entire line of products or organizational capabilities, obviously the value created for each product line adds
to the positioning value. In this regard, the decision to establish an e-business
is a positioning option. It adds an additional organizational capability that
advances the ability of the firm to engage in a new form of interacting with
and offering services to customers and suppliers; it provides a novel value
proposition for the firm that will be beneficial across product lines and
across departments. It will assist in streamlining manufacturing, supply
chains, and inventory management; provide a novel infrastructure for marketing and open new distribution channels, and enable the organization to
offer new services to its customers with a growing focus on individualized,
customized solutions. The overall vision associated with this project is summarized in Figure 7.8.

The challenge is to value these mostly intangible benefits and also determine the critical cost to invest. To this end, the vision needs to be transformed into distinct branches of the binomial asset tree that carry timelines,
bear probabilities, and identify sources of value creation. Figure 7.9 provides
the basic outline of the binomial asset tree.

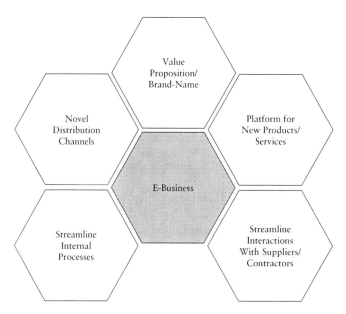

FIGURE 7.8 The positioning vision

The five basic branches do not necessarily run in parallel but may be structured sequentially, as shown in Figure 7.10.

The investment may start with a pilot project that focuses on streamlining internal processes, followed by an integration step with external contractual partners, followed by building novel distribution channels and ultimately the offering of novel products. At each level the value proposition of leveraging organizational capability and brand name across the organization and across geographical areas is maintained. During the implementation of each phase, management has the option to learn and evaluate. After completion of each phase, management may either take the project to the next level or terminate the project at the current level and abandon the idea of further expanding the e-business strategy across the organization.

By initiating the e-business strategy internally to streamline internal transactions, initial investment costs are quite limited, but the opportunity to gain experience and learn is very valuable. Management may feel confident in assigning probabilities of success to the e-business initiative internally, having full knowledge of organizational structures and procedures. The experience gained in this phase will be helpful in implementing the next phase.

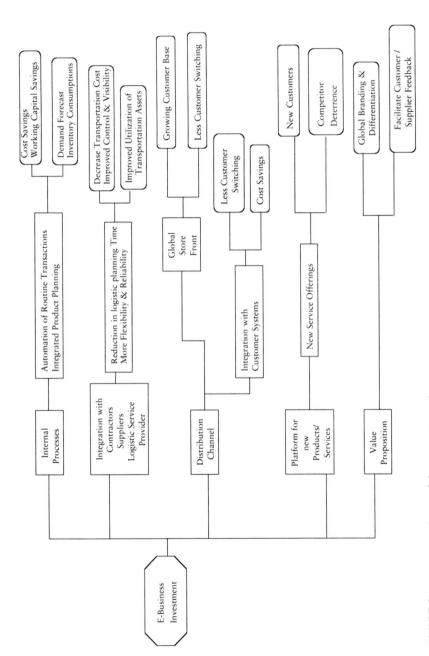

FIGURE 7.9 The binomial tree of the strategic options

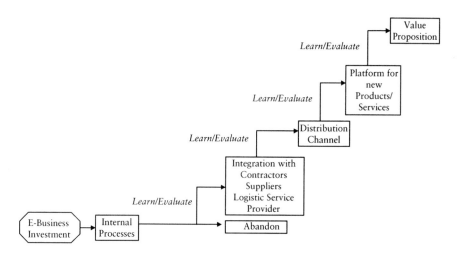

FIGURE 7.10 The staged investment strategy

Further, it will be instrumental in extrapolating basic data sets to the next phase and making more informed assumptions as to the likely time line of implementation and probabilities of success when extending the e-business initiative to the outer circle of contractors, the next phase, which is likely to involve a bigger cost outlay.

PORTFOLIO MANAGEMENT

The fundamental objective of portfolio management, writes David Swenson, the CFO of Yale and in charge of a 7 billion dollar endowment, lies in faithful implementation of long-term policy targets.[33] Portfolio theory is concerned with tools and systems that permit investors to classify, estimate, and control both the nature and extent of expected risk and return. It is of crucial importance to the strategic framework of an organization to incorporate a decision-making framework and procedures that proactively attend to the collective risks, their nature, their size, their implications, and their management, be it internally or externally.

In 1990, the three economists to receive the Nobel prize included Harry M. Markowitz, the founder of modern portfolio theory. Markowitz won the award for work he had published in 1952.[34] He had proposed that the risk of a financial security should not be measured at the individual level but in the context of the entire security portfolio. Selecting a set of securities that are negatively correlated and therefore will respond to future uncertain changes in the market by moving in opposite directions helps the portfolio owner to diversify and therefore minimize exposure to risk while preserving returns. Asset allocation decisions emerged as the key to manage risk and return for investment securities—and for investment projects.

The quantification of the relationship between risk and return as well as the notion that investors must be compensated for taking on risks are at the heart of modern portfolio theory. The relationship between individual securities within a given portfolio dictates the overall risk-return profile of the portfolio; understanding and managing this relationship becomes more important than the analysis of an individual security.

Corporate portfolio decisions cover acquisitions and divestments; allocation and re-allocation of resources between projects, extensions, and contractions; insourcing and outsourcing decisions; and management of fixed assets such as plants, buildings, and machines, as well as intangible assets including brand names and intellectual property. Portfolio design and portfolio decisions work across departments and across the organization; they are fundamental to the formulation and execution of corporate strategy.

Financial portfolio theory recommends four basic steps to evaluate security investments:

1. *Security valuation*—describing a universe of assets in terms of expected return and expected risk
2. *Asset allocation*—determining how assets are to be distributed among classes of investment such as stocks or bonds
3. *Portfolio optimization*—reconciling risk and return in selecting the securities to be included
4. *Performance measurement*—dividing each stock's performance (risk) into market-related (systematic) and industry/security-related (residual) classifications

The same principles are applicable to corporate project portfolio analysis and design.

1. *Opportunity analysis*—describing the wealth of investment opportunities, their risk and return profiles, aligned with corporate strategy and vision
2. *Allocation decision*—allocating human, financial, and asset resources to portfolio projects, including the withdrawal of corporate resources

3. *Project mix*—defining the combination of projects that maximize profit but minimize risk, aligned with corporate strategy and vision and supported by corporate core competence
4. *Performance review*—characterizing and monitoring the specific private risks associated with individual projects and across the project portfolio; managing those risks and leveraging them across projects; defining the exogenous risks any project portfolio will face and understanding how different project portfolios are likely to respond to those risks.

For financial securities, the generic recommendation for portfolio management is to include three asset classes: equities, real estate, and fixed income.[35] The underlying rationale for investments in each class is relatively simple, as briefly summarized in Figure 7.11.

For project portfolio investments, criteria are not only much more complex but also conflicting. They include time to completion, fit into corporate strategy, drivers of risk, probabilities of success, expected costs, revenue and profit profiles, competitive strength, and inter-project leverage. In addition, there is allocation of resources to sustain existing core businesses (fixed income, cash cows) as well as to maintain existing assets. Depending on overall corporate strategy and the risk-comfort zone of the organization, as well as assumptions on future uncertainties and market developments, there will not be just one but several corporate project portfolios that may address conflicting objectives and a set of different uncertain futures.

The first prominent strategic management frameworks for portfolio management include matrix-based approaches, such as the Boston Consulting Group Matrix and the McKinsey and Company Matrix. The key dimensions of the McKinsey matrix are industry attractiveness on the x-axis and the current position of individual business units on the y-axis. Industry attractiveness is captured by market size, market growth, industry profitability, and cyclicality. The strength of the business unit is measured by its market position, that is, market share; by its competitive position; by judging, for example, brand name, quality, technology innovation, manufacturing ability, distribution network, and cost structure; and by return on sales.

Asset Class	Equity	Fixed Income	Real Estate
Rationale	• Risk Premium • Dissimilar price movements	• Current Income • Stability	• Stability

FIGURE 7.11 Financial portfolio approach

Both dimensions serve to position the business unit. From that position derives the portfolio management recommendation: Grow units that are at the higher end of both dimensions, hold what is in an intermediate position, and harvest, that is, maximize cash flows but minimize future investments, which is at the lower end of both dimensions.

The Boston Consulting Group (BCG) matrix offers a similar framework. It divides the corporate portfolio into stars, question marks, cash cows, and dogs. Stars provide high earnings with growth potential and need to be grown. Question marks provide low earnings at rapid growth, and plenty of uncertainty as to future earnings. They need to be analyzed and ultimately transformed into dogs or stars. Dogs deliver poor, unstable earnings and little cash flow; they better be divested. Cash cows deliver high cash flow, and need to be milked. Subsequent to Boston Consulting Group and McKinsey, A.D. Little created the "Strategic Condition Matrix." It positions the elements of the portfolio along technology maturity or product life cycle on the x-axis and competitive positioning or strength along the y-axis. Competitive strength is defined by the current market share, the strength of the technology, the availability of investment resources, the cost structure, or other managerial competitive advantages.

The value of these models lies in their simple design. Even a complex multinational and multi-business unit can capture its business units and their relative position and contribution to corporate wealth in a single diagram. These matrixes are designed to provide "exformation." Tor Norretranders,[36] the Danish science writer, invented this term in his book *The User Illusion*; it stands for the quintessence that remains after the wealth of information has been analyzed, incorporated, and then discarded; exformation is *explicitly discarded information*. For exformation to work effectively, or work at all, the two parties, the sender and recipient of exformation, need to have a shared body of knowledge. Only then, in a shared context, will exformation make sense. Otherwise, it is illegible, impalpable, not understandable.

Compressing corporate portfolio exformation in a two-dimensional static matrix based on this kind of analysis bears some disadvantages. Only a few parameters go into the analysis. Key drivers that will impact on the future strength of an organization, such as the ability to adopt technology changes and the flexibility to respond to sudden changes in the economic environment, as well as intangible organizational capabilities, are not visibly and explicitly included, therefore, they cannot be explicitly addressed.

More importantly, the matrix view fosters a silo approach to business strategy: interactions between business units or projects that synergize or antagonize in building corporate strength are not visualized or analyzed in a matrix approach. The matrix models offer little help in prioritizing projects that occur in subsequent stages, have inter-project leverage features, different time lines and time constraints, different probabilities of success, and different risk profiles leading to distinct risk/return ratios, and need to be realized in a financially constrained environment with uncertain competitive pressures. Finally, the matrix approach does little to assist in planning for multiple what-if scenarios. It seduces the organization into thinking in static boxes rather than thinking about processes in a fluctuating environment with emerging and expiring real options. Portfolio management has to be a very active and dynamic process that involves monitoring and responding to changes that alter the outlook and composition of the corporate real option portfolio.

Real option thinking is in many ways an ideal tool for portfolio management; in fact business strategy has been likened to a "Portfolio of Real Options,"[37] simply because cash flows are not static and fixed, but evolving and declining, subject to sudden "jumps" caused by competitive entry or new technology evolution. Business investment decisions are a series of options that evolve or expire, grow or diminish. To use another analogy from the arts: Business strategy does not look like a painting by Mondrian, with distinct squares and boxes, clearly separated, in an orderly flow; business strategy resembles more closely the *Catalanian Journey* by Miro, where everything is in flux, and new opportunities arise all the time, while perceived opportunities may expire.

In a far less artistic representation, Figure 7.12 shows that real option portfolio strategy takes into account that the future is not only uncertain,

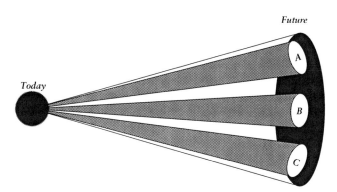

FIGURE 7.12 The portfolio of future options

but that there are different futures for which the organization needs to prepare itself.

Time for another borrowing from the biological sciences: Biologists ascribe the highest probability of survival to organisms or species, or even individual molecules, that have best preserved their ability to adopt and respond, adaptive systems that keep many options open for a long time and engage in few irreversible commitments.

Real option theory suggests that the project portfolio that best preserves managerial flexibility to respond to future unknowns should be elected. Today's organizational capabilities and resources have to be developed so that they can target those futures. That implies the use of different technologies, a changing competitive environment, and a changing customer base with changing needs. Ideally, today's resources should be complementary, but not necessary related; they should be diversifiable and flexible to adapt to future needs.

The value of real option analysis to advance portfolio management is instantly and intuitively apparent. Real option analysis facilitates a fair risk-comparison among projects. It is an ideal tool to display the interaction of options that can be synergistic, additive, interactive, prohibitive, interfering, or even mutually hedging. Therefore, real option analysis can be very helpful in finding the risk-minimizing, value-maximizing project portfolio that also accommodates the optimal timing strategy under existing or perceived competitive pressures. It will assist in identifying options that can be delayed versus those that will be killed by waiting. Option analysis, in short, helps in mapping and quantifying the portfolio matrix along multiple dimensions.

Lint and Pennings[38] provide a real option approach to the product development portfolio. Their analysis is based on the conceptual framework of the BCG matrix. In brief, real option valuation is instrumental in grouping the portfolio of early R&D projects in four boxes, those with low and high uncertainty and negative or positive market payoff, respectively. Projects that have completed the R&D stage then enter a second portfolio, designated the product launch portfolio, again designed after the BCG model. Here, the real option valuation of the portfolio projects is instrumental in differentiating the projects according to high or low market uncertainty that are either below or above the critical threshold to invest. Both portfolios are used to prioritize R&D and product launch projects, respectively.

Childs and colleagues[39] investigated the importance of project interrelationship in order to elect the best investment opportunity among mutually exclusive projects. The insight provided in this analysis is that for highly correlated projects, a sequential rather than parallel development plan is favorable to maximize the return/risk ratio. As projects become less correlated and the variance between the expected revenues increases, a parallel development is preferential, as it makes it possible to quickly select the better of the two projects. The authors also point out that in case of sequential development, it may be advisable to start with the less valuable project if this offers an information advantage and more resolution of uncertainty than the more valuable project. Parallel project development is, on the contrary, advisable for projects with low market uncertainty upon completion, high irreversibility, and long development times.

Efficient corporate portfolios need to consider corporate strategy, goals, and vision; they need to acknowledge internal and external risks and uncertainties, resource constraints, and corporate risk preference. Optimized, real option-based portfolio analysis provides an understanding of the most efficient project portfolios that preserve managerial flexibility for future uncertainties. It includes what-if scenarios, pays attention to project dynamics and timing, interaction, emerging and resolving risks and uncertainties, it identifies future trade-off scenarios and discovers inter- and intra-project and portfolio hedges. It also leaves room to identify, discover, or acquire additional, complementary value-adding or risk-minimizing options internally and externally. An ideal portfolio strategy comes up with a mix of portfolios that rank top projects but accommodate a range of future uncertainties when doing so. Because the real option framework incorporates interaction between projects and values managerial flexibility when responding to future uncertainties, it not only facilitates project ranking across multiple dimensions and risk drivers but also makes it possible to determine the risk-return profile of the entire project or investment options portfolio.

For example, in Chapter 6 we investigated the option to learn. When valuing the abandonment option in this scenario, we initially included only the cost saved by the learning exercise. We valued the project and the investment decision for a standalone project. However, in a corporate budgeting decision scenario, that decision is likely to fall into the context of overall corporate resource allocation. The costs saved by deciding against the investment opportunity as a result of the learning experience is—in the corporate context—not just the value of the money not invested in this opportunity. To a greater extent, it is also the opportunity value gained by investing in another project that creates option value.

Corporate project portfolio management takes place at both the operational as well as the strategic level. At the operational level, all existing projects are tracked and managed to control progress, costs, resources, and maintenance of deadlines, timing, and maintenance of a project pipeline At the strategic level, additional layers of complexity are added: market uncertainty and market variability, competitive entry, technology advances, corporate vision and positioning, as well as the corporate composite risk comfort zone. Operational portfolio management, if done well, gives management at each point in time a snapshot of the number of projects, their state of development, the project pipeline status, and the current and projected allocation of resources. Strategic portfolio analysis provides insight into the time, risk, and value proposition of the program collection.

In its basic form, portfolio management of investment decisions in real assets involves selection of the best project among two or more mutually exclusive projects. As an illustration of how to approach this within the real option framework using the binomial approach, consider the following scenario. A firm has budgeted $50 million for a new product development program. It has four projects in early stages of the pipeline from which to pick one to take forward. These four projects have different technical probabilities of success and different market payoff scenarios, as summarized in Table 7.1.

Product A imposes—from the technical product development perspective—no real challenges; at 90% probability, it will succeed. The market payoff is, however, at the lower end, with little upside potential. Project B is more risky, but also offers more upside potential, with a higher overall market and a higher probability of capturing a significant proportion of this market of 50%. Product C has a 50/50 chance of succeeding; the upside market potential is twice that of product A. Project D, finally, has an 80% chance of failing. However, if it can be implemented, it has a high likelihood of getting a significant fraction of a very attractive market. For each product, we assume a total cost of $50 million and a time of completion of two years. Which one is the better option?

Considering the technical likelihood of success, the worst case scenario value to achieve for each project is 0, that is, the project fails. The best case scenario to achieve reflects the best market payoff scenario and success in product development. The expected value derives from this minimum and

TABLE 7.1 The project portfolio

	Technical Success (%)	Min Payoff ($)	Max Payoff ($)	Market Risk (%)
A	90	200	300	40
B	70	200	400	50
C	50	300	600	60
D	20	300	800	70

TABLE 7.2 The option value of portfolio projects

	Technical Success (%)	Min Payoff ($)	Max Payoff ($)	Expected Value ($)	Risk-Neutral Probability p	Call ($)	Costs ($)
A	90.00	0	240	216	0.963	152	50
B	70.00	0	300	210	0.749	146	50
C	50.00	0	480	240	0.535	174	50
D	20.00	0	650	130	0.214	71	50

maximum asset value achievable, taking in account market risk and technical risk. From there we calculate the risk-neutral probability and, considering the exercise price for each project of $50 million in development costs, the value of the call option on each project, as summarized in Table 7.2.

Under the initial set of assumptions, project C is the clear winner, followed by A, B, and then D. In order to rescue project D it needs to be brought up to the same value as project C, and management undertakes a sensitivity analysis to determine the main value drivers of project D. Figure 7.13 summarizes the analysis by changing the assumptions about technical and market risk.

Management may want to include a few more parameters to evaluate the four project opportunities in the context of competitive strength, contribution to future growth options, the value added to existing product lines

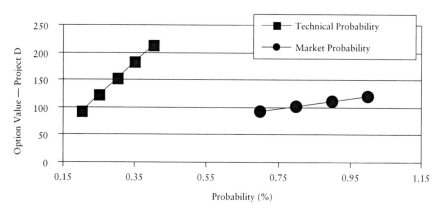

FIGURE 7.13 Project D option value sensitivity

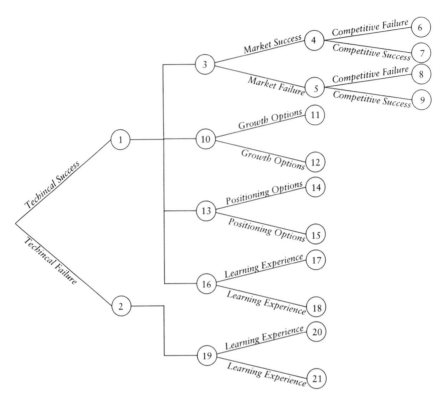

FIGURE 7.14 The binomial asset tree of embedded project portfolio options

through synergies or positioning, or the learning value of the projects. Figure 7.14 depicts the binomial asset tree for embedded options.

Assume the four projects are subjected to the diverse likelihood of competitive threats that will result in distinct losses of market share as summarized in Table 7.3.

The competitive threat will only materialize once the product has reached the market. That implies that the maximum payoff is either the maximum market payoff in the absence of competitive entry (node 6, Figure 7.14) or the payoff reduced by the loss of market share under competitive entry (node 7). Similarly, the minimum payoff is either the envisioned worst case market scenario in the absence of competitive entry (node 8) or the one reduced by additional loss of market share if the competitor succeeds (node 9), leading to the best case market payoff (node 4) or the worst case market payoff (node 5).

TABLE 7.3 Susceptibility of portfolio projects to competitive threats

	Probability of Competitive Entry (%)	Loss— Min Payoff ($m)	Loss— Max Payoff ($m)	Loss (%)	Loss— Expected ($m)
A	60	80	120	40	57.6
B	50	50	100	25	37.5
C	70	105	210	35	117.6
D	10	90	240	30	19.5

Which one of these will materialize will depend on the market risk allocated to each of the projects (Table 7.1) and drives the expected value at node 3. The technical success probability assigned to each project (node 1) determines the expected value at node 2; in case of failure, the asset value is zero (node 2), which drives the expected asset value at node 3 from which the risk-free probability p is calculated, as well as the call of the option at node 0 for the four different projects. Table 7.4 summarizes the data.

Given these assumptions of competitive threat, project B becomes the most valuable project. How does the risk/return profile of the four projects compare? We determine return R in the good state of nature as the ratio of market payoff in the future to today's expected asset value. The current asset value S_0 is today's expected value of the investment opportunity, derived from the future payoff, the costs it takes to develop the asset, the probabilities of success and discounted to today's value depending on the anticipated time of development. The future asset value S_1 is the maximum return management expects to achieve, that is, the expected market payoff, assuming 100% technical success and 0% competitive entry. The implied volatility, as discussed in Chapter 2, in the binomial option model is calculated using the following formula:

$$\sigma_1 = \frac{1n\ R_1}{\sqrt{t1}}$$

The cumulative risk for each project consists of market risk, technical risk, and risk of competitive entry. Figure 7.15 plots the return for each project against the implied volatility (left panel) and the cumulative risk (right panel). Non-competitive conditions are indicated by closed symbols; competitive conditions are represented by open symbols.

As the binomial model predicts, return is correlated with the implied volatility. The cumulative risk, however, indicates that the worst risk/return

TABLE 7.4 Option value of portfolio projects under competitive threats

	Min Value after Loss ($m)	Max Value after Loss ($m)	Expected Min Value (node 5) ($m)	Expected Max Value (node 4) ($m)	Expected Value (node 3) ($m)	Expected Value (node 2) ($m)	Expected Value (node 0) ($m)	Risk-Free Probability p	Call ($m)
A	120	180	152	228	182	0	164	0.963	103
B	150	300	175	350	263	0	184	0.749	121
C	195	390	227	453	362	0	181	0.535	119
D	210	560	291	776	631	0	126	0.214	68

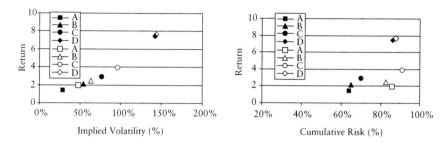

FIGURE 7.15 Portfolio project return in relation to implied volatility and cumulative risk

profile is achieved for project A that offers under competitive conditions a 2.0-fold return at a cumulative risk of 85.6%. The option value of the four investment options can then be plotted against the cumulative risk associated with each investment opportunity, as shown in Figure 7.16 for competitive conditions.

As we would have expected, the option value increases as the cumulative probability to succeed increases. However, the risk/return ratio as determined from the option value and the cumulative probability to succeed differs markedly across the four different investment opportunities. If we draw a trend line through the four data points, we can separate over-performing projects (on and above the trend line) from under-performing (below the trend line) projects. Project A, for example, displays a marginally increased probability of success compared to project D, but offers a much larger option value.

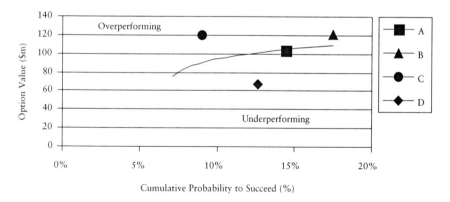

FIGURE 7.16 Option value of portfolio projects as a function of cumulative project success probability

TABLE 7.5 Expected asset value of additional options embedded in portfolio projects

	Technical Success (%)	Growth Options ($)	Learning Options—Success ($)	Positioning Options ($)	Synergy Value with Existing Options ($)	IP Options ($)	Learning Options—Failure ($)	Additional Value—Success ($)	Additional Value—Failure ($)
A	90.00	0.10	0.10	2.00	10.00	0.10	0.10	12.30	0.10
B	70.00	4.00	2.00	2.00	8.00	2.00	0.10	18.00	0.10
C	50.00	6.00	3.00	3.00	5.00	3.00	0.50	20.00	0.50
D	20.00	60.00	20.00	30.00	0.00	10.00	10.00	120.00	10.00

If other options embedded in each of the four investment projects are also included, the risk/return profile is likely to change again. Consider the following assumptions about the expected value of embedded growth options, learning options, and the carry-over effect to other projects via positioning options or via synergies with existing product lines for the four investment opportunities, as summarized in Table 7.5 (in $ million).

All but the learning options will materialize only if the projects succeed. Only for the learning options do the engineers and management feel confident that, even in the case of failure, valuable experience and knowledge can be gained that will be useful for future projects. In the organizational learning curve, each of the projects is positioned differently. Project A would not add much to creating novel organizational expertise, but in essence would benefit from existing organizational benefits and wisdom. Project D would provide the organization with the greatest learning opportunity. Even if the project fails, there will be value for future developments that could build on the experience to be gained when project D is undertaken.

How does the addition of other embedded option value alter the risk/return profile of the four individual projects? Figure 7.17 shows the results; the solid symbols represent the option value without the additional embedded options; the open symbols option value with embedded options.

The addition of embedded options does not change the outcome of the analysis significantly. This makes sense intuitively since we have not altered the risk profile of each of the opportunities but only increased the return. With embedded growth options included, projects D and A are now definitely in the unfavorable zone, while projects C and B are positioned in the favorable risk/benefit zone with C being the clear winner. Whether or not

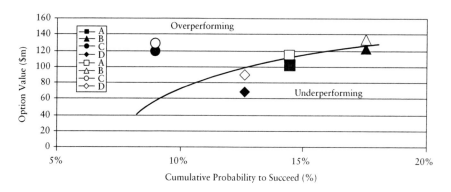

FIGURE 7.17 Option value of portfolio projects in relation to cumulative success proability

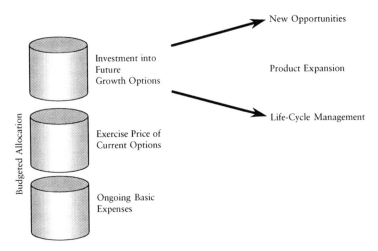

FIGURE 7.18 The basic corporate budget buckets

the firm wants to go for project B or project C or may even envision a staged initial investment in each option will depend on the overall resources available, the time to maturity applicable for each option, that is, the likelihood of each option to be killed effectively by competitive entry, and the suitability of each option for a staged investment, potentially with the option to slow and thereby reduce investment costs per period without endangering the option.

So far, we have only undertaken a comparative analysis of the four competing products but we have not yet put the investment decision into the context of the entire firm portfolio. Consider the firm's budget to be allocated to three main areas (Figure 7.18): Ongoing expenses to maintain the current businesses and infrastructure, exercise price for options in place, and investments in the acquisition of future growth options. The latter fall into life-cycle management of existing product lines, such as expanding those product lines into new markets or developing second- or third-generation products, and into the expansion of existing product lines, as well as the creation of new markets and products.

Assume now that a firm is faced with the following investment decision scenario, as shown in Figure 7.19.

The firm has currently an asset in place that is expected to generate between $800 million and $600 million in revenues over its remaining lifetime, with an expected asset value of $700 million. There is a 50% probability that a competitor may enter in approximately two years from now, and if so, then those revenues are likely to drop to $500 million in the best case and

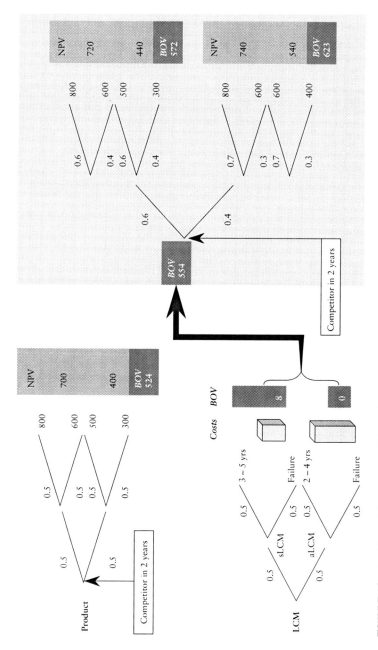

FIGURE 7.19 The binomial asset tree: Life-cycle management versus new product development

$300 million in the worst case scenario, leaving an expected value of this asset in place of $400 million. Under these uncertainties, the asset in place currently has an option value of $524 million to the firm. Assume now that the firm has the opportunity to invest in a life-cycle management (LCM) program that will lead to a novel product that is complementary to the existing product.

In fact, there are two versions, a "standard" version, designated sLCM, and an accelerated version, designated aLCM. The standard version will take between three and five years to complete and create option value of $8 million at the projected costs of $50 million. The accelerated version will be completed between two and four years, cost about $75 million, and under the given market payoff assumptions for the project will create no option value. The option for the accelerated product development version is out of the money.

Assume now that by engaging in either of the two possible LCM programs, management will send out a strong signal to the market that has some deterrence effect. Management assumes that the likelihood of the competitor to enter the market drops to 40% from 50% in the absence of such a signal, thereby reducing the chances that competitive entry will take away market share from the existing asset in place to 40%. Management also believes that if it engages in the standard LCM program, the resulting product will support the market position of the current asset in place and lift the chances for the better market outcome, both in the presence and absence of competitive entry from 50% to 60%. If it were to embark on the accelerated program, the effect might be even more pronounced, with a projected likelihood of realizing the better market payoff for the existing product of 70%.

Without changing the overall assumptions about the best and the worst market payoff scenario, and simply by altering the likelihood of competitive entry and the best case market scenario to occur, the standard LCM lifts the option value of the current asset in place to $572 million and the accelerated LCM even to $623 million, creating additional option value by improving the position of an existing product of $48 million and $99 million, respectively.

Contemplated in isolation, the accelerated LCM appears to be the more favorable option to forward, as it creates more than twice as much option value as the standard LCM. However, management also may want to consider that acquiring the aLCM option is about twice as expensive as the sLCM option. From a budget perspective with limited resources, this implies that there will be few resources left to acquire any of the other growth options introduced above as projects A, B, C, and D. Table 7.6 summarizes the strategic alternatives for the budget including the calculated option value for

TABLE 7.6 The corporate allocation alternatives: Portfolio project's option values and cumulative risks

Strategy	no LCM		"standard" LCM		"accelerated" LCM			
	Option Value ($)	Cumulative Project Risk (%)	Option Value ($)	Cumulative Project Risk (%)	Option Value ($)	Cumulative Project Risk (%)	Option Value ($)	Cumulative Project Risk (%)
Asset in Place	524	75.0	572	64.0	623	58.0	623	58.0
sLCM	—	—	8	70.0	—	—	—	—
aLCM	—	—	—	—	0	75.0	0	75.0
Project A	114	82.5	114	82.5	114	82.5	114	82.5
Project B	134	85.6	134	85.6	—	—	134	85.6
Project C	129	91.0	—	—	129	91.0	—	—

each project, as well as the cumulative risk for each project that consists of market risk, competitive risk, and technical or private risk.

Management may now want to determine the overall option value that is created by each strategic portfolio as well as the cumulative risk inherent in each project portfolio. The portfolio risk is calculated similar to the calculation of a security portfolio risk.[40] The variance or risk of a portfolio of two securities is calculated by multiplying the proportion invested in each security with the security's variance and summing up all those products, provided these securities have no covariance. If the securities have covariance, then one has to add to the above the product of the proportion invested in each individual security, the variance of each individual security, and the covariance of all securities.

We use this simplification and assume that the individual risks in the project portfolio are not correlated, that is, the covariance is set at zero. Under these simplifying assumptions the total portfolio risk then is the sum of the weighted individual risk of each project added to the portfolio. Figure 7.20 depicts the option value for each project portfolio against the portfolio risk. It identifies the portfolio consisting of no life-cycle management but acquisition of project A, B, and C as the most rewarding choice. For a less risk-taking organization, the accelerated life-cycle management program in conjunction with project B and A is a good alternative. Investing in a standard LCM program and in project A and B is the worst of all alternatives.

In the above analysis we have assumed the covariance of individual projects to be zero. The real option framework does, however, also allow including covariance of individual projects. For example, the market risk of

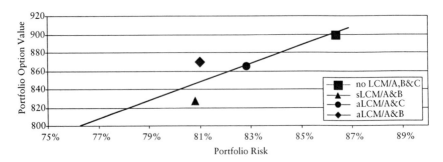

FIGURE 7.20 The optimum corporate portfolio: Portfolio option value versus cumulative portfolio risk

either of the LCM programs is likely to be co-varied with the market risk of the existing product in place whose revenues the LCM program is designed to support. Imagine further that two of the new product development programs rely on similar technologies or address similar customer groups. In this case part of the technical or private risk as well as part of the market risk is positively correlated, and addition of both projects to the portfolio would do little to diversify the portfolio risk. Alternatively, one of the new product development programs may utilize a more risky but completely new technology that would also add a new product line to the firm. Such a program would have a negative covariance with existing components of the corporate portfolio and could reduce overall portfolio risk.

This simple example has shown that an option-based portfolio analysis facilitates project ranking across several dimensions, each of which contribute to the overall risk/return ratio, both with their respective risk-profile and with their contribution to the composite option value of any given project. The benefit of the option-based portfolio analysis includes the preservation of the conventional risk/return ratio, while all conceivable risk factors as well as all conceivable returns are considered. Note, for example, that in the project ranking of projects A to D, we allowed for value creation from learning even in the case of project failure.

NOTES

1. R.P. Rumelt, D. Schendel, and D.J. Teece, "Strategic Management and Economics," *Strategic Management Journal* 12:5, 1991.

2. M. Amram and N. Kulatilaka, *Real Options. Managing Strategic Investment in an Uncertain World* (Harvard Business School Press, 1999).

3. J.A. Belohav, "The Evolving Competitive Paradigm," *Business Horizons*, March–April, 11, 1996.

4. R. Kaplan and D. Norton, "The Balanced Scorecard—Measures That Drive Performance," *Harvard Business Review*, 1992.

5. R. Kaplan and D. Norton, "Leading Change with the Balanced Scorecard," *Financial Executive* 17:64, 2001.

6. R. Kaplan and D. Norton, "Transforming the Balanced Scorecard from Performance Measurement to Strategic Management, Part II," *Accounting Horizons* 15:147, 2001; R. Kaplan and D. Norton, *The Strategy Focused Organization: How Balanced Scorecard Companies Thrive in the New Business Environment* (Harvard Business School Press, 2001).

7. P. Brewer, "Putting Strategy into the Balanced Scorecard," *Strategic Finance* 83:44, 2002.

8. G. Hamel and C.K. Prahalad, *Competing for the Future* (Harvard Business School Press, 1994).

9. J. Barney, "Firm Resources and Sustained Competitive Advantage," *Journal of Management* 17:99, 1991; I. Dierickx and K. Cool, "Asset Stock Accumulation and Sustainability of Competitive Advantage," *Management Science* 35:504, 1989; S. Lippman and R. Rumelt, "Uncertain Imitability: An Analysis of Interfirm Differences in Efficiency Competition," *The Bell Journal of Economics* 13:418, 1982; B.A. Wernerfelt, "A Resource-Based View of the Firm," *Strategic Management Journal* 5:171, 1984.

10. P. Selznik, *Leadership in Administration* (New York: Harper and Row, 1957); E.G. Penrose, *The Theory of the Growth of the Firm* (New York: John Wiley, 1959).

11. P. Berger and E. Ofek, "Diversification's Effect on Firm Value," *Journal of Financial Economics* 37:39, 1995; H. Servaes, "The Value of Diversification During the Conglomerate Merger Wave," *Journal of Finance* 51:1201, 1996.

12. B.A. Wernerfelt, "A Resource-Based View of the Firm," *Strategic Management Journal* 5:171, 1984; M. Peteraf, "The Cornerstones of Competitive Advantage: A Resource-Based View," *Strategic Management Journal* 14:179, 1993.

13. R. Nelson and S. Winter, *An Evolutionary Theory of Economic Change* (Harvard University Press, 1982); D.C. Mowery, J.E. Oxley, and B.S. Silverman, "Strategic Alliances and Interfirm Knowledge Transfer," *Strategic Management Journal* 17:77, 1996.

14. R. Henderson and I. Cockburn, "Measuring Competence? Exploring Firm Effects in Pharmaceutical Research," *Strategic Management Journal* 15:63, 1994.

15. G. Hamel and C.K. Prahalad, *Competing for the Future* (Harvard Business School Press, 1994).

16. D. Leonard-Barton, *The Wellspring of Knowledge. Building and Sustaining the Sources of Innovation* (Harvard Business School Press, 1994).

17. R. Nelson and S. Winter, *An Evolutionary Theory of Economic Change* (Harvard University Press, 1982).

18. B. Kogut and U. Zander, "Knowledge of the Firm, Combinative Capabilities, and the Replication of Technology," *Organization Science* 3:383, 1992; B. Kogut and U. Zander, "Knowledge of the Firm and the Evolutionary Theory of the Multinational Corporation," *Journal of International Business Studies* 24:625, 1993.

19. See for example, "Battling blockbusters" (*Business Week*, January 11, 1999, 105).

20. B.A. Wernerfelt, "A Resource-Based View of the Firm," *Strategic Management Journal* 5:171, 1984; D. Leonard-Barton, *The Wellspring of Knowledge. Building and Sustaining the Sources of Innovation* (Harvard Business School Press, 1994).

21. D.J. Teece, "Capturing Value from Knowledge Assets: The New Economy, Markets for Know-How, and Intangible Assets," *California Management Review* 40:55, 1998.

22. K.P. Coyne, S.J.D. Hall, and C.P. Gorman, "Is Your Core Competence a Mirage?" *McKinsey Quarterly*, Winter 1997, p. 40.

23. M.T. Nolan, "Improving Patient Care Through Data Competence," *Nursing Economics* 18:250, 2000.

24. J. Barney, "Firm Resources and Sustained Competitive Advantage," *Journal of Management* 17:99, 1991; D.J. Teece, "Capturing Value from Knowledge Assets: The New Economy, Markets for Know-How, and Intangible Assets," *California Management Review* 40:55, 1998.

25. D. Leonard-Barton, "Core Capabilities and Core Rigidities: A Paradox in Managing New Product Development," *Strategic Management Journal*, Summer Special Issue 13:111, 1992.

26. D. Dougherty, "Managing Your Core Incompetencies for Corporate Venturing," *Entrepreneurship: Theory and Practice* 19:113, 1995.

27. D. Lei, M.A. Hitt, and R. Bettis, "Dynamic Core Competences Through Meta-Learning and Strategic Context," *Journal of Management*, Winter 22:549, 1996.

28. B. Kogut and N. Kulatilaka, "Capabilities As Real Options," *Organization Science* 12:744, 2001.
29. D. Epstein, N. Mayor, P. Schonbucher, E. Whalley, and P. Wilmott, "The Value of Market Research When a Firm Is Learning. Real Option Pricing and Optimal Filtering," in L. Trigeorgis, ed., *Real Options and Business Strategy. Applications to Decision-Making* (Risk Books, 2001).
30. E. Major, D. Asch, and M. Cordey-Hayes, "Foresight As a Core Competence," *Futures* 33:91, 2002.
31. L. Baruch, "Rethinking Accounting," *Financial Executive* 18:34, 2002.
32. R. McGrath, "A Real Option Logic for Initiating Technology Positioning Investments," *Academy of Management Review* 22:974, 1997.
33. D.F. Swenson, *Pioneering Portfolio Management* (New York: The Free Press, 2000, p. 132).
34. H. Markowitz, "Portfolio Selection," *Journal of Finance*, March 1952, pp. 77–91.
35. I.S. Rothenberg, "Financial Planning Forum: The Advantages of Modern Portfolio Theory," *Accounting Today*, April 26, 1999.
36. T. Norretranders, *The User Illusion* (Penguin Group, 1999).
37. T. Luehrman, "Investment Opportunities as Real Options: Getting Started on the Numbers," *Harvard Business Review*, July–August, 1998, p. 51.
38. O. Lint and E. Pennings, "R&D As an Option on Market Introduction," *R&D Management* 28:279, 1998; O. Lint and E. Pennings, "An Option Approach to the New Product Development Process: A Case Study at Philips Electronics," *R&D Management* 31:163, 2001.
39. P.D. Childs, S.H. Ott, and A.J. Triantis, "Capital Budgeting for Interrelated Projects: A Real Options Approach," *Journal of Financial and Quantitative Analysis* 33:305, 1998.
40. R.A. Brealey and S.C. Myers, *Principles of Corporate Finance* (New York: McGraw-Hill, 1996).

CHAPTER 8

Managing Relationships with Real Options

As much as the real option framework requires an organizational mindset and culture to flourish, equally it also drives and changes managerial and organizational behavior. In its most simple form, contracts and agreements with embedded real options may be designed to spur certain behaviors while penalizing others. A point in case is the bidding auction for the Antamina mine.[1] The Peruvian government had set up an auction whereby participants were asked to submit bids for the right to explore the mine as well as for the planned expenditures to develop the mine following a two-year exploration period. Figure 8.1 provides a cursory outline.

The auction design incorporated embedded real options, namely the option to defer the decision to commit mine exploration, until after a two-year

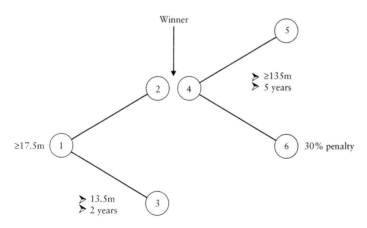

FIGURE 8.1 The strategic options in the Antamina mine auction

exploration period (nodes 2/3), a novelty in the mining industry. Tradition-
ally, mining auctions imply a bidding process for the upfront fee that enti-
tles the winner to the right, but not the obligation, to explore the mine, a
scenario that led to one of the first real option valuations.[2] The rules proposed by the Peruvian government, instead, asked bidders to bid for both the
option premium, that is, acquisition of the right to explore (node 1) as well
as the exercise price that would lead to acquisition of the best-case scenario
(node 5).

This auction structure produced very specific incentives designed to in-
duce certain behavior among the bidders. First of all, it created a strong
motivation for bidders to propose high investments for the actual mine development, the exercise price of the second stage of the compound option.
Thereby, however, the layout of the bidding process also increased the probability that the option will move out of the money in the second stage and
that the project will be abandoned by the successful bidder at node 4. However, the abandonment comes at a price: The successful bidder has to pay
30% of the proposed exercise price as penalty if she fails to commit.

The successful bidder was defined by the value of the initial bid plus
30% of the commitment bid for mine development. This way, bidders could
win by making high commitments for the second stage and the present value
of 30% would go into identifying the winner, but by making low commitments for the first stage. The winner would commit to a high exercise price
but only a small option price for acquiring the option. This structure facilitated the participation in the bidding of smaller firms that lacked the resources today to engage in the auction but could win based on the promise
of future payments.

The penalty clause for the second stage, on the contrary, creates disin-
centives: It may be an invitation to purchase extra assets to circumvent the
penalty but re-deploy those assets for other uses or to use inflated transfer
prices to increase the recorded investment sum. Moel and Tufano also point
out that the structure of the auction may not actually help the Peruvian government to achieve its proclaimed goals: attracting major world-class firms,
while the rules could favor also smaller, less resourceful players; and obtaining instant cash proceeds, while the auction structure would permit a
bidder to win mostly on the promise of future cash commitments in stage II.

Real option analysis, as the bidding auction of the Antamina mine already suggests, is a very valuable framework to evaluate transactions with
customers, business partners, vendors, or employees. Contractual relationships serve multiple purposes. They provide access to technology; share risk
in product development; set the foundation for future growth options; limit
exposure to future uncertainty by fixing conditions for mutual delivery of

products, services, or input resources; and provide incentive structures aligned with corporate vision and strategy. In each context, both sides of the contractual equation have distinct and often different expectations, assumptions, and perceptions about future uncertainties. And yet, if they engage in an agreement, both sides have to see value in the agreement and feel confident that their mutual risks and uncertainties are taken care of adequately and fairly.

When exercising a real option by engaging in a contractual arrangement, negotiating partners also need to think about hedging tools to mitigate the risk associated with those transactions. Real options, while often embedded in these agreements, are usually not necessarily explicitly recognized or valued as such. Real option analysis provides the framework to accommodate future uncertainties, to preserve attractiveness of the agreement to both sides in view of these uncertainties, or to manage divergent, sometimes disparate assumptions shared by each partner. Incorporating real option analysis contributes significantly to managing relationships in the face of uncertainty and irreversibility by preserving flexibility.

Failure to accommodate future uncertainties into contractual agreements can be quite costly. Consider the example of the U.S. life insurance industry. Many of these companies failed in the late 1960s to recognize the impact uncertain interest rates might have on the contractual conditions presented to clients. Standard policies at the time offered policy owners the opportunity to borrow money against the cash value of the insurance at a fixed interest rate. Some of these policies had a very long expiration date, and during this time to maturity, interest rates not just fluctuated but steadily climbed up to 13%, up to four percentage points above the fixed interest rates granted in the insurance contracts. This development created an excellent arbitrage opportunity for policyholders. They borrowed cash against the insurance policy and invested it at a 4% higher rate. Many policyholders took advantage of this option embedded in their policies, leading to bankruptcy of some insurance companies.

More recently, other firms have not only recognized the value of real options in structuring license agreements but in fact made it a core competence to develop tailored products for their customers from high-tech industries. Within high-tech industries innovative product design and development often entails the need to access intellectual property rights from third parties. Those licensing agreements constitute ideal opportunities for real option valuation. Cadence Design System, a Silicon Valley-based electronic design product and service firm has recently developed an options-based license valuation service product.[3] The benefits as seen here include better integration of variable and uncertain market payoff outcomes in the deal structure, as well as implementation of a fast track to bring both sides of the table to a mutually agreeable consensus on the deal structure terms based on a common framework—and mindset.

Contractual agreements regularly contain real options related to the transfer of products, services, or other assets. Sourcing of services has become an integrated part of operations in firms across industries. Those agreements enhance flexibility in the firm's cost structure but by the same token also increase exposure to other, often external uncertainties, including exchange risks, liability risks, and timing risks. Frequently firms engage in contractual agreements to jointly develop or market a product or service. Those deals need to reconcile a diverse set of working assumptions about the probabilities of success, time frames, cost scenarios, and the ultimate market payoff shared by either of the partners. Contract embedded clauses are designed to function as performance incentives, such as milestones, or penalties. Identifying and valuing those embedded real options assists in refining deal structures and terms, aligning them with internal strategies and assumptions, and helps to identify risk, as well as upside potential associated with contractual agreements, and to value expansion or growth options inherent in those agreements.

For example, a joint venture on a product development program can be viewed as a sequential compound option whereby after the initial learning experience one of the partners makes an equity investment in the other partner. Successful product development during the joint venture creates the option to expand the agreement to include sales or distribution rights and may ultimately create the incentive—and real option—to acquire the joint venture partner. These types of agreements are frequent in high-tech industries such as semiconductors, software development or biotechnology, which feature high R&D intensity and high levels of technical uncertainty.

A recent article in *Red Herring* alludes to IBM's changing chip strategy, which now involves a series of investments in start-up companies in exchange for equity.[4] Similarly, Intel participated in an early round investment in a start-up firm called VxTel, an investment that can be viewed as the acquisition of a growth option. This growth option was exercised when Intel finally acquired VxTel for an exercise price of $550 million.

These examples also extend to other industries. Anheuser-Busch, the global brewery, within the past few years has initiated a novel strategy of growth option acquisitions by making small equity investments in local breweries in foreign markets.[5] These investments given Anheuser both growth options as well as learning options: By participating in the small breweries, Anheuser learns quickly about the market structure, demand,

and growth potential of these markets, thereby reducing much of the noise that would otherwise cloud assumptions about the attractiveness of these markets. This, in turn, facilitates informed decisions as to which of those growth options should be exercised by acquiring target firms in proliferating markets.

A joint venture creates the option to learn about technical and market uncertainty by preserving a stake in the development program. It provides the opportunity to participate in the upside potential while also sustaining enough flexibility to exit at low costs if the project fails. Those partner strategies that build on sequential investments constitute an important part of corporate strategies. They avoid the risk inherent in premature acquisition of a technology firm prior to obtaining a good understanding of the feasibility of the emerging technology and its market acceptance.

An agreement between two partners, be it to jointly develop a new product or to provide for product or service supply, should allow for sufficient embedded options and flexibility to sustain a fair and just allocation of obligations and rewards to each party for both the current conditions, under which the agreement is closed, and a set of future uncertainties. In other words, the agreement should create a Pareto optimal allocation of risks and reward in the face of uncertainty: there is no other allocation in which some other individual is better off and no individual is worse off. It implies that both parties can benefit equally from future upsides and are equally protected against downside risks. Contract embedded options that permit fair risk and reward sharing during the presumed lifetime of the agreement under a set of future uncertainties are likely to stabilize and sustain the relationship between the two parties.

One solution to the problem of future uncertainties is contingent contracts. In a contingent contract, some of the deal terms are not finalized but are left open for future events, that is, the contingencies, to occur. Those contingencies may relate to uncertain market payoffs, the success of a joint project, or the costs it may take to complete a task. Real options are a great analytical tool to reconcile disparate assumptions and expectations in the structure of a contingent contract.

In another context, contract embedded options are designed to create behavioral incentives or penalize unwanted actions. These include delivery contracts with penalty clauses for delays or employment contracts that entail incentive options.

This chapter will provide several examples of a real option analysis in contractual relationships between two parties: a delivery contract for a service product with uncertain development time; a supplier contract for assets with short lead times such as fashion goods with market uncertainty; and a joint venture agreement to co-develop a new drug with significant technical and market payoff uncertainty.

DELIVERY CONTRACTS

In a delivery contract two parties engage in an agreement by which one side wants to secure delivery of a product or service for a specified period of time in a specified amount or at a specified price. The other side, the recipient, seeks to protect herself against price increases, product shortages, or delay. The deliverer is motivated to engage in the contract to secure demand and to facilitate production planning and resource requirement planning (queuing, input prices). The recipient seeks to secure reliability and stable pricing structure. She will attempt to terminate the contract and switch to another partner if the pricing or quality of the opponent appears more favorable. The deliverer perceives liquidity of the recipient as a major uncertainty against which to protect. Routinely, the time frame of these contracts is limited and subject to periodical review and renewal or termination.

In option terminology, such a framework is similar to a European Swapt-option: The exercise time is pre-determined. The option owner has the right to swap for another agreement if certain conditions are met. Swapt-options are frequently used for interest rate options. At predetermined dates the option owner has the right, but not the obligation, to enter into an interest rate swap and thereby either pay or receive a fixed swap-option.

Consider the following scenario: A software developer engages in a contract with a bank to develop a novel analytical system. Both parties agree on a fixed price of $500,000 and time to completion of 100 days. As the project is crucial to the client's organizational effectiveness and performance, as well as future business planning, the client proposes a penalty clause for potential delays. Specifically, the client suggests a fee that is 6% of the contract value for every day the completion of the business is delayed.

Prior to signing up for the job, the software development firm may want to evaluate the risk of this deal structure in light of internal assumptions and data. It may also want to determine the value hedging the risk of penalties through outsourcing. After internal discussions with the software developers, management has gained a good understanding of the various components of the product development plan. Its engineers have produced best and worst time line scenarios for project completion and identified several risk factors and uncertainties that drive those scenarios and time lines. Three sce-

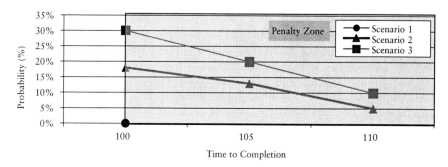

FIGURE 8.2 Time to completion scenarios

narios are being entertained, and the assumptions about probability of completion for those scenarios are depicted in Figure 8.2.

With those data in hand, management now needs to work out how these time frames translate into risk, given the suggested penalty. The key question to answer is: What is the value of the contract under the current risk profile with and without the mitigation of risk? The cumulative probability of completing the project over time (solid lines) and the corresponding payoff functions (dashed lines) are shown in Figure 8.3.

Under scenario 1, even though the expected time to completion is longer, there is no probability assigned to the development time exceeding the 100 days deadline. Hence, in scenario 1, the expected payoff will be the full sum of $500,000. Although under scenario 2 the expected time to completion is below 100 days, there is an accumulated 10% chance that the

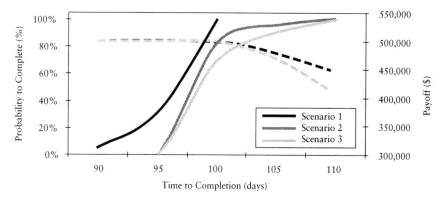

FIGURE 8.3 Cumulative probability of project completion and payoff function

software developer will be late, and this reduces the expected payoff. In fact, there is a cumulative probability of 1% to be delayed by as much as 10 days, reducing the payoff to as little as $455,000. In scenario 3 that probability is as high as 30%, and the expected payoff is reduced to $425,500, amounting to a 9% and 15% loss of the maximum payoff, respectively.

This analysis motivates management to explore alternative options in order to mitigate the risk, including the option to outsource some of the work in a later stage of the project. The software engineers assure senior management that after half the time into the project, that is, on day 50, they will have a much better understanding as to how the residual time line will evolve. They will then be able to predict reliably the probability of completing the project within the 100 days deadline. They will, however, not be able to predict how many days the project may be late if the deadline cannot be met.

If there is a chance that the project cannot be completed in time with the help of all the internal resources, management has the option to engage external help, either by employing part-time engineers or by outsourcing part of the work to another third party. Either alternative would imply additional cost and reduce the anticipated payoff, but it would also guarantee project completion in time and hence avoid the penalty payment. The cost of outsourcing or engaging part-time workers is estimated to be $20,000.

Clearly, the value of the outsourcing option then depends on the costs for the service as well as on the penalty payments saved. These, in turn, depend on the anticipated number of days the implementation of the software may be delayed beyond the 100 days deadline. The strategic options are captured in the binomial model presented in Figure 8.4.

To calculate the value of the contract option at node 1, we start at the end of the binomial tree and work backwards. At node 3, the value of the call

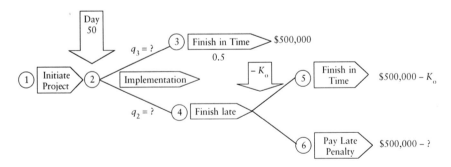

FIGURE 8.4 The binomial asset tree of managerial options

option is driven by the internal cost assumptions. Management believes it will cost $150,000 to complete the project. The value of the asset at node 3 is hence $350,000.

At node 4, management knows the project will be completed late but does not know how late. The value of the strategic options is driven by the probability function of completing the project late and the costs to be incurred for being late (node 6) and for outsourcing (node 5). The cost estimate for outsourcing is $20,000. The implication is that the software will be developed in time and the invoice will be paid in full. The asset value of the contract at node 5 hence becomes $500,000 – $150,000 – $20,000 = $330,000.

The value of the option at node 6 depends on the probability function of completing the project beyond the 100 day deadline and the additional penalty cost deriving from that.

For scenario 3, the penalty amounts to $0 in the best case and $90,000 in the worst case, and based on the probability function of delay, to $33,000 in the expected case. For scenario 2, the best case is also a $0 penalty, the worst case is $54,000, and the expected penalty is $12,255.

At node 4, management does not know which of the two scenarios may materialize, so for now each is assumed to be equally likely. The expected penalty payment therefore is $0.5 \cdot \$12,255 + 0.5 \cdot \$54,000$ or $22,627, more than the costs for outsourcing. The expected asset value at node 6 then becomes $500,000 – $150,000 – $22,627 = $327,372.

What then is the value of the option to outsource? Figure 8.5 shows the option scenario. By outsourcing management mitigates the risk of losing

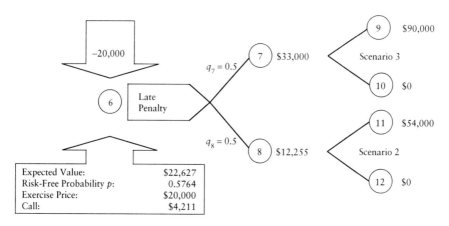

FIGURE 8.5 The binomial asset tree for the outsourcing option

$22,627, the expected value at node 6, at the exercise price of the outsourcing costs, i.e., $20,000. The minimum loss at node 6 is the expected penalty payment under scenario 2, the maximum loss the expected penalty payment under scenario 3. Those data give rise to a risk-free probability of $p = 0.5764$ and the value of the call on outsourcing then becomes $4,211.

What are the most important value drivers for the option outsource? If the penalty payment can be negotiated down from currently 6% to 4.956% of the contract value per day and the costs for outsourcing remain fixed at $20,000, the option to outsource moves out of the money. The critical penalty premium that moves the option to outsource out of the money is calculated by solving the equation for the call at node 6 for the premium range that makes the call value zero. This is done either by using the solver function in Excel or by repetitive iteration of the premium percentage.

If the penalty payment can be re-negotiated to 4.95% or less, management will be—from a financial perspective—better off to risk a delayed delivery and pay the penalty rather than to commit to outsourcing. From a corporate perspective, however, this strategy puts the reputation and brand name of the firm at risk. Failing to deliver a promised service in time and thereby causing major inconvenience for the customer is likely to enhance the hurdle for future customer recruitment or may even lead to losses within the current customer base.

If management agrees to outsource, this will provide a downside hedge to the contract, and the option to outsource is in the money as soon as the suggested penalty payment rises above 4.956%. There will be no need to negotiate. Management could almost offer an even higher penalty payment to signal to its client that the firm has confidence in its ability to complete the project without delay. While such a strategy may impress the client, it also bears the risk of sending the wrong incentive signals to its employees. They may view the outsourcing as a hedge against failure and may feel that—for the future—since this option is always open to management, they do not have to really keep tight deadlines. Such a move may therefore reduce motivation and commitment of the internal workforce.

How sensitive is the option to outsource to timing uncertainty, then? At an assumed cost of $20,000 and at a penalty rate of 6% per delayed day, the value of the option to outsource is $4,211. Figure 8.6 shows how outsourcing option value changes as the expected probability of delay declines. We let the probability to complete the project beyond the 105 and 110 days time frame decline for both scenario 2 and scenario 3 in parallel at incremental steps of 1%.

As soon as the probability of delay beyond 110 days drops to 4.5%, the option to outsource moves out of the money. Likewise, as soon as the prob-

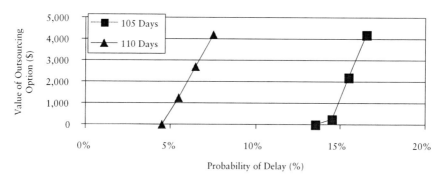

FIGURE 8.6 Sensitivity of the outsourcing option to the probability of delay

ability to delay beyond 105 days drops to 14% and below, the option to outsource also moves out of the money.

What is the message to management from this analysis? Any attempt within the organization to improve organizational processes and procedures and to motivate its employees to make accurate and reliable predictions on time projections and enforce organizational discipline to meet those time frames will pay off. It will also eliminate the need to negotiate around any penalty payment or to outsource and thereby create value for the organization: dividend value by eliminating penalty or outsourcing payments and competitive value by creating a reputation for timely and reliable service delivery.

SUPPLIER CONTRACTS

Often, two parties interested in engaging in a deal to pursue common interests not only entertain disparate expectations about future payoffs but also face very different, if not opposite, uncertainties and risks that can easily stand in the way of a successful deal closure. Michael Porter coined the terms supplier and buyer power and ascribed two of his five forces that shape industry dynamics to these parties. Even without exercising supplier or buyer power, even within a power equilibrium, negotiations between supplier and buyer create much room for dispute and need to reconcile distinct motivations and expectations.

In the fashion retail industry, for example, retailers and manufacturers need to interact in a mutually dependent relationship, facing the same uncertainties, but deriving distinct if not disparate risks from those uncertainties (Figure 8.7).

Retailers rely on being able to respond to fast and sudden as well as somewhat unpredictable demand changes from their retail customers. Being able to deliver the desired fashion goods when they are in high demand at an acceptable price is key to the business. It provides a strong incentive to engage in delivery contracts with fashion manufacturers that guarantee rapid, reliable delivery of potentially huge quantities of goods at ideally short notice. The fashion manufacturer, on the other hand, faces as a result of these market dynamics, a different set of uncertainties and risks: She has to have sufficient capacity to respond to high demand, balance expensive inventory with short lead times and flexible responses to changing market demands, and find ways to deal with unwanted goods. She also has to manage cost uncertainty for raw material and labor.

This situation poses major challenges to the management of expectations and to the structure of the supply and delivery conditions that have to accommodate several sources of uncertainties with differential impact on both parties.

How can real option analysis assist in creating fair and flexible deal terms that incorporate uncertainties? In the supplier-buyer scenario, the retailer has to preserve flexibility in order to respond to demand uncertainty; the manufacturer has to preserve flexibility to adjust capacity and plan for the purchase of raw material and inventory build-up. It is the responsibility of the retailer to produce a market forecast as well as a timing schedule for sales. The forecast will provide a best and a worst case sales scenario. The worst case scenario constitutes the minimum amount of goods the retailer is willing to commit to purchase. The best case scenario is the amount of goods the retailer likes to have an option on. The expected case reflects the as-

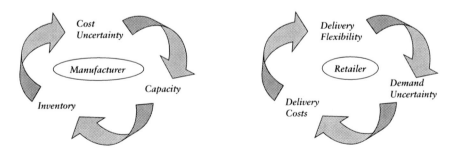

FIGURE 8.7 Uncertainty sources for fashion retailer and manufacturer

sumptions about the best or the worst case scenario to occur. Consider the outline of a basic supplier-buyer agreement that is summarized in Figure 8.8.

The minimum purchase provides the floor for the manufacturer. If the retailer finds demand less than the assumed worst case scenario, he agrees to pay a penalty if he fails to purchase the minimum amount of goods. The penalty compensates the manufacturer for inventory costs and expenses incurred for purchasing raw material. The forecasted expected case provides the upper limit of the total order, which is composed of a fixed order, the minimum, and a flexible amount, which is optional. It will be up to the manufacturer to prepare and plan for the optional delivery. The retailer agrees to pay up front a small option fee of $0.2 per unit of the flexible amount. If demand is low, that option will remain unexercised; if demand goes up, the option will be exercised by paying an additional $1.00 per unit for the flexible amount.

In addition, there is a third bucket that will materialize only if demand increases the expected case. In this scenario, for orders beyond the expected case that may come at short notice and require short delivery times, there will be a premium order price per item. The premium compensates the manufacturer for sudden capacity switches and purchase of additional material at potentially higher prices and potential overtime for his employees.

Both parties may have different sets of expectations on future demand uncertainty, but both have exact knowledge of their internal cost and revenue structure under different scenarios. What does such a concept look like in a real option framework, and how does the option analysis help both parties to refine the best part forward?

The retailer assumes that the market demand will be anywhere between 50,000 pieces at the minimum and 200,000 pieces at maximum but has really very little understanding as to what scenario may play out. He is unsure as to whether to order the 50,000 items now at a price of $1 each and commit to additional items as an option at an option fee of $0.2 and exercise

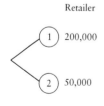

Retailer		Revenue	Price		Costs	Revenue	Manufacturer	
1	200,000	1.5	1.5	Premium	0.9	0.6	200,000	1
		1.8	1.2	Option	0.7	0.5		
2	50,000	2.0	1.0	Minimum	0.5	0.5	50,000	2
		−0.6	0.6	Penalty	0.5	0.1		

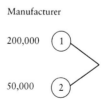

FIGURE 8.8 Outline of the deal structure I

price of $1.00 each if demand is favorable, leaving still the option to pur-chase at a premium of $1.50 each if demand becomes extraordinary. Alter-natively, he may order what is likely to be halfway between the worst and the expected demand, risk paying a penalty if he is unable to sell the goods and has to return them to the manufacturer, but save the option and the pre-mium payment. Finally, he may just buy what he views as the expected de-mand and increase the risk of paying a penalty, but further reduce the number of additional items to be bought as an option or as a premium. How does the option value of such a contract look to the retailer? Figure 8.9 summarizes the option value of the payoff scenarios from the retailer's perspective.

Shown is the option value on net payoffs as a function of an increasing amount of minimum orders on the *x*-axis and a series of market risks. These range for a probability of 20% to 90% for the highest market demand sce-nario to occur. It is assumed that the retailer will sell each item at a fixed price of $3.

At high market risk, that is, low probability of meeting the best case sce-nario of 200,000 sales, the option value for the retailer declines with in-creasing minimum orders. This reflects the penalty payments on returned goods as well as the option fee on the flexible units as those options remain unexercised due to low demand. As market risk declines and the probability to meet the best sales forecast increases, management becomes increasingly better off by ordering a very high minimum amount of goods. With low market uncertainty, the probability to pay penalty for oversubscribed units declines. The probability of all options on flexible units to be exercised in-creases, and hence there will be no additional loss due to option fee pay-ments, while at the same time the number of extra units that need to be

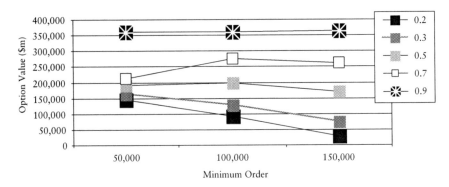

FIGURE 8.9 The option value for the retailer under market uncertainty

purchased at a premium becomes smaller the higher the initial minimum order is. The volatility increases as the market risk increases. For very low market risk, i.e., $q = 0.9$, the difference in option value for a high minimum order versus a low minimum order is 1.2%, but 80% for the high market risk of 0.2. In other words, given the high market uncertainty, management can lose more than gain by ordering the high minimal amount.

The option value is also sensitive to the proposed penalty, shown in Figure 8.10. At high market risk, that is only a 20% probability for the best case demand scenario to come through, an increase in the proposed penalty payment per unit from $0.2 to $1.5 leads to even further decline of option value as the minimum order increases, shown in solid squares in Figure 8.10. In fact, at a penalty payment of $1.50 per unit and a minimum order of 150,000, the option is out of the money for the retailer under conditions of high market risk. On the contrary, when market risk is low and the best case demand scenario has a 90% chance of being realized, the penalty payment has little effect on option value for the retailer, shown in solid circles in Figure 8.10. While this result is not surprising and intuitively makes sense, the sensitivity analysis itself does provide guidance for the retailer when negotiating the contract and deciding on the minimum order amount.

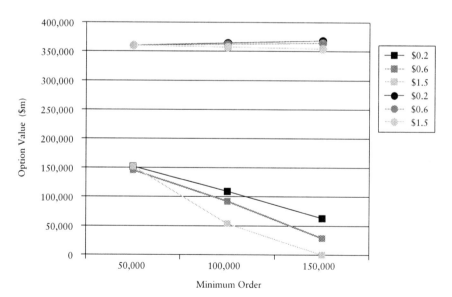

FIGURE 8.10 Option sensitivity to penalty payments—the retailers perspective

From the manufacturer's perspective, the option value of the agreement displays quite an opposite behavior. Figure 8.11 summarizes in the upper panel the option value of the contract to the manufacturer under the same market risk scenarios.

First, the manufacturer does not benefit from larger minimum orders if market expectations are high; the value of the contract option declines as the minimum order increases. This reflects the fact that under the agreement the manufacturer would gain incremental revenues/item if the retailer were to purchase goods at a premium price. The higher the minimum amount the retailer agrees to order, however, the fewer items he will have to purchase at a premium, even under excellent market conditions. On the other hand, the smaller the minimum order and the higher the probability of high market demand, the greater the likelihood for the retailer to purchase additional items at the premium becomes, and the option value for the manufacturer increases.

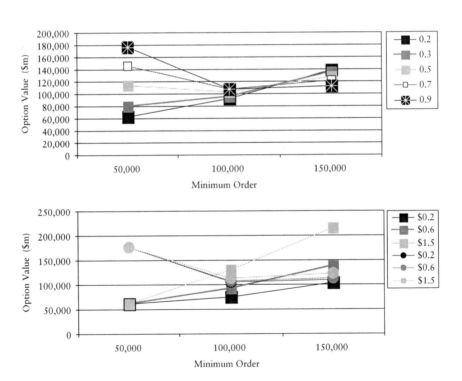

FIGURE 8.11 The option value for the manufacturer under market uncertainty

For low market expectations, the manufacturer increasingly benefits from higher minimum orders. This reflects the penalty payments imposed on the retailer for units ordered but returned if market demand is low. If market expectations are ambiguous, that is, a 50% chance for the high demand and a 50% chance for the low demand scenario, either a low minimum or high minimum order work best for the manufacturer. In the first instance, option value derives from the premium for additional orders, in the second instance from penalty payments on returned goods.

How sensitive is the option value to penalty payments from the manufacturer's perspective? This is shown in the lower panel of Figure 8.11. Under low market risk conditions (solid circles), there is little sensitivity of option value to an increase in the proposed penalty payment. Overall, with an increasing minimum order, the option value declines. Under high market risk conditions (shown in solid squares), on the contrary, the manufacturer increasingly benefits from larger penalty payments as the minimum order goes up. Again, this makes intuitive sense but provides the manufacturer with guidelines for his negotiation strategy.

This deal structure really enforces an already conflicting exposure to uncertainties and risks. Is there an alternative contract structure that could align the interests of both manufacturer and retailer and allow both to benefit from the market upside potential and share the market risk? The retailer may attempt to share the risk of demand uncertainty with the manufacturer: If demand falls below the expected case scenario assumptions, the manufacturer agrees to reduce the price to allow for a more substantial rebate of the goods at the retailer. If demand exceeds the expected case scenario, the retailer will share some of the profit with the manufacturer. This way the deal structure becomes contingent on the resolution of demand uncertainty and is designed to allocate risk and reward equally. Figure 8.12 shows the outline of the revised deal structure.

Both parties agree on a minimum order of 50,000 items at a purchase price of $1 per item. If demand is higher, the manufacturer will charge an additional 10% per item for each 25,000 additional items beyond the minimum order of 50,000 the retailer will purchase. If demand is lower than 50,000, the manufacturer agrees to offer a 10% reduction per item for each 5,000 items below the minimum order of 50,000. The retailer still expects to sell at $3 per item, and the manufacturer still expects to incur additional manufacturing costs for each item if demand goes up significantly, depending on the lag time and on the amount of additional items requested. Therefore, the basic operating assumptions have remained the same. Figure 8.13 depicts how the altered deal structure translates into real option value for

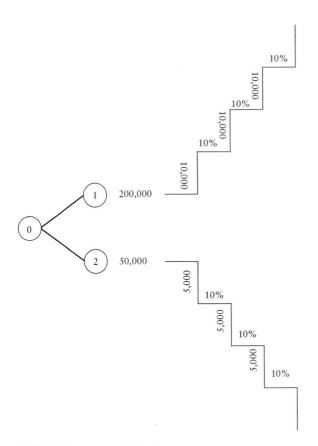

FIGURE 8.12 Outline of the deal structure II

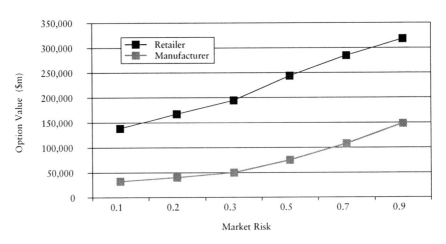

FIGURE 8.13 Option value for both parties under market uncertainty

each partner for a range of market uncertainties. Both parties now benefit from the upside of the market risk; their incentives are aligned.

DEAL STRUCTURING—MANAGING EXPECTATIONS IN A JOINT VENTURE OR ALLIANCE

Across industries, as market and technology uncertainty increase, an effective hedging strategy for many companies is to engage in joint R&D ventures to explore multiple technologies simultaneously, creating a portfolio of early stage R&D options, some of which can be turned into future growth options. These agreements have to reconcile different motivations, different assumptions, and different expectations to lead to a contractual agreement that helps to manage expectations on both sides, in the face of high uncertainty. Figure 8.14 depicts the major hurdles.

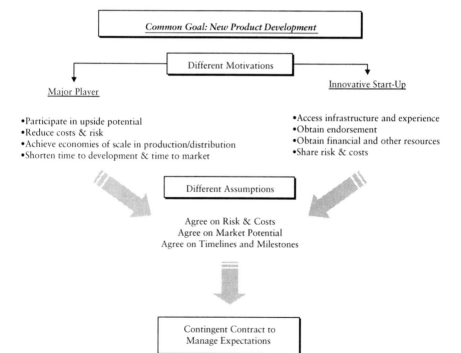

FIGURE 8.14 Challenges of a new product development joint venture

Deals of this nature often involve quite heterogeneous partners: a large established pharmaceutical or software company and an emerging biotech firm or software start-up. The motives to engage in an alliance or joint venture are diverse on both sides. The more established player seeks to fill his early product pipeline and to obtain with little investment and at low risk the option to participate in future growth options. The small start-up seeks for independent validation and endorsement of its technology by partnering with an established firm, gaining access to experience and knowledge and financial as well as other help in developing the product.

Naturally, both sides have different sets of assumptions about the main value drivers in this arrangement. The main purpose of the deals is to share the risks and the costs as well as future payoffs. The challenge is in defining what sharing entails, and this challenge is fostered by two components: high uncertainty as to whether the product will be developed and what features it will have, and how these will translate into market penetration and market potential, in reference to both technical uncertainty, market requirement uncertainty, and competitive entry.

In addition, both sides have different assumptions and expectations regarding each of these uncertainties. Often, the bigger, more mature, and also more experienced organization is more prudent with respect to market size and probability of technical success. The smaller, innovative company that invented the technology, on the contrary, is a strong believer and also wants to sell access to its core business at a high price. The smaller player expects from the successful deal closure rapid flow of cash as an award for bringing the technology to its current state as well as milestones and future royalties to participate in the upside commercial potential. The bigger player wants to increase the pool of options in the early pipeline without enhancing the overall corporate risk too much and without hitting its balance sheet with R&D expenses that are too high.

Failing to manage the expectations and reconcile the assumptions can easily lead to a breakdown of the negotiations. For example, when Jean-Louis Gassee, the founder of the operating system maker Be Inc., and Apple, the computer manufacturer, initially discussed a deal that would make the Be computer operating system (Be OS) the core of a new Macintosh computer operating system, the negotiations eventually broke down. Be felt that its technology—at the current state—was worth at least $285 million, while Apple would not offer more than $100 million.[6] Had both parties agreed to a contingent contract with embedded real options, those differences could have been handled within the agreement.

If two parties negotiate within a real option framework, divergent assumptions can in fact be very constructive and useful. First, they help in further understanding and exploring the drivers of risk and uncertainty and risk. Second, the different assumptions about key risk and value drivers do not become the basis of prolonged and potentially tiresome deal discussions. Instead, they simply are incorporated as best and worst case scenarios into the deal structure. Third, those assumptions, a bet of each partner on the uncertain future, will help define the contingencies of the deal structure that make it possible to share risk and reward equally even for a range of uncertain future outcomes.

Imagine a joint R&D program between a small start-up company, designated SU, with an exciting technology, and a big biotech company, designated BB, with much experience in bringing products to the market but in need of early-stage pipeline products. Both want to engage in a joint venture to develop a new drug, whereby the small company provides the technology, and the larger player the financial resources as well as infrastructure and expertise for clinical development, marketing, and distribution. The basic framework of the program that should serve as the core of the deal to be structured is shown below in Figure 8.15.

Both firms operate with a divergent set of assumptions that relate to all aspects of the program and affect the key drivers of the option valuation. The start-up firm SU believes in a better market outcome both for the best and the worst case scenarios, yielding distinct assumptions about the ex-

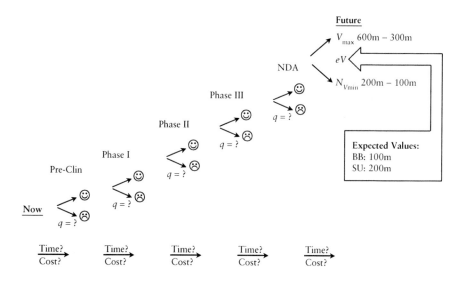

FIGURE 8.15 The binomial asset tree of the product development compound option

TABLE 8.1 Assumptions on private risk

Assumptions on Technical Success Probability

	BB (%)	SU (%)
Target	25	30
Lead	80	90
Validation	70	75
Pre-Clinical	40	50
Phase I	60	70
Phase II	50	60
Phase III	70	80
FDA	90	95

pected value of the asset both players want to generate in cooperation. The start-up also believes that there is an overall cumulative probability of technical success of 3.03%, while the big biotech firm BB, having seen too many apparently promising technologies fail before, estimates the cumulative probability of success at the pre-clinical stage not to exceed 1.06%. Table 8.1 summarizes the diverse set of estimates on the technical probability of success for the various stages of development from each perspective.

Both parties also have slightly divergent assumptions as to how much it will cost to bring the product through the development program; Table 8.2 summarizes those assumptions (figures are given in $ million).

Both SU and BB, however, agree on the time it will take to get to market, i.e., 7 years. The option value of this investment opportunity obviously looks different for both players, as shown in Figure 8.16.

Obviously, the diverse sets of assumptions also determine what each party views as the critical cost to invest, that is, the maximum amount of resources to be spent that drives the option at the money, but not yet out of the

TABLE 8.2 Assumptions on product development costs

	Target	Lead	Validation	Pre-Clinic	Phase I	Phase II	Phase III	FDA
BB Assump-tions R&D	0.3	0.4	0.5	0.5	5	12	20	5
SU Assump-tions R&D	0.2	0.4	0.5	0.5	4	8	14	5

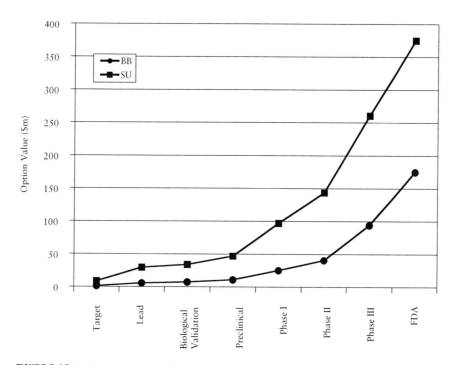

FIGURE 8.16 Disparate option values of the opportunity

money. As before, we calculate the critical cost *K* to invest by setting the equation for the call to zero and solving for *K*. Figure 8.17 summarizes the results.

The art of deal making now is to find a deal structure that is perceived as fair and just by both sides and meets the assumptions and expectations of both sides. The general structure of a typical R&D joint venture entails one or all of the following elements:

- Up-front payment for access to the technology
- Milestone payments for certain, pre-defined R&D achievements
- A share of costs
- Royalties upon successful product development and launch

These are the basic tools that can be used by both parties to arrive at a deal settlement that under the diverse sets of assumptions makes the deal structure an equal and just real option for each player. BB, approaching the

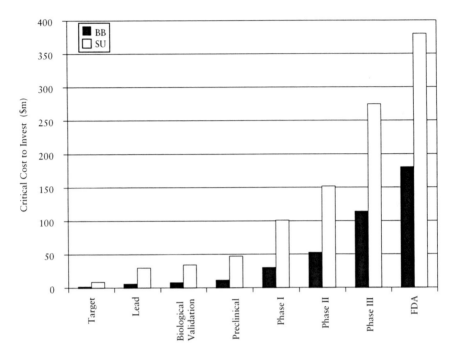

FIGURE 8.17 Disparate investment thresholds for the opportunity

scenario from its own assumptions, proposes to pay the following milestone payments upon successful completion of each stage, as shown in Table 8.3 (in $ million).

BB assumes that the gross margin of the product will be 35%. Both parties agree, as the assumptions about the final market potential vary, to stage the proposed royalty rate, depending on future market payoff. The royalty rate BB will pay SU will increase as the sales increase, as outlined in Table 8.4.

TABLE 8.3 The milestone payments of the deal

	Lead ($)	Pre-Clinical ($)	Phase II ($)	FDA Submission ($)
Milestones	1.0	2.5	5.0	7.5

TABLE 8.4 The royalty payments—
contingent on revenues

Sales ≤	$200m	$400m	$600m
Royalties	5%	10%	15%

How does this deal structure look as a real option for both parties, using the respective sets of assumptions? SU assumes a market potential of $400 million and will therefore model the deal using a 15% royalty rate. BB assumes a total market potential of no more than $200 million, and will therefore operate with a 5% royalty rate. As both parties also have different ideas as to the probability of technical success, each incorporates in their evaluation of the deal different probabilities of actually paying or receiving the milestone payments. Therefore, the maximum and minimum asset value and the expected value that represents market uncertainty and technical success probability are distinct in the frameworks that each party assumes. Finally, as cost assumptions also vary, the exercise price for each stage of the compounded option will be different in each party's real option evaluation.

Each party now wants to understand what the option value looks like for both partners under the internal set of assumptions. Figure 8.18 depicts in the left panel the value of the option to each player using BB's assumptions; in the right panel, the option value of the deal to both parties using SU's assumptions.

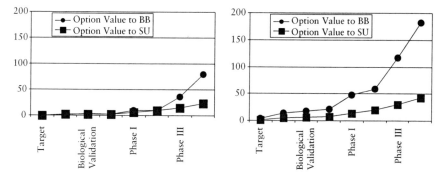

FIGURE 8.18 The option value of the opportunity—to each partner under each set of assumptions

Under both sets of assumptions, BB clearly will enjoy much more of the upside potential than SU will, and this is more pronounced as the project proceeds successfully through the development stages and also more pronounced using SU's set of assumptions (right panel). SU is strongly motivated to re-negotiate the royalty rate to achieve a better share of the upside potential in the later stage of program development. Again, both parties go back to their own drawing boards to determine under what conditions the value of the investment option would be equal after the product reaches the market. Figure 8.19 summarizes the results for increasing royalty rates for total sales.

Under BB assumptions, that equilibrium is reached at 22.5%, and under SU assumptions, it is reached at 27%. These figures define the boundaries for further negotiation. BB, while attracted by the upside potential in the long term is not prepared to entertain such high royalty rates. Given the overall cost structure of the future product, an uncertain future competitive environment that may require additional expenses for marketing and distribution this option starts to look less attractive than some other opportunities BB could entertain instead. BB, to strengthen its negotiation position, would like to obtain an understanding of how, in the current deal structure, risk and return are related for each of the players. While BB recognizes that it will have a more significant share of the upside potential, it also emphasizes that the risk in the early stages of the development is really not shared. BB will pay for the development program and will pay milestones, while SU will not incur any further costs.

We discussed in Chapter 2 how the binomial model makes it possible to calculate the implied volatility as well as the risk and return ratio. While both parties participating in this deal may not be able to agree on the basic assumptions, they are likely to be able to agree that each party should receive a fair return for the perceived risk. BB clearly has a higher risk as-

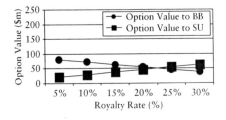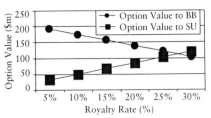

FIGURE 8.19 Alignment of option value by changing royalty rates

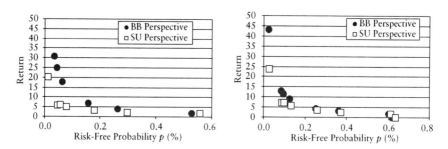

FIGURE 8.20 The risk-return profile for both parties under each set of assumptions

sumption than SU. How is this correlated with the expected return under the given deal scenario? We have already explained how the original Cox, Ross, and Rubinstein binomial option model looks at risk and return. In the good state of the world, the return R at the end of the next period will be a multiple of the current value of the underlying asset. In the bad state of the world, the return R will go down and only be a fraction of the current value of the underlying $1/R$. We follow the basic conceptual outline as presented in previous work[7] and calculate the return R for each development phase as the value at the end of that phase in the good state of nature. This is the maximum asset value to be achieved under optimal market conditions and assuming no technical failure. The return R is divided by the asset value reached at the end of the previous development phase, which is the expected asset value. We then investigate the relationship between the return and the risk-neutral probability of success. The risk-neutral probability p therefore serves as a proxy for risk. The left panel in Figure 8.20 shows the deal from both perspectives using the assumptions of BB; the right panel shows the deal from both perspectives using the assumptions of SU.

The current deal structure very well aligns the risk and return ratios for both partners, irrespective of the underlying assumptions. However, from both perspectives using both sets of assumptions, the risk-return profiles appear somewhat more favorable to BB than to SU. The two partners may consider adjusting the incremental royalty rates for the various revenue brackets or the milestones to bring the risk-return curves for each party into complete alignment under both sets of assumptions. The mutual benefit from the real option analysis is a better understanding of the respective risks and concerns of the business partners. It also improves ways to acknowledge that risk and allow for provisions—even if both parties operate under disparate sets of assumptions.

NOTES

1. A. Moel and P. Tufano, "When Are Real Options Exercised? An Empirical Study of Mine Closings," *The Review of Financial Studies* 15:35, 2002; A. Moel and P. Tufano, "Bidding for the Antamina Mine: Valuation and Incentives in a Real Option Context," in M.J. Brennan and L. Trigeorgis, eds., *Project Flexibility, Agency and Competition* (Oxford University Press, 2001).
2. J. Paddock, D. Siegel, and J. Smith, "Option Valuation of Claims on Physical Assets: The Case of Offshore Petroleum Leases," *Quarterly Journal of Economics* 103:479, 1988.
3. CFO staff, "Getting Real—Want to Take More Uncertainty Out of Capital Investment Decisions? Try Real Options," *CFO Magazine*, November 1, 1999.
4. S. Silverman, "Big Blue Goes Ape on Sand Hill Road," *Red Herring*, February 20, 2001.
5. T. Arnold, "Value Creation at Anheuser-Busch: A Real Options Example," *Journal of Applied Corporate Finance* 14:52, 2001.
6. P. Burrows, "How Apple Took Its NeXT Step," *Business Week*, January 13, 1997, p. 36.
7. T.J. Seppae and T. Laamanen, "Valuation of Venture Capital Investments: Empirical Evidence," *R&D Management* 31:215, 2001.

CHAPTER 9

Real Options—A Mindset to Share and Communicate

The value creation in Real Options—compared to a static, inflexible NPV analysis—derives from preserving flexibility. How much of these ideas and concepts have actually been tried in practice? How much empirical evidence exists for the use of real options by financial markets? What are the organizational challenges for implementing real option concepts and mindsets, and how can corporate real options be communicated to investors? This chapter will touch on these questions.

REAL OPTIONS AND ORGANIZATIONAL DESIGN AND BEHAVIOR

The Mutual Interplay

The real option framework is not simply another financial tool for the finance department; it is an organizational mindset that has to penetrate the organization to make a successful and helpful tool. Certain organizational requirements have to be met before any given firm can successfully put the real option framework into action. Implementation of the real option framework is intricately interwoven with organizational design and organizational behavior, as Figure 9.1 shows.

Careful thought processes across the organization are required to identify all options, their interactions, and the uncertainties that drive their value. Dependable and valuable real option analysis relies on a detailed set of assumptions that require the collective organizational knowledge to arrive at the most prudent input parameters. Finally, real option value can only be created and made real if the options are properly exercised. This, in turn, calls for the right incentives for managerial and organizational behavior to be in place.

Organizational Culture

Identifying & Framing

Organizational
Infrastructure & Design

Analyzing & Valuing

Organizational
Behavior & Incentives

Executing

FIGURE 9.1 The real option framework and organizational design

Organizational culture has a significant impact as to what is recognized as a real option. Two players in the same industry and exposed to the same exogenous, regulatory uncertainties may easily come to opposite conclusions as to what that uncertainty means for their business decisions. One player argues that in a tightly regulated environment flexibility really is of little help, as actions are largely externally determined. The other player, on the contrary, feels that, because of the narrow regulatory environment, creating space for flexibility is extremely important. In his view it will protect him against being driven by those exogenous circumstances and help him sustain the ability to respond in a flexible fashion. Both organizations are likely to identify, create, and exercise option value in a dramatically different fashion and extent.

The cultural dimensions of an organization also direct which options a firm identifies and how it exercises those options. Remember: real options do not value uncertainty per se, but only in conjunction with flexibility. Managerial skills that can be used to create that flexibility coupled with organizational ability to execute the flexibility are mandatory. Further, real options do not value uncertainty that results from noisy signals. On the contrary, the ability of the organization to receive information, share and utilize it, and transform it into exformation and defined input parameters for real option analysis adds great merit and soundness to the real option analysis.

The value of any given option will also be different to each owner, as the organizational capabilities to execute the real option, drive the upside potential but limit or eliminate the downside risk are distinct for different organizations. The same business opportunity will have real option value for one organization, but not for the other. Further, future decisions are contingent on current decisions. This is the Markov property of the real option. The Markov property, as you will remember from Chapter 1, means that the next step is contingent on the preceding one, but not on the one before that. To create option value, an organization must be capable of envisioning and executing those steps.

Consider the following example from the utility industry.[1] Two players, the UK-based energy and general service provider Centrica, and the global oil giant Shell, express interest in entering the Texas and Ohio electricity retail markets following deregulation. Centrica has established several product and service lines to serve the retail customer, including a credit card, retail insurance policies, and gas and electricity services. On the contrary, the multinational oil company Shell is known primarily for its achievements as a global oil company. It is one of America's leading oil and gas producers, manufacturers, and marketers of oil and chemical products. It has produced and delivered natural gas to utilities for several decades. In 1998, Shell formed a subsidiary, Shell Energy Services, with the intention of expanding its customer base for natural gas residential and small business customers.

Both Centrica and Shell attempted to enter the electricity markets in Texas and Ohio after deregulation, but soon Shell exercised its abandonment option. Clearly, the two corporate business models and the capabilities built over time kept the Texas and Ohio markets alive as an attractive real option for Centrica, but not for Shell. Centrica had taken steps before that and made the decision to enter the market in Texas and Ohio a natural progression, contingent on the capabilities built into the organization. It had the right experience, skill set, and cost structure in place to drive the real option of entering these two markets into the money. Shell, on the other hand, argued when announcing its decision to withdraw that the pace of electricity deregulation was too slow in the U.S. for them to reach an adequate size that would allow them to become profitable in a reasonable length of time.[2]

What had happened? Let's view Shell's market entry into the electricity market in Texas and Ohio as a learning and growth option, shown in Figure 9.2.

The decision to embark on a new business development program by entering the residential electricity markets in Texas and Ohio (node 1) derived

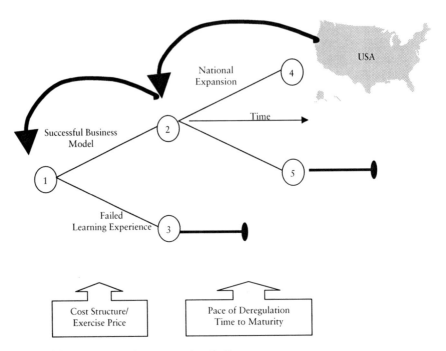

FIGURE 9.2 The binomial asset tree for Shell

much of its value from the prospect of expanding this business model nationwide, the upside potential at node 4. In other words, the future sequential nationwide market expansion factored into the real option evaluation and drove the option for Texas and Ohio into the money. Texas and Ohio, as independent market entities, might not have been "in the money real options" on their own for Shell, but only as part of the initial learning and experience gathering stage of a sequential compound option. The press release also points to two drivers of uncertainty identified by senior management that led to abandoning of the real growth option: (1) exercise price of the growth option, that is, the cost structure of the operation on a small scale versus the anticipated cost structure on the large scale following nationwide adoption of the electricity retail offer, and (2) time to maturity: uncertainty regarding the pace of national deregulation might have pushed time to maturity further out, driving the real option for Shell, with its given cost structure, out of the money (node 5). Shell settled for a joint venture with a smaller partner[3] to cover the Ohio market. This joint venture may well deliver the learning dividends Shell had been seeking in the first place. It may also be the exercise price Shell has to pay for the right to defer the decision of entering the electricity retail market at a later point in time, when more of the regulatory uncertainty has been resolved.

Real options are at the interface of organizational flexibility, capability, and resources, as symbolized in Figure 9.3. Those three elements form a very dynamic arpeggio, competing as well as synergizing. The option value of corporate resources is related to the firm's ability to exploit emerging opportunities that are created by the uncertain evolution of the environment. Alternative courses of action are available and must be sustained for the company to preserve strategic competitiveness. Flexibility also implies redefining capabilities and utilizing existing resources for more creative product and service design.

However, there is a trade-off decision to be made: building organizational flexibility and acquiring many real options while at the same time preserving a core focus, a core competence and a unique skill set. If the use of real options is too aggressive and if an organization acquires too many growth options, there is a danger of over-commitment, and ultimately failure to execute. The organization is at risk of losing focus and the ability to build and nourish core competence. The organization is also at risk of becoming unable to monitor all available options carefully and exercise as required.

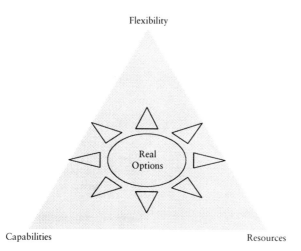

FIGURE 9.3 The organizational real option triad

Real Options—Being Shaped by the Organization

Organizational design is key to support real option analysis and execution. To be able to take full advantage of all organizational real options, organizational design must support the four key dimensions of the real option framework: identifying, mapping, execution, and communication, shown in Figure 9.4.

The organization is at risk of not fully realizing its entire real option potential by failing to fully identify all inherent options, failing to recognize and map out the important drivers of uncertainty, and failing to execute because of agency conflicts and dissonance of incentive alignment. Finally, the organization may simply leave money on the table by failing to communicate acquired options and options in place to investors. Additional operational weaknesses can further aggravate the inability of an organization to identify, value, and execute its real options. This includes inappropri-

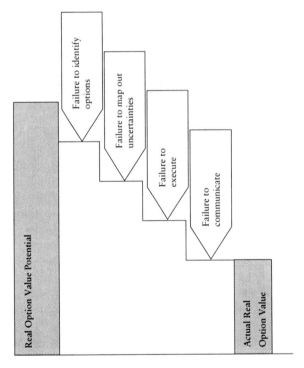

FIGURE 9.4 Organizational risks to full exploitation of the corporate real option potential

ate management systems that do not facilitate flexible decision-making processes, the internal cost structure that inhibits flexible shifting and adjusting of business activities, and an organizational culture and communication hardware that does not promote or smooth the progress of fast and complete information sharing.

Optimal integration of the real option mindset relies strongly on the organizational ability to access, digest, and integrate information. Sensitivity analysis documents where the important drivers of uncertainties lie, and what the option space is. This should provide sufficient guidance and incentive to try to fill the information gaps. It may even invite a careful look into historic patterns within the organization and the industry, for lessons to be learned. Remember, financial option pricing is based on predicting the future by studying the patterns of the past. Useful information can come from expense records, bills, and project accounting documents. Interviews with internal and external experts help to identify options as well as define the boundaries of uncertainty. Data from the balanced scorecard performance reviews can turn into corporate treasuries in the context of the real option framework. Data simulation, using Monte Carlo simulation, Crystal Ball, or other software programs also may be helpful. Useful estimates may also come from public records. For example, in an attempt to put a value on an R&D program, one might well study how in the past similar R&D programs have fared by looking into joint venture, license, or alliance agreements that put a value on comparable programs in distinct stages of development.[4] From these data one can prepare a probability function of the future payoff. That probability function reflects the stage of the development as well as the range of possible market values comparable programs have achieved in the past. This probability function not only gives guiding estimates as to the best and the worst case market payoff scenario but also to the expected market value, from which the binomial option value can be easily calculated.

Other sources of information are financial markets; after all, the real option approach is about aligning strategy with financial markets. This may not be applicable for all real options, but for some. For example, historic volatilities of securities traded in the financial market may serve as a proxy for project-specific volatilities, provided there are enough commonalities between the two.[5] When valuating unextracted natural resources such as oil, one may derive estimates for future prices by observing the market for futures on oil.[6] Such an approach also takes care of the no-arbitrage argument: Prices will fluctuate until arbitrage opportunities are exhausted.

There is no restriction to creativity in finding reliable and guiding input parameters. Cross-departmental planning groups involving strategy, finance, regulatory, operations, portfolio management, and intellectual property and other legal experts will be very helpful in recognizing all options but also in defining and refining all uncertainties as well as real organizational flexibilities. However, ultimately, the organizational architecture will shape how real options are recognized, framed, analyzed, and exercised. This relates to the processes and procedures in place to make decisions, to measure performance, and to allocate rewards.

An organization with many layers of approval processes, for example, may arrive at ultimate approval for a real option too late, when the time to maturity has already expired. Operational flexibility and cost structure to exercise that flexibility need to be in place to allow management to adjust to changes, adopt the flexible option path, and thereby mitigate risk. In the absence of sufficient flexible management systems, real options are at great risk not to be exercised or out of the money most of the time because of unfavorable cost-structures. Organizational culture and communication hardware both are mandatory for fast and complete information sharing, the essence and foundation of real option analysis.

Real option analysis can only be successful and help the organization to better cope with uncertainty if it is followed by proper exercise of the identified real option. After all, the market will value only the execution, not the analysis or valuation of the real option. Trivial but true: The most sophisticated but unexecuted real option analysis and valuation is worth far less than the least sophisticated but well executed NPV analysis. Implementing flexibility in the project valuation, appraisal, and execution procedure needs to be matched with organizational design.

The value of using real options to improve managerial decisions grows as the general sense of fast pace and uncertainty grows across industries. Firms operating in these environments are likely to adopt certain organizational structures. Business cycles tend to change faster; new technologies arrive faster and tend to change fundamental assumptions and industry structures. The arrival of the Internet, for example, has challenged basic assumptions in the information, newspaper, and media industries. The increasing availability of information technology has over the past decade facilitated deep-seated changes in the organization of most workplaces. Self-directed teams and cross-functional projects characterize the emerging workplaces. There is also an increasing tendency to integrate suppliers and customers at the organizational periphery.[7]

Cultural dimensions of an organization also direct how options are being recognized, implemented, and executed. They drive the shape of the organizational risk comfort zone that will dictate the choice among multiple available real options. Consider, for example, the learning option we discussed in previous chapters. It derives its value from reducing uncertainty and facilitating better informed managerial decisions. From the perspective of an established firm, a joint venture with a technology platform company is, for example, such a learning option: It makes it possible to acquire insight and knowledge about an emerging technology without committing full resources and accepting full risk. This learning option can be executed by acquiring a joint venture partner. Cultural dimensions, such as described by Hofstede,[8] may influence the value of a learning option of this nature, how that value is derived, what the organizational risk comfort zone is, and how the learning option is executed. Hofstede describes four dimensions of national culture, including power distance, uncertainty avoidance, masculinity, and individualism. A survey of 173 joint ventures and minority equity collaborations in the biotech industry revealed that firms from cultures with high power distance and high uncertainty avoidance, as is characteristic of the Japanese business system, tend to exercise the acquisition option more often.[9] Further, firms that learn better or more efficiently in a hierarchical structure are also more likely to acquire their joint venture partner. Here, organizational design and culture leads the decision maker to believe that the incremental rate of learning and the perceived learning benefit are higher under acquisition and complete control rather than in a joint venture scenario. Therefore, the investment value of the real option to acquire is increased, and the critical cost to invest is decreased compared to a joint venture scenario.

Cultural attributes such as power distance and uncertainty avoidance also drive organizational architecture and function.[10] These, too, control whether an organization is more comfortable with outsourcing, leasing, or learning in a joint venture or requires acquisition and control to maximize the learning experience. Along these lines, a recent study[11] suggests that firms from countries with higher power distance and more uncertainty avoidance are more likely to seek majority ownership in foreign subsidiaries. Internalizing the partner firm may increase the efficiency of knowledge transfer, thus enabling the firm to reduce future R&D costs so that growth options can be exercised at a lower cost.

As cultural distance between two partners increases, perceived transaction costs to overcome those cultural hurdles and achieve good communication and a sense of control also increase. Here, one may argue that perceived transaction costs that arise from cultural differences are higher in a joint venture than in an acquisition and therefore move the acquisition option sooner into the money than the joint venture option.

There is also empirical support for the notion that firms from a high uncertainty avoidance culture prefer licensing agreements over acquisition strategies.[12] Licensing agreements are much more a low-risk, staged investment approach with a small exercise price compared to an acquisition strategy that requires a higher commitment. Finally, cultures that accept and value uncertainty also value and cherish managerial personalities that display a strong champion character. At least four distinct champion personalities are well described in the literature, such as the network facilitator, the transformational leader, the organizational maverick, and the organizational buffer. Again, empirical evidence supports the notion that acceptance of those personalities in organizations from an uncertainty accepting cultural background facilitates and increases overall innovation.[13]

Firms engaged in innovative R&D projects also tend to choose different paths, depending on their cultural background and their stage of organizational maturity. Japanese pharmaceutical firms, for example, choose to enter into foreign R&D by establishing foreign subsidiaries and utilizing them to engage in collaborative R&D projects.[14] Cultural dimensions may further guide the design of the corporate R&D project portfolio.[15] Japanese firms, for example, tend to allocate more R&D resources to basic research and pre-emptive or strategic research than to applied research. This decision appears to be informed by the traditional emphasis on long-term strategic views within the Japanese business system. Long-term competitive advantage is likely to result from basic research rather than from applied research. Australian firms, on the contrary, focus much more on short-term goals (that is, options with short time to maturity) and correspondingly spend a large proportion of their R&D resources on applied research. This may reflect a more short-term approach to business, one that is much more informed by Anglo-Saxon business systems.

The leadership role of the United States in the biotech and life-science industry has also been explained by the real option approach to investments.[16] For high-risk and lengthy R&D projects such as those leading to innovative novel drugs, the investment approach is staged. We have previously characterized projects of this nature as sequential compound options. Concurrent investment into subsequent stages depends on the level of uncertainty that determines the critical cost to invest. At least two sources of heterogeneity between the U.S. and Europe, so goes the argument of this study, have helped the U.S. to identify and execute real options in the emerging biotech industry while preventing the EU from doing so. Regulatory uncertainty, as one key uncertainty in the drug development and approval process, has been higher in Europe than in the U.S., and has elevated the critical threshold to invest in for innovative R&D projects. For one, European drug approval agencies were less structured and slower in the approval rate than the FDA in the U.S. Further, consumer concerns about the merits of modern biotechnology were much stronger in Europe. In addition, as the drug development process tends to be a lengthy one, the rate of investment for the time to build option is crucial for the option owner to fully execute all sequential steps of the compounded real options. In the U.S., at least within the early stages of the emerging biotech industry, there was much more capital, and specifically risk capital, available to support these real option owners.

Real Options—Shaping Organizational Behavior

The option mindset can be instrumental in structuring relationships among stakeholders: partners, customers, suppliers, and shareholders. Specifically, they can be instrumental in resolving or reducing agency conflicts between managers and shareholders.[17] Incentive structures need to be altered or created to align with the real option framework so the organization becomes fully capable of exercising its real options. The rational exercise of options, as a purely mathematical analysis might indicate, has its human limitations: managers are not rational value maximizing robots.

Only recently an analysis was completed that looked for empirical support for one of the first theoretical real option concepts developed in the mid-eighties: the decision to open and close mines and thereby exercise deferral as well as switching options.[18] Seventeen years after publication of the pioneering academic papers by Brenner and Schwartz on real options in the mining industry, Tufano and Moel provided an empirical validation by examining 285 mine opening and closing decisions between 1988 and 1997.[19] The authors find both validation as well as loopholes of the real option model.

They are able to confirm—in line with the theoretical considerations of the 1985 paper by Brennan and Schwartz—the decision to exercise the option to open a mine depends on prices: higher prices increase the likelihood of mines being open. In addition, however, the study also provides empirical support for the notion of hysteresis in the decision to open and close. This hysteresis between the opening and closing of a mine is reflected in the observation that the likelihood of opening or closing is influenced by the mine status in the preceding period. Again, this is just what Markow suggested: The next movement is conditional on the previous step, but not so much on the steps preceding the previous one.

The decision to open or close a mine also depends—as the real option model predicts—on the costs of maintaining the open mine and preserving the closed mine, as well as the switching costs involved in closing or opening. Additional factors that guide the decision are stakeholder concerns; the background of the decision maker, such as his professional experience and

education, age, and compensation; the organizational structure; prior experience in abandoning; the overall organizational profitability; regulatory and
legal costs, that is, transaction costs that go along with exercising the option
either way, as well as the overall financial impediments such as the level of
debt.

In addition, the authors identify several other factors that influence the
opening-closing decision that are not part of the Brennan and Schwartz real
option model, nor are they incorporated in the real option models developed
since. This includes communication with stakeholders as well as negotiations with co-owners; the majority of mines are not owned by a single firm
but by several owners.

Interestingly, too, and much in line with portfolio theory, the individual
mine opening-closing decision is made in the context of its effect on the entire mining portfolio in place. The incentive to close also will depend on
hedging strategies in place: Empirical evidence suggests that well-hedged
firms tend to delay the decision to abandon even in very unfavorable times
with low prices.[20] A hedging strategy elevates the critical cost to invest that
moves the option out of the money. While the option value of abandoning
may be higher than the value of continuing operations, a well-designed
hedging strategy may permit management to justify continuous operations
as the options still remain in the money.

For example, assume an oil company produces oil at a cost per barrel of
$100 and sells it for $80. Clearly, the option to continue that operation is
out of the money. However, if the firm has a hedge for $120 a barrel, it can
produce at $100 and make a profit of $20 per barrel. While the more valuable option would still be to close the operation, buy the oil at $80, and sell
at $120, the operating option is still in the money and there is less pressure
on management to abandon.

In this context, there is a well-known and described managerial incentive to spend cash flow on growth options to increase the number of assets
under control.[21] This spending pattern also includes financial hedging strategies to mitigate business risks. These have enjoyed increasing popularity in
recent years among the large corporations. While hedging strategies mitigate
risk, they also reduce or eliminate corporate discipline to avoid ongoing execution of real options that are out of the money. Those out of the money
options, can, if properly hedged by financial hedging strategies, still be in the
money! However, greater shareholder value would derive from a real option
that is deep in the money without a hedging strategy. Further, cash-flow
hedging eliminates the need to seek finance from investors and banks, and
thereby also eliminates an important control element of the choice and execution of corporate real options. Risk hedging strategies avert risk; as man-

agers are risk averse and want to limit their personal exposure to bad news, corporate risk management becomes career risk or employment risk management. Financial hedging as an effective risk management tool has the potential to inflate agency conflicts, specifically those related to the exercise of the abandonment option of failing projects, as it permits managers to keep those projects for too long.

There is a rich literature on agency conflicts, and some of that work also includes the real option framework. Agency conflicts may, for example, play out in what is being recognized and valued as an option. The perception of a real option or business opportunity is guided by the mental and organizational framework that an agent or an organization is operating in. Consider the following scenario:[22] A firm engages a consultant with expert knowledge and access to non-public information to evaluate the cost of a new opportunity the firm is interested in pursuing and also to contribute to the implementation. Assume that the agent is being paid based on a percentage of the investment costs required to implement the opportunity. This obviously creates a strong incentive for the agent to signal investment costs higher than those that are true or to delay completion of the project to increase costs. Asymmetric information, in this scenario, creates flexibility costs.

Incentive fees for managers may also be viewed as a call exchange option with the manager's performance against a pre-determined benchmark acting as the exercise price.[23] If the incentive fee simply depends on realized performance in relation to a benchmark, its value is calculated as a European exchange call option. In this instance, as shown in Margrabe's valuation of the exchange option, increasing the volatility of the underlying asset, that is, the managerial performance, increases the value of the call. That, in turn, creates an incentive for the manager to elect more risky investments in an attempt to increase the volatility of his performance and therefore increase the upside potential of his incentive fee.

Alternatively, the incentive fee could be based on both absolute and relative performance, whereby the absolute performance is measured against a pre-determined threshold. Now we have a multi-contingency option pricing problem, whereby the volatilities of relative and absolute performance as well as their correlation have ambiguous effects on the option price. Assume that the performance measure is the market value of the firm. The incentive fee can then be calculated as the premium of a compound barrier call option on a European down-and-out call. In other words, if the market value of the firm's capital falls below a pre-determined threshold, the incentive fee expires. The firm's market value derives from the current value of the firm's assets, and the strike price is the face value of the firm's debt. The lower, down-and-out barrier, is the current market value of the firm's capital.[24]

This model does an excellent job of aligning shareholder and managerial interests and incentives when applied to a firm's debt and assets. However, as asset volatility becomes very high, this incentive fee structure entices managers to engage in a more conservative investment approach, thereby failing to go for the value maximization investment strategy. Hence, even the multi-contingency compound call option framework does not resolve the traditional agency conflict.

Managerial limitations also encompass how many options can be monitored, handled, and managed effectively. As investors in financial securities aim at finding the right mix of stable and volatile securities to match their personal risk comfort zone, managers making budget decisions across project portfolios have to find the right mix to match the corporate comfort risk zone as well as the corporate ability to exercise. Remember: real options will only create real value when they are properly exercised. Depending on corporate resources, individual firms have distinct capacities to exercise growth options. For each given firm there is likely to be an optimum growth option portfolio. Growth options can easily be acquired in large numbers either as probing investments in the exploration of novel technologies, or as joint ventures or equity acquisition in small firms with either promising technology or an interesting geographical location. These early stage options often come at very small prices.

However, the corporate and organizational challenge lies in exercising those options. What is the optimum portfolio of growth option for a firm? Just as the individual investor considers the impact on overall portfolio risk and return when adding a new security to her portfolio, the corporate manager also has to consider how adding a new growth option affects the overall risk profile of the corporate project portfolio, the resource allocation over time, and management's ability to execute this as well as all the existing real options in the corporate portfolio. Laamanen, studying the growth option portfolio of Finnish firms on acquisition expeditions, reasoned that a small growth option portfolio sets narrow limits to the perceived expected, future value of the firm, while a large growth option portfolio offers risk reduction through enhanced variability and diversification.[25] However, once the acquisition portfolio exceeds a certain size, option interactions set in and restrict the expected value of the growth option portfolio.

What is observed here in the context of an acquisition strategy obviously has a more general meaning for the overall composition of the firm's real option portfolio in terms of risk, return, timing, resource leverage potential, and alignment with the corporate strategy and vision. Option acquisitions add to portfolio diversification and enhance variability; they can also function to hedge competitive uncertainties in related markets. There are constraints as to the coordination capacity of management,[26] and there is a threshold where increasingly complex interactions of multiple embedded and created real options do not add further value.[27] The firm will reach a limit where the acquisition of additional options—in the absence of the ability to fund, monitor and exercise them—will actually decrease value of the total corporate option portfolio.

A real option-based budgeting process is a very dynamic approach that requires continuous and careful monitoring of both internal as well as external value and uncertainty drivers. A great deal of organizational discipline is compulsory, and in fact it is assumed in the academic literature that it goes into action once triggers or thresholds are hit. As the real option value is driven by both parts of the equation, external uncertainty and internal flexibility to respond, the value of a real option may easily change as the competitive environment or—more generally—the external environment changes. Internal changes and new information created internally also drive the value of individual or several real options. For example, the request by one group of the R&D department to permit over-budget expenditures may have implications for the cost assumptions made for several related R&D projects. Some of these may move out of the money if an unforeseen event increases the budgeted costs above the critical cost to invest.

It is important that this information not just be shared but also utilized by decision makers, and it is equally important that those who convey the information are not being penalized. Options may move in and out of the money, seamlessly, and unnoticed by senior management, if processes and procedures for continuous monitoring of the corporate option portfolio or the discipline to act are not in place. Adoption of real options requires both flexibility as well as a very stringent organizational discipline directed at observing those uncertainty drivers constantly, so as not to miss a trigger being set off that changes a "go" into a "no-go" decision, and vice versa.

Along these lines, there is yet an additional request for organizational discipline and culture that—if realized—is likely to have significant impact on the quality of the real option analysis: the ability of an organization to seek information that challenges conventional, habitual organizational assumptions and beliefs. In order to prepare the organization best for unforeseeable future uncertainties that have the potential to both create and destroy option value, the organization must enforce discipline in seeking signals and information that do not match conventional expectations and perspectives but challenge those beliefs. It must avoid the emergence of monitoring and observing routines that will only find confirmative information. That, in fact, may be the biggest hurdle in implementing a meaningful real option valuation framework.

There must be an organizational openness and willingness to discuss risks individually; this provides insights into avenues to mitigate risk. All sources of uncertainty need to be discussed and compared on an even field to identify the true business risk. In the real option framework, there is no place for a black-box discount rate across the lifetime of a project or across projects. Only by understanding all risks and making them comparable across projects can the organization succeed in optimizing its asset and option portfolio, while also building risk-mitigation synergies across projects. Framing the situation and thinking carefully through the strategic alternatives in the face of future uncertainties is the most essential step in the real option analysis. Strategic frameworks such as SWOT can provide valuable assistance in identifying low uncertainties (strength), high uncertainty (weakness), upside potential (opportunities), and downside risks (threats).

Real options analysis cannot be done in a cook-book fashion; it is not about implementing a financial software that permits easy calculation of complex option prices, including exotic options. Such an approach would miss out on the thought process that adds the value to the analysis and is mandatory to identify, discover, and value the real options that are individual to any given firm. In the 1997 survey among UK firms about their experience with the real option framework,[28] managers furthermore noted that not everybody feels comfortable with the notion of embracing uncertainty. The built-in abandonment option, the option to terminate a project once the technical success probability drops beyond a certain threshold, may be viewed as an "escape route for bad investments" and in fact exercise an adverse influence on motivation and commitment if staff members know there is room for maneuver if projects take a bad turn.

REAL OPTIONS AND WALL STREET

Empirical studies point to the notion that financial markets are already embracing the concept of real options when valuing firms. The concept became especially popular with the arrival of Internet firms at the stock markets that had no income but lots of—real or perceived—growth potential. Smit finds empirical evidence for the market valuation of growth options:[29] Firms operating in industries with high market uncertainty, high R&D intensity, and therefore high private uncertainty, tend to have a higher proportion of their market value attributed to growth options than those operating in income industries. The former include pharmaceuticals, electronics, and information technology firms that enjoy between 70% and 92% contribution of growth options to overall market value. The latter entail transportation, chemicals, and electric power firms that are rewarded by the market with 38% to 62% growth option value.

Laamnen[30] studied the market reaction to the acquisition of growth options. He based his analysis on mergers and acquisition in the Finnish telecommunication industry. His analysis confirmed that a high market-to-book ratio implies that the stock market has high growth expectations. He also noticed that the higher this ratio, the more negative the stock market reacts to acquisition of additional growth options.

The financial market also is quite sensitive to the creation of growth options through internal R&D initiatives. An empirical study in the information technology industry,[31] for example, showed not only that the market reacts to corporate announcements on technology innovation but that the market also is quite sensitive in judging whether those technology innovations are true growth options or merely life-cycle management options. Technology announcements that relate to a competitive defense strategy and are designed to improve existing technologies are not perceived as growth options and do not lead investors to increase future earnings-per-share expectations. Further, investors also do not put much short-term value on the announcement of technology innovations in very immature, just emerging branches of the industry. In this scenario, the perceived market risk is very high as long as leader and followers are not clearly defined and industry standards are only emerging. This market risk suppresses the short-term option value of those announcements. However, in the longer-term five-year earnings forecasts, those announcements are valued, to some small extent. Investors realize and recognize that even if the future market payoff is highly uncertain, the organization has acquired learning options with the potential to create knowledge and expertise. Thus, investors value the learning option inherent in technology announcements in the early, fermentation state of an emerging industry.

Others have studied the effect of R&D announcements both at the innovation and commercialization stage of development and arrived at similar results:[32] Investors value R&D announcements as growth options, but early stage R&D is—given the uncertainty surrounding technical feasibility and market potential—valued less than R&D in the commercialization stage. However, investors also put more real option value on an R&D initiative by a technology-driven firm than for a product-driven firm—possibly recognizing that this is the core competence of the former, and that the organizational capabilities and skill set that drive successful implementation of an early stage R&D project in a technology platform firm are stronger, decreasing the private risk of those endeavors. Further, investors value R&D

announcements, which create the basis of future growth and expansion options, more highly when made by small firms compared to big firms.

Lambrecht and Perraudin[33] studied the volatility of biotech firms from 1988 to 1998, during which time the biotech industry first emerged. They found high volatilities of returns and kurtosis coefficients with positive skewness but at the same time negative returns for market indexes such as the Standard & Poor 100 index. They also found that firm volatility declines over time, as the firms mature, and that competitor risk makes up a substantial fraction of firms' volatilities. Finally, the authors provided evidence that the threat of preemption in this industry accelerates investment on average by six months, substantially decreasing the value of the deferral option.

If financial markets have already adopted, consciously or intuitively, the concept of real option valuation in their investment appraisals, then it will be the challenge and opportunity for firms to communicate clearly and effectively the real options in place as well as the value and uncertainty drivers. Investors and corporations interact in a circle of mutually influencing and reinforcing feedbacks, as shown in Figure 9.5.

Through managerial actions, balance sheets, quarterly financial reports, and its public relations strategy, the firm communicates both directly and indirectly to its stakeholders its ability to cope with external uncertainties, to create value, and to manage risk. Based on information from and about the firm as well as on the general exogenous environment, stakeholders, in turn, including investors, form their own perceptions about key value drivers and the sources and extent of risk and uncertainty, as well as the ability of the

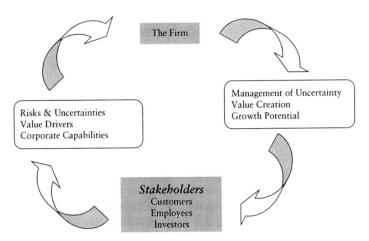

FIGURE 9.5 Market valuation of corporate real options—A complex interplay

firm to manage those risks and create value. Those perceptions and assumptions drive the firm's value in the market place. Consider the following example: Early in 2001 the computer chip maker Intel issued a warning that its second-quarter revenues would remain flat. At the same time, the company reported an 82% decline in its first-quarter earnings. The company's stock price rose by $2.93 per share. The two bad news items were presented along with the good news that in the firm's view the personal computer chip market was stabilizing and that the normal ordering pattern was expected going forward.[34] Clearly, the market appreciated the reduced risk of future downturns.

If we are looking into how real option application plays out in today's corporate world in the valuation of firms, we have two sources of information: empirical evidence as provided by the stock market that communicates investors' views on the creation and execution of corporate real options, as well as corporate communications. Pioneers for real option application can be found in both camps.

Michael Mauboussin, chief strategist with the research department of Credit Suisse First Boston (CSFB), advises analysts to use discounted cash flow to value a company's current businesses, then add the value of the real options they have created.[35] Others have claimed that real options are best at valuing the "next big thing," such as dotcom companies, where the major part of the valuation is derived from perceived growth options in future markets, in the absence of current cash flows. Mouboussin has stimulated at least two of CSFB's analysts to apply the real option concept in practice when valuing securities. Laura Martin covers the entertainment sector. She recognizes the real option value inherent in the cables lying in the ground and started incorporating these real options in her analysis in the summer of 1999.[36] Those cables, she argues, do not just contribute to current cash-flow generation. Moreover, they have real growth option value as the same cables can and will be used for new applications.[37] Likewise, she argues, traditional valuation methods for the entertainment industry ignore the growth option value that is derived from archived films, the film library. Technology innovation is constantly occurring in the entertainment industry: from TV to color films to cable, via VCRs and DVDs. Classical movies therefore retain growth option value long after they have left the box offices. These classical movies will all benefit from the technology innovation: They will become available on TV, as video and now as DVD and create the potential for new cash flows with each technology innovation reaching the market.

Pierre Chao, who covers aerospace and defense for CSFB, realized that a defense contractor, who is developing government-funded weapons, may ultimately develop a technology or a product that will be very useful for civilian commercial applications. A point in case is RF Microdevices, a North Carolina-based firm. This firm transformed gallium arsenide semiconductors, which were originally designed and developed for spy satellites, into chips for cell phones. While these analysts take a proactive approach and almost educate the firms they cover about their inherent real option value, other firms, such as Intel, take the reverse road and educate their analysts about the use of real options and what it means to arrive at the appropriate value for assets in place and future growth options.

Others have collected empirical evidence for intuitive use of real options in real markets, concerning real decisions. Quigg[38] was first to investigate the predictive power of the real option framework. She showed—based on a large sample of market prices—that the real option to defer land development is included in the market real estate valuation: The transaction prices are over the intrinsic value of the land; the difference represents the option premium for the flexibility to defer land development. In the example under investigation, that option premium is 6%.

In a conceptually similar study, Davis[39] looked at empirical evidence of option premiums in a survey of published literature on mineral asset mining. He found that these studies, which value several forms of managerial flexibility such as timing the investment, that is, the option to delay, to shut down, to build inventory, or to expand, explain around 20% and 50% of the value gap between the market value and a DCF-based appraisal of developed and not-yet-developed projects, respectively. This analysis suggests that option valuation is, at most, of secondary, if of any, importance in asset valuation. In fact, for North American gold mines, for example, each 1 percent change in the gold price causes a 2 percent change in the stock price.[40] If valuation is based on only the DCF method, it is likely to overestimate the exposure to gold price volatility and to ignore managerial flexibility and hedging strategies that would mitigate those risks for the individual firm.

Davis identified five methodological weaknesses to explain the discrepancy between the market value and a DCF-based appraisal. These encompass failure to take in a comprehensive analysis of all managerial options such as the value generated by future projects including growth options, that any given firm owns via the firm-specific organizational capabilities, as well as incomplete analysis of all sources of uncertainty. All the studies surveyed by Davis focus on volatile prices for minerals as the only source of uncertainty. Davis, on the contrary, pointed out that environmental catastrophes are another source of very real uncertainty that creates an almost unlimited downside risk. Davis also enlisted three methodological weaknesses that may contribute to the observed discrepancy. These include the fundamental assumption of option pricing that options are exercised at the optimal time, while in reality, preemptive pressure may force the real option owner to exercise prematurely. Obviously, a comprehensive option analysis would include competitive entry as a major uncertainty that drives option value, just as we have shown in Chapter 5. Further, the empirical studies all assume that the price of the mineral is driven only by the current spot price, but not by other variables, such as inventory, and also assume that prices are lognormally distributed. Both assumptions are not confirmed by reality. Inventory, for example, also impacts on price movements as do reserves.

Seppae and Laamanen were the first to validate the real option concept as applied by venture capitalists and financial markets.[41] Conceptually, this work built on an earlier paper by Willner,[42] who proposed a real option valuation model for start-up ventures. Willner developed a jump valuation formula to value start-up firms as growth options. The jumps reflect that start-up firms derive their value from the number of break-through discoveries they make and the additional value created as a result of those discoveries and their implementation. The Willner jump-option pricing model valued start-up ventures based on two components: the NPV of assets in place and growth options whose valuation allows for variations in the expected frequency of discoveries and in the expected increase of value as a result of those discoveries.

Seppae and Laamanen studied empirical evidence for intuitive use of the real option application by using the binomial option pricing model to determine risk and return patterns of 597 investment rounds undertaken by a total of 176 U.S. venture-capital financed companies that went public in 1998 or 1999. The analysis confirms several hypotheses based on surveys among the venture capital industry: Risk-neutral probabilities are smaller in earlier stages and increase as start-ups mature. The implied volatility calculated from the Cox, Ross, and Rubinstein binomial model is higher in earlier stages and declines as the venture matures. The analysis also shows that the risk-neutral probability decreases as time length between venture rounds increases. In other words, the risk-free probability is smaller as steps between stages become bigger and increases as steps between financing stages decline. Further, as the number of rounds for a given venture increases, the risk-free probability increases, and the implied volatility declines. These findings are very much in line with previously published qualitative empirical observations of risk-return behavior in the venture capital industry. The study provides strong support for the validity of the binomial option pricing model to analyze risk-return profiles of venture investments, or other staged investments such as in R&D projects, and to in fact assist in predicting actual future valuations.

Berger, Ofek, and Swary[43] provided empirical evidence for the notion that financial markets do in fact value the abandonment option. The real abandonment option is an American put option whereby the underlying asset value is uncertain, that is, the cash flows derived from the assets in place, as well as the exercise price is uncertain, that is, the salvage price. The value of a firm, correspondingly, is the value derived from assets in place that may generate future cash flows as well as assets that create more value when being abandoned. The salvage value of the latter should reflect the degree of specialization of the asset to be abandoned, with less specialized, more generalized assets being of more value. Building on a database of more than 7,000 firms during the years of 1984 and 1990, the authors found—in line with theoretical considerations—that indeed there is a positive correlation between the market value of a firm and the exit value, that is, the abandonment option. The abandonment option value is defined in this study by the percentage by which the salvage value exceeds the value of future cash flows. The authors further found that the market value is driven not just by the book value but also by the nature of the assets that comprise the book value, that is, more generalized assets drive the market value of the abandonment option higher than more specialized assets do. Option theory also suggests that the value of the abandonment option, and hence the market valuation of the firm, should become more sensitive to volatility in the value of the underlying asset, that is, the exit value, when the likelihood of that option to be exercised increases. The probability of the abandonment option to be exercised is driven by the likelihood of financial distress for the firm as well as by the perception of managerial willingness to exercise the abandonment option. The analysis of the empirical data suggests that the exit value is valued indeed more highly by the market with increasing likelihood of financial distress as well as for firms whose management has proven in the past—by significant divestures—its willingness to execute the abandonment option.

EMPIRICAL EVIDENCE

The basic notion of real option analysis, the value of flexibility in the face of uncertainty, is suitable for use primarily in industries and projects that display one or several of the following characteristics: large investment projects with long time frames and significant uncertainty such as investments into natural resources; high-risk investments with uncertain technology in rapidly changing markets, which is frequent in high-tech industries including computers, semiconductors, pharmaceuticals, biotech, and chemicals; strategic growth options to explore new markets: geographical, products, and technologies that allow for sequential compounded options, options to engage in joint ventures or R&D collaborations; knowledge options that include investments in learning, establishing processes and procedures or in the acquisition of intellectual property rights, licenses, copyrights, and brand names; flexibility options by changing the amount and mix of input and output; and capability investments in technologies, infrastructure, distribution channels, or other corporate capabilities, such as transportation, information technology, and R&D technologies.

In the academic literature, real options have been instrumental in valuing investment opportunities in a broad range of industries and applications. Papers on the real option valuation of investment decisions have appeared for the biotech and pharmaceutical industry, the energy and utility sector, and natural resource exploration such as mining and forestry or environmental protection.[44]

How does the explosion in the academic literature relate to the use of real options in practice? After all, real option valuation, according to the *Wall Street Journal* in 1990, is the next best thing to "gut feeling"; it allows companies to act on their intuition again.[45] In fact, managers do use their intuition when valuing opportunities as growth options; however, in the absence of a formal framework, option valuation lacks consistency.[46]

In the UK, corporations expressed interest in using options pricing methods for capital budget decisions starting in the early '90s. McKinsey claimed that it used the real option framework for its clients to value R&D projects.[47] Notable examples included British Petroleum's approach to investing in a high-risk oil exploration project in the North Sea. Given the volatile nature of oil prices, the uncertainties of oil reserves, and the technological challenges associated with oil drilling in the North Sea, the idea of drilling in the North Sea would never have found any support based on a DCF analysis. Intuitive application of the real option concept, however, invited management to take a more aggressive attitude towards a high-risk project.[48]

Others report that some sophisticated energy firms have entire departments devoted to asset valuation and optimization for risk management and valuation, "quant shops" with people from diverse educational backgrounds including physics or mathematics or operations research who craft valuation methods and risk management tools.[49] For these firms, asset valuation and optimization have become a core competence. Similarly, mining companies have reportedly used the real option concept successfully.[50] Firms in both industries are dealing with commodities. Others, on the contrary, have failed to collect empirical evidence that real options are in fact used for R&D applications in the same industries,[51] although much of the early academic literature is concerned with the real option valuation of natural resource R&D projects.

The assessment of both research and development opportunities and manufacturing plant investment by Merck and Company has long been noted. Merck had been a strong advocate of real options thinking across the broad range of their R&D and manufacturing enterprises since the mid 1990s. In the words of the company's CFO Judy Lewent, "When you make an initial investment in a research project, you are paying an entry fee for a right. To me all kinds of business decisions are options." Presentations at some recent international real option meetings suggest that real option analysis has become an integrated analytical tool at several major pharmaceutical or biotech firms, including Eli Lilly, Genentech, Amgen, or Genzyme.

Microsoft has more recently adopted the real option framework to make visible to its current and future customers the value derived in the form of cost savings by using the Windows 2000 software. Building on the help and audit of industry analysts, the initiative is designed to help customers identify which IT investment will be the most valuable "real options" for their respective organizations.[52] Several blue chip companies including BHP Billiton, a global resource commodity provider; NAB, The National Association of Broadcasters; Airbus; Lucent; Credit Suisse; Amazon; and Hewlett-Packard (HP) use real options.[53] HP started experimenting with real options to evaluate its manufacturing procedures beginning in the early 1990s, advised by Stanford Professor Corey A. Billington.[54] A recent survey suggests that 27 percent of U.S. companies are using real option valuation for corporate budgeting decisions; a consultant working in the field estimated that $30 to $40 billion worth of corporate transactions were evaluated and executed based on a real option analysis in the year 2000 alone.[55]

Despite the intuitive and theoretical advances of using real options for capital budgeting decisions and for aligning corporate strategy with financial markets, there is still mixed evidence as to the actual use of real options. A recent study[56] suggests two reasons for the limited actual use of real options: unfamiliarity with the theoretical and mathematical concepts and the requirement for modeling assumptions where there is little or no data on those parameters. Obviously, any organization that thinks about implementing real options needs to think also about the kind of numerical data needed, as well as ways to retrieve those data, either from historical records or by ensuring mechanisms and procedures for cross-organizational data collection. Any organization that likes to believably and reliably communicate its real option value to investors needs to ensure that data that feed the assumptions underlying the real option pricing are reliable and sound.

A survey among FTSE 100 companies in the UK[57] pointed to several organizational and behavioral aspects that accompany the implementation of flexibility in the valuation process. Again, despite the intuitive and rational appreciation of real options as an analytical tool, the surveyed managers for the most part acknowledged that few methodologies were in place in their organizations to actually value uncertainty and flexibility, and that they felt uncomfortable in doing so. Embedded options were recognized intuitively and, specifically, acknowledgment of the flexibility to postpone led to the sanction of investment projects in around 50% of the cases. The option to abandon, on the other side, received very little attention and valuation. Some managers expressed concerns that prominent valuation of flexibility within the organization could actually decrease motivation and commitment.

However, on the other side, managers also emphasized that the real option framework as an analytical tool helped internally to reconcile assumptions, expectations, and conflicting ambitions across the organization. Thus, even without implementing the quantitative part of real option valuation, the analytical and strategic part of real option analysis was perceived to be very helpful in arriving at better decision making. Managers recognize the growing need for flexibility as uncertainty grows and as the time frames of pending uncertainties extend. They also recognize the need to appreciate organizational and behavioral effects, which uncertainty as well as dealing with it through preserving flexibility imposes. But then, there is, too, a notion of frustration when attempting to implement the real option framework: More than half of the U.S. firms that experimented with the framework ended up rejecting it, according to the results of a recent survey.[58]

Part of the problem includes that the option framework requests many input variables. Option models that build on partial differential equations and stochastic processes, as provided in many academic papers, impose major challenges on managers if they are asked to estimate the variance of future revenues. In addition to mathematical complexity, some of the real option valuation models offered in the academic literature still are very simplistic in structure, which in turn necessitates many simplifying assumptions. These make the real option valuation of a real capital budget decision look very unreal. Pairing mathematical complexity with simplifying assumptions will give any manager a very hard time when attempting to communicate the decision scenario and guideline to the executive board.

The academic literature also provides at least one post-mortem analysis of a well-known and well-publicized real option application: The valuation of a drug development program at Merck.[59] The authors illustrate a key challenge in implementing real options: a potential discordance between strategic analysis results and assumptions going into a real option analysis. Obviously, the value of the real option analysis is driven by the validity of the assumptions going into the analysis, as well as the overall match between the option model and the strategic decision scenario. Real option analysis will not work if there is a discordance between the real option and the strategic framework regarding the value and impact of uncertainty parameters, such as time to maturity. The real option framework, if strictly adopted from the financial framework, suggests that increasing time to maturity enhances the value of the option. The strategic framework for a drug development company, on the contrary, clearly indicates that a delay in time to maturation, that is, a delay in drug development time, is an adverse event that reduces the value of the investment opportunity. Valuable patent time expires unused as the drug reaches the market with delay; competitors may enter with an alternative product and erode market share. We have in an earlier chapter already discussed this dissonance.

Some of these thoughts as well as growing experience in overcoming organizational and other challenges in implementing the concept are echoed more strongly in a more recent survey across various industries including consumer and industrial products, financial services, high-tech and information, life sciences, energy, real estate, and transportation in the U.S.[60] This survey made very clear that many organizations perceive real options not just as an analytical tool but equally as a "way of thinking" as well as an organizational process. Based on the survey results, the authors also refined a common path to successful implementation of real options that consists of four key steps:

- Gaining initial experience by experimenting with the use of real options in one or more pilot projects
- Obtaining support and buy-in from the senior management level
- Establishing a scalable process for routine real option use—based on the pilot experience and integrating established organizational processes and procedures
- Expanding the tools and the concept enterprise wide

NOTES

1. G.L. Ridderbusch, "Running the Option," *Energy Customer Management*, December 2001.

2. Press release by Shell, September 4, 2001: "Shell Energy withdraws from Ohio and Texas Electric Power Markets."

3. Press release by Shell, October 2, 2001: "Coral Reaches Agreement with ESG in Preparation for Texas Electric Choice Program. Shell Affiliate to Target Industrial and Large End-Use Customers."

4. M.A. Brach and D.A. Paxson, "A Gene to Drug Venture: Poisson Options Analysis," *R&D Management* 31:203, 2001.

5. M. Amram and N. Kulatilaka, *Real Options. Managing Strategic Investment in an Uncertain World* (Harvard Business School Press, 1999).

6. M. Lehocky and D.A. Paxson, "Arbitrage-Free Evaluation of Exhaustible Resource Firms," *Journal of Business Finance and Accounting* 25:1363, 1998.

7. H. Kolodny, M. Liu, B. Symne, and H. Denis, "New Technology and the Emerging Organizational Paradigm," *Human Relations* 49:12, 1996.

8. G. Hofstede, *Cultures and Organizations: Software of the Mind* (Berkshire, UK: McGraw-Hill, 1991).

9. T.B. Folta and W.J. Ferrier, "The Effect of National Culture on Partner Buyouts in Cross-Border Biotechnology Alliances," *Journal of High Technology Management Research* 11:175, 2000.

10. L. Hoecklin, *Managing Cultural Differences: Strategies for Competitive Advantage* (Wokingham, UK: Addison-Wesley, 1995).

11. K. Erramilli, "Nationality and Subsidiary Ownership Patterns in Multinational Corporations," *Journal of International Business Studies* 27:225, 1996.

12. S. Shane, "The Effect of National Culture on the Choice Between Licensing and Direct Foreign Investment," *Strategic Management Journal* 15:627, 1994.

13. S. Shane, "Uncertainty Avoidance and the Preference for Innovation Championing Roles," *Journal of International Business Studies* 26:47, 1995.

14. J. Penner-Hahn, "Firm and Environmental Influences on the Mode and Sequence of Foreign Research and Development Activities," *Strategic Management Journal* 19:149, 1998.

15. Z. Liao and P.F. Greenfield, "Corporate R&D Strategy Portfolio in Japanese and Australian Technology-Based Firms: An Empirical Study," *IEEE Transactions on Engineering Management* 45:323, 1998; R. Whiteley, *Business Systems in East Asia* (Sage Publications, 1994); R. Whiteley, *European Business Systems* (Sage Publications, 1994).

16. B. Lavoie and I.M. Sheldon, "The Comparative Advantage of Real Options: An Explanation for the U.S. Specialization in Biotechnology," *AgBioForum* 3:47, 2000. Available on the World Wide Web: http://www.agbioforum.org.

17. F.M. Paris, "A Compound Option Model to Value Moral Hazard," *Journal of Derivatives* 9:53, 2001; M.P. Kritzman and D. Rich, "Risk Containment for Investors with Multivariate Utility Functions," *Journal of Derivatives* 5:28, 1998; D. Mauer and S. Ott, "Agency Cost, Under-investment and Optimal Capital Structure: The Effect of Growth Options to Expand," in M.J. Brennan and L. Trigeorgis, eds., *Project Flexibility, Agency and Competition* (Oxford University Press, 2001); J. Maeland, *Valuation of Irreversible Investments: Agency Costs* (Norwegian School of Economics and Business Administration). Paper presented at the Real Option Conference, Cambridge, UK, 1999.

18. M. Brennan and E. Schwartz, "Evaluating Natural Resource Investments," *Journal of Business* 58:135, 1985.

19. A. Moel and P. Tufano, "When Are Real Options Exercised? An Empirical Study of Mine Closings," *The Review of Financial Studies* 15:35, 2002.

20. M. Nicholls, "Reality Strikes Gold Miners," *Risk Magazine*, September 1997, p. 7.

21. P. Tufano, "Agency Costs of Corporate Risk Management," *Financial Management* 27:67, 1998.

22. J. Maeland, *Valuation of Irreversible Investments: Agency Costs* (Norwegian School of Economics and Business Administration). Paper presented at the Real Option Conference, Cambridge, UK, 1999.

23. F.M. Paris, "A Compound Option Model to Value Moral Hazard," *Journal of Derivatives* 9:53, 2001.

24. See note 11.

25. T. Laamanen, *Growth Option Company Acquisitions: In Search for an Optimal Option Portfolio* (Real Option Conference, Cambridge, UK, 1998).

26. E. Penrose, *The Theory of the Growth of the Firm* (Basil Blackwell, London, 1959).

27. L. Trigeorgis, "The Nature of Option Interactions and the Valuation of Investments with Multiple Real Options," *Journal of Finance and Quantitative Analysis* 28:1–20, 1993.

28. J.S. Busby and C.G. Pitts, "Real Options and Capital Investment Decisions," *Management Accounting* 75:38, 1997.

29. H.T.J. Smit, *Empirical Characteristics of Growth Options*. Presented at the Real Option Group Conference, Cambridge, 1999.

30. T. Laamanen, *Growth Option Company Acquisitions: In Search for an Optimal Option Portfolio* (Real Option Conference, Cambridge, UK, 1998).

31. J.H. Pardue, E. Higgins, and T. Biggart, "Impact of New Product Announcements on Firm Value in Information Technology Producing In-

dustries. An Examination of Industry Level Evolutionary Eras," *The Engineering Economist* 45:144, 2000.

32. K.K. Kelm, V.K. Narayanan, and G.E. Pinches, "Shareholder Value Creation During R&D Innovation and Commercialization Stages," *Academy of Management Journal* 38:770, 1995.

33. B. Lambrecht and W. Perraudin, *Real Options and Preemption under Incomplete Information* (Real Option Group Conference, Cambridge, UK, 1999).

34. D. Goodin, "Intel Net Dropped 82% in First Quarter," *Wall Street Journal*, April 18, 2001, P A3 & A10.

35. M.J. Mauboussin, "Get Real: Using Real Options in Security Analysis," *CSFB Equity Research*, June 23, 1999.

36. M.A. Desai, P. Tufano, and Laura Martin, *Real Options and the Cable Industry* (Harvard Business School Case 201-004).

37. L. Martin, *Using Real Options on Wall Street* (IQPC Real Options Conference, March 2001).

38. L. Quigg, "Empirical Testing of Real-Option Pricing Models," *Journal of Finance* 48:621, 1993.

39. G.A. Davis, "Option Premiums in Mineral Asset Pricing. Are They Important?" *Land Economics* 72:167, 1996.

40. P. Tufano, "The Determinants of Stock Price Exposure: Financial Engineering and the Gold Mining Industry," *Journal of Finance* 53:1015, 1998.

41. T.J. Seppae and T. Laamanen, "Valuation of Venture Capital Investments: Empirical Evidence," *R&D Management* 31:215, 2001.

42. R. Willner, "Valuing Start-Up Venture Growth Options," in L. Trigeorgis, ed., *Real Options in Capital Investment* (Westport, CT: Praeger, 1998, pp. 221–239).

43. P. Berger, E. Ofek, and I. Swary, "Investor Valuation of the Abandonment Option," *Journal of Financial Economics* 42:257, 1996.

44. N. Nichols, "Scientific Management at Merck: An Interview with CFO Judy Lewent," *Harvard Business Review*, Jan.–Feb., p. 88, 1994; S. Mason and C. Baldwin, "Evaluation of Government Subsidies to Large-Scale Energy Projects: A Contingent Claims Approach," *Advances in Futures and Options Research* 3:169, 1988; R. Morck, R. Schwartz, and D. Stengeland, "The Valuation of Forestry Resources under Stochastic Prices and Inventories," *Journal of Financial and Quantitative Analysis* 24:473, 1989; M. Walsh, "Potential for Derivative Instruments on Sulfur Dioxide Emission Reduction Credits," *Derivatives Quarterly* 32, 1994.

45. A.M. Naj, "In R&D, the Next Best Thing to a Gut Feeling," *Wall Street Journal* (European Edition), May 22, 1990.

46. S.D. Howell and A.J. Jagle, "Laboratory Evidence on How Managers Intuitively Value Real Growth Options," *Journal of Business Finance and Accounting* 24:915, 1997.

47. T. Copeland, T. Koller, and J. Murrin, *Valuation: Measuring and Managing the Value of Companies* (John Wiley and Sons, 1998, p. 362).

48. K.J. Leslie and M.P. Michaels, "The Real Power of Real Options," *The McKinsey Quarterly*, 1997 number 3.

49. J.P. Lukens, "Increasing Price Volatility Sparks Interest in Energy Finance Area," *Houston Business Journal*, June 1, 2001, p. 34.

50. P. Coy, "Exploiting Uncertainty," *Business Week*, June 7:118–122, 1999.

51. J.E. Smith and K. McCardle, "Valuing Oil Properties: Integrating Option Pricing and Decision Analysis Approaches," *Operations Research* 46:198, 1998.

52. C. Waltner, "Payback in a Hurry—Microsoft's New Operating System Offers a Host of Money-Saving Management Features," *e-Directions*, Winter 2000.

53. D. Parker, "The Real Thing: The Theory of Real Options is Steadily Finding Its Way into the Strategic Plans of Australian Companies," *Australian CPA*, March 2002; A. Triantis and A. Borison, "Real Options: State of the Practice," *Journal of Applied Corporate Finance* 14:8, 2001; IQOC Real Option Conference, March 2001; October 2001.

54. P. Buxbaum, "The Accidental Real Optionist," *Computerworld*, January 7, 2002.

55. C.L. Culp: Real Options: A Case Study & Primer. Derivatives Week, May 13, 2001.

56. D.M. Lander and G.E. Pinches, "Challenges to the Practical Implementation of Modeling and Valuing Real Options," *Quarterly Review of Economics and Finance* 38:537, 1998.

57. J.S. Busby and C.G. Pitts, "Real Options and Capital Investment Decisions," *Management Accounting* 75:38, 1997.

58. *The Economist*, April 22, 2000, p. 64.

59. N. Nichols, "Scientific Management at Merck: An Interview with CFO Judy Lewent," *Harvard Business Review*, Jan.–Feb., p. 88, 1994; E.H. Bowman and G.T. Moskowitz, "Real Option Analysis and Strategic Decision Making," *Organization Science* 12:772, 2001.

60. A. Triantis and A. Borison, "Real Options: State of the Practice," *Journal of Applied Corporate Finance* 14:8, 2001.

CHAPTER 10

The Real Option Future

NOVEL CONCEPTS IN REAL OPTION APPLICATION

From mining to high-tech projects, the real option concept has infiltrated valuation problems in several areas.[1] Real option concepts have been developed to value worker flexibility created through cross-training, or composite risks in a manufacturing environment including demand uncertainty, production risks, including uncertain input costs, and operating risks such as the likelihood of system breakdowns. Technology uncertainty is not only a challenge for product development, but is also a challenge for customers. In times of high technology uncertainty and frequent arrival of novel technologies, customers, too, need to evaluate carefully their product needs as well as their options to preserve asset flexibility. For a supplier of customer services that entails weighing the option to acquire versus the option to lease to balance cost structure and flexibility.

The investment in training and education of local sales representatives in an emerging market is an example of a real human resource option. While the operation itself may lose money, it provides the organization with the opportunity to learn that will be very valuable if the market in the local economy grows. Along the same lines, all investments into training and education of employees generate real option value by creating and strengthening organizational capabilities. This, in turn, alters the exercise price of future corporate real options or accelerates and improves future product development programs.

The real option framework is also very helpful in evaluating network expansion opportunities.[2] These include, for example, airlines seeking to expand into new markets, investments in a utility distribution infrastructure, the expansion of data networks or product line extensions in traditional industries by offering additional products for the same customer segment. The option value derives from new network effects and network externalities, including a value increase of the individual good as the number of units using the good increases. A good example is the use of email or the FAX. Further option value is gained from economies of scale, strategic and positioning values including connectivity or brand image, as well as operational value drawn from the leverage of the existing infrastructure.

Others have proposed long options for emerging markets as an alternative to the acquisition of growth options in the form of minority stakes and acquisitions.[3] Diversification facilitates corporate risk hedging strategies and is often done by buying minority stakes. That, however, so goes the argument, ties up too much capital and offers little leverage. A long option, on the other hand, gives the owner the right, but not the obligation, to buy the opportunity at some time in the future. The underlying asset for the long option is the present value of future synergies.

In the manufacturing context, real options were instrumental in arriving at an optimal quality control strategy:[4] external data that capture market dynamics are integrated with internal data on operational aspects of the manufacturing process in a real option valuation model to identify the optimum control chart decision at the single plant level. Evolutionary real options were designed for staged investments in uncertain markets with high technical uncertainty.[5] Here, two drivers of uncertainty, namely technical uncertainty and market uncertainty, are simulated as separate stochastic processes using Monte Carlo simulation. Those datasets are then taken through an evolutionary programming procedure that ultimately identifies the optimum decision rule.

Exotic options such as barrier options on exchange rates have been instrumental in modeling production or sales delocalization flexibility under exchange uncertainty under competitive conditions.[6] In this scenario the exchange rate creates the option pseudo-barrier for the firm: The firm contemplates selling or producing its products abroad. Multinational firms such as manufacturers of cars, clothing, or chips engage in firm migration. The global infrastructure provides the firm with the managerial flexibility to choose the production location and benefit from the upside potential of cheap labor or more favorable exchange rates, creating a competitive advantage. The decision to delocalize is triggered by the exchange rate, which obviously is determined externally and constitutes exogenous, non-private uncertainty. The option will be exercised if a certain barrier of the exchange rate is reached. In a situation with asymmetric information, the investment opportunity is valued as a pseudo-barrier option. The incentive to switch and delocalize is generated once a predetermined barrier level of exchange rate or labor cost is reached. This threshold is from the firm's perspective the value-maximizing threshold beyond or below which alternative strategic options create the most value. This scenario is comparable to a perpetual American call option. However, different from the financial call, the American call on the real asset is exercised early under competitive conditions with asymmetric information. Firms have incomplete information on different firms' cost structures. This motivates them to choose a strategic threshold, or pseudo-barrier, that is different from the threshold a monopolist would choose. It lies between the NPV and American perpetual monopoly threshold. The pseudo-barrier threshold under competitive conditions depends on the individual information available to the firm. The difference between the perpetual American call and the pseudo-barrier call option is the cost of preemption under competitive conditions with asymmetric information.

Margrabe was first to derive a model to price the option to exchange one asset for another.[7] The same paradigm has been used to value timber-harvesting decisions or debt-for-nature swaps. Chambers,[8] for example, valued the option to preserve natural goods in the form of debt-for-nature swaps. Governmental organizations introduced debt-for-nature swaps in an attempt to assist less-developed countries in environmental protection efforts. In this framework, non-governmental organizations (NGOs) engage in the protection and preservation of natural goods and the environment. They negotiate the conditions of a swap by which the donor purchases commercial debt from a recipient country at a discount from its creditors in secondary markets. This discount usually reflects the commercial banks' rather reduced expectations for repayment by debtor countries. The debt is then converted into local currency according to the agreement. The recipient country pays the donor more than the market value but less than the face value of the debt. The difference is used for environmental protection activities. The option value for the environmental protection organizations arises from the agreement terms with the debtor country. The value of the option to preserve land is driven by the land preservation value, the time to maturation of the option as well as the relationship between the value of preservation, and the value of developing and their respective volatilities.

Another exotic option concept explored for real option application is the chooser option. The financial chooser option gives the owner the right to choose between a put versus a call on the same security. In essence, a chooser option is an option on an option, just like the compound option. In the real option world, a chooser option has been instrumental in devising the optimal investment strategy for a software developer who needs to license a technology for his product.[9] The software company can either agree to pay a variable fee based on the future market value or engage in a fixed license fee today. Its choice is not between a put and a call but between two alternative strategies. In this specific scenario, the software developer who owns the chooser option will always choose the lesser of two possibly correlated delivery assets at the time of exercise to minimize her costs.

Rapid technology innovations and changes accelerate economic depreciation. Economic depreciation is defined as the change in service potential of an asset and the change in service value of the same asset. Rapid economic depreciation affects the option to defer and wait.[10] First, the opportunity cost lost due to deferring the investment decision and product launch is particularly high in the imminent period, while it declines in later periods. Second, if economic depreciation is fast, the implication is that the value of the asset declines rapidly. If, then, for example, demand (that is, asset value) is expected to decline, the option to defer has no more value. Firms will either invest instantly if the option is still in the money or will exercise the abandonment option. On the other hand, firms are motivated to defer an investment if they perceive that the market is still expanding. In this instance, the investment trigger is hit as soon as the rate of economic depreciation has reached zero. This insight argues against the use of an exogenous rate of depreciation, as initially proposed by Dixit and Pindyck. It also argues for the idea that data generated by real option valuation models can be used and reinterpreted as models for predicting economic depreciation.

More recently, extensions of the application of the real option analytical framework to intangible assets have been suggested. These include brand names, firm reputation, organizational capabilities, know-how and expertise, the existing market position, infrastructure, distribution channels, employees, and contractual agreements including licenses and leases, all of which are an integral part to the organizational ability to preserve flexibility and respond to future uncertainties.

Virtual options are options on information. They entail options to purchase or to process information. Their value, just as we have discussed in the context of the learning option, stems from improvement in decision support. The fundamental difference to options on real assets is that virtual real options can be exercised multiple times. They also are subjected to higher volatility and more jumps. Combined, those two effects can drive the value of virtual options very high. This may explain the high market value of information-based companies.

"Our primary assets, which are our software and our software-development skills, do not show up on the balance sheet at all," says Bill Gates.[11] Valuation based on real options analysis, as the FASB also recognizes, may be "the most promising area for valuation of intangible assets";[12] and it is a very important challenge. In 1978, the average U.S. company had a book-value-to-market-value ratio of 95%; in 1998 it was a mere 28%. Some firms, such as Amazon or Microsoft, have book-value-to-market-value ratios of less than 10% in recent years. Even the market value of "old economy" companies exceeds their book value as defined by the balance sheet by some five or six times.[13] Traditional accounting systems often fail to capture the intangible value of knowledge-based assets inherent in the modern organization, although the importance of knowledge as a strategic asset of the corporation has long been recognized[14] and although the importance of knowledge management for sustainable growth is placed high. "The most valuable asset of a 21st century institution will be its knowledge workers and their productivity."[15]

The strategic management literature has increasingly adopted a knowledge-based perspective. With knowledge as the most strategic critical resource of the firm,[16] the management of intellectual capital emerges as a source of competitive advantage, and learning evolves as a key capability for the organization. The quality of technology knowledge relates to the organizational ability to excel in product and process innovation that reduces private risks and enhances real option value. Others have pointed out how radical changes in technological patterns can destroy the value of some given areas of corporate knowledge.[17] The integration of the existing knowledge base, the strategy for the acquisition of future knowledge, and its management and valuation in relation to the overall business strategy seems mandatory.

Sources and types of knowledge include tacit knowledge that resides in employees, in processes and procedures, based in experience and not easily transferable or imitable; databases of information; and process-based knowledge, as well as intellectual property. Instruments to leverage knowledge include licensing agreements, subscription to databases, patents as barrier to entry, and access to a monopoly rent. Much of the organizational knowledge, however, will contribute in ways that are difficult to value in terms of enhancing organizational competitiveness, capability, and ability to create and execute real options.

While there is a rich literature on knowledge management that describes and advances the cognitive techniques of an organization, that is, the processes and procedures that facilitate the understanding and increase the intra-organizational dissemination of information, little has been published on the economic value of knowledge. The valuation of knowledge is still in its infancy but the need to determine the economic value is acknowledged. Pakes[18] uses an option valuation model to value patents. He views a patent as a right but not an obligation to renew the patent by paying the patent fees. Looking at the actual renewal rates for a series of patents, he then estimates the underlying value distribution of the patent value. His work provides evidence for a large amount of inherent option value. Lanjouw[19] takes this concept a step further by including not just patent renewal but also patent litigation. He assumes that the propensity of a firm to engage in an expensive defense strategy for existing patents that involve litigation in court reflects the perceived value of the patent. The highly skewed nature of patent value is well recognized: a large proportion of the patented inventions are worth very little, whereas a small number of patents are extremely valuable. A 1998 study by Schankerman indicates that a median value of patent rights (in 1980 U.S. dollars) is $1,631 in pharmaceuticals, $2,930 in mechanical, and $3,159 in electronics patents (for U.S. and major European countries). The top 1% of patents accounts for 12% of the total value of patent rights in pharmaceuticals and 21% and 24% for mechanical and electronic patents. The top 5% of patents accounts for 34% of total value in pharmaceuticals, and 50% and 55% for mechanical and electronics patents.

But what is the market value of corporate expertise? Real option analysis may provide a good framework to get this started.[20] The valuation of knowledge needs to tie in with the appreciation of incremental cash flows generated by knowledge. Real options create the bond between knowledge and operational benefits such as an increase in potential returns, a decrease in the cost of learning, and an increase in the probability of success. Those links provide a direct connection to the income statement. These incremental cash flows stem from various sources: knowledge that forms the basis of future growth opportunities or helps in exploiting new markets or product developments, and knowledge that contributes to increased profits by improving product distribution or product features and creates new revenue sources by making corporate knowledge available to others through patent or technology licenses.

Valued are both the creation and application of knowledge as well as the management of knowledge. The organizational ability to create growth opportunities depends on creating new knowledge, exploiting existing knowledge in new ways, and protecting valuable knowledge from exploitation by competitors. These are seed-growth opportunities from which growth opportunities can emerge.

Knowledge-based real options share with real options on tangible assets the significant amount of uncertainty that will prevail even at the time of exercise of the option. Further, costs to acquire knowledge-based options may be even more difficult to identify than costs that are incurred on tangible, real assets. Also, the value derived from acquiring or creating knowledge options will depend to a significant degree on the organizational ability to utilize and integrate the knowledge across the firm. It is hence endogenously driven to a great extent and the uncertainty derives from organizational structure and design, not from exogenous market uncertainty.

Real options have also been explored as a way to value investments in other intangible assets such as corporate sustainability.[21] Consider a hypothetical mining company that contemplates investing $5 million in its current operations with the goal of making these operations more acceptable to society than those run by its competitor and thereby win the "social license to operate." There is a 50% chance that this will actually be achieved with the investment. The challenge is to define the potential value created by social acceptability and to refine the estimates for that value.

EXTENSION OF THE CONCEPTS

The past few years have witnessed an explosion in creative real option applications. How much of those ideas and models will infiltrate day-to-day managerial practice remains to be seen. There are two components in the contribution of the academic real option work: insights and methodology. The insights derived from often very abstract and highly analytical work are likely to infiltrate managerial decision making first. The methodology applied, however, may find it harder to make its way into corporate offices. Mathematical accessibility, translational value of the models given complexity and sometimes rigidity of the underlying assumptions and input parameters will drive penetration from theory into practice. Of course, success of real option application cannot be measured by penetration alone; the most important parameter to evaluate success of the concept will be its contribution to improved decision making and fair market valuation of the firm's assets in place and growth options. In view of many of the inconsistencies and non-analogies between financial and real options, it is still unclear how, when and which of the basic concepts can be meaningfully translated into practical real option frameworks. Despite much enthusiasm, real options valuation is challenging, but not impossible, to put into practice.

Financial option concepts and valuation methodology deserve great credit for bringing a new tool to the evaluation of corporate decision making that has—more than any other method—the potential to function as a true and solid bridge between finance, strategy and the organization. However, in order for the real option framework to become fully integrated and truly valuable to corporate executives, it may have to emancipate itself from the strict analogies to financial options. That emancipation is likely to take place along two dimensions: methodology and concepts. Financial options really play out only along two scales: time to maturity and the observable difference between exercise price and stock price. Real options, on the other hand, have many dimensions. Slowly but surely more of those dimensions find integration into the theoretical foundations of applied real option work.

Much of the pioneering work on real options assumes options were proprietary and not shared, and that the expiration time was known and definitive, just as for financial options. More recently, uncertain time to maturity was introduced, and more attention is paid to investigating the interaction between options and the impact of competitive scenarios.

A significant extension of the real option concept that is based on uncertainty, irreversibility, and the flexibility to delay includes the notion of partial reversibility, which does not exist for financial options.[22] Partial reversibility becomes effective, for example, with the option to abandon. When the option to abandon a project against salvage price is included in the investment appraisal, the critical cost to invest declines and the incentive to invest increases. We have shown this in a simple example in Chapter 3. Similarly, if the firm has the option to expand, this provides the firm with additional flexibility after the initial commitment and also lowers the critical investment threshold. Both options challenge the notion of irreversibility, both offer partial reversibility, and both options reduce the incentive to delay.

Further, during waiting, the cost of capital may increase, adding additional costs to the option to defer. Increase in the cost of capital also makes the option of later expansion more costly. On the other hand, if the obtainable salvage price for abandonment is also volatile and at risk to decline, the value of the put option also declines. Obviously, the option to abandon and the option to defer on the same asset correlate to some degree. Remember the example of the car manufacturer in Chapter 3. If the demand for cars declines, the incentive to sell the plant goes up. However, if the demand for cars declines universally and the plant can only be used to manufacture cars, then the salvage value for the plant will also decline. Also remember that there is empirical support for the notion that investors do value the abandonment option, but that they will differentiate between specialized assets, whose value is expected to correlate more with market demand, and generalized assets, which can be utilized for production in other, uncorrelated markets.[23]

Ultimately, the decision to defer the investment or to invest now is dictated by the dynamic interplay of these three options: waiting, abandoning, and expanding.

Uncertainty and irreversibility create the option value of delay; this was the initial insight and emphasis of the real option concept as presented by Dixit and Pindyck. The cost of delay is—for the owner of a monopoly option—the revenue forgone by deferring the investment. For the owner of a shared option, the option to defer may kill the entire investment opportunity under competitive pressure. The option to abandon and the option to expand offer an exit from this dilemma. With the publication of the work of Abel and colleagues, that intuitive notion has formally entered the economic literature. The authors link real option pricing to macroeconomic theory, specifically to Tobin's q, which is defined as the ratio of the market value of the firm to the replacement cost of its capital. q measures the incentive of a firm to invest in capital, which goes up as the value of capital increases relative to the cost of capital. Linked to real option pricing, the incentive to defer or to expand declines as the cost of capital goes up.

Assume that you are interested in finding out the value of several different options on two assets that are correlated. You may then want to consider using three-dimensional binomial trees. Figure 10.1 illustrates the concepts (adapted from Espen Gaarder Haug[24])

In essence, the binomial pyramid reconciles two independent but correlated geometric Brownian motions. Such a scenario is applicable, for example, if the investment in one project will create in the future two distinct assets that will both generate independent cash flows, but only one of the two assets will be taken to the market. Both assets address distinct customer segments but within the same market and therefore face largely the same market risk. Therefore, their payoff functions are correlated. This scenario represents an option on two underlying assets where only the asset with the maximum payoff will be realized.

More recently, artificial neural networks (ANN) have emerged as an option pricing method that is an alternative to Black-Scholes. An ANN attempts to address one critical shortcoming of the Black-Scholes model, namely the severe restrictions it imposes on the nature of the underlying asset and the markets in which the asset is traded. Those conditions make application of Black-Scholes challenging, not only for real options, but sometimes also for financial options. These restrictions include the following conditions: returns have to be log-normally distributed, stocks need to trade continuously, and the volatility of the underlying asset remains constant over time.

FIGURE 10.1 The three-dimensional binomial option. Source: Haug.

ANNs are sets of mathematical models that mimic some of the properties of mammalian brains and nervous systems. The mammalian brain has several very desirable features that are so far unmatched by the computer; they include the ability to process large datasets even with incomplete and noisy information. Another feature is the ability to develop algorithms and learn from experience in doing so. Moreover, the mammalian brain is extraordinarily quick to adapt to changes in the environment. Artificial neural networks, too, have the ability to learn. They possess millions of densely interconnected processing elements, analogous to the neurons in the nervous system. This constitutes a novel structure of information processing systems, which enables neural networks to learn and distinguishes them from "normal" computer programs.

Neural networks emerged in the late '50s mainly as attempts to model behavioral and brain processes. Since then neural networks have become very sophisticated and have been applied to a variety of technical problems, including data mining and image analysis in medicine and bioinformatics, speech and signal recognition, modeling of complex physical processes, regulation of input controlled processes, and for predictions about stocks, options, and futures. They have succeeded in pricing financial options with greater accuracy than Black-Scholes and have also been explored as a way to value real options.[25]

Much of the academic real option work relies on geometric Brownian motions to model future stochastic behavior of the asset value as well as costs. This approach assumes that past volatility is indicative for future volatility, and that the future will simply be an extrapolation of the past. That assumption usually causes concerns among corporate executives. It is often viewed as a doubtful simplification of the challenges real investment decisions face, ill suited to convince anyone of the value of this methodology for budgeting decisions.

An emerging alternative is the use of fuzzy numbers, subjective estimates to express understanding of the future cash flows that come as a family of fuzzy numbers or as possibility distribution.[26] Fuzzy numbers had their entrée into financial mathematics in 1987, and more recently have been applied to value real options.[27] They represent not just a single number, but rather a quantity whose value is hazy, not exact. A fuzzy number is a function in itself, and all exact numbers that are part of that function are members of the fuzzy number. Fuzzy numbers encompass probability distributions of different shapes, including a bell-shaped, log-normal distribution but also a trapezoid, triangular or any irregular membership function. The notion of a fuzzy number is likely to have more intuitive appeal to managers than a log-normal stochastic approach.

LIMITATIONS OF THE REAL OPTION CONCEPT

The real option concept offers several intriguing benefits for the appraisal of investment decisions and significant advantages compared to a static DCF-based NPV appraisal process. These are summarized in Figure 10.2.

However, the real option concept and method also has pitfalls and shortcomings that need to be taken into consideration to ensure the best use of the paradigm. There are obvious limitations if one were to literally adapt the financial option pricing to real option pricing. We have already discussed several reasons that should discourage the use of the Black-Scholes formula to value a real option. For example, the returns must be log-normally distributed, securities must be continuously traded, and there must be complete markets that provide an unlimited number of options to trade with. For most real options, returns are exponential; sometimes they come in jumps, in both upward and downward jumps. For products with a short life-cycle the log-normal distribution is entirely out of place.[28] Black-Scholes requires that units and fractions of units on securities can be traded. There are no units on investment projects, a phenomenon referred to as the "Brooklyn Bridge."[29] There is no way one can sell a unit of a project that one does not own. Still, Black-Scholes can be applied to value vacant land if one assumes complete markets and the existence of a market portfolio that is perfectly correlated with the vacant lot.

The increasingly pronounced "volatility smile" after the 1987 stock market crash highlighted a central problem with Black-Scholes, namely, the assumption that volatility does not change over time. As a consequence of this assumption, one must deduce in the Black-Scholes world that all options on

DCF - Traditional	Real Options
Operating decisions will not change in the future	Directional changes pending arrival of new information
Base case set of expected cash flows	Cash flows contingent on future uncertain conditions
Static, sensitivity and scenario analysis	Managerial flexibility to react to changing conditions

FIGURE 10.2 DCF versus real options

the same asset have the same implied volatility. However, the Black-Scholes implied volatilities tend to vary depending on the exercise price and also depending on the time to maturity. This phenomenon became very prominent after the stock market crash in 1987. It has invited other scholars to come up with novel models for option pricing that do not require that assumption anymore but rather propose a deterministic volatility function.[30] It is a great advantage of the binomial option pricing model that it does not require volatility to remain constant. Instead, it allows for the volatility to change in each phase of the project, as we have seen for the compound option.

For real options—as well as for the DCF framework—the assumption must be made that there is a traded security or a portfolio of securities whose risks and payoffs mimic exactly the expected risks and payoffs of the investment project to model the future payoff. This has prompted some to demand that real options can only be applied to situations where those traded securities can be found—ignoring that managers who use the DCF approach do not routinely search the market for traded securities to find the matching twin either.

The need and desire to utilize real options as a tool to align investment decisions with financial markets has also prompted the search for twin securities whose past stock volatilities could serve as a proxy for the future volatility of a corporate investment project. To many corporate executives, this approach lacks intuition and appeal in rapidly changing environments where overall the past gives little guidance as to the future. Further, and maybe more importantly, the purchase and exercise of the financial options is unlikely to alter the payoff dynamics of the replicating portfolio consisting of stocks and bonds. Applying the same principle to real option analysis largely ignores that firms operate in a competitive and highly interactive environment. Steps taken or not taken by any individual firm are likely to have an immediate impact on the action of its competitors and on the overall market equilibrium. We could call this the Heisenberg uncertainty principle of the real option.

Heisenberg, in his 1927 paper on uncertainty, wrote that "The more precisely the position is determined, the less precisely the momentum is known." What he meant was the following: In an attempt to determine the position and motion of a particle, a measurement is being made. However, the same measurement disturbs untouched nature and changes the motion. Adapting to the world of corporate strategic investments and the real option valuation thereof: A company that replicates an investment decision with a perfectly matching traded security in order to price the value of its real option is likely to alter the momentum of that same security by exercising its real option and entering the market with its product.

Take, for example, an oil firm that relies on the volatility of oil stocks, futures or oil prices to replicate its real option on exploring a new oil field. The firm, when acquiring the option, becomes immediately part of the dynamics that govern the twin security, which is meant to function as a riskless replicating portfolio. Its decision to explore the oil field will already send out a signal to comparable firms and alter their investment decisions. Once the real option is exercised and the well is ready to deliver oil, the additional supply may further alter the market dynamics and stock volatilities of the comparable "twin security." Other real options, such as the investment in developing wearable computers, have no precedent yet in the market and will therefore be difficult to model with existing traded twin securities. Instead of finding the replicating portfolio in the traded securities, one may model the expected payoff for wearable computers by assigning probabilities of market behavior based on market research and past experiences of market penetration for products that were similarly innovative when they first came out—and recruit to fuzzy numbers.

Financial option pricing assumes future values of the underlying asset based on stochastic processes. If we eliminate those stochastic processes and replace them with other tools, we have to acknowledge the human limitation to make predictions. Predictions about the future are based on past experience; they also are made in an organizational and cultural context. A useful tool for real option analysis is scenario planning and scenario learning. For real option analysis, scenario planning approximates what volatility is for financial option pricing. It builds on existing knowledge and past experience to create a range of plausible scenarios for the future, just as financial options rely on past volatilities when predicting future volatilities. Scenario planning addresses three challenges: uncertainty, complexity, and paradigm shifts.[31]

Scenario planning is mostly about organizational learning.[32] So is real option analysis: It is scenario planning—defining the options under various scenarios—as well as scenario learning—shaping and monitoring the evolution of the real option. Scenario planning relies on imagining the future rather than extrapolating from the past. So does real option analysis: We shape the binomial tree of the future, the dream-tree, and work back to today. Most important, scenario planning forces the organization to think about more than one future. So does and so should real option analysis. We have mentioned the portfolio of real options for a portfolio of futures. Scenario planning helps in the seeing, creating, evaluating, and timing of options.

"I think there's a world market for maybe five computers," predicted Thomas Watson, Chairman of IBM, in 1943. Still, almost 40 years later, in the early '80s, the corporate executives of IBM did not anticipate that computer demand could exceed roughly 250,000 pieces, not worth major investments for IBM in basic technologies. So the firm gladly outsourced the development of operating systems and chips and gave Microsoft all the profits in exchange for the development costs of the DOS operating system. Imagine what would have happened if IBM had used real option analysis and ascribed a probability of just 1% to an upside scenario that envisioned the sale of 40 million computers by the year 1990. At a price of $5,000 per computer this scenario would have contributed roughly $1 billion in option value to the deal negotiation in the early '80s, and might have altered the deal structure between IBM and Microsoft.

Uncertainties are the center of attention in scenario planning, and remedies to enhance competitive advantage across a range of uncertain futures. Scenario planning enforces systematic exploration and evaluation of possible future changes and threats. Several useful tools have been developed to support scenario analysis, including emerging pattern monitors (EPM). These entail a whole arsenal of technologies to pour over ongoing economic, political, technological, and cultural developments in an attempt to identify patterns just as the financial markets do. EPM also embraces simulation, such as Monte Carlo analysis, as a tool to guide the human mind in shaping the future.

Scenario planning separates what is believed to be certain and observable in trends from what is uncertain and subject to change. Once the drivers of change are identified, the rules of interaction can be defined and can lead to the evolution of multiple scenarios. For those who share the author's view that real life cannot easily be squeezed into a log-normal view of the world but still embrace the notion of mathematically guided rather than human-predicted future scenarios, there are several other planning tools available that can easily be linked to a real option analysis, such as the Gompertz analysis, the growth limit analysis, or learning curve techniques.

For financial options, the relationship between the various input parameters and option value is well defined, as summarized in Figure 10.3.

For real options, those relationships are much more complex. Time to maturation does not increase the value of the real option because of the time value of revenue streams forgone and because of competitive threats. Different sources of uncertainty or volatility drive the value of the real option, and they do not per se increase the value of the real option at all. First, there are risks and uncertainties that diminish option value, as others have shown[33] and we have reproduced with the binomial model for market variability and competitive entry uncertainty. Second, uncertainty that derives from noisy signals is of no value at all; it interferes with managerial ability

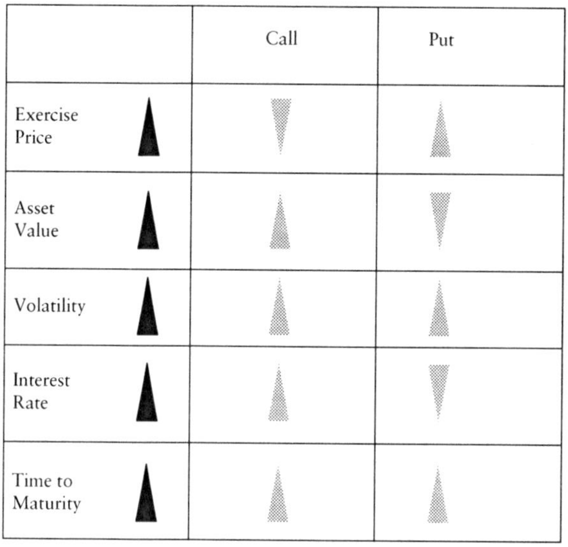

	Call	Put
Exercise Price ↑	▼	▲
Asset Value ↑	▲	▼
Volatility ↑	▲	▲
Interest Rate ↑	▲	▼
Time to Maturity ↑	▲	▲

FIGURE 10.3 Drivers of financial option value

to make good, well-informed decisions. Third, real options do not value uncertainty; they only value flexibility in response to uncertainty.

Potential upside or knockout provisions are inherent to many real options, and they must be incorporated in the valuation. Failing to do so can easily exaggerate the value of these investment options. Options, by definition, are always positive or zero. However, even financial markets have discovered negative option values.[34] As for real options, management can acquire options that are out of the money and thereby will destroy value. Moreover, the money invested in an out-of-the-money option is forgone for an opportunity that might be well in the money, increasing corporate regret. Corporate managers are increasingly at risk of being regretful when the limits of forecasting are not accepted and alternative scenarios are ignored. The critical cost to invest does provide one sanity check for investment decisions. However, one may want to explore whether for real options the exercise price should be complemented by an insurance premium to protect against the downside risk. That downside risk does not exist for financial options, as the exercise price is paid after the value of the asset has been observed.

Further, there are human limitations involved in the rational exercise of real options—even if all uncertainty and value drivers are continuously monitored and the investment trigger is under constant observation. A well-studied phenomenon, termed the Concorde fallacy, often gets in the way of the rational exercise of real options. Unlike animals and young children, grown ups tend to hold onto previous investments, even if reason tells them not to.[35] It may have to do with the adult desire not to waste anything. In fact, failure to exercise abandoning options might have contributed to the decline of ancient societies, such as the Pueblos.[36] It has been suggested that the Pueblos failed to abandon existing settlements that had taken a great deal of time and effort to build. In fact, it appears that they stuck to existing settlements even when resources became scarce as a result of drought and additional related and unrelated socioeconomic factors.

In addition to the technical challenges, such as the lack of tradability and liquidity and the issues around risk-neutrality as well as the challenges of arriving at reliable estimates for revenues and costs, there are also conceptual limitations to the real option framework that need to be acknowledged and considered when using real options in practice.

Financial options are exercised under observable prices for the underlying stock. Real options, on the contrary, need to be exercised when the value of an underlying asset is still evolving. Financial options benefit from uncertainty, that is, volatility, as increasing volatility opens the avenues for bigger upside potential while the downside risk remains limited.

As to real options, the downside risks of real options are not limited. Think about liabilities that may arise sometime in the future as the result of real options exercised today. Further, real options can still move out of the money once they have been exercised. Finally, once the real option has been acquired and the exercise has been paid, management has to work hard to create and materialize the envisioned upside potential. Therefore, real options do not benefit from uncertainty per se, but only from flexibility to respond to future uncertainty. From this fundamental conceptual difference between real options and financial options derives the generic rule on the value and exercise of real options shown in Figure 10.4.

Real option flexibility is tightly linked to operational flexibility and uncertainty. Operational uncertainty, in fact, reduces flexibility and diminishes real option value. If operational uncertainty can be resolved prior to the exercise of the real option, it will not impact the real option value. However, if operational uncertainty is only resolved after decisions have been made and resources have been committed, operational uncertainties reduce flexibility and real option value.[37] Those operational uncertainties include budget constraints, future market payoffs, private risk related to product performance, and market risk related to product performance of competing products, as well as uncertain time to project completion. The value of the

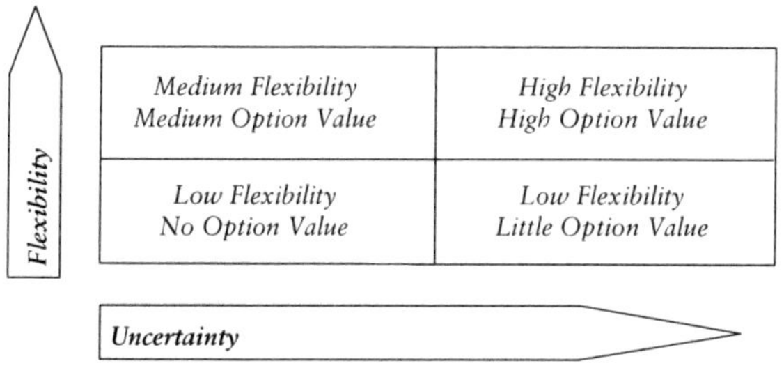

FIGURE 10.4 The real option value matrix

underlying asset is driven by both exogenous, market uncertainty, and by endogenous, technical or private uncertainty. The latter can only be completely resolved by committing and investing. Even if the project fails, the organization will still derive value from learning and collecting expertise that will help in reducing the probability of failure in the future.

Real option value can only be created if the organization is capable of executing. It requires discipline in mapping out the uncertainties, but even more discipline in mapping out the organizational flexibilities to respond. These organizational flexibilities reflect exogenous constraints as well as constraints derived from the organizational design. While the static DCF analysis suffers from the lack of innovation and variability, the real danger of real options lies in getting lost in a self-inflicted option jungle that can no longer be executed.

The value creation in real options, compared to the NPV analysis, stems from preserving the right to get involved without having the obligation to do so. Value creation in the real option framework is intricately linked and interwoven with the organizational culture and design, the organizational mindset, communication structures and organizational understanding of uncertainties, procedures to monitor internal and external value drivers, and incentives to execute, as shown in Figure 10.5.

However, for each real option, any future decision is conditional and dependent on today's decision. An organization that is capable of envisioning several futures can create a portfolio of options to preserve maximum flexibility to respond to those futures. It will be able to choose from a set of opportunities those that are the most valuable, depending on the future state, and when executing that choice create and maximize value. An organization that fails to envision and plan for future contingencies or has insufficient operational plasticity lacks the appropriate flexibility and will have few if any real options in the money to exercise.

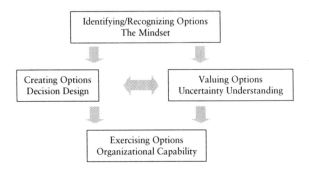

FIGURE 10.5 Drivers of real option value

CONCLUDING REMARKS

Real options is a very dynamic valuation method; it works best if used consistently throughout the organization and if integrated well with other, complementary financial and strategic tools. Real options have a natural life-cycle, the option life-cycle, shown in Figure 10.6, which consists of seed, fermentation, formulation, launch, growth and maturity, and then decline. This life-cycle needs to be closely followed and observed.

Real options work best in organizations that encourage open discussions and broad, comprehensive data collection. Some of the companies that had little success with the real option approach and abandoned it in frustration did so because there were too few data to measure risk. Many data and much information smolder unused in corporate filing cabinets and harddrives. Designing and implementing a proactive data collection and data warehouse system to capture benchmarks on historic and ongoing projects to directly drive assumptions about real option analysis or to feed into Monte Carlo simulations can be a very helpful endeavor. Another pitfall is inconsistent application of the framework, which prevents fair comparison of corporate-wide risks, costs, and opportunities and is a sure recipe for organizational frustration, withholding of critical information, and failure to come up with a comprehensive corporate dream-tree, the predecessor of the binomial asset tree.

One last reminder: A real option is any investment in physical and intangible assets, in human competence, and in organizational capabilities that help the organization to envision and respond to future contingent events.

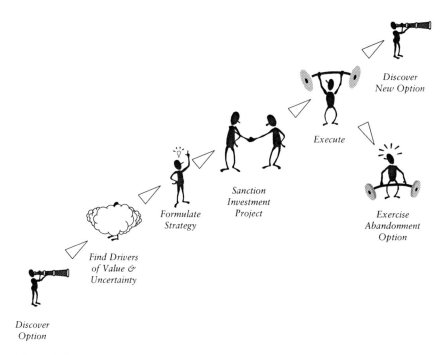

FIGURE 10.6 The life-cycle of a real option

NOTES

1. H. Nembhard, "Real Option Modeling for Valuing Worker Flexibility," *IERC Abstract 2107*, 2001; B. Kamrad and S. Lele, "Production, Operating Risk and Market Uncertainty: A Valuation Perspective on Controlled Policies," *IIE Transactions* 30:455, 1998.
2. M.I. De Miranda, *Analysis of Investment Opportunities for Network Expansion Projects: A Real Option Approach*. (Fifth Real Options Group Conference, Los Angeles, May 2001).
3. M. Raynor, *Real Options on Synergies and Long Options in Acquisitions*. Presented at the Fifth Annual Real Options Group Conference, July 11, 2001, Los Angeles, California.
4. H. Nembhard, L. Shi, and M. Aktan, "A Real Options Design for Quality Control Charts," *The Engineering Economist* 47:28, 2002.

5. M.A.G. Dias, *Selection of Alternatives of Investment in Information for Oilfield Development Using Evolutionary Real Option Approach* (Fifth Real Options Group Conference, Los Angeles, 2001).

6. P. Botteron, M. Chesney, and R. Gibson-Asner, *An Application of Exotic Options to Firm's Strategic Delocalisation Policies under Exchange Rate Risk* (Real Options Group Conference, Cambridge, 1998).

7. W. Margrabe, "The Value of an Option to Exchange One Asset for Another," *Journal of Finance* 33:177, 1978.

8. C.M. Chambers, P.E. Chambers, and J.C. Whitehead, "Conservation Organizations and the Option Value to Preserve: An Application to Debt-for-Nature Swaps," *Ecological Encomics* 9:135, 1994.

9. H. Erdogmus, *Management of License Cost Uncertainty in Software Development: A Real Option Approach* (Fifth Real Options Group Conference, Los Angeles, 2001).

10. H. Ergas and J.P. Small, *Real Options and Economic Depreciation*, working paper (University of Auckland, March 2000).

11. "Business: A Price on the Priceless," *The Economist*, June 12, 1999, pp. 61–62.

12. W.S. Upton, *Business and Financial Reporting, Challenges from the New Economy*, special report (Financial Accounting Series, No. 219-A, April 2001).

13. L. Baruch, *Knowledge Management: A Fad or a Vital Need?* (Vanguard Technology Transfer Institute Conference, "Where Technology and People Meet," November 6–7, 2000, Atlanta, GA).

14. S.G. Winter, "Knowledge and Competence as Strategic Assets," in D.J. Teece, ed., *The Competitive Challenge*, 1987; M.H. Zack, "Developing a Knowledge Strategy," *California Management Review* 41:125, 1999.

15. F. Drucker, "Knowledge-Worker Productivity: The Biggest Challenge," *California Management Review* 41:79, 1999.

16. D.J. Teece, "Capturing Value from Knowledge Assets: The New Economy, Markets for Know-How, and Intangible Assets," *California Management Review* 40:55, 1998; M.H. Zack, "Developing a Knowledge Strategy," *California Management Review* 41:125, 1999; P. Yates-Mercer and D. Bawden, "Managing the Paradox: The Valuation of Knowledge and Knowledge Management," *Journal of Information Science* 28:19, 2002; R.M. Grant, "Toward a Knowledge-Based Theory of the Firm," *Strategic Management Journal* 17:109, 1996; R.G. McGrath, M.H. Tsai, S. Venkataraman, and I.C. MacMillan, "Innovation, Competitive Advantage and Rent: A Model and Test," *Management Science* 42:389, 1996.

17. M.L. Tushman and P. Anderson, "Technological Discontinuities and Organizational Environments," *Administrative Science Quarterly* 31:439, 1986; R.M. Henderson and K.B. Clark, "Architectural Innovation: The Reconfiguration of Existing Product Technologies and the Failure of Established Firms," *Administrative Science Quarterly* 35:9, 1990.

18. A. Pakes, "Patents as Options: Some Estimates of the Value of Holding European Patent Stocks," *Econometrica* 54:755, 1986.

19. J.O. Lanjouw, "Patent Protection in the Shadow of Infringement: Simulation Estimations of Patent Value," *Review of Economic Studies* 65: 671, 1998.

20. R.W. Coff and K.J. Laverty, "Real Options on Knowledge Assets: Panacea or Pandora's Box?" *Business Horizons* 44:73, 2001.

21. D.J. Reed, *Stalking the Elusive Business Case for Corporate Sustainability* (World Resources Institute, 2001, 15).

22. A.A. Abel, A.K. Dixit, J.C. Eberly, and R.S. Pindyck, "Options, the Value of Capital and Investment," *Quarterly Journal of Economics* 111:753, 1996.

23. P. Berger, E. Ofek, and I. Swary, "Investor Valuation of the Abandonment Option," *Journal of Financial Economics* 42:257, 1996.

24. E.G. Haug, "3-Dimensional Lattice Models." http://home.online.no/ ~espehaug/3DLattice.html.

25. H. Amilon, *A Neural Network versus Black Scholes. A comparison of Pricing and Hedging Performance*, working paper (University of Lund, Sweden); A. Taudes, M. Natter, and M. Trcka, "Real Option Valuation with Neural Networks," *International Journal of Intelligent Systems in Accounting, Finance and Management* 7:1, 1998; R. Gencay and M. Oi, "Pricing and Hedging Derivative Securities with Neural Networks: Bayesian Regularization, Early Stopping, and Bagging," *IEEE Transactions on Neural Networks* 12:726, 2000; E.W. Saad, D.V. Prokhorov, and D.C. Wunsch, "Comparative Study of Stock Trend Prediction Using Time Delay, Recurrent and Probabilistic Neural Networks," *IEEE Transactions on Neural Networks* 9:145, 1998.

26. D. Dubois and H. Prade, *Possibility Theory* (New York: Plenum Press, 1988).

27. J.J. Buckley, "The Fuzzy Mathematics of Finance," *Fuzzy Sets and Systems* 21:257, 1987; L. Calzi, "Towards a General Setting for the Fuzzy Mathematics of Finance," *Fuzzy Sets and Systems* 35:265, 1990; Z. Zmeskal, "Application of the Fuzzy-Stochastic Methodology to Appraising the Firm Value as a European Call Option," *European Journal*

of Operational Research 135:303, 2001; C. Carlsson and R. Fuller, "Project Scheduling with Fuzzy Real Options," *Cybernetics and Systems* 33:511, 2002.

28. N.P.B. Bollen, "Real Options and Product Life-Cycle," *Management Science* 45:670, 1999.

29. S.K. Turnbull and C.F. Sirmans, "Vacant Land Options: A Theoretical Analysis," *Regional Science and Urban Economics* 20:213, 1990.

30. E. Derman and I. Kani, "The Volatility Smile and Its Implied Tree," *Quantitative Strategies Research Notes.* Goldman Sachs, 1994; B. Dupirie, "Pricing with a Smile," *Risk* 7:18, 1994; M. Rubinstein, "Implied Binomial Trees," *Journal of Finance* 49:771, 1994.

31. P.J.H. Schoemaker, "Scenario Planning: A Tool for Strategic Thinking," *Sloan Management Review*, Winter 1995, p. 25.

32. K. van der Heijden, *Scenarios: The art of Strategic Conversation* (Wiley, 1995).

33. A. Huchzermeier and C.H. Loch, "Evaluating R&D Projects as Learning Options: Why More Variability Is Not Always Better," in H. Wildemann, ed., *Produktion und Controlling* (München: TCW Transfer Centrum Verlag, 185–197, 1999).

34. F.A. Longstaff, "Are Negative Option Prices Possible? The Callable U.S. Treasury-Bond Puzzle," *The Journal of Business* 65:571, 1992; B.D. Jordan and D.R. Kuipers, "The Impact of Treasury Bond Futures on the Cash U.S. Treasury Market," *Journal of Financial Economics* 46:67, 1997.

35. H.R. Arkes and P. Ayton, "The Sunk Cost and Concorde Effects: Are Humans Less Rational Than Lower Animals?" *Psychological Bulletin* 125:591, 1999.

36. M.A. Janssen, M. Scheffer, and T.A. Kohler, *Sunk-Cost Effects Made Ancient Societies Vulnerable to Collapse*, working paper (Indiana University).

37. A. Huchzermeier and C. Loch, "Project Management Under Risk: Using the Real Options Approach to Evaluate Flexibility in R&D," *Management Science* 47:85, 2001.

bibliography

Abel, A.A.; A.K. Dixit; J.C. Eberly; and R.S. Pindyck. "Options, the Value of Capital and Investment." *Quarterly Journal of Economics* 111:753, 1996.

Amilon, H. *A Neural Network versus Black Scholes. A Comparison of Pricing and Hedging Performance*, working paper. University of Lund, Sweden, 2001.

Amram, M., and N. Kulatilaka. *Real Options. Managing Strategic Investment in an Uncertain World.* Harvard Business School Press, 1999.

Arkes, H.R., and P. Ayton. "The Sunk Cost and Concorde Effects: Are Humans Less Rational Than Lower Animals?" *Psychological Bulletin* 125:591, 1999.

Arnold, T. "Value Creation at Anheuser-Busch: A Real Options Example." *Journal of Applied Corporate Finance* 14:52, 2001.

Arrow, K.J., and A.C. Fisher. "Environmental Preservation, Uncertainty and Irreversibility." *Quarterly Journal of Economics* 88:312, 1974.

Bachelier, L. *Theorie de la Speculation.* Annales Scientifiques de l'Ecole Normale Superieure, III-17:21(86), 1900. Thesis for the Doctorate in Mathematical Sciences (defended March 29, 1900). Reprinted by Editions Jacques Gabay, Paris, 1995. English translation in P. Cootner, ed., *The Random Character of Stock Market Prices*, pp. 17–78. Cambridge: MIT Press, 1964.

Baldwin, C.Y., and B.J. Clark. "Capital-Budgeting Systems and Capabilities Investments in U.S. Companies after the Second World War." *Business History Review* 68:73, 1994.

Baness, J. "Elements of a Theory of Stock-Option Value." *Journal of Political Economy* 72:163, 1964.

Barney, J. "Firm Resources and Sustained Competitive Advantage." *Journal of Management* 17:99, 1991.

Baruch, L. "Rethinking Accounting." *Financial Executive* 18:34, 2002.

Basili, M. *Quasi-Option Values—Empirical Measures*, working paper. University of Sienna, 1999.

Bazerman, M.H., and J.J. Gillespie. "Betting on the Future: The Virtues of Contingent Contracts." *Harvard Business Review* Sept.–Oct., 1999, 77:155.

Belohav, J.A. "The Evolving Competitive Paradigm." *Business Horizons*, March–April, 11, 1996.

Benaroch, M., and R.J. Kauffman. "A Case for Using Real Options Pricing Analysis to Evaluate Information Technology Project Investments." *Information Systems Research* 10:70, 1999.

Berger, P., and E. Ofek. "Diversification's Effect on Firm Value." *Journal of Financial Economics* 37:39, 1995.

Berger, P.; E. Ofek; and I. Swary. "Investor Valuation of the Abandonment Option." *Journal of Financial Economics* 42:257, 1996.

Berk, J.B.; R.C. Green; and V. Naik. "Optimal Investment, Growth Options and Security Returns." *Journal of Finance* 54:1553, 1999.

Berk, J.B. "A Simple Approach for Deciding When to Invest." *The American Economic Review* 89:1319, 1999.

Berk, J.B.; R.C. Green; and V. Naik. *Valuation and Return Dynamics of New Ventures*, working paper. Haas School of Business, December 2000.

Bernardo, A.E., and B. Chowdhry. "Resources, Real Options, and Corporate Strategy." *Journal of Financial Economics* 63, 2002.

Berrada, T. *Valuing Real Options When Time to Maturity is Uncertain*. Third Real Options Group Conference, Cambridge, UK, 1999.

Black, F., and M. Scholes. "The Pricing of Options and Corporate Liabilities." *Journal of Political Economy* 81:637, 1973.

Bollen, N.P.B. "Real Options and Product Life-Cycle." *Management Science* 45:670, 1999.

Boltzmann, L. *Vorlesungen Äuber Gastheorie*. J.A. Barth, Leipzig, 1896. Published in two volumes, 1896 and 1898. Appeared in French in 1902–1905, *Leçons sur la Theorie des Gaz*, Gauthier-Villars, Paris. Published in English by Dover, New York as *Lectures on Gas Theory*, 490p.

Botteron, P.; M. Chesney; and R. Gibson-Asner. *An Application of Exotic Options to Firm's Strategic Delocalisation Policies under Exchange Rate Risk*. Real Options Group Conference, Cambridge, 1998.

Bowen, T.S. "Committing to Consultants: Outside Help Requires Internal Commitment and Management Skills." *InfoWorld* 20:61, 1998.

Bowman, E.H., and G.T. Moskowitz. "Real Option Analysis and Strategic Decision Making." *Organization Science* 12:772, 2001.

Boyle, P.P. "Options: A Monte Carlo Approach." *Journal of Financial Economics* 4:323, 1977.

Brach, M.A., and D.A. Paxson. "A Gene to Drug Venture: Poisson Options Analysis." *R&D Management* 31:203, 2001.

Brealey, R.A., and S.C. Myers. *Principles of Corporate Finance.* McGraw-Hill, 1996.

Brennan, M., and E. Schwartz. "Evaluating Natural Resource Investments." *Journal of Business* 58:135, 1985.

Brewer, P. "Putting Strategy into the Balanced Scorecard." *Strategic Finance* 83:44, 2002.

Brown, R. "A Brief Account of Microscopical Observations Made in the Months of June, July, and August, 1827, on the Particles Contained in the Pollen of Plants; and on the General Existence of Active Molecules in Organic and Inorganic Bodies." *Philosophical Magazine* 4:161, 1828.

Buckley, J. J. "The Fuzzy Mathematics of Finance." *Fuzzy Sets and Systems.* 35: 265, 1990.

Bunch, D.S., and R. Smiley. "Who Deters Entry? Evidence on the Use of Strategic Entry Deterrents." *Review of Economics and Statistics* 74:509, 1992.

Burrows, P. "How Apple Took Its NeXT Step." *Business Week*, January 13, 1997, p. 36.

Busby, J.S., and C.G. Pitts. "Real Options and Capital Investment Decisions." *Management Accounting* 75:38, 1997.

Buxbaum, P. "The Accidental Real Optionist." *Computerworld*, January 7, 2002.

Calzi, L. "Towards a General Setting for the Fuzzy Mathematics of Finance." *Fuzzy Sets and Systems.* 35: 265, 1990.

Carew, E. *Derivatives Decoded.* Allen and Unwin, St. Leonards, Australia, 1995.

Carlsson, C., and R. Fuller. "Project Scheduling with Fuzzy Real Options." *Cybernetics and Systems* 33: 511, 2002.

Carr, P. "The Valuation of Sequential Exchange Opportunities." *Journal of Finance* 43:1235, 1988.

Carr, P. "Randomization and the American Put." *Review of Financial Studies* 11:597, 1998.

Cassano, M.A. "How Well Can Options Complete Markets." *The Journal of Derivatives* 7, 2001.

Chambers, C.M.; P.E. Chambers; and J.C. Whitehead. Conservation Organizations and the Option Value to Preserve: An Application to Debt-for-Nature Swaps." *Ecological Encomics* 9:135, 1994.

Chang, S.J. "International Expansion Strategy of Japanese Firms: Capability Building Through Sequential Entry." *Academy of Management Journal* 38(2):383–407, 1995.

Chesney, M.; M. Jeanblanc-Pique; and M. Yor. "Brownian Excursions and Parisien Barrier Options." *Advances in Applied Probability* 29:165, 1997.

Childs, P.D.; S.H. Ott; and T.J.Riddiough. "Valuation and Information Acquisition Policy for Claims Written on Noisy Real Assets." *Financial Management* 30:45, 2001.

Childs, P.D.; S.H. Ott; and A.J. Triantis. "Capital Budgeting for Interrelated Projects: A Real Options Approach." *Journal of Financial and Quantitative Analysis* 33:305, 1998.

Childs, P.D.; T.R. Riddiough; and A. Triantis. "Mixed Uses and the Redevelopment Option." *Real Estate Economics* 24:317, 1996.

Chorn, L.G., and A. Sharma. "Valuing Investments in Extensions to Product Lines and Services Offerings When Facing Competitive Entry." Draft 06/30/2001. Fifth Real Options Conference, 2001.

Coff, R.W., and K.J. Laverty. "Real Options on Knowledge Assets: Panacea or Pandora's Box?" *Business Horizons* 44:73, 2001.

Copeland, T.; T. Koller; and J. Murrin. *Valuation: Measuring and Managing the Value of Companies*. John Wiley and Sons, 1998.

Copeland, T., and V. Antikarov. *Real Options—A Practitioner's Guide*. Texetere, 2001.

Cortazar, G., and E.S. Schwartz. "A Compound Option Model of Production and Intermediate Inventories." *The Journal of Business* 66:517, 1993.

Cox, J., and M. Rubinstein. *Options Markets*. Prentice-Hall, Englewood Cliffs, NJ, 1985.

Cox, J.C., and S.A. Ross. "The Valuation of Options for Alternative Stochastic Processes." *Journal of Financial Economics* 3:145, 1976.

Cox, J.C; S.A.Ross; and M. Rubinstein. "Option Pricing: A Simplified Approach." *Journal of Financial Economics* 7:229, 1979.

Coy, P. "Exploiting Uncertainty." *Business Week*, June 7:118–122, 1999.

Coyne, K.P.; S.J.D. Hall; and C.P. Gorman. "Is Your Core Competence a Mirage?" *McKinsey Quarterly*, Winter 1997, p. 40.

Culp, C.L. "Real Options: A case study and primer." *Derivatives Week*, May 13, 2001.

Davis, G.A. "Option Premiums in Mineral Asset Pricing. Are They Important?" *Land Economics* 72:167, 1996.

Day, G.S., and P.J. Shoemaker. *Managing Emerging Technologies*. Wiley, 2000.

Dembo, R.S., and A. Freeman. *Seeing Tomorrow: Rewriting the Rules of Risk*. John Wiley and Sons, 1998.

De Miranda, M.I. "Analysis of Investment Opportunities for Network Expansion Projects: A Real Option Approach." Fifth Real Options Conference, Los Angeles, May 2001.

Derman, E., and I. Kani. "The Volatility Smile and Its Implied Tree." *Quantitative Strategies Research Notes.* Goldman Sachs, 1994.

Deutsch, C.H. "Software That Makes a Grown Company Cry." *New York Times,* Nov. 8, 1998.

Dias, M.A.G. "Selection of Alternatives of Investment in Information For Oilfield Development Using Evolutionary Real Option Approach." Fifth Real Options Conference, Los Angeles, 2001.

Dierickx, I., and K. Cool. "Asset Stock Accumulation and Sustainability of Competitive Advantage." *Management Science* 35:504, 1989.

Dixit, A. "Entry and Exit Decisions under Uncertainty." *Journal of Political Economics* 97:620, 1989.

Dixit, A.K., and R.S. Pindyck. *Investment under Uncertainty.* Princeton University Press, 1994.

Dos Santos, B. "Justifying Investments in New Information Technologies." *Journal of Management Information Systems,* 7, 4:71, 1991.

Douggie, D. *Future Markets.* Prentice-Hall, 1989.

Dougherty, D. "Managing Your Core Incompetencies for Corporate Venturing." *Entrepreneurship: Theory and Practice* 19:113, 1995.

Drucker, F. "Knowledge-Worker Productivity: The Biggest Challenge." *California Management Review* 41:79, 1999.

Dubois, D., and H. Prade. *Possibility Theory.* Plenum Press, 1988.

Dupirie, B. "Pricing with a Smile." *Risk* 7:18, 1994.

Eeckhoudt, L., and P. Godfroid. "Risk Aversion and the Value of Information." *Journal of Economic Education* 31:382, 2000.

Einstein, A. "Uber die von der molekularkinetischen Theorie der Wärme gefordete Bewegung von in ruhenden Fluessigkeiten suspendierten Teilchen." *Annalen der Physik,* 17:549, 1905. Reprinted in A. Einstein, *Investigations on the Theory of the Brownian Movement,* edited with notes by R. Faurth, translated by A.D. Cower, London: Methuen, 1926. This English translation appears also in Dover, New York, 1956.

Epstein, D.; N. Mayor; P. Schonbucher; E. Whalley; and P. Wilmott. "The Value of Market Research when a Firm Is Learning. Real Option Pricing and Optimal Filtering." In L. Trigeorgis, ed., "Real Options and Business Strategy." *Applications to Decision-Making.* Risk Books, 2001.

Erdogmus, H. "Management of License Cost Uncertainty in Software Development: A Real Option Approach." Fifth Real Options Group Conference, Los Angeles, 2001.

Ergas, H., and J.P. Small. *Real Options and Economic Depreciation*, working paper. University of Auckland, March 2000.

Erramilli, K. "Nationality and Subsidiary Ownership Patterns in Multinational Corporations." *Journal of International Business Studies* 27:225, 1996.

Faulkner, T.W. "Applying 'Options Thinking' to R&D Valuation." *Research Technology Management* May–June, 1996, pp. 50–56.

Fisher, I. *The Rate of Interest: Its Nature, Determination and Relation to Economic Phenomena*. New York, 1907.

Folta, T.B. "Governance and Uncertainty: The Tradeoff between Administrative Control and Commitment." *Strategic Management Journal* 19:1007, 1998.

Folta, T.B., and W.J. Ferrier. "The Effect of National Culture on Partner Buyouts in Cross-Border Biotechnology Alliances." *The Journal of High Technology Management Research* 11:175, 2000.

Ford, B.J. "Brownien Movement in Clarkia Pollen: A Reprise of the First Observations." *The Microscope* 40:235, 1992.

Fries, S.; M. Miller; and W. Perraudin. "Debt Pricing in Industry Equilibrium." *Review of Financial Studies* 10:39, 1997.

Gencay, R., and M. Oi. "Pricing and Hedging Derivative Securities with Neural Networks: Bayesian Regularization, Early Stopping, and Bagging." *IEEE Transactions on Neural Networks*. 12:726, 2001.

Geske, R., and K. Shastri. "Valuation by Approximation: A Comparison of Alternative Option Valuation Techniques." *Journal of Financial and Quantitative Analysis* 20:45, 1985.

Geske, R. "The Valuation of Compound Options." *Journal of Financial Economics* 7:63, 1979.

Geske, R. "The Valuation of Corporate Liabilities as Compound Options." *Journal of Financial and Quantitative Analysis* 12:541, 1977.

Gould, J. "Risk, Stochastic Preference and the Value of Information." *Journal of Economic Theory* 8:64, 1974.

Grabowski, H.G., and J.M. Vernon. "Returns to R&D on New Drug Introduction in the 1980's." *Journal of Health Economics* 13:383, 1994.

Graham, A. "The Place of Reason in the Chinese Philosophical Tradition." in Raymond Dawson, ed., *The Legacy of China*, pp. 28–56, 1964.

Graham-Tomasi, T. "Quasi-Option Value." in D.W. Bromley, ed., *Handbook of Environmental Economics*. Blackwell, Oxford, UK and Cambridge, USA, 1995.

Grant, R.M. "Toward a Knowledge-Based Theory of the Firm." *Strategic Management Journal* 17:109, 1996.

Grenadier, S. "Valuing Lease Contracts. A Real-Options Approach." *Journal of Financial Economics* 38: 297, 1995.

Grenadier, S. *Game Choices. The Intersection of Real Options and Game Theory.* London: Risk Books. 2001.

Grenadier, S.R., and A.M. Weiss. "Investment in Technological Innovations: An Option Pricing Approach." *Journal of Financial Economics* 44:397, 1997.

Hamel, G., and C.K. Prahalad. *Competing for the Future.* Harvard Business School Press, 1994.

Haug, E.G. 3-Dimensional Lattice Models. http://home.online.no/~espehaug/3DLattice.html.

Hayes, R., and D. Garvin. "Managing As if Tomorrow Mattered." *Harvard Business Review* May–June, 71, 1982.

Hayes, R.H., and W.J. Abernathy. "Managing Our Way to Economic Decline." *Harvard Business Review*, September–October, 67, 1980.

Henderson, R., and I. Cockburn. "Measuring Competence? Exploring Firm Effects in Pharmaceutical Research." *Strategic Management Journal* 15:63, 1994.

Henderson, R.M., and K.B. Clark. "Architectural Innovation: The Reconfiguration of Existing Product Technologies and the Failure of Established Firms." *Administrative Science Quarterly* 35:9, 1990.

Henry, C. "Investment Decisions under Uncertainty: The Irreversibility Effect." *American Economic Review* 64:1006, 1974.

Herath, H.S.B., and C.S. Park. "Real Option Valuation and Its Relationship to Bayesian Decision Making Methods." *Engineering Economist* 46:1, 2001.

Herath, H., and C.S. Park. "Multi-Stage Capital Investment Opportunities as Compound Real Options." *Engineering Economist* 47:27, 2002.

Hilton, R. "Determinants of Information Value." *Management Science* 27:57, 1981.

Hoecklin, L. *Managing Cultural Differences: Strategies for Competitive Advantage.* Wokingham, UK: Addison-Wesley, 1995.

Hofstede, G. *Cultures and Organizations: Software of the Mind.* Berkshire, UK: McGraw-Hill, 1991.

Howell, S.D., and A.J. Jagle. "Laboratory Evidence on How Managers Intuitively Value Real Growth Options." *Journal of Business Finance and Accounting* 24:915, 1997.

Huchzermeier, A., and C.H. Loch. "Evaluating R&D Projects as Learning Options: Why More Variability is Not Always Better." in H. Wildemann, ed., *Produktion und Controlling*, München: TCW Transfer Centrum Verlag, 185–197, 1999.

Huchzermeier, A., and C. Loch. "Project Management Under Risk: Using the Real Options Approach to Evaluate Flexibility in R&D." *Management Science* 47:85, 2001.

Hull, J.C. *Options, Futures and Other Derivatives.* Prentice-Hall, 1997.

Ingersoll, J.E., and S.A. Ross. "Waiting To Invest: Investment and Uncertainty." *The Journal of Business* 65:29, 1992.

Janssen, M.A.; M. Scheffer; and T.A. Kohler. *Sunk-Cost Effects Made Ancient Societies Vulnerable to Collapse*, working paper. Indiana University, 2002.

Jensen, M.C., and W.H. Meckling. "Theory of the Firm: Managerial Behavior, Agency Costs and Ownership Structure." *Journal of Financial Economics* 3:305, 1976.

Jordan, B.D., and D.R. Kuipers. "The Impact of Treasury Bond Futures on the Cash U.S. Treasury Market." *Journal of Financial Economics* 46:67, 1997.

Kamien, M., and N. Schwartz. *Market Structure and Innovation.* Cambridge University Press, 1982.

Kamrad, B., and S. Lele. "Production, Operating Risk and Market Uncertainty: A Valuation Perspective on Controlled Policies." *IIE Transactions* 30:455, 1998.

Kaplan, R., and D. Norton. "The Balanced Scorecard—Measures That Drive Performance." *Harvard Business Review*, 1992.

Kaplan, R., and D. Norton. "Leading Change with the Balanced Scorecard." *Financial Executive* 17:64, 2001.

Kaplan, R., and D. Norton. "Transforming the Balanced Scorecard from Performance Measurement to Strategic Management: Part II." *Accounting Horizons* 15:147, 2001.

Kaplan, R., and D. Norton. "The Strategy Focused Organization: How Balanced Scorecard Companies Thrive in the New Business Environment." *Harvard Business School Press*, 2001.

Kellogg, D.; J.M. Charnes; and R. Demirer. "Valuation of a Biotechnology Firm: An Application of Real-Options Methodologies." Third Real Options Conference, 1999.

Kelm, K.K.; V.K. Narayanan; and G.E. Pinches. Shareholder Value Creation during R&D Innovation and Commercialization Stages." *Academy of Management Journal* 38:770, 1995.

Kensinger, J. *Project Abandonment as a Put Option: Dealing with the Capital Investment Decision and Operating Risk Using Option Pricing Theory*, working paper 80-121. Cox School of Business, October 1980.

Kensinger, J.W. "Adding the Value of Active Management into the Capital Budgeting Equation." *Midland Corporate Finance Journal*, Spring, p. 31, 1987.

Kester, ,W.C. "Today's Options for Tomorrow's Growth." *Harvard Business Review*, March–April 18, 1984.

Kogut, B. "Joint Ventures and the Option to Expand and Acquire." *Management Science* 37: 19, 1991.

Kogut, B., and N. Kulatilaka. "Capabilities as Real Options." *Organization Science* 12:744, 2001.

Kogut, B., and U. Zander. "Knowledge of the Firm, Combinative Capabilities, and the Replication of Technology." *Organization Science* 3:383, 1992.

Kogut, B., and U. Zander. "Knowledge of the Firm and the Evolutionary Theory of the Multinational Corporation." *Journal of International Business Studies* 24:625, 1993.

Kolodny, H.; M. Liu; B. Symne; and H. Denis. "New Technology and the Emerging Organizational Paradigm." *Human Relations* 49:12, 1996.

Kritzman, M.P., and D. Rich. "Risk Containment for Investors with Multivariate Utility Functions." *The Journal of Derivatives* 5:28, 1998.

Kulatilaka, N. "The Value of Flexibility: The Case of a Dual-Fuel Industrial Steam Boiler." *Financial Management* 22:271, 1993.

Kulatilaka, N., and A. Marcus. "General Formulation of Corporate Real Options." *Research in Finance* 7:183, 1988.

Kulatilaka, N., and E.C. Perotti. "Strategic Growth Options." *Management Science* 44:1021, 1998.

Laamanen, T. "Growth Option Company Acquisitions: In Search for an Optimal Option Portfolio." Real Options Conference, Cambridge, UK, 1998.

Lambrect, B. "Strategic Sequential Investments and Sleeping Patents," in M. Brennan and L. Trigeorgis, eds., *Project Flexibility, Agency and Competition*. Oxford University Press, 2001.

Lambrecht, B., and W. Perraudin. *Option Games*, working paper. Cambridge University, and CEPR, UK, August 1994.

Lambrecht, B., and W. Perraudin. *Real Option and Preemption*, working paper. Cambridge University, Birkbeck College (London) and CEPR, UK, 1996.

Lambrecht, B., and W. Perraudin. *Real Options and Preemption under Incomplete Information*. Real Options Group Conference, Cambridge, UK, 1999.

Lander, D.M., and G.E. Pinches. "Challenges to the Practical Implementation of Modeling and Valuing Real Options." *Quarterly Review of Economics and Finance* 38:537, 1998.

Lanjouw, J.O. "Patent Protection in the Shadow of Infringement: Simulation Estimations of Patent Value." *Review of Economic Studies* 65:671, 1998.

Lavoie, B., and I.M. Sheldon. "The Comparative Advantage of Real Options: An Explanation for the US Specialization in Biotechnology." *AgBioForum* 3(1), 47–52, 2000. Available on the World Wide Web: http://www.agbioforum.org.

Leahy, J.V. "Investment in Competitive Equilibrium: The Optimality of Myopic Behavior." *Quarterly Journal of Economics* 108:1105, 1993.

Lee, J., and D.A. Paxson. "Valuation of R&D Real American Sequential Exchange Options." *R&D Management* 31:191, 2001.

Lehocky, M., and D.A. Paxson. "Arbitrage-Free Evaluation of Exhaustible Resource Firms." *Journal of Business Finance and Accounting* 25:1363, 1998.

Lei, D.; M.A. Hitt; and R. Bettis. "Dynamic Core Competences through Meta-Learning and Strategic Context." *Journal of Management*, Winter, 22:549, 1996.

Leland, H.E., and M. Rubinstein. "The Evolution of Portfolio Insurance," in Don Luskin, ed., *Dynamic Hedging: A Guide to Portfolio Insurance*. John Wiley and Sons, 1988.

Leonard-Barton, D. "Core Capabilities and Core Rigidities: A Paradox in Managing New Product Development." *Strategic Management Journal*, Summer Special Issue, 13:111, 1992.

Leonard-Barton, D. *The Wellspring of Knowledge. Building and Sustaining the Sources of Innovation*. Harvard Business School Press, 1994.

Leslie, K.J., and M.P. Michaels. "The Real Power of Real Options." *The McKinsey Quarterly*, 1997, number 3.

Liao, Z., and P.F. Greenfield. "Corporate R&D Strategy Portfolio in Japanese and Australian Technology-Based Firms: An Empirical Study." *IEEE Transactions on Engineering Management* 45:323, 1998.

Lint, O., and E. Pennings. "R&D as an Option on Market Introduction." *R&D Management* 28:279, 1998.

Lint, O., and E. Pennings. "An Option Approach to the New Product Development Process: A Case Study at Philips Electronics." *R&D Management* 31:163, 2001.

Lippman, S., and R. Rumelt. "Uncertain Imitability: An Analysis of Interfirm Differences in Efficiency Competition." *The Bell Journal of Economics* 13:418, 1982.

Loch, C.H., and K. Bode-Gruel. "Evaluating Growth Options as Sources of Value for Pharmaceutical Research Projects." *R&D Management* 31:231, 2001.

Longstaff, F.A. "Are Negative Option Prices Possible? The Callable U.S. Treasury-Bond Puzzle." *The Journal of Business* 65:571, 1992.

Luehrman, T. "Investment Opportunities as Real Options: Getting Started on the Numbers." *Harvard Business Review*, July–August, 1998, p. 51.

Lukens, J.P. "Increasing Price Volatility Sparks Interest in Energy Finance Area." *Houston Business Journal*, June 1, 2001, p. 34.

MacDonald, R., and D. Siegel. "The Value of Waiting to Invest." *Quarterly Journal of Economics* 101:707, 1986.

Maeland, J. *Valuation of Irreversible Investments: Agency Costs*. Norwegian School of Economics and Business Administration. Paper presented at the Real Options Conference, Cambridge, UK, 1999.

Majd, S., and R.S. Pindyck. "Time to Build, Option Value, and Investment Decisions." *Journal of Industrial Economics* 18:7, 1987.

Major, E.; D. Asch; and M. Cordey-Hayes. "Foresight as a Core Competence." *Futures* 33:91, 2002.

Margrabe, W. "The Value of an Option to Exchange One Asset for Another." *Journal of Finance* 33:177, 1978.

Markowitz, H. "Portfolio Selection." *Journal of Finance*, March 1952, pp. 77–91.

Martzoukos, S.H. "Real R&D Options with Endogenous and Exogenous Learning." Forthcoming in D.A. Paxson, ed., *Real R&D Options*, Butterworth–Heinemann Quantitative Finance Series.

Mason, S., and C.W. Baldwin. "Evaluation of Government Subsidies to Large-Scale Energy Projects: A Contingent Claims Approach." *Advances in Futures and Options Research* 3:169, 1988.

Mauboussin, M.J. "Get Real: Using Real Options in Security Analysis." *CSFB Equity Research*, June 23, 1999.

Mauer, D., and S. Ott. "Investment under Uncertainty: The Case of Replacement Investment Decisions." *Journal of Financial and Quantitative Analysis* 30:581, 1995.

Mauer, D., and S. Ott. "Agency Cost, Underinvestment and Optimal Capital Structure: The Effect of Growth Options to Expand," in M.J. Brennan and L. Trigeorgis, eds., *Project Flexibility, Agency and Competition*. Oxford University Press, 2001.

McCardle, K. "Information Acquisition and the Adoption of New Technology." *Management Science* 31:1372, 1985.

McCormack, J., and G. Sick. "Valuing PUD Reserves: A Practical Application of Real Option Techniques." *Journal of Applied Corporate Finance* 13, Volume 4, Winter 2001.

McGrath, R.G.; M.H. Tsai; S. Venkataraman; and I.C. MacMillan. "Innovation, Competitive Advantage and Rent: A Model and Test." *Management Science* 42:389, 1996.

McGrath, R. "A Real Option Logic for Initiating Technology Positioning Investments." *Academy of Management Review* 22:974, 1997.

McGrath, R.G. "Falling Forward: Real Options Reasoning and Entrepreneurial Failure." *Academy of Management Review* 24:13, 1999.

Merton, R.C. "Theory of Rational Option Pricing." *Bell Journal of Economics and Management Science* 4:141, 1973.

Merton, R.C. "Option Pricing Where the Underlying Stock Returns are Discontinuous." *Journal of Financial Economics* 3:449, 1974.

Merton, R.C. "On the Option Pricing of Contingent Claims and the Modigliani-Miller Theorem." *Journal of Financial Economics* 5:241, 1977.

Moad, J. "Finding the Best Cultural Match for Software." *PC Week*, September 8, 1997.

Moel, A., and P. Tufano. "When Are Real Options Exercised? An Empirical Study Of Mine Closings." *The Review of Financial Studies* 15:35, 2002.

Moel, A., and P. Tufano. "Bidding for the Antamina Mine: Valuation and Incentives in a Real Option Context," in M.J. Brennan and L. Trigeorgis, eds., *Project Flexibility, Agency and Competition*. Oxford University Press, 2001.

Morck, R.; R. Schwartz; and D. Stengeland. "The Valuation of Forestry Resources under Stochastic Prices and Inventories." *Journal of Financial and Quantitative Analysis* 24:473, 1989.

Mowery, D.C.; J.E. Oxley; and B.S. Silverman. "Strategic Alliances and Interfirm Knowledge Transfer." *Strategic Management Journal* 17:77, 1996.

Myers, S.C. "Determinants of Corporate Borrowing." *Journal of Financial Economics* 5:147, 1977.

Myers, S.C. "Finance theory and financial strategy." *Midland Corporate Finance Journal* 5:5, 1987.

Myers, S.C., and S. Majd. *Calculating Abandonment Value Using Option Pricing Theory*. Sloan School of Management. Working Paper. May 1983.

Myers, S.C., and S. Majd. "Abandonment Value and Project Life." *Advances in Futures and Option Research* 4:1, 1990.

Nelson, R., and S. Winter. *An Evolutionary Theory of Economic Change*. Harvard University Press, Cambridge, 1982.

Nembhard, H. "Real Option Modeling for Valuing Worker Flexibility." *IERC Abstract 2107*, 2001.

Nembhard, H.; L. Shi; and M. Aktan. "A Real Options Design for Quality Control Charts." *The Engineering Economist* 47:28, 2002.

Newton, D.; D.A. Paxson; and A. Pearson. "Real R&D Options." in A. Belcher, J. Hassard, and S.D. Procter, eds., *R&D Decisions: Strategy, Policy and Disclosure*. London: Routledge, 1996, 273.

Newton, D.P., and A.W. Pearson. "Application of Option Pricing Theory to R&D." *R&D Management* 24:83, 1994.

Nicholls, M. "Reality Strikes Gold Miners." *Risk Magazine*, September 1997, p. 7.

Nichols, N. "Scientific Management at Merck: An Interview with CFO Judy Lewent." *Harvard Business Review*, Jan.–Feb., 1994, p. 88.

Nolan, M.T. "Improving Patient Care Through Data Competence." *Nursing Economics* 18: 250, 2000.

Norretranders, T. *The User Illusion*. Penguin Group, 1999.

Ottoo, R.E. "Valuation of Internal Growth Opportunities: The Case of a Biotech Company." *The Quarterly Review of Economics and Finance* 38:615, 1998.

Paddock, J.; D. Siegel; and J. Smith. "Option Valuation of Claims on Physical Assets: The Case of Offshore Petroleum Leases." *Quarterly Journal of Economics* 103:479, 1988.

Pakes, A. "Patents As Options: Some Estimates of the Value of Holding European Patent Stocks." *Econometrica* 54:755, 1986.

Panayi, S., and L. Trigeorgis. "Multi-Stage Real Options: The Cases of Information Technology Infrastructure and International Bank Expansion." *Quarterly Review of Economics and Finance* 38:675, 1998.

Pardue, J.H.; E. Higgins; and T. Biggart. "Impact of New Product Announcements on Firm Value in Information Technology Producing Industries. An Examination of Industry Level Evolutionary Eras." *The Engineering Economist* 45:144, 2000.

Paris, F.M. "A Compound Option Model to Value Moral Hazard." *Journal of Derivatives* 9:53, 2001.

Parker, D. "The Real Thing: The Theory of Real Options Is Steadily Finding Its Way into the Strategic Plans of Australian Companies." *Australian CPA*, March 2002.

Penner-Hahn, J. "Firm and Environmental Influences on the Mode and Sequence of Foreign Research and Development Activities." *Strategic Management Journal* 19:149, 1998.

Pennings, E., and O. Lint. *Market Entry, Phased Rollout or Abandonment? A Real Options Approach*. Working Paper. Erasmus University, 1998.

Pennings, E., and O. Lint. "The Option Value of Advanced R&D." *European Journal of Operational Research* 103:83, 1997.

Penrose, E.G.: *The Theory of the Growth of the Firm*. New York, 1959.

Peteraf, M. "The Cornerstones of Competitive Advantage: A Resource-Based View." *Strategic Management Journal* 14:179, 1993.

Pindyck, R.S. "Irreversible Investment, Capacity Choice and the Value of the Firm." *American Economic Review* 79:969, 1988.

Pindyck, R.S. "A Note on Competitive Investment under Uncertainty." *American Economic Review* 83:273, 1993.

Pope, P.F., and A.W. Stark. *Are Equities Really Options? Understanding the Size, Book-to-Market and Earnings-to Price Factors.* Third Real Options Group Conference, 1999.

Porter, M. "Capital Disadvantage: America's Failing Capital Investment System." *Harvard Business Review*, September–October 65, 1992.

Quigg, L. "Empirical Testing of Real-Option Pricing Models." *Journal of Finance* 48:621, 1993.

Reed, D.J. *Stalking the Elusive Business Case for Corporate Sustainability.* World Resources Institute, 2001, 15.

Rich, D.R. "The Mathematical Foundations of Barrier Option-Pricing Theory." *Advances in Futures and Options Research* 7:267–311, 1994.

Ridderbusch, G.L. "Running the Option." *Energy Customer Management*, December 2001.

Roberts, K., and M. Weitzman. "Funding Criteria for Research, Development and Exploration Projects." *Econometrica* 49:1261, 1981.

Rothenberg, I.S. "Financial Planning Forum: The Advantages of Modern Portfolio Theory." *Accounting Today*, April 26, 1999.

Rubinstein, M., and E. Reiner. "Breaking Down the Barriers." *Risk Magazine* 8:28, 1991a.

Rubinstein, M., and E. Reiner. "Unscrambling the Binary Code." *Risk Magazine* 9:37, 1991b.

Rubinstein, M. "Double Trouble." *Risk Magazine* 4:73, 1992.

Rubinstein, M. "Implied Binomial Trees." *Journal of Finance* 49:771, 1994.

Rumelt, R.P.; D. Schendel; and D.J. Teece. "Strategic Management and Economics." *Strategic Management Journal* 12:5, 1991.

Ryrie, T. "What's ERP?" *Charter* 70:46, 1999.

Saad, E.W.; D.V.Prokhorov; and D.C. Wunsch. "Comparative Study of Stock Trend Prediction Using Time Delay, Recurrent and Probabilistic Neural Networks." *IEEE Transactions on Neural Networks* 9:145, 1998.

Samuelson, P. "Rational Theory of Warrant Pricing." *Industrial Management Review* 6:13, 1967.

Schary (Amram), M. "The Probability of Exit." *Rand Journal of Economics*, Vol. 22, No. 3, 1991, pp. 339–353.

Schoemaker, P.J.H. "Scenario Planning: A tool for strategic thinking." *Sloan Management Review*, Winter 1995, p. 25.

Schwartz, E.S., and M. Moon. "Evaluating Research and Development Investments," in M. Brennan and L. Trigeorgis, eds., *Project Flexibility, Agency and Competition*. Oxford University Press, 2000.

Selznik, P. *Leadership in Administration*. New York: Harper and Row, 1957.

Seppae, T.J., and T. Laamanen. "Valuation of Venture Capital Investments: Empirical Evidence." *R&D Management* 31:215, 2001.

Servaes, H. "The Value of Diversification during the Conglomerate Merger Wave." *Journal of Finance* 51:1201, 1996.

Shane, S. "The Effect of National Culture on the Choice Between Licensing and Direct Foreign Investment." *Strategic Management Journal* 15:627, 1994.

Shane, S. "Uncertainty Avoidance and the Preference for Innovation Championing Roles." *Journal of International Business Studies* 26:47, 1995.

Sharpe, W.F. *Investments*. Prentice-Hall, 1978.

Siegel, D.; J. Smith; and J. Paddock. "Valuing Offshore Oil Properties with Option Pricing Models." *Midland Corporate Finance Journal*, Spring 1987, p. 22.

Silverman, S. "Big Blue Goes Ape on Sand Hill Road." *Red Herring*, February 20, 2001.

Smets, F. *Exporting versus FDI: The Effect of Uncertainty, Irreversibility and Strategic Interactions*. Working Paper, Yale University Press, 1991.

Smit, H.T.J. *Empirical Characteristics of Growth Options*. Presented at the Third Real Options Group Conference, Cambridge, 1999.

Smit, H.T.J., and L.A. Ankum. "A Real Options and Game-Theoretic Approach to Corporate Investment Strategy Under Competition." *Financial Management* 22:241, 1993.

Smit, H.T.J., and L. Trigeorgis. "Growth Options, Competition and Strategy: An Answer to the Market Valuation Puzzle?" in L. Trigeorgis, ed., *Real Options and Business Strategy: Applications to Decision Making*, Risk Books, 1999.

Smit, H.T.J., and L. Trigeorgis. *R&D Option Strategies*. Fifth Real Options Conference, Los Angeles, 2001.

Smit, H.T.J., and L. Trigeorgis. *Flexibility and Competitive R&D Strategies*. Working Paper, Erasmus University, 1997.

Smith, J.E., and K. McCardle. "Valuing Oil Properties: Integrating Option Pricing and Decision Analysis Approaches." *Operations Research* 46:198, 1998.

Spencer, B.J., and J.A. Brander. "Pre-Commitment and Flexibility: Applications to Oligopoly Theory." *European Economic Review* 36:1601, 1992.

Swenson, D.F. *Pioneering Portfolio Management*. New York: The Free Press, 2000.

Taudes, A.; M. Natter; and M. Trcka. "Real Option Valuation with Neural Networks." *International Journal of Intelligent Systems in Accounting, Finance and Management* 7:43, 1998.

Teece, D.J. "Capturing Value from Knowledge Assets: The New Economy, Markets for Know-How, and Intangible Assets." *California Management Review* 40:55, 1998.

Triantis, A., and A. Borison. "Real Options: State of the Practice." *Journal of Applied Corporate Finance* 14:8, 2001.

Trigeorgis, L., and S.P. Mason. "Valuing Managerial Flexibility." *Midland Corporate Finance Journal* 5:14, 1987.

Trigeorgis, L. "Real Options and Interactions with Financial Flexibility." *Financial Management* 22:202, 1993.

Trigeorgis, L. "The Nature of Option Interactions and the Valuation of Investments with Multiple Real Options." *Journal of Financial and Quantitative Analysis* 28:20, 1993.

Trigeorgis, L. "A Conceptual Options Framework for Capital Budgeting." *Advances in Futures and Options Research* 3:145, 1988.

Trigeorgis, L. *Real Options—Managerial Flexibility and Strategy in Resource Allocation*. MIT Press, Cambridge, MA, 1996.

Tsekrekos, A.E. "Investment under Economic and Implementation Uncertainty." *R&D Management* 31:127, 2001.

Tufano, P. "Agency Costs of Corporate Risk Management." *Financial Management* 27:67, 1998.

Tufano, P. "The Determinants of Stock Price Exposure: Financial Engineering and the Gold Mining Industry." *Journal of Finance* 53:1015, 1998.

Turnbull, S.K., and C.F. Sirmans. "Vacant Land Options: A Theoretical Analysis." *Regional Science and Urban Economics* 20:213, 1990.

Tushman, M.L., and P. Anderson. "Technological Discontinuities and Organizational Environments." *Administrative Science Quarterly* 31:439, 1986.

Tzu, S. *The Art of War*. Oxford University Press, 1988.

Upton, W.S. "Business and Financial Reporting, Challenges from the New Economy." Special Report. *Financial Accounting Series*, No. 219-A, April 2001.

van der Heijden, K. *Scenarios: The Art of Strategic Conversation*. Wiley, 1995.

Walsh, M. "Potential for Derivative Instruments on Sulfur Dioxide Emission Reduction Credits." *Derivatives Quarterly*, 32, 1994.

Waltner, C. "Payback in a Hurry—Microsoft's New Operating System Offers a Host of Money-Saving Management Features." *e-Directions*, Winter 2000.

Weeds, H. "Reverse Hysteresis: R&D Investments with Stochastic Innovation." Working Paper. 1999.

Weeds, H. "Strategic Delay in a Real Options Model of R&D Consumption." *Review of Economic Studies*, in print, 2002.

Wernerfelt, B.A. "A Resource-Based View of the Firm." *Strategic Management Journal* 5:171, 1984.

Whiteley, R. *Business Systems in East Asia*. Sage Publications, 1994.

Whiteley, R. *European Business Systems*. Sage Publications, 1994.

Willinger, M. "Risk Aversion and the Value of Information." *Journal of Risk and Insurance* 56:320, 1989.

Willner, R. "Valuing Start-Up Venture Growth Options," in L. Trigeorgis, ed., *Real Options in Capital Investment*. Westport, CT: Praeger, 1998. pp. 221–239.

Wilmott, P. *Derivatives. The Theory and Practice of Financial Engineering*. John Wiley & Sons, 1999.

Winter, S.G. "Knowledge and Competence as Strategic Assets." in D.J. Teece, ed., *The Competitive Challenge*. New York: Harper and Row, 1987.

Yates-Mercer, P., and D. Bawden. "Managing the Paradox: The Valuation of Knowledge and Knowledge Management." *Journal of Information Science* 28:19, 2002.

Zack, M.H. "Developing a Knowledge Strategy." *California Management Review* 41:125, 1999.

Zhu, K.X. "Strategic Investment in Information Technologies: A Real-Options and Game-Theoretic Approach." Unpublished Doctoral Dissertation, Stanford University, 1999.

Zmeskal, Z. "Application of the Fuzzy-Stochastic Methodology to Appraising the Firm Value as a European Call Option." *European Journal of Operational Research* 135:303, 2001.

index

Printed in the United Kingdom by
Lightning Source UK Ltd., Milton Keynes
140250UK00002B/23/A

9 780471 263081